D0991239

Modernizing the American War Department

Modernizing the American Wa

Daniel R. Beaver

Department

Change and Continuity in a Turbulent Era, 1885–1920

The Kent State University Press
Kent, Ohio

Library of Congress Catalog Card Number 2006018816
ISBN-10: 0-87338-879-8
ISBN-13: 978-0-87338-879-5
Manufactured in the United States of America

10 09 08 07 06   5 4 3 2 1

Frontispiece: Eisenhower Executive Office Building
Center of Military History, Washington, D.C.

Library of Congress Cataloging-in-Publication Data
Beaver, Daniel R., 1928–
Modernizing the American War Department :
change and continuity in a turbulent era, 1885–1920 / Daniel R. Beaver.
       p. cm.
    Includes bibliographical references and index.
    ISBN-10: 0-87338-879-8 (hardcover : alk. paper) ∞
    ISBN-13: 978-0-87338-879-5 (hardcover : alk. paper) ∞
    1. United States. War Dept.—History—19th century.
    2. United States. War Dept.—History—20th century. I. Title.
UA23.6.B43   2006
355.60973'09041—dc22   2006018816

British Library Cataloging-in-Publication data are available.

For Barb, Dan, Susan, and Will,
and in memory of Catherine

CONTENTS

PREFACE

This book is not about the Spanish American War or the Great War. It is not about the coming of World War II. It is not a simple, linear administrative history. It is about the adjustment of certain representative nineteenth-century War Department organizations to the managerial, technological, and policy challenges of a new day. It examines concurrently the offices of the secretary of war, the commanding general (later the chief of staff), the quartermaster general, the chief of ordnance, the chief signal officer, and, on occasion, the chief of engineers. Although it concentrates on the critical years 1885–1920 and examines critically the challenges of the Progressive Era and the First World War, it ranges from the days when John C. Calhoun established the foundations of the nineteenth-century American military system to 1940 when, with its structure modified through four decades of past experience, the War Department was poised to meet its greatest test since 1861.

The War Department had, or so it seemed, a straightforward mission—to raise, organize, train, supply, equip, deploy, and commit to battle the military forces of the republic in support of national policies under the control of Congress and the direction of the president of the United States. The most difficult personal and organizational issues, however, were involved in building effective systems that would help achieve those purposes. Each part of the organization, though a piece of the whole, had a distinct history. The story of how the members of each part saw themselves and made connections with each other and with the members of the other parts, some of them outside the War Department, and made the system work involves an examination of the historical challenges encountered in building and managing a complex, multipurpose organization. The story unfolds against a background of massive industrial and technological change, as the country moved from a traditional rural-agricultural and market-based commercial system toward a more integrated national order characterized by interconnected corporate enterprises. During the Progressive Era, interest groups—some traditional and some recently constructed, with often contradictory agendas—vied for control of the country's potential in ways that would shift the organizational balance of power, at first subtly and later more directly, from local authorities toward the federal government and unleash political tensions as old as the republic.

☆ ☆ ☆

There are certain terms used systematically in this volume that require definition. *Modernization* involves the process of incremental change that continued throughout the era. Parts of the vocabulary of the current "organizational synthesis" are used to describe the political processes through which nineteenth-century bureaucratic coalitions, which emphasized informal connections and individual consultation, were modified to become formal twentieth-century corporate systems, which used factory and machine metaphors to stress the importance of rationality, efficiency, predictability, and unambiguous lines of command and control. The terms *periphery, center,* and *connection* are used to discuss these conditions. *Periphery* defines the decentralized local, state, and regional authority in the nation and the post, bureau, and departmental levels in the army. *Center* defines the centralized federal authority in the nation and the authority concentrated in the office of the secretary of war, the commanding general, and later, the chief of staff in the War Department, and the army. *Connection* describes those points where representatives of various groups met and made decisions, often informally, without even the creation of temporary new agencies.

Viewed from the top, American modernization has been described as a traditional contest between the center and the periphery in which the forces of change are concentrated at the center. One can reach quite different conclusions, however, by examining conditions from the middle—from the perspectives of the leaders of the War Department and its various bureaus and departments—that reveal the continuing importance of traditional institutions as well as the power and significance of the periphery. Before the Civil War, the country operated politically through pressure groups organized, often informally, into separate spheres with parallel paths where the critical connections rested at local court houses and state capitals. The relative importance of such groups was substantially changed by the transformations in communications and industry that had already precipitated a market revolution and continued throughout the nineteenth century. In the twentieth century connections were made more often in Washington, as American political leaders combined traditional private institutions with a modestly expanded and interventionist public sector in an attempt to meet the challenges of the day without incurring the threats to liberty posed by massive, centralized, bureaucratic authoritarianism, which they believed was developing in the rest of the industrialized world.

The term *organizational modernization* is used to describe the transition in the War Department from a nineteenth-century bureaucratic system characterized by informal, decentralized, horizontal, organic, and familial connections based on community and consultation and aimed at achieving harmony and cooperation, in favor of a twentieth-century system characterized by formal, centralized, vertical, architectural, and corporate managerial structures integrated through a clearly defined hierarchy whose decisions were supported by rational planning and directed at clearly definable and predictable outcomes. The symbolic language of nineteenth-century soldiers stressed the periphery and emphasized family, community, and horizontal cooperation. The twentieth-century military modernizers emphasized the center, and some described the War Department and the army as simply another corporate enterprise with, perhaps, a different definition of profit, hierarchically organized and symbolized by the factory and the machine.

To help explain the bureaucratic politics involved in the transition, the terms *professionalism, culture, reform,* and *reorganization* are often employed. Although officers in the combat arms, engineers, technicians, and supply and logistical experts were all soldiers, they were not the same kinds of soldiers. *Professionalism* is used when describing the activities of officers from any department or bureau in the War Department or branch of the army who possessed specialized knowledge and were supported by a formal or informal educational system that transferred that knowledge from those who possessed it to those who would become members of the organization. The organization's definition of "professional" was revealed by the ways in which it approached issues, as well as by the systematic practices and procedures that were followed regularly in routine problem solving and, less often, in crisis management. In the War Department and the army, soldiers were often members of several departmental, bureau, or branch interest groups, each with different, if not unique, definitions of professionalism. *Culture* is used in a similar way. In this study, the term refers to the habits of mind and traditional behaviors of groups of professionals that shape the ways they respond to challenges and either encourage or discourage the development of connections within common organizations. Before the Civil War, the War Department and the army achieved such connections informally. To believe that in such a traditional environment the creation of formal twentieth-century command and control systems would end previous practices would be naive. Little disappeared from the way the military made decisions. The untidy nature of customary power relationships was simply masked by the illusion that they were systematically and rationally organized.

Two other terms help explain the organizational perplexities of the Progressive Era. *Reform* denotes significant changes in perceptions of institutional realities within and among professional and cultural interest groups. *Reorganization* includes external political and architectural adjustments of organizations to clarify authority in order to perform assigned tasks efficiently. Theoretically, a reorganization is the result of a reform, but it is just as often a political response that creates an illusion of change in order to retain the reality of traditional professional and cultural associations. The most effective War Department leaders understood that very well. They responded to new challenges by maintaining their connections with those who continued to defend informal, consultative traditions and had to be persuaded, not coerced, if the new arrangements were to be successful. Bureaucratic and departmental reorganizations occurred with monotonous regularity, but reform occurred only after internal professional and cultural perceptions changed, and that seldom happened except in crisis periods. Even then reform tended to be incremental rather than revolutionary. War Department reorganizations and reforms often occurred simultaneously. Affairs moved with great speed at some levels and with near-glacial slowness at others, and the results were kaleidoscopic. Not much really disappeared; it simply reappeared, some would say metastasized, in other modified forms and became complicated and incremental rather than simple, linear, and revolutionary, bringing one to conclude that bureaucratic organizations, like old soldiers, never die. Sometimes they don't even fade away.

People both define and are defined by the organizations to which they belong, and the power of personality endures regardless of structural modifications. War Department leaders were talented but, like all human beings, fallible. They had to navigate the treacherous bureaucratic channels carefully if officers in the various branches and departments were to be brought to cooperate, possibly at the risk of sacrificing their own carefully guarded authority, in enterprises that, in their minds, might at best only marginally enhance military effectiveness. The most successful leaders were pragmatic problem solvers rather than organizational theoreticians, and they followed two apparently contradictory prescriptions. The first was that sound management required efficient, systematically constructed organizations with a clear hierarchy of command. The second was that effective exercise of that power of command required consultation. Those paradoxical imperatives had to be carefully combined, and the most gifted administrators balanced the extremes of hierarchy and consultation, creating an organizational equilibrium that allowed flawed people in imperfect organizations to function effectively. The problems they faced were more difficult during the long peacetime periods of small budgets, garrison duty, constabulary action, and intense bureaucratic infighting when the nastier elements in the human character emerged than in the years of large-scale war when vital questions of national interest served to unite people of diverse character and conflicting ambitions in a common endeavor. Their responses to managerial and organizational challenges involved shades of difference rather than theoretical or ideological systems. They knew that pure hierarchy bred resentment and, except in crisis situations, caused disruption of the organization, whereas pure consultation led to inaction. Some creative and imaginative leaders understood that organizational modernization could be accomplished in a number of ways. For others, the idea that there might be more than one kind of system that could achieve administrative order and efficiency was profoundly unsettling.

Only the most fervent ideologues would deny that the introduction of new military technology did not add other dimensions to an already complex organizational situation. Between 1840 and 1870, the United States Army adopted single-shot breechloading rifles, repeating pistols, and rifled field artillery, and after 1880, in a very compressed time frame, it acquired more new weapons and equipment than at any other time in American history. A relatively uncomplicated method is used to discuss those issues. Technology is one of the elements that connect military groups through one or more energy sources to make a military-technological system. Over time such a system becomes not only a set of tools but also a body of ideas and methods of organizing, integrating, and applying the tools in effective ways. Single innovations seldom change whole systems, but they do create ripples that affect relationships among parts of systems and between them and the whole. Systems themselves move through phases of stability, dislocation, and restabilization until a critical mass of innovations or a new energy source or a new set of ideas forces a change that restructures the entire system.

Until 1940, there were only two complete military-technological systems. The first, or preindustrial system (prior to 1840) was powered by wind, water, and animal power to feed, equip, supply, and support armies that used weapon systems propelled by torsion, tension, and muscle, and later by black powder. The second, or industrial system (after 1840) which is the one of greatest concern in these chapters, built incrementally on new energy sources (coal, oil, and electricity), improved propellants and weapons, and began to overlap the first system. Between 1840 and 1880, a critical mass of technological innovations transformed and modernized the conduct of war in the West. The steel plow and the reaper expanded agricultural production, freed labor from the farm, and made unprecedented numbers of men available for military service. The factory system of industrial production supplemented water power with steam, multiplied manufacturing potential, and made it possible to arm and equip the troops. The steamship and the railroad provided the means to move them and increased strategic speed and mobility. The telegraph and telephone provided the forces, at first only on land, with the means for rapid communication.

Innovations in military weaponry moved slowly as armies adopted the single-shot breechloading rifle and the repeating pistol. After 1880, with the appearance of magazine rifles, machine guns, quick-firing artillery, and smokeless powder, the process accelerated. Motor trucks and airplanes, powered by internal combustion engines, expanded tactical mobility, while wireless radio extended both tactical and strategic communication at sea as well as on land. The airplane introduced a whole new dimension of warfare. Within the accelerating yet unsynchronized second system, each part moved through three phases—fragile, volatile, and robust—similar to, but faster than, those that shaped the preindustrial era before the modernized second, or industrial, system was integrated into armies like those fielded by the United States and Great Britain during the Second World War.

The adoption of such a vast amount of new equipment in such a short time raised significant issues involving fighting doctrine and disturbed traditional connections between all the combat arms and supporting agencies. The term *fighting doctrine* is profoundly political and cultural. It involves the development of methods through which military technology becomes connected with and affects the structure of existing military forces. In the army, the possibility that fighting doctrine could drive technology was an innovative idea, and it did not take hold until just before the Great War. Late-nineteenth- and early-twentieth-century soldiers understood that technological times had changed, but they had difficulty rethinking and conceptualizing the connections between time, space, and firepower. It took time to design, produce, and field effective weapons. It took time to integrate the new weapons, construct new formations, and develop controls to coordinate them in battle. It also took time to develop the industrial capacity to provide the fuel, weapons, ammunition, and equipment that were consumed at a prodigious rate. The intellectual challenges were unprecedented, and the second military technological system was organizationally more fragile and doctrinally more complex and than the one it supplanted.

One of the criticisms of the "New Military History" is that it often neglects the connections between military organization, administration, and technological developments and the actual conduct of armies in the field. *Doctrine,* the ways that technologies are linked and applied on the battlefield, is of relatively recent origin, but that does not mean that soldiers had not previously employed thoughtful and innovative combinations of heavy and light infantry, artillery, and cavalry. *Policy,* the political objectives to be attained in war, *strategy,* the general coordination and application of military power to secure policy objectives, *operations,* the coordination and application of military power in a single theater, and *tactics,* the methods used by large and small units to conduct battle, may not all have been parts of the nineteenth-century military lexicon, but American politicians and soldiers understood their meaning very well.

I am a traditional historian. I can discern no predetermined patterns in history, only one emergency following another, and only one safe rule: recognition of the role of the unexpected. My approach is narrative, descriptive, and analytical rather than theoretical and predictive. Human institutions are profoundly resilient, and change is most often contingent and incremental rather than revolutionary. People do make a difference. So do chance and luck. The study of the impact of immediate events, rather than assertions about inevitable historical forces, shapes my judgments, making them, most often, contextual attempts to clarify the actions of men in organizations at particular moments. The book is built on published documents, records collections in the National Archives and at the Library of Congress, and research materials at the United States Military History Institute at the Army War College and at other libraries throughout the country. It reflects in its notes and "Essay on Sources" the excellent work of other scholars in the field. It is organized into eleven chapters. Each chapter consists of a set of interconnected topical essays. Together, they provide a more positive appreciation than has usually been offered of the patterns and textures of War Department life during a turbulent, transitional era.

☆ ☆ ☆

Years ago the Mershon Center of Ohio State University awarded me a postdoctoral fellowship to begin to study this topic, and this volume consolidates, integrates, and synthesizes the work of that seminal year. Without the encouragement of the late Edgar M. Furniss Jr., I could never have begun a project that has become, unexpectedly, a lifetime undertaking. During a year as Harold K. Johnson Professor at the United States Army Military History Institute at the United States Army War College at Carlisle, Pennsylvania, I had the time to explore its unrivaled collection of nineteenth-century *militaria Americana* and to think about what I was trying to write. Two years in residence at the United States Army Center of Military History in Washington, D.C., allowed me to write about those and other important army issues. At the Military

History Institute, staff members Louise Arnold-Friend, David Keough, John Slonaker, and Dennis Vetock and chief archivist Richard Sommers gave me the benefit of their unrivaled knowledge of the nineteenth- and early-twentieth-century American military establishment. Without the assistance of Professor Dennis Showalter of Colorado College, Dr. Edgar Raines of the Center of Military History, Edward M. Coffman, professor emeritus at the University of Wisconsin, Professor John K. Ohl of Mesa College, Arizona, and Dr. David F. Trask, former chief historian at the Center of Military History, this book would never have seen the light of day. Professors George F. Hofmann, Thomas Sakmyster, John Alexander, James Cebula, Joseph Foster, and Herbert Curry of the University of Cincinnati were always helpful and supportive. Professor Allan Millett of Ohio State University read the first draft of the book, and I have benefited from his astute criticism. In addition, the Charles Phelps Taft Committee of the University of Cincinnati awarded me substantial grants to carry on my research and to help publish the volume. In 1974 I first met James E. Hewes Jr. of the Center of Military History, and he told me he had planned to write a two-volume history of the War Department but could only publish a single volume concentrated on the years since 1940. When I told him what I was working on, he replied, "Go to it." This book is only part of the debt I owe Dennis, Mac, Dave, John, Ed, Jim, and all those other good and helpful people.

I also wish to thank the Firestone Library at Princeton University for permission to quote from the papers of Bernard Baruch. Although most of the cited and quoted material in the book is from President Wilson's papers, housed in the Library of Congress, Princeton University Press has granted permission to quote short excerpts from volumes 51 and 52 of Arthur S. Link, ed., *The Letters and Papers of Woodrow Wilson*. I am grateful to the editors of the *Journal of Military History* for permission to quote from Robert Stohlman's *The Powerless Position: The Commanding General of the Army of the United States, 1864–1903*. Ellis Hawley, Edgar Raines, and William Roberts have also kindly given me permission to quote from their unpublished essays. Finally, I want to thank Joanna Hildebrand Craig and Tara C. Lenington, my editors at the Kent State University Press, for their unfailing support during the production of this book.

For more than twenty years my wife, Barbara, has read, criticized, and corrected each of the many variations of this manuscript. My oldest son, Dan, associate professor of English history at Pennsylvania State University, read the original draft and helped me keep the project in perspective. My youngest son, Will, had to deal with this enterprise from kindergarten through his college years. They reminded me often of what was really important.

Able people working in accordance with a sound, clear-cut plan of organization are prime requisites to successful administration. Having both you can't miss. With only one you are seriously handicapped. Without either, God help you!

—HAROLD ICKES

CHAPTER 1

SEPARATE SPHERES AND PARALLEL PATHS

THE WAR DEPARTMENT AND THE ARMY, 1820–1885

On July 5, 1814, Brigadier General Winfield Scott's brigade attacked the British at the little Canadian junction of Chippewa. The roads in northern New York state were atrocious, and during the previous months Scott had been plagued by shortages of quartermaster and ordnance supplies. Horses, mules, and oxen were in short supply. Hurriedly ordered transport wagons fell apart. The food was rotten. The troops carried muskets of various makes and calibers. Not only did they have to conserve scarce small arms and artillery ammunition, but they also had to wear nonregulation gray wool uniforms in the hottest season of the year. The troops proved effective, but their support was dreadful. Command and control also left much to be desired. During the previous year and a half, President James Madison, Secretary of War John Armstrong, and Secretary of State James Monroe had applied themselves to military affairs without much effect. The president and the secretary of state even appeared on the field themselves at Blandensburg. After Monroe took over at the War Department, despite his reorganizations in 1813 and in 1814, conditions did not improve much. Postwar investigations revealed dishonesty bordering on treason and inefficiency in military management and leadership of unsurpassed magnitude. Difficulties ranged from cynical exploitation of the government by fraudulent contract merchants to Eli Whitney's failure to fulfill his infamous musket contract with the War Department. The abominable transportation and communications conditions accounted for many of the failures of military command, but they only highlighted the poor performance of those who should have taken such difficulties into account. The events of the war exposed a dark, bankrupt side of American military affairs.[1]

Congressional investigations in 1815 and 1816 revealed the inadequacy of the connections between the War Department and the army and brought substantial bureaucratic reorganization. The chief architect was John C. Calhoun, one of America's great nineteenth-century administrators. Appointed secretary of war on October 10, 1817, to succeed William Crawford of Georgia, Calhoun, who was both reformer and modernizer, struck at the organizational residue of the eighteenth century. The original system, based on the tradition of "no standing army" and characterized by a citizen militia and civilian control of the military at every level from the periphery to the center, had been transferred to the federal government virtually intact after the Revolutionary War. At command levels it had its roots in earlier political and administrative practices. At supply and logistical levels it was dominated by civilian contractors who operated beyond military control under the oversight of local, politically appointed intendants who considered a public office a species of property to be exploited for personal or family advantage. Their contracting and purchasing methods brought corruption and mismanagement in administration, finance, logistics, general supply, and procurement.[2]

Calhoun was convinced that wartime failures had been caused by both poor organization and poor executive management. He argued for an expansible peacetime regular army to enhance and possibly replace the citizen militia. He recommended that dependence on civilian contractors in the field should be ended and that the finance, subsistence, supply, production, and procurement agencies of the War Department should be militarized and made clearly accountable. He advised that the War Department should be so organized and connected that nothing need be changed or improvised in an emergency. The secretary of war appointed to positions of leadership young reform-minded officers who were committed to improving command and control and establishing accountability. The Calhoun reforms reflected the administrative modernization that reshaped the capacity of the state in Europe and America to meet new organizational and technological challenges during the nineteenth century and endured, with minor changes, until the first decade of the twentieth century. Their institutional and professional cultures had to be reckoned with far longer.[3]

☆ ☆ ☆

During the years before the Civil War, the secretary of war, assisted by a small civilian staff, commanded the army in the name of the president and ensured the revolutionary tradition of civilian supremacy over the military. The power of the Office of Commanding General, established in 1821 in part to remedy wartime deficiencies, was intentionally made ambiguous and nonstatutory. The position, first filled almost inadvertently by Jacob Brown (1821–1828) and then, before the Civil War, by Alexander McComb (1828–1841) and Winfield Scott (1841–1861), represented the warrior tradition—honor, duty, obedience, courage—as well as commitment to a single, hierarchical chain of command. Officers of the combat arms asserted that the only purpose of an army was achieved on the field of battle and that their special training and virtue required that they command the whole army, including the War Department staff. Aside from McComb, an astute and sensitive military politician, every commanding general argued that he reported directly to the president of the United States, that he commanded all the army, including the bureau chiefs, and that he was coequal with the secretary of war, whose task was merely to coordinate the War Department bureaucracy.[4]

Soldiers of the staff in the technical and supply bureaus did not take such assertions from the line without a rejoinder. Part of the new technological and managerial leadership of the nineteenth-century industrial revolution, they designed and made the guns, procured the supplies, built the roads, transported the army, and, in their depots and armories, managed the problems of the early industrial era. Officers of the Ordnance Department in particular were innovative inventors, technocrats, and industrial managers before the Civil War. Their relationships with certain civilian cannon founders, powder makers, and small-arms producers, their open-door policy at federal arsenals, and the free movement they allowed craftsmen from their workshops into private factories made the department a net exporter of technology into American industry. This did not make them any more agreeable to congressmen, whose pleas for favors were rejected, to private entrepreneurs, who considered the bureaus business rivals, or to line officers, who considered them mere tinkerers and mechanics. Accepted as equals by the civilian entrepreneurial, intellectual, and academic communities, they found professional legitimacy in the War Department through the development of special schools and apprenticeships.[5] They pointed out that they took the same oath to defend the Constitution as officers of the line and were also soldiers of the republic. Children of the age of iron and steam, they seldom achieved command, but they did demand consultation.

The issue of command and control between the secretary of war, the commanding general, and the bureau chiefs disturbed relations in the War Department for generations. Winfield Scott was utterly inflexible, and in the early 1850s his attitude poisoned relations between the president, the commanding general, and the secretary of war. All the secretaries of war insisted that the commanding general reported to them, not, as Scott believed, directly to the president. They argued that too much was made of the alleged powerlessness of the commanding general. If his arrogance or narrowness of view did not blind him, they stated, he could work informally through them as their chief military adviser. In 1857 Secretary of War John B. Floyd, who got along with Scott better than most of his contemporaries, conceded the general's point and recommended that the commanding general receive statutory power over the bureau chiefs.[6]

Every secretary of war also insisted that he must have personal contact with every element in the organizational hierarchy. The doctrine of equal access generated friction between members of the War Department staff, who insisted they must be at least consulted, and the commanding general, who claimed that they were all under his command. What ultimately developed was a War Department staff consisting of the bureau chiefs, who had direct access to the secretary of war, and a commanding general of the army, also with access to the secretary but with no direct control over the officers in the bureaus. Always somewhat artificial organizationally, it was an ingenious system of divide and rule that maintained civilian control of the military and granted no statutory overall command power to any soldier, bureaucrat, or line officer.[7] It encouraged cohesion and stability at one level and fostered separatism at another. It ensured that the secretary of war had access to multiple sources of information about departmental matters, but it also increased jurisdictional conflicts. Like members of any traditional community or extended family, to which army officers often compared themselves, soldiers exploited their political connections and knew each other's strengths, failures, and weaknesses. If occasion demanded, they were prepared to exploit all of them.[8]

Two significant civilian interest groups also played roles in the system. War Department supply experts, logisticians, and weapons technocrats worked closely, though not always harmoniously, with a relatively small number of client firms—civilian mercantile houses, freighting and transport concerns, and arms manufacturers—that formed important political interest groups. A number of officers resigned from the service to accept important jobs in such businesses. It seemed easier for an officer to become a businessman than it was for a businessman, except in wartime, to adjust to the values and procedures of army life. Few businessmen showed any interest in becoming regular army officers.[9] Individual businessmen and soldiers played significant, often adversarial, roles as they strove for satisfactory outcomes as members of one or more of the interest groups involved, and on several occasions private small-arms makers sought to have public arsenals of production abolished. It was in the House and Senate Appropriations and Military Affairs committees and on the floors of Congress that those questions were resolved. Congressmen and senators involved themselves intimately with the most minute matters of army business and especially during peacetime, when the army was budget driven, their micromanagement required the vast amount of paperwork about which War Department bureaucrats complained. Thus, before the Civil War, a set of "patron-client" relationships between the War Department, members of congressional committees, food, clothing, equipment, forage, and transportation firms, and small-arms and heavy-metals producers comprised a small national defense sector of the economy.[10]

☆ ☆ ☆

Until 1840 the American organizational landscape was relatively stable. Business and technological enterprises were characterized by either single entrepreneurships or simple partnerships whose members exercised personal control. A representative firm produced a line of products with a local or, at most, a regional clientele. Such traditional business organizations lacked a body of salaried middle managers who supervised the day-to-day activity of the business and were directly accountable to the owners. Ownership and management were directly linked. Some traditional firms reached considerable size and encountered problems of scale and control that, in many cases, accounted for their demise. Before 1840 there was little institutional innovation in private American business. As long as the processes of production and distribution remained dependent on men, animals, and water and wind power, there was little pressure to change. Such sources of energy could not generate the volume of output in production and the number of transactions in distribution large enough to require organizational innovation. The slow rate of production and the slow movement of goods through the system allowed control by small, personally owned and managed enterprises. Although the economy was expanding, the agencies of growth were the myriad small producers, middlemen, merchants, and traders whose numbers increased to meet the needs of the growing population and whose activities were determined by price and market forces. After 1840, important innovations associated with the second industrial revolution—steam-powered machinery, the steamboat, the steam locomotive, and the electric telegraph—substantially began to influence traditional forms of production, transportation and communication and move the country toward a more expansive market economy.[11]

By modern standards the War Department was a small-scale organization. It appeared to operate hierarchically through army regulations and War Department general orders. Although army officers, bound by the soldier's oath and dedicated to the defense of the republic, rejected the cash-nexus mentality of the contemporary business community, they still reflected the society they served.[12] The military establishment was a national institution, but its power structure, like that in the country, was diffuse, decentralized, and obstinately, at times frustratingly, plural. Although organized and administered through geographic divisions and departments, the army was inhibited operationally and conceptually by the slow pace of transportation and communication. Command and management involved politically appointed civilians and career officers. Civilians came and went, but military appointments were permanent. Promotion was by seniority within the separate regiments and bureaus, and, until the Civil War, there was no military retirement system. Soldiers considered their bureaus and branches independent domains and interagency communication a privilege, not a requirement. The army and the War Department were separate hierarchical structures, but they could and did interact. When matters arose that transcended a single organization or involved outsiders, they could cross interior and exterior administrative barriers with ease. They were isolated neither from each other nor from the civilian communities with which, on many occasions, they worked. They operated through boards and councils, informal consultation, and personal contact. But in an era of small independent businessmen, loosely connected communities, and prickly personalities, commands, if they were to be heeded, were couched in comradely and conciliatory terms. Connections were personal. Even inside the separate branches and bureaus, careful consultation and negotiation preceded the appearance of regulations and general orders.

The War Department administered the force, produced many of its own supplies and much of its own equipment in its own depots, arsenals, and armories, and, under the Militia act of 1808, supplied a small portion of the arms for the state militias. Although the Act of 1808 provided $200,000 a year in federal money for the arming of the militia, state legislatures in New York and Massachusetts, under pressure from their own private small-arms manufacturers, created "state defense sectors" and equipped their troops with the products of their own factories instead of weapons produced in the national armories. This was perfectly legal, for the Act of 1808 was unclear, retaining a provision from the militia act of 1792 that specified that the only common characteristic of military small arms should be caliber.[13]

Before the Civil War, the topographical engineers explored the country while other engineers, in cooperation with the Quartermaster Bureau, built roads, army posts, and coastal fortifications and improved waterways. Ordnance technicians, through metallurgical experimentation and the development of interchangeable manufacture by machinery, played a role in advancing the industrial revolution in America. Army combat elements were organized into regiments, but they were scattered in penny-packet units along the coast and frontier. Soldiers of the line acted as a buffer between whites and Indians on the frontier and provided rallying points for economic development. Never really at peace, their strength ranged from roughly 6,000 troops in 1825 to a little more than 16,000 men in 1860. With no powerful enemies within striking distance, there was no need for mobilization planning or large federal forces. In war the nation relied on the regular army and United States volunteers, and on the state militias, for local defense and occasional short service in the field. There was time to prepare after hostilities began against any conceivable foreign threat.[14] The nineteenth-century military order was one of separate spheres yet parallel paths. Such a decentralized, consultative system maintained political and organizational equilibrium, but it moved slowly, increased paperwork, and reinforced the prejudices of parochial, narrowly specialized officers in all the branches and bureaus.[15]

The Civil War marked the greatest test of the nineteenth-century system as well as its greatest triumph.[16] The story of Abraham Lincoln and his generals is a familiar one. The federal command system during the first two years of the war revealed all the problems that had surfaced during the Scott controversy in the 1850s. Scott, still active and still adamant about his power, was too old to exercise field command, and when George McClellan became commanding general, he left Washington, as Scott had done earlier in the expedition to take Mexico City. McClellan never really escaped the narrow perspectives of the Army of the Potomac and, with troops in action on multiple fronts, a vacuum grew in Washington that Secretary of War Edwin M. Stanton attempted to fill by creating a "War Board" headed by Ethan Allen Hitchcock.[17] The war board remained until Lincoln finally found his general in Ulysses S. Grant. It was then absorbed into a special staff headed by Henry Halleck and Quartermaster General Montgomery Meigs.

The president coordinated the war effort through an informal war council composed of Secretary of War Stanton, other cabinet members, and members of Halleck's special staff. Grant headed a unified command that coordinated multiple armies on multiple fronts. When he became commanding general in 1864, he moved his headquarters out of Washington into the field where he accompanied George Gordon Meade and the Army of the Potomac until the end of hostilities. As commander in chief, Lincoln communicated with the commanding general in any way he wished. Most often it was through Stanton and Halleck, but occasionally he simply went directly to Grant's headquarters himself.[18]

The Civil War was fought by armies of regulars and United States volunteers. Both the Union and the Confederacy passed conscription laws, but with their bounties, exemptions, and commutation fees, they served more to encourage volunteering than to raise armies.[19] In the North, after the militia draft legislation of 1862, new troops were raised locally and sent forward to federal depots, where they were supplied and equipped by national authorities. At a time when intricate industrial and manufacturing issues had not yet become important elements in national mobilization, the record of the Civil War bureaus was impressive. Ordnance, quartermaster, and subsistence added appropriate procurement divisions and commissioned experienced private businessmen to meet the challenge. Between 1861 and 1865, they supplied an army that expanded from 16,215 officers and men organized into ten infantry regiments, three cavalry regiments, and two artillery regiments to a massive force of 446,000 men organized into 1,696 infantry regiments, 272 cavalry regiments, and 78 artillery regiments. By 1863 the army had so many supply and escort wagons that they were a logistical embarrassment. Federal forces had so much food that the waste alone could have fed another quarter million men. Supplies of uniforms and leather gear expanded until the government was able to outfit the troops from its own expanded production alone. Northern weapons factories delivered 1,700,000 small arms; the national arsenal at Springfield, Massachusetts, alone completed 200,000 small arms a year. Northern foundries cast 7,892 cannon of all calibers. After eighteen months the War Department returned to its traditional practice of requiring competitive bids on army contracts. On July 3, 1863, during the Gettysburg battle, federal supply depots held reserve small arms, artillery, uniforms, and equipment sufficient, if necessary, to re-equip the entire Army of the Potomac.[20]

The Lincoln government dominated the center of the nineteenth-century system. The president did not contemplate building a complex, formal bureaucracy to run the war, and the War Department civilian staff remained relatively small. The raw materials required for the conflict comprised a modest percent of the total national resources and no formal allocation and production priorities were needed. Most problems were met by informal adjustment of market variables.[21] Indirect government encouragement through tariff protection and attractive contracting arrangements were, in most cases, sufficient to increase production.[22]

Most of American industry was still in a precorporate stage of development. Factories in the iron and textile industries engaged work forces of fewer than a hundred people each. Labor, when it was organized at all, was shifting from guilds to craft unions. Agriculture was in transition from self-sufficiency and labor-intensive production to more mechanized forms, and there was, at first, no national control of the creation and control of credit. Only in land and water transport and wire communication did federal authorities develop a central control system. The government regulated the railroads and on occasion ran them to expedite the shipment of troops and supplies. It ran its own lines in the active military zones and administered its own river boat and telegraph systems.[23]

During 1863, prodded by the humorless, single-minded Stanton, army supply officers and logisticians divided the North into two major supply regions. Western armies drew supplies from sources west of the Allegheny Mountains. Eastern armies drew from the industrial base east of the mountains. Because of the concentration of the small-arms industry in the Connecticut Valley and upper New York state, those regions became the source of small arms for the whole army. Supplies were shipped by rail and water in bulk and stored at general depots from Washington to Nashville. Cannon manufacturing moved beyond Pittsburgh to Cincinnati, where Miles Greenwood established the first cannon foundry in Ohio in 1862. Uniform manufacture expanded at Philadelphia and spread to "Union Halls" from Cincinnati to Jeffersonville, Indiana, where, among others, the widows and dependents of Union soldiers toiled to supply the army. The system worked through informal connections that were established between ordnance, quartermaster, department commanders, and local business leaders. Chambers of commerce and boards of trade in the various western cities coordinated manufacturing schedules and transportation by river, while the assistant secretary of war's office organized railroad transportation.[24]

The armies fought primarily east of the Mississippi river, where strategic transportation and communication had been revolutionized already by the railroad, the steamboat, and the telegraph, and where manufacturing facilities were available to supply equipment rapidly. Tactical communication, however, depended on animal and human power. Weapons were relatively simple. Although small arms and ammunition were in mass production with some interchangeable parts and some progress had been made in metallurgy, empirical and practical methods were the rule. Complex, modern artillery was still two decades in the future. In 1861 casting a muzzleloading artillery tube was a simple process, and field guns could be provided in quantity in a matter of a few months. Ammunition expenditures were large by Napoleonic standards but small by twentieth-century measurements. It was an infantryman's war and the War Department knew what had to be produced and how to procure it.

The most significant wartime doctrinal and tactical problems were generated by the possession by both sides of the muzzleloading rifle, which quadrupled the lethal range of small arms, drove infantry into entrenchments, forced artillery away from the line of battle, and ended the mass charge of cavalry. The rifle, by expanding the battlefield, made tactical communication difficult but increased defensive power. Entrenched infantry could concentrate fire on an advancing opponent, while the attacker, in close order to secure mass and velocity, was shot to pieces in the lethal zone, two hundred yards in front of the defensive line. Unfortunately, an army board that had toured Europe in 1854 and seen the impact of rifle fire during the Crimean War had not deemed it important enough for comment.[25]

During the first year of the war, private soldiers seemed to learn about the new rifle faster than officers. It made traditional line and column attack tactics suicidal and drove infantry to cover. By late 1864, Emory Upton's newly developed tactical system of fire and maneuver, even when used with muzzleloaders, reduced casualties and gave the attackers some hope of success.[26] Upton's tactics and a good breechloading rifle to concentrate firepower rather than people meant the offense might neutralize the advantages of the defense. Some field soldiers demanded breechloaders immediately. They bought them for their troops on the private market. Others thought they were still unreliable. They argued that soldiers were unfamiliar with them and nothing should be changed during the war. Some inventors wanted to go even further and introduce entirely new repeating weapons. Technicians, who knew the problems of building new models with existing manufacturing technologies, feared they would be caught short and resisted change until an adequate reserve of standard rifles was available. Logisticians wanted to wait until adequate supplies of metallic cartridges were available. Thus, mixed signals from the field, the uneven state of technological development and concern over production induced bureau technicians to delay and moved the small-arms boards, which met continuously during the war, toward conservatism. It was 1864 before the Ordnance Bureau considered introducing a standard breechloader into the service. Modest contracts had already been awarded to client companies to identify practical problems in producing the new rifles in quantity, and ammunition contracts for improved metallic ammunition had been negotiated to build up an initial supply. When everything was proceeding systematically the main production effort would shift from muzzleloaders to breechloaders, but the war was over before a breechloader was adopted and issued to the troops.[27]

The Confederate government was never able to establish the balance between the center and the periphery that the Lincoln government achieved so successfully. With few of the advantages that were available to the Union, the Confederacy had to organize from the ground up, but it finally mobilized about two-thirds of the military manpower available to the Union. Although the Confederacy was the first to introduce conscription, President Jefferson Davis resisted unity of military command until 1865. Outside of the active forces there was a very small pool of managerial talent. From the first moments the Confederacy faced a war of scarcity. The industrial base was modest, and it suffered throughout the war from shortages of machine tools. Too much land had gone into cotton and too little into foodstuffs; in a short time, the Confederates faced a shortage of corn and hogs in a country where the land and the weather were most favorable to their production. The textile industry was small and there was little hope to expand it. Without the North's luxury of finite demands and infinite supplies, Southerners turned by necessity to a command economy. It was to the credit of Confederate bureaucrats that the army did not suffer any more than it did from shortages of arms and ammunition. Battlefield pickups during the first two years of the war helped—foreign imports were also important—but demand was beyond supply, and the economy had to be converted, by force where necessary, to ordnance and supply production. There was nothing except the French Revolutionary model to serve as a precedent. The Virginia maximum price for food was consciously modeled on the "Revolutionary Maximum of 1793." For the Confederacy, however, successful prosecution of the war would require the coordination of the entire economy. Supplies had to be allocated from theater to theater and between soldiers and civilians from some central point. This flew in the face of Southern ideology, and political power remained obstinately decentralized. It was with the greatest difficulty that state and local authorities were coordinated. The Confederate government had only the powers of national confiscation, and commandeering and implementing them aroused fierce local resistance. It was never able to integrate the railroads and supply them with rolling stock, engines, and rails. Advancing Union armies cut off necessary supplies and ruined the transportation net. When Lee surrendered his starving army, virtually naked and shoeless, at Appomattox Court House, unused supplies of grain, meat, and clothing lay in Georgia depots. The Confederacy had the resources for a long war, but it could not, in view of Southern ideological commitments, develop the tools to put them to the best use.[28]

☆ ☆ ☆

After the Civil War the American organizational landscape expanded dramatically. Although small-scale business and agriculture still remained characteristic of the American economy, as the century neared its end large-scale corporate enterprise grew more significant. From the end of the Civil War to the turn of the twentieth century, the number of businesses with capital in excess of $5 million that produced for national and international markets grew substantially. The national rail network approached completion. Capital and credit, some self-generated, some from abroad, and some provided through the new national banking system, were available. The growing urban marketplace encouraged great new merchandising firms to compete with older local enterprises through mail-order houses and nationally controlled local outlets. Advertising on a national scale maximized profits by exciting consumer demands for new goods and services. Applied science and technology, especially in the electrical and chemical industries, were brought to the service of marketing, creating new products to attract the buying public's dollars. By 1890 command and control of their growing resources posed unprecedented organizational problems for the generation of American businessmen who had built the colossus.

Yankee inventors and tool makers continued to innovate, but their discoveries often first found application abroad. The electronics and chemical industries, nascent enterprises on the cutting edge of emerging technologies, were open to new methods, but the older basic industries followed, rather than led, the drive for improved industrial techniques. Americans had been net importers of technology before the Civil War, and American entrepreneurs as a group preferred to continue to use established procedures. Europeans could innovate and the Americans would carefully tailor successful ventures to home conditions. Their creative contributions would come elsewhere.

By the mid-1880s it was clear to many businessmen that neither traditional single entrepreneurship nor simple partnerships could cope with the vast scale of American industrial development. It was also clear that some form of organization had to be created that combined centralized control of policy with decentralized operations. During the early 1890s the solution was found in the integrated and diversified corporation. Early corporations were merely mechanisms for risk sharing among entrepreneurs. The great transformation of the late nineteenth century changed the corporation from a legal and financial device to a managerial tool. The transition had begun with the railroads in the 1850s and continued through the organizational innovations of such early masters of enterprise as John D. Rockefeller, Andrew Carnegie, and the brothers Gustavus and Edwin Swift. The movement was from horizontal or vertical structures organized as trusts or holding companies to consolidated and integrated corporations. The motivation was to eliminate or control competition and to improve productivity by maximizing the use of costly capacity. The process began in the years after the panic of 1893 and culminated just before the Great War with a new form of business organization. In business, at least at the national level, power was moving toward the centralized and departmentalized integrated corporation. Enormous benefits awaited those who could systematize the operations of the burgeoning industrial giants; the challenges and rewards spawned a generation of professional industrial managers who were confident they could organize production, marketing, and consumption into efficient, comprehensive systems. Like the traditional guild members in medicine and law and newer status seekers in academe, government, and commerce, they formed professional associations to establish their exclusiveness and expertise. Engineers in all their myriad forms moved into the industrial world while whole colleges provided managers and administrators to fill the growing market for experts in an expanding and increasingly organized society.

Technical and managerial specialization was necessary to meet the organizational challenge. By 1914 a system of expanded management practices had appeared, supported by colleges of business administration and departments of industrial engineering, whose faculties were graduating a group of self-consciously professional industrial managers and technicians who believed they could rationalize, organize, and streamline the process of manufacturing and link it successfully with logistics and marketing. They created laboratories to develop new products and generated demands where none had existed before. Control of the national social environment was the objective. People in some sectors of the American educational and corporate communities, especially engineers and business managers associated with the new science-based industries, came to believe that homogenizing and integrating American society within a framework of values associated with corporate cost-effectiveness and efficiency were realizable goals. Their "New American System" of rationally controlled large-scale enterprises challenged still viable nineteenth-century networks of small producers and local markets. Walter Gifford of American Telephone and Telegraph, one of the new breed of industrial managers, claimed in a typical outburst of enthusiasm that the system, melded with creative use of new psychological testing procedures, might be used to organize the world in the interests of human happiness and efficiency. Supporters labeled this fundamental process "modernization," an effort to move power from the periphery toward the center to plan, mobilize, and rationalize the use of resources to achieve greater control and efficiency.[29]

☆ ☆ ☆

The War Department and the army were not unaffected by the postwar changes in the organizational landscape. Faced with no immediate military threats, however, they basked in the reflected light of the great Union victory. The public arsenals, no longer among the largest factories in the country, suffered relative decline as centers of production and invention. Innovators could succeed only with the cooperation of powerful, often antagonistic, groups, some within the military establishment and many entirely beyond the realm of the War Department. Despite an apparatus of vertical command, which gave it a corporate appearance, the War Department and the army remained nineteenth-century American institutions. The issues of command and control and communication that had shaped the debate within the military establishment for more than fifty years became part of another debate that involved two apparently irreconcilable concepts of organizational efficiency—one corporate and hierarchical and the other community centered and cooperative—inside a complex, multipurpose, multicultural institution. The antebellum compromise had achieved organizational balance by harmonizing relationships among staff and line officers in the same ways they might be handled in an extended family or, perhaps, a local political courthouse ring. The system fed on improvisation, negotiation, connection, and consultation. Imprecise and unscientific as they were, such traditional familial and community-powered organizations proved successful in a great national crisis, providing the means by which the armies of volunteers that saved the republic were armed, fed, supplied, transported, and led to battlefield success. During the Civil War the system was modified to meet expanded requirements. After the war it remained intact, its members hailed as the organizers of Union victory. Formal command and control remained in the hands of the president and the secretary of war. Military officers were permanently assigned to staff and line duties. The line, with its hierarchical structure and self-conscious professionalism, continued to define "soldier" narrowly as involving only the expertise of the warrior and championed the heroic tradition of battlefield command. With their civilian and congressional allies they argued that the only task of the army was to fight; War Department supply, technical, and logistical organizations were mere supporting agencies. But the line, with no branch chiefs, could speak only through the commanding general. The technicians, administrators, and supply specialists in the bureaus, with their own powerful congressional and civilian lobbies, had several organizational voices and continued to insist that they should be treated as equals. They associated themselves as much with engineers, factory managers, merchants, lawyers, doctors, and administrators in civilian life as with the combat soldiers with whom they served. Proud of their expert knowledge and often dictatorial in their own organizations, they resented their ambivalent places in the military system. They did not quarrel with the line's view of the function of an army, but they resisted all efforts to bring them under the sole authority of the combat arms. They wanted to be consulted on broad issues of military affairs and were comfortable with the informal system of boards and councils that had been developed earlier in the era.

The staff bureaus retained their traditional "patron-client" relationships with the civilian economy and connections remained contractual and often adversarial. Some manufacturing firms resented the War Department, but the engineers, in particular, had cordial contacts with local construction magnates. The perennial transportation, food, fodder, and clothing requirements of the Subsistence and Quartermaster bureaus brought their representatives into regular negotiations with railroads and freight companies, textile brokers, regional suppliers of animals, and agricultural middlemen. Ordnance continued its connections with the private arms makers, but cordiality declined after the war as smaller appropriations brought few government orders for guns to the industry. Cut-throat competition in the small-arms field led to efforts by private producers to eliminate public competition. Ordnance officers, far less pragmatic than quartermaster and subsistence officers, were the chief ideological proponents of government manufacture of military hardware. Private arms makers were convinced the bureau unjustly favored certain suppliers, imposed unreasonably high quality standards on the private trade, and interfered with capital flow by holding large sums of money in litigation over small matters of compliance. Field soldiers and civilians alike were convinced that ordnance favored its own designs over those submitted by any outsiders. When hard times struck the small-arms industry after the war, driving many famous firms into bankruptcy or merger, private producers lobbied Congress to end government manufacturing of ordnance and place the work in the hands of private contractors.

In 1878 "Colonel" Eli Whitney, president of the Whitney Arms Company and spokesman for the group that included Winchester, Remington, Sharpes, Ames, the Union Metallic Cartridge Company, and the Providence Tool Company, argued that private manufacturers had ample capacity to meet government needs in peace and war and that private arms were of equal if not superior quality and cost less per unit than arsenal arms. Some congressmen and businessmen claimed that ordnance officers had developed an intellectual "not-invented-here" attitude that made them invulnerable to innovative ideas from the outside, and during the panic and business depression of 1873 legislators whose constituents were in the small-arms trades were especially keen to transfer work from government factories into the private sector. Resentful that a government-designed small arm had been selected for the army in 1873 and that tests in 1878 had resulted only in experimental orders for new rifles, all of which were built under royalty in the Springfield plant, civilian arms makers continuously agitated to abolish the government factories. The debate over public and private arms production played a role in the slow development of the small-arms arsenal at Rock Island, Illinois, and hindered the adoption of a new breechloading rifle. The contest spilled over into foreign affairs, when charges by private arms makers that Chief of Ordnance Alexander Dyer had compromised the United States government by engaging illegally in the international traffic in arms brought on a congressional investigation. In the meantime, lobbying by the Association of Manufacturers of Arms, Ammunition, and Equipment led the Joint Committee on the Reorganization of the Army (known as the Burnside Committee) to recommend in 1878 that the government end production of small arms and ammunition. The Ordnance Bureau responded with figures from its own experts. Lieutenant Colonel J. G. Benton, superintendent of the Springfield Arsenal and an effective member of previous small-arms and ordnance boards, asserted that government-manufactured arms were less expensive than those from the private makers. Although Colonel Benton claimed that questions of private and public production involved "questions of political economy . . . which I shall not pretend to discuss," he implied that arms constructed in public arsenals were of much higher quality than anything available on the private market. The attempt to abolish government small-arms manufacturing was turned aside, and the section was removed from the bill submitted to the Congress.[30]

After 1885, at a time when historians have claimed the country was most committed to private entrepreneurship, the Ordnance Bureau moved for the first time to develop its own facilities to finish the new steel artillery tubes and began a running feud with artillery producers that sputtered until the Spanish-American War. Ordnance always had depended on the private sector for field artillery and coastal artillery tubes, and the wrought iron Parrot rifles and great cast iron Rodman and Dahlgren smooth bores of the 1850s had made American ordnance a world leader. American steel makers, however, had little interest in military contracts. Congress insisted on regular competitive bidding, which eliminated the fiscal predictability that could justify investment in plant and machinery. Even when experimental guns were authorized, the market for gun steel remained too small to justify the investment. The big profits were in the expanding civilian market for wire, cable, rail, plate, and mild steel structural forms, and it would take very favorable government action in the form of subsidies and even more tariff protection to induce American producers to enter the high-risk armaments business. The attitudes of the steel men played into the hands of the iron founders who had a vested interest in military business. They lobbied to prevent the shift over to steel guns, and America's late entry into the field can at least in part be blamed on the iron mongers opposition to new technology.

Lieutenant Colonel Silas Crispin, constructor of ordnance until 1881, was of little help. Crispin, who had commanded the New York Arsenal during the French arms affair, resisted the introduction of steel guns into the American inventory. He was a pragmatic, parsimonious administrator whose most important goal seemed to be to modify in some way and use up all the surplus wrought iron and cast iron guns still under ordnance control. Perhaps it was his concern about reliable sources of supplies, his apprehension about prematurely introducing an untested technology, his long association with the iron founders at West Point and South Boston, or, as his critics claimed, his vested interest in his own designs for improved cast iron artillery. Whatever the reason, it was not until his guns blew up under pressure from increased powder charges and Congress pressed an investigation into the selection of his designs that he reluctantly adopted the new steel technology.[31]

In the 1880s the thrust toward corporate control, with its emphasis on integrated organizations and formal vertical and horizontal lines of authority, made such traditional structures as the War Department and the army appear obsolete. Congress, although most interested in cutting the budget and reducing the officer corps, called twice before 1885 for reorganization of the command and control agencies of the military establishment with little success. The naval hysteria of the mid-eighties brought some money for coastal fortifications, housing and new equipment for the regular army, but the navy got the bulk of the appropriations. There was little chance of wide popular support for army reorganization and reform without the challenge of overt hostilities.

For fifteen years whatever criticism occurred was only part of the traditional struggles of the line to assert command and control over the staff and of the latter to achieve military respectability and recognition as soldiers of the republic. Officers of the line fought with Indians and bureau chiefs, kept their fences mended with influential friends, and fretted over promotion; officers in the subsistence, supply, and technical bureaus worked and tested, jousted with the line over petty matters of administration, kept their legislative fences mended, and fretted over promotion. With opportunities for recognition scarce, ambitious officers seeped from the service into more promising civilian careers. Both future chief signal officer George Owen Squier and future general of the armies of the United States John J. Pershing thought seriously about leaving the service during the early years of their careers.[32]

Commanding General William T. Sherman (1869–1883) was no complacent timeserver. He pressed consistently for systematic reforms in organization, education, and training, but his insistence on a hierarchical command system made his efforts as much a problem as a solution. He resented what he called civilian intervention in military affairs and once in exasperation even suggested that the office of secretary of war be abolished. Before a congressional committee in 1874, when asked who commanded a particular part of the military establishment—in this case the engineer battalion at Willet's Point—he replied, "God only knows for I do not." A little later, complaining of his "powerless position," he took himself and his headquarters off to Saint Louis.[33]

Sherman, whose shade dominated the army until the First World War, denigrated the roles of army support elements. Alluding at one time to the work of the Signal Corps, he said they were "no more soldiers than the men at the Smithsonian Institution. . . . What does a soldier care about the weather?" he asked. "Whether good or bad, he must take it as it comes." He called the Ordnance Bureau "the softest place in the army" and a good spot for "sons and nephews . . . with influential congressional friends." Sherman denied that technical and supply officers were legitimate soldiers and his coterie felt the same way. In 1876, at Sherman's request, John M. Schofield, who was at the time superintendent of the military academy at West Point, headed a committee that revised army regulations to require all officers of the War Department staff to report to the commanding general rather than to the secretary of war. Opposition from all the bureau chiefs, who lobbied against them in Congress, forced deletion of that section and prevented the appearance of a new set of army regulations until 1881.[34]

Sherman encouraged the intellectual development of certain younger combat officers who supported his views of military command. In particular, he kept a close eye on Emory Upton, who had been brevetted for bravery during the Civil War and who had helped modernize American infantry tactics. Upton was serving as commandant of cadets at West Point when Sherman sent him on a mission to study foreign military systems. In two important books, *The Armies of Asia and Europe* (New York: Appleton, 1878) and *The Military Policy of the United States* (circulated privately among line officers for over two decades before its official publication by the War Department in 1904), Upton championed a "modern" American army similar to the expansible force proposed by John C. Calhoun a half century earlier. A nationally controlled force based on the armies of Europe and headed by professional officers and a professional general staff, the new army would replace the old confederation of regulars, militia, and state volunteers, which, in his view, had brought on so much misery and military mischief in the past.[35] Uptonian thinking was soon apparent in the journals of the new military professional associations such as the *Journal of the Military Service Institution of the United States* and the *Cavalry Journal*. It also found a place in the curriculum of the army postgraduate school for infantry and cavalry officers being revitalized at Fort Leavenworth, Kansas, but it was not until the last cohort of soldiers who had served in the Civil War came to power, bringing with them a new group of ambitious officers, that conditions really began to change. Led by Commanding General John Schofield, they began a process that between 1885 and 1900 modified existing connections in the War Department and later brought significant reorganization and reform.[36]

CHAPTER 2

THE WAR DEPARTMENT, 1885–1916

SEARCHING FOR A MODERN COMMAND-AND-CONTROL SYSTEM

On the Fourth of July 1883, holiday crowds flocked to the memorial park at Gettysburg to celebrate the great crusade that had saved the Union. The armies had marched for days toward the battle; the celebrators came by interurban trains in hours. They lodged at the tourist hotels that had sprung up like toadstools in the town and gathered at the commercial pavilions that had created a carnival atmosphere that many claimed desecrated the site of the great federal victory. They bought souvenirs for their romping children, scoured the ground for memorabilia, and toured the battlefield in narrow-gage rail cars. Citizens, on this twentieth anniversary of the battle, listened to oratory commemorating the sacrifices of youths, now grown older, who had fought there. The park was dedicated to the nation, but the sentimental Victorian monuments that were rising within the grounds were dedicated to the heroic officers and volunteer soldiers of the sovereign states. Memorials paid for by voluntary contributions—many of them from school children from Pennsylvania, Massachusetts, New York, Ohio, Maine, and Connecticut—honored the coalition of small-town companies and state regiments that had joined together to stem the rebellion. Gettysburg Park represented not only the current taste and institutional memory of the American people, but also their reactions to what had been happening to them and their country since the Civil War. The loose confederation of local communities that had fought the war was metamorphosing; speed in transportation, communication, and production was steadily driving the fulcrum of power in American life from the periphery toward the center. Nineteenth-century society, where the important things happened in neighborhoods and communities, was changing into another kind where economic and political decisions made in New York or Chicago or Washington, D.C., affected life in Camden, Ohio, or Knoxville, Tennessee, or Sacramento, California, in ways that had previously been inconceivable. The process was incremental and filled with tension as the country's political institutions were modified to deal with economic and social challenges on a national scale. Supporters later labeled it Progressivism, an effort to create a new organizational balance to rationalize the use of resources to achieve greater control and efficiency. Opponents called it a conspiracy to turn communities rooted in history into machines—factories with interchangeable parts, human and material—adrift in time and space.[1]

☆ ☆ ☆

The War Department responded to the same challenges that confronted the rest of American society. Always a complex, multipurpose institution, it had been shaped by peacetime military missions and the ambitions of bureaucrats as well as by wartime crises. In peace problems of command and control had been resolved informally through consultation, either individually or through boards and committees. In war they had been dealt with through ad hoc councils. To assure civilian authority over the military, the commanding general exercised control by order of the secretary of war. As Secretary Robert Todd Lincoln made clear to Commanding General Philip H. Sheridan (1883–1888) in early 1885,

> My understanding of your command is that . . . you are authorized to give direction, subject to the President, who is represented in the War Department by the Secretary of War, to all Division Commanders, and through them, to all under their orders. That includes all the regiments of the Army, and all officers of the Staff Departments detailed by the Secretary of War to serve under you, or under officers subject to your command, subject, of course to such restrictions as may be contained in the Army Regulations, or as may result from special orders of the Secretary of War. . . . In practice the Commanding General is the adviser of the Secretary of War in a multitude of matters.[2]

Generals Sheridan and Sherman understood the system very well and, like Winfield Scott before them, despised it. Lieutenant General John M. Schofield (1888–1895) accepted it and knew how to use it efficiently and effectively. Nelson Miles (1895–1903), the last commanding general, fought the system, often in dramatic ways, and the effects were disastrous. When the shift to an allegedly modern, corporate general staff took place in 1903, little really changed. Secretary of War Elihu Root (1899–1904) understood that changes in title did not mean changes in perception and tried to modify and systematize traditional nineteenth-century practices. Chief of Staff J. Franklin Bell (1906–1910) understood the human variables involved and, like Schofield, tried to use them in the service of the country. Neither Chief of Staff Leonard Wood (1910–1914) nor Adjutant General Fred C. Ainsworth (1904–1912), who had both entered the army as contract surgeons, were capable of seeing beyond their own interests.

General Schofield, an artilleryman and a successful combat soldier, was among the last of the band of brothers who had led Union armies to victory in the Civil War. He had a sophisticated understanding of human affairs and a superb grasp of how the War Department really worked. After the war he served as a diplomat, as superintendent of the military academy at West Point, and, at the direction of General Sherman in 1877, as the head of a committee of officers that attempted unsuccessfully to revise army regulations. He had no use for War Department "purveyors of pork and beans," but he had witnessed the unsuccessful efforts of Sherman and Sheridan to command the War Department staff directly and escape the authority of the secretary of war. He wrote in his memoirs that he considered formal power of that kind inconsistent with military subordination and good citizenship. Until his retirement in 1895, through indirection, accommodation, and diplomacy, he gave the army and the War Department staff consistent and effective leadership.[3]

One of Schofield's first moves upon becoming commanding general of the army was to inform Adjutant General Richard C. Drum that, in the future, all orders that had formerly been circulated under the name of the commanding general should go out under the secretary of war's signature. Schofield held regular meetings with the bureau chiefs to solicit their advice and counsel. He asserted that all were soldiers of the republic and their common goals were to serve the nation effectively. Privately, Schofield never changed his mind about the bureau chiefs. He simply understood that they had to be accommodated. He saw the significance of Secretary of War Robert Todd Lincoln's words and acted quickly to renounce direct command. He would be chief of staff and adviser to his civilian superiors and friend to and coordinator of the work of those he acknowledged as fellow soldiers in the bureaus. He knew how to ask for advice and understood the mellowing effects of consultation. He decentralized control over financial affairs. As president of the new Board of Ordnance and Fortification, he established formal methods of cooperation and doctrinal coordination in the army and among the bureaus.[4] In five years, filling old bottles with new wine, he accomplished his task. In his *Annual Report* for 1893, Schofield wrote that a new era had begun in the War Department. Interdepartmental interests had been harmonized to carry out the "orders of the President and the Secretary of War."[5]

Everyone profited from Schofield's attention.[6] The engineers, with their unique involvement with civil works, improved their traditional good relations with chambers of commerce and business lobbyists. The Corps of Engineers' new flood control and navigation work became technically more systematic. The congressionally mandated Mississippi River and Missouri River commissions gave the engineers the opportunity to plan long-range construction projects under continuing contracts. In the 1890s the corps began the work of flood control on tributaries of the Mississippi, like the Tennessee River, where George W. Goethals got much of the experience that prepared him for his work in Panama. Meanwhile, selecting, building, and arming the Endicott fortifications increased the visibility of the Ordnance Bureau and the Quartermaster Bureau. Even the new Signal Corps reinforced its already significant presence around the major coastal cities. Selecting sites, negotiating the sale of land with local developers, building emplacements, and installing the guns gave everyone work and recognition.

Chief of Ordnance Stephen Vincent Benét blossomed. Between 1885 and his retirement in 1891, Benét presided over the construction and deployment of a new breechloading, steel, 3.2-inch light field gun and the design of a family of modern coastal artillery. He began the process that resulted in the testing and adoption of a new magazine rifle. He experimented with smokeless powder and worked with the Dupont Company to supply it. Old civilian clients such as the West Point, the South Boston, and the Allegheny foundries disappeared, but new industrial partners such as Midvale Steel, Carnegie Steel, and Bethlehem Steel proved ready and able to do business. Much material for the new guns still came from Europe, but the end of foreign dependency was in sight. The Ordnance Bureau finally secured its own gun factory, where it could fulfill its traditional role, setting quality standards for the industry and creating a cost-measuring stick to protect the public. Benét was well pleased. He even implied later in his report that Schofield actually did command the whole army and not simply its combat arms.[7]

General Schofield served for seven years under two presidents, Grover Cleveland and Benjamin Harrison, and four secretaries of war, William C. Endicott, Redfield Proctor, Steven B. Elkins, and Daniel S. Lamont. In his honor, President Cleveland reestablished the rank of lieutenant general, which was bestowed upon Schofield when he retired in 1895. Schofield was one of those who understood that one served himself best by serving others.

He put the interests of the whole before the interests of the parts and the concerns of those over whom he held power before his own. He established the power, at least during his tenure, of the commanding general, forwarded his own interests, and secured a place of esteem and honor. In his memoirs he wrote,

> Long study of the subject, at the instance of Generals Grant and Sherman, earnest efforts to champion their views, and knowledge of the causes of their failure . . . led me to the conclusion . . . that under the government of the United States an actual military commander of the army [was] not possible unless in an extreme emergency like that which led to the assignment of Lieutenant General Grant in 1864; and that the general-in-chief, or nominal commanding general, [could] at most be only a "chief of staff,"—that or nothing,—whatever may be the mere title under which he may be assigned to duty by the President. The way to success in rendering efficient public service does not lie through any assumption of authority which the nation may have given to another, even if not most wisely, but rather in zealous, faithful and subordinate efforts to assist that other in doing what the country has imposed on him. . . . "Be ye wise as a serpent and as harmless as a dove" is the only rule of action I have ever heard of that can steer a soldier clear of trouble.[8]

☆ ☆ ☆

In August 1895 Secretary of War Daniel S. Lamont called Major General Nelson A. Miles to Washington to succeed Schofield. The son of a New England small farmer and abolitionist, Miles, to whom celebrity came perhaps too early, joined the army in 1861 and rose from lieutenant of Massachusetts Volunteers to brevet brigadier general before he was twenty-five. After the war he remained in military service and distinguished himself as commander of the Fifth Infantry during the Indian campaigns of the late sixties and seventies. In 1877 he helped run Chief Joseph and the Nez Percé to ground. In 1886 he commanded the forces that captured Geronimo and the remnants of his Apache band in Arizona and in 1891 led army troops in one of the last tragic acts of the Indian wars, the Ghost Dance fight at the Pine Ridge Reservation. In 1894, after much grumbling, he reluctantly commanded the federal troops that contained the Pullman Strike in Chicago. Miles understood the limits of military force in controlling social change. He sympathized with labor and, ironically, supported Native American rights. Among the few Democratic army officers, "Cump" Sherman's son-in-law remained something of an out-sider in an army whose officers were predominantly Republican. He was well known in Washington and often testified before congressional committees. He served in 1873 on the small-arms board that adopted the Springfield "trap door" rifle. In 1878 he lobbied strenuously but unsuccessfully for the introduction of a new magazine rifle and campaigned for steel guns for the artillery. But if Gilbert and Sullivan had written for the American stage, they would have satirized Miles, who loved flamboyant uniforms, as one of their "Modern Major Generals." Miles advocated all except one of the popular military reforms, and his opposition to that one was so interlocked with his hubris that it ultimately led to his political destruction. Miles believed the commanding general must directly command. He was a difficult man who had no use for, if he could even understand, Schofield's brilliant indirect solutions to the problems of the office. He lacked interpersonal skills, and, as sensitive about his own reputation as he was oblivious to those of others, he left a trail of quarrels and shattered friendships behind him. He was a publicity seeker and a dandified posturer who was right about so many things during his life that he alienated most of his friends.[9]

Until the end of the second Cleveland administration in 1897, little distin-guished the new commanding general from his predecessor. Cordial connec-tions with the secretary of war and the supply and technical staffs, so carefully nurtured by General Schofield, continued. On Miles's recommendation the secretary of war tried unsuccessfully to convince the Congress that the army's infantry regiments should be reorganized into multibattalion units capable of immediate wartime expansion. Secretary Lamont worked to concentrate the army on fewer posts near central railheads to enhance strategic mobility. Lamont and Miles also pressed Congress for funds to complete the coastal fortifications and recommended a new permanent construction board with representation from all interested arms and agencies. Miles was the first to suggest creation of a regiment of bicyclists and the purchase of "motor wagons." The strength of the army had not changed substantially since 1875, and among Miles's more interesting recommendations was one to fix the size of the army in relationship to national population and national wealth as defined through the decennial census. Miles recommended a minimum peacetime strength of one soldier for each two thousand population and a maximum peacetime strength of one soldier per each one thousand population. The secretary of war submitted such schemes to the Congress every year, but they got no further than the House and Senate Military Affairs committees.[10] Miles was abroad doing the circle of

European military maneuvers during the early months of the administration of President William McKinley when the new secretary of war, Russell A. Alger, settled into office.

☆ ☆ ☆

The United States met the crisis of the Spanish-American War with traditional nineteenth-century methods. In 1898, the system of separate spheres and parallel paths still prevailed, and a coalition of regulars and United States volunteers fought the war while the state militias recruited volunteers and provided home defense. The war was too short for major difficulties with state governors and local authorities to emerge. With no formal institutional ways to coordinate the war effort, the president conducted the battle through an informal war council and directed the army and navy by telephone and telegraph from his "War Room" in the executive mansion.[11]

The army consistently reacted to events. War Department planners headed by General Miles recommended in March 1898 that the regular army concentrate near the gulf coast and carry out a "reconnaissance in force" into Cuba during the summer to establish contact with the Cuban patriot army. That would allow the Americans to use the malarial rainy season to mobilize, equip, and train a modest force to invade the island and capture Havana during good weather in the fall. Seizure of Havana would bring about the collapse of the rest of the Spanish Caribbean empire. During May 1898, however, affairs slipped out of the War Department's control and U.S. volunteers were raised more quickly than expected. By June, almost a quarter million men were headed for camp and clamoring for equipment.

President McKinley was under great pressure to undertake an immediate movement against the Spaniards. An experienced volunteer officer from the Civil War, McKinley adopted an indirect strategy. He ordered attacks on the margins of Spanish power in the Caribbean and the Pacific rather than a possibly costly assault against Havana.[12] The president, who abhorred casualties, defined American objectives carefully and sought peace with Spain at the earliest possible moment. Secretary Alger, like William L. Marcy during the Mexican War and Edwin M. Stanton during the Civil War, coordinated the war effort through an ad hoc War Department council of bureau chiefs and administrators and cooperated with Secretary of the Navy John D. Long through the president's war council.[13]

The war was waged on three fronts—Cuba, Puerto Rico, and the Philippines—and required close coordination of the army and navy. Unfortunately, Miles, who was no Grant, abdicated the role of coordinator and blustered off to lead an invasion of Puerto Rico, and there was no Henry Halleck in Washington to act in his name to manage the army and coordinate the campaign. Adjutant General Henry Corbin (1898–1904) undertook that task, gained the ear of the president and the secretary of war, and further undermined Miles's authority.

For the administrators and technicians in the War Department, Civil War organizational models proved adequate. Mobilization moved at a quicker pace than in 1861, while the scale of battle did not require industrial conversion or assignment of production priorities among a number of competing agencies. General William R. Shafter, who commanded the Cuban expedition, may have had no use for telegraphers, but President McKinley and Secretary Alger did, and Chief Signal Officer Adolphus Greely had no trouble getting wire and communications equipment. There was no need to seize the national telegraph or telephone lines. With the cooperation of private firms, Greely linked Washington with the Atlantic, Gulf, and Pacific coasts by multiple telegraph and telephone lines and, in his report for 1898, proclaimed that the age of strategic military communication had arrived.[14]

Connections between the combat arms and the supply, technical, and logistical agencies within the War Department remained informal and consultative. The Ordnance Department expanded small-arms and ammunition production at Springfield and Frankford and bought or made personal accouterments for more than a quarter million men at Rock Island Arsenal in Illinois. Chief of Ordnance Daniel Flagler decentralized contracting and had orders for ordnance equipment placed directly by regional arsenal commanders. When the war began, reserves of small arms and artillery were out of balance. There were more artillery tubes than carriages and more tubes and carriages than ammunition. Even the most experienced civilian contractors could not deliver small arms or artillery of government pattern in less than six months, and the arms that were delivered during the war came from government arsenals. Ordnance shortages appeared because the army was thrown into battle more quickly than anticipated and the war ended abruptly before supply could be synchronized.[15] Captain F. E. Hobbes, inspector of ordnance at Watervliet Arsenal, reported that his efforts to procure artillery and ammunition at the American Ordnance Company, Bridgeport, Connecticut, and at the Driggs-Seabury Company, Derby, Connecticut, had been unsuccessful.[16]

In September 1898, an Ordnance Board headed by Major Stanhope Blunt of the Rock Island Arsenal interviewed regular army combat officers at Camp Wikoff, Long Island. None had commanded volunteers during the Santiago campaign, and none had experience with troops armed with the model 73

Springfield. All, however, condemned the lack of uniformity in small arms types and calibers. The Blunt Board concluded that, aside from shortages of smokeless powder and artillery ammunition, the scarcity of Krag-Jorgensen .30-caliber rifles, and some other minor failures, the bureau's performance had been adequate. "Taken as a whole . . . ordnance equipment for artillery, cavalry and infantry, including ammunition . . . stood admirably the test of the most severe field service, and received high commendation from officers who . . . observed it on the march and in action."[17] When Chief of Ordnance Flagler reviewed the lessons of the war, he concluded that the Civil War experience had been repeated. He anticipated no change in general military policy. In his annual report for 1898 he wrote, "A nation that does not keep a standing army ready equipped is still less likely to undergo the great cost of changing arms in store in order to be always ready to furnish the latest and most improved patterns immediately." State troops, he continued, had arrived poorly equipped and had to be supplied from federal resources. It would be better, he concluded, to have them leave all their material behind as the Civil War volunteers finally did and be supplied "with new stores furnished by the United States in perfect condition and ready for active service." Flagler stressed the need for a general war reserve. He recommended that public rifle-producing capacity be increased to 2,500 a day by fully equipping the Rock Island Arsenal with manufacturing machinery and that a supply of at least 100,000 rifles be accumulated quickly after each equipment change. Rifle production should be continued at a rate of 30,000 a year to replace losses. Flagler also recommended a reserve of field and siege artillery for an army of 500,000 men with a three-month supply of ammunition.[18]

Using the traditionally decentralized system of regional procurement, Commissary General Charles P. Eagan oversupplied the army rather than poisoned or starved it, and by the end of the summer of 1898, stateside camps and depots were full of deteriorating and rotting subsistence.[19] Although there was some confusion at first in getting the men to the mobilization camps, Quartermaster General Marshall I. Ludington managed to clothe, feed, equip, and shelter more than a quarter million and mount three major overseas expeditions in six months. Only the hastily organized expedition to Cuba stumbled. There were difficulties with railroad shipping priorities during May and June and congestion on the single-track line to Tampa, Florida. Transports intended to house troops for a few days had to shelter them for more than a week. The Puerto Rican campaign, which was launched within weeks of the landings at Daiquiri, Cuba, was well supported, and the San Francisco quartermaster expeditiously moved an adequately equipped American force to the Philippines.

Departmental quartermasters contracted for clothing and transport region-ally and expanded production at the bureau's facilities in Philadelphia, Jeffer-sonville, and San Francisco. Civil War models of contracting out precut cloth were continued, but for the first time Philadelphia seamstresses agreed to use sewing machines. The wagon industry was not prepared for mass production, so getting wagons made to army specifications would take nine months. Clem Studebaker, when asked by Secretary of War Alger to supply 200 six-mule wagons and 1,000 escort wagons in two months, replied, "I couldn't agree to turn out 200 six mulers in a year. When you people sold off all your big wagons some two years ago, we used up all our stock. Now we have neither material nor machinery to make them." He complained that the army wagon was too difficult to manufacture. The wagon industry supplied farm wagons of their own designs made from green lumber, and those that were delivered fell apart quickly. The post office made up some of the canvas shortages by making mail bags into tents. The first deliveries of tent canvas, uniform cloth, and boots were substandard and wagons were always short, but nothing like the "shoddy" scandals of the Civil War occurred. In part, the performance was the result of the improved state of the American textile industry and, in part, the result of the work of superb quartermaster inspectors who followed former Quartermaster General Samuel B. Holabird's list of standard specifi-cations.[20] In his report for 1898, Ludington asked for the passage of stronger federal legislation to control the railroads in wartime and recommended that a quartermaster war reserve for 500,000 men be maintained and kept current through annual issues to regular troops and state militias.[21]

Until recently the historiography of the Spanish-American War reflected the views of disgruntled line officers such as General Miles or enthusiastic modern-izers inside and outside the army who sought to shape early twentieth-century military legislation. The temporary congestion at Tampa, the filthy, disease-ridden mobilization camps of the U.S. volunteers, the August "skedaddle" of the Fifth Corps from Cuba to Montauk Point, Long Island, pursued by yellow fever and malaria, and Miles's sensational "embalmed beef" charges against Commissary General Eagan contributed to the view that the war was a colos-sal botch. After months of testimony, however, a commission of former Civil War officers led by Major General Grenville M. Dodge praised the army for accomplishing a "herculean" task in spite of general unpreparedness. The report was no whitewash. It revealed weaknesses that had plagued the War Depart-ment and the army for decades. Small units had operated effectively in the field. In the short time they had to accomplish their missions, the Ordnance, Quartermaster, and Commissary departments had performed adequately. The problems lay in command, control, planning, and coordination. There were no formal connections between the army and navy, and Miles had deserted his post in Washington to lead an attack on a secondary objective, leaving President McKinley to conduct a multiservice, multifront war with a hastily assembled war council. There had been insufficient reserve supplies and no real War Department preparation for general military mobilization. Embarrassing conflicts between the army and the War Department staff had plagued the war effort. In its conclusions, the Dodge Commission suggested that in conducting the war against Spain, the nineteenth-century command-and-control system had reached the limits of its capacity.[22]

☆ ☆ ☆

In August 1899, a new secretary of war, Elihu Root, supported by a critical mass of army, congressional, and public opinion, moved confidently to resolve the issues raised by the war. Root championed neither line supremacy nor consolidated military command, but he sought to settle the argument about the relationship between the commanding general and the secretary of war and formalize the chain of command between the president of the United States, the secretary of war, and the army. If Miles had not been commanding general, affairs would possibly have taken a quite different turn. Miles's arrogance and posturing alienated Secretary Root, President McKinley, and, after McKinley's death, President Theodore Roosevelt. Root was determined that no single personality should ever again have such capacity to influence the conduct of American military affairs. The office of commanding general was abolished, not reformed, and the new chief of staff was given the power to coordinate War Department activities, but not to command. As he wrote in his report for 1903, the new system would recognize historical realities and civilian supremacy would be assured. The president would command through the secretary of war, and the new chief of staff would act, as Schofield had done, in the secretary of war's name. Backed by President Roosevelt, Assistant Adjutant General William H. Carter, and several distinguished Civil War soldiers, including former Commanding General Schofield, Root successfully confronted General Miles; and in 1903, shortly after Miles's retirement and after much lobbying, Congress passed legislation creating an American general staff.[23]

Root quickly implemented other important changes. With little desire to destroy traditional relationships, he began to explore ways to harmonize the multiple agencies in the War Department and the army. He moved cautiously toward formalizing war planning and improving interservice cooperation. In his first *Annual Report* in 1899, he offered the viewpoint championed by every

prominent line officer since the Civil War that "it is a fundamental proposition
. . . that the real object of having an army is to provide for war" and called for
careful study of army administration and planning. In 1900, on the advice of a
board of officers chaired by Brigadier General William Ludlow, he established
a permanent War College Board to modernize officer postgraduate education
and study military policy.[24] The Army War College, created two years later,
became a war planning agency and a division of the general staff. Through an
understanding with the secretary of the navy, the army was connected formally
with the navy by a joint army-navy planning board.[25]

In a landmark decision, Secretary Root ended permanent assignments to the
War Department staff and replaced them with a system of rotation between
staff duty and line service, which was intended to integrate technological
competence with combat proficiency. The detail system aimed ultimately
to homogenize the army and establish a single professional identification
of "soldier" as an expert on all phases of the conduct of war. But Root also
recognized the significance of the previous arrangement of separate spheres
and parallel paths and understood that there would be great resistance in both
the staff and the line to the new detail system. He wisely continued to allow
departmental administrators, technicians, and supply officers direct access to
his office.

It has been argued that the new legislation introduced a partnership between
the secretary of war and the chief of staff that replaced an alleged nineteenth-
century alliance of the secretary and War Department bureau chiefs, but
that seems to be an oversimplification.[26] Schofield had already done that.
It is also tempting to place Root within that body of opinion characterized
by Ellis Hawley as "corporatist." Root was a corporation lawyer and saw the
need for systematic approaches to national problems. He was also a child of
the nineteenth century. His metaphors and similes revealed his ambivalence
about the new doctrines of industrial efficiency. They were often traditionally
organic and anatomical, as when he referred to the "brain of an army," but
they were sometimes mechanical and architectural, as when he referred to the
army as a military machine. Most often, however, he saw the War Department
as an efficiently administered law office like his own New York firm, where the
clerks were bright and well behaved, the junior partners excelled in their own
specialties, and the senior partners refereed disputes, planned for the future,
and set the general tone of the enterprise.[27]

The manner in which Secretary Root manipulated the reform impulse
revealed his political methods and priorities. He was aware of the multipurpose
nature of and the myriad interest groups in the War Department and the

army and the threats they posed to effective reform. He may have wanted a federal reserve force that would make it unnecessary to deal with the states on matters involving the militia and the National Guard, but he knew that such a proposal would create a hornets nest of opposition and settled for the Militia Act of 1903. The Dick Act, as it was called, brought the first substantial reform in the reserve force since 1792. The act retained the universal obligation to serve contained in the original legislation but recognized the National Guard—which was for the first time identified in federal legislation—as the official army reserve. The act also made available sufficient funds to provide general military stores and arms to standardize the guard's tables of organization and equipment and made National Guard officers eligible to attend army postgraduate schools. Regular army officers were to be assigned to help train and inspect the guardsmen, and a provision was made for annual joint maneuvers when funds were available. It was not the whole loaf, but it was a very nice half one.[28]

Root was even more cautious when he dealt with the supply, technical, and logistical departments. In 1902, he proposed a bill to Congress to create a department of supply, but, realizing that any radical attempt to reorganize the existing departments would raise unnecessary difficulties, he quickly withdrew it and postponed reform to another day. Root's political caution had costs, and throughout the Progressive Era general coordination of logistics and supply remained fragmented and difficult. In 1908, Chief of Staff J. Franklin Bell wrote a letter to President Roosevelt recommending a single department of supply and logistics. Bell, however, was a realist and an accomplished practitioner of congressional and interbureau politics. He realized that such a proposition was utopian. Perhaps, he continued, the bureau chiefs, most of whom were reform minded and open to persuasion, might be brought to modify the nineteenth-century system and form some sort of supply council in the War Department. Supply reform, he concluded, was more complex than general staff reform, and War Department leaders must reshape the bureau system incrementally as opportunities arose.[29]

The General Staff Act of 1903 combined nineteenth-century military institutions and early-twentieth-century organizational practices and marked a stage in the continuing effort to define the nature of command and control of the American military establishment. The conflicts in the War Department over organization and management during the Progressive Era were not between antimodernists in the bureaus and modernizers in the general staff. Everyone was a modernizer. They were not between corporatist rationalizers and anticorporatist traditionalists. Everyone understood that it was necessary to coordinate the work of the military establishment in the interest of the nation. The argument was between an assertive minority, including Secretary of War Henry Stimson (1911–1913), who saw the army as an industrial machine with interchangeable and scientifically articulated parts, and a more conventional majority represented by Secretaries Root and William Howard Taft, who held that the army was a community or possibly an extended partnership. The differences were more than those of mere management style. In a community or partnership interests were harmonized; in an industrial machine assignments were scientifically defined and controlled. A community comprised groups of people who had to be persuaded, cajoled, and ultimately brought to commit themselves to a task, a mission, or a cause. The situation was ripe for political conflict. Leo S. Rowe, a student of management at the University of Pennsylvania, wrote in 1905 that institutional change was very slow and older traditions would, even in the midst of a reform period, reassert themselves, often in different guises.[30] This was what happened. Branch and bureau leaders protected their interests while appearing, through the use of the language of fashionable trendsetters in the factories, the board rooms, and the engineering schools, to be on the cutting edge of management and organizational theory.[31] Using a common rhetoric that stressed modernization, efficiency, reform, and reorganization, bureau professionals and their supporters championed the traditional cause of separate spheres and parallel paths with its virtues of consultation, cooperation, and harmonization, while the line and its allies argued for a vertically constructed corporate chain of command. All the old tensions and drives for dominance by the line and the countervailing thrust for recognition and equal status by War Department administrators and technicians continued. Tables of organization were reorganized, but conditions remained much the same. Technicians and administrators in the bureaus, field soldiers, and military and civilian reformers and reorganizers sought increased status in the revitalized army and, if possible, expanded influence in making military policy.

In the bureaucratic wars of the Progressive Era, alliances shifted constantly, but officers in the combat arms, many of whom seldom saw beyond branch advantage, supported a hierarchical chain of command under a chief of staff whose formal power would resemble that which Scott, Sherman, Sheridan, and Miles had unsuccessfully sought for the old commanding general of the army. The bureau chiefs clung to the consultative definition developed by Schofield and a consultative approach to the problem of command with the chief of staff acting as a sort of "chairman of the board." Only Root, Taft, and Chief of Staff Bell saw the opportunity to combine contemporary management with nineteenth-century conventions and verities. In their view the new chief of staff would be first among military equals and the official conduit through which the president and the secretary of war communicated with the army. In 1904, Paymaster General Alfred E. Bates, a survivor of many bureaucratic battles and a shrewd observer of the secretary's careful manipulations, wrote of the politically adroit Root that he had "at last placed the Army on a scientific business basis."[32]

When Chief of Staff Bell wrote his prudent letter to Theodore Roosevelt in 1908 about organizing a supply department, he could not anticipate that in a few years a mean-spirited, old fashioned personal feud would threaten a decade of incremental improvement and bring distress to the supporters of War Department reform, regardless of their management philosophies. The controversy between Chief of Staff Leonard Wood and Adjutant General Fred Ainsworth (1904–1912), which was the exception to the generally cordial relations that existed between the bureau chiefs, the chief of staff, and the secretary of war before the First World War, has dominated much of the literature about the period. Root and Taft had avoided a confrontation with Ainsworth, but both had played a part in precipitating the battle. Root had decided that he did not want the War Department staff tied up in detail and combined the adjutant general's office and the pension and records office into a new office of military secretary headed by Ainsworth. Secretary of War Taft, in a significant political blunder, named the military secretary the acting secretary of war when he or the assistant secretary of war was out of Washington, thus making Ainsworth, on occasion, superior to the chief of staff. When the military secretaryship was abolished and the adjutant general's office re-established, Ainsworth apparently believed that he still wielded such authority.[33]

Wood succeeded Bell in 1910, and in May 1911 Stimson became secretary of war. Just before Taft, who was by then president, asked Stimson to replace the departing secretary, Jacob M. Dickinson, a friend had written Stimson that he should accept the offer because the War Department, in his view no longer a place for time servers, would present "interesting problems" for a talented man.[34] A volunteer soldier during the war with Spain and a member of former Secretary Root's law firm, Stimson was sympathetic to the new War Department reforms. Soon, however, he fell under Wood's influence. Wood was Stimson's sort of man. An outdoorsman and a progressive, he had all sorts of plans to reorganize and reform the army. He also had a potentially disastrous relationship growing with Ainsworth.

Neither Ainsworth nor Wood really cared about the current debates concerning War Department management and the role of a general staff. Both were medical doctors—Ainsworth had received his degree from the University of the

City of New York (later New York University), whereas Wood had graduated from Harvard Medical School a decade later—and had begun their careers as contract surgeons. Neither had served with troops at the company level and both had advanced their prospects by manipulating the political system. Both had risen to prominence in unconventional ways, Ainsworth as an expert in business methods, first in the records and pensions office and later as military secretary and adjutant general, and Wood as a friend and physician to presidents and a colonial administrator. Both loved to command but hated to be commanded. Ainsworth had taken the measure of more than one secretary of war, including the formidable Root, and Wood had outmaneuvered more than one commanding officer. At the time of his appointment as chief of staff, Wood was known, at least to Ainsworth, as an opponent of the general staff system. Both men had reputations as efficient administrators and each was hell bent on having his own way. Both were full of hubris and adamant in pursuit of personal power and would use even the president of the United States, the secretary of war, and the Congress to further their personal ambitions. The struggle for supremacy between the adjutant general and the chief of staff left nothing but wreckage behind.

Wood was an authoritarian. Committed to a hierarchical chain of command, he had little interest in being a board chairman. Like Winfield Scott, he wanted to be commanding general of the army. A charming and charismatic leader with powerful friends, he was a formidable opponent. On the other hand, a fellow officer once described Ainsworth as the only completely evil man he had ever known. Ainsworth, who had invested wisely and well, was independently wealthy. He used all his means as a manipulator and bureaucratic politician to control the War Department. Neither Wood nor Ainsworth understood Schofield's admonition that to make the military system function one had to consult rather than command and that power in a mutlipurpose organization had to be shared if it were to be effective.

The precipitating issues in the Wood-Ainsworth affair were trivial, involving the assignment of officers to recruiting duty and the simplification of departmental paperwork. In both the recruiting case and the muster roll affair, the adjutant general argued that the chief of staff was interfering illegally in the affairs of his department. Ainsworth fought Wood with every political weapon at his command, but he finally overreached himself. A memorandum, sardonic and impolitic, opened him to Wood's attack. The adjutant general retired "voluntarily" before a court martial could find him guilty of insubordination. Wood's success, however, was illusionary—Ainsworth was not an old soldier who simply faded away. He changed his command post after President

Taft approved his retirement and held court in his spacious apartment at the Concord Hotel in Washington, D.C., where he entertained congressmen and disgruntled officers. In 1912 he began to take his revenge. He and his associates in Congress turned Root's detail system upside down. The "Manchu Law" of 1912 modified legislation passed in 1910 and denied officers of the line below the rank of major appointment to detached service unless they had spent two of the preceding six years with their home units. Four years later, during the debates over the National Defense Act of 1916, Ainsworth struck again when he helped Congressman James Hay of Virginia cut the strength of the general staff and restrict its authority. Meanwhile, Wood ended his tour as chief of staff in 1914 and took command of the Eastern Department. In spite of his work supporting military reform during the preparedness campaign, he never achieved the fame and position he desired. Secretary of War Newton D. Baker called him his most insubordinate subordinate and prevented him from gaining glory and advancement during the First World War.[35]

The Wood-Ainsworth affair was a disaster. Brigadier General Tasker H. Bliss lamented that Wood had abused his power. In a letter to Judge Advocate General Enoch H. Crowder, Bliss, echoing Schofield's views of two decades before, declared that the chief of staff must be the servant of the army, not its master. Only by institutionalizing and depersonalizing the office could its real potential for control be realized. The secret of command lay in balancing hierarchy and consultation, and Bliss believed that neither Ainsworth nor Wood even knew there was a question, much less that it might have an answer. Wood might have clarified relations with the bureau chiefs, but he perpetuated the kind of personal administrative interference that had weakened the career of Nelson Miles. Bliss, like Schofield, understood that balancing hierarchy and consultation in managing the War Department was an art that involved power sharing and brought satisfaction and success to all who served.[36]

CHAPTER 3

THE WAR DEPARTMENT, 1900–1916

GENERAL SUPPLY AND MILITARY TECHNOLOGY

After the war with Spain, the redefined and expanded mission of the army brought much work and some money for the bureaus and gave logisticians and technicians challenging tasks. Quartermaster General James Aleshire and Commissary General Henry Sharpe were imaginative administrators. Chief of Ordnance William Crozier gained a reputation as a military manager and efficiency expert, while Signal Corps officers Adolphus Greely, James Allen, George P. Scriven, and George O. Squier were outstanding innovators and technicians. Colonel George W. Goethals of the engineers gained fame as the builder of the Panama Canal. By 1916, War Department scientists, technicians, and industrial managers had achieved national and international recognition as leaders in their fields.[1]

A revisionist description of the War Department bureau chiefs as imaginative innovators runs the risk of creating a portrait as far from reality as older, line-dominated interpretations that define them as reactionary, incompetent obstructionists.[2] The Quartermaster Bureau at first resisted reform. Quartermaster General Luddington, who remained in control until 1903, and Charles F. Humphrey, who succeeded him, were suspicious of the new general staff and, in particular, opposed Root's new detail system, which would regularly interchange officers of the line and bureau technicians. Humphrey argued that detailing from the line would undermine the professionalism of quartermaster officers and asserted that such a system flew in the face of contemporary business practices and fostered military amateurism. Humphrey also resisted general staff supervision, and a short time later Secretary of War William Howard Taft and President Theodore Roosevelt manipulated his retirement from the army.[3]

On July 1, 1907, James B. Aleshire became the new quartermaster general. Aleshire was a new kind of bureau chief. After graduating from West Point in

1880, he spent fourteen years on the frontier in the First Cavalry Regiment. He made a reputation on the plains as an administrator and logistician, but his most spectacular success came during the great Ohio River flood of 1884, when he supplied victims between Parkersburg, West Virginia, and Ironton, Ohio, with food, shelter and clothing. Aleshire subsequently served as secretary of the Infantry and Cavalry School at Fort Leavenworth, Kansas. Still a lieutenant in 1895, he transferred to the Quartermaster Department to gain promotion and to support his growing family. Aleshire combined a cavalryman's interest in big, handsome horses with a quartermaster's concern with breeding and quality. He served during the Spanish-American War as chief purchasing agent for horses and mules for the army. In 1900 he became quartermaster of the China Relief Expedition and went from there to the Philippines as Chief Quartermaster Humphrey's assistant in charge of the Manila Quartermaster Depot. When Humphrey became quartermaster general in 1903, he took Aleshire with him to Washington. During the next four years Aleshire practiced his specialty. He recommended that a system of remount depots for the army be established where horses would be bought young and prepared for service. His work brought him to the attention of President Roosevelt, and when Humphrey fell from grace Aleshire was prepared to step into his place.

The Aleshire years at the Quartermaster Bureau were the most creative since the days of Montgomery Meigs. Like the other bureau chiefs, the new quartermaster general regarded the detail system as an attack on bureau professionalism and a bid for line supremacy, but he chose to work quietly toward its elimination rather than confront Chief of Staff J. Franklin Bell outright. Aleshire extended the authority of local and regional quartermasters. Each year he apportioned funds to officers in the field who then allotted supplies to the troops in their territorial departments. In 1908 he became the first bureau chief to prepare and submit an itemized budget to Congress. After consulting field soldiers, the Philadelphia Quartermaster Depot designed and issued a new olive-drab winter uniform and cooperated with private textile firms in an attempt to develop a light, fixed-color summer uniform. After merger with the Commissary Bureau, he ordered continued experiments with rations and field kitchens and established the cooks and bakers schools that Commissary General Henry Sharpe had championed for years. Although officer training continued in the apprentice tradition, after the quartermaster field service was created in 1912 Aleshire established a quartermaster school for enlisted men.

The Quartermaster Bureau was traditionally responsible for transportation. In 1906 Aleshire attempted to strengthen the emergency power of the military over the railroads. Shortly before he assumed command, federal legislation gave troop and supply trains transportation priority in emergencies, and in 1907 Aleshire called a conference of railroad men in Washington to work out contingency plans. The railroaders paid lip service to the War Department's needs but resisted the idea that penalties should be imposed on violators. Although Aleshire attempted to clarify the grounds on which penalties could be levied, he was not sanguine. After his experience with sidetracked trains during the mobilizations on the Mexican border in 1912, he became convinced that effective rail operation could not be secured without punitive legislation. He also opposed, successfully in the Philippines and unsuccessfully in the Caribbean, attempts by shippers to dismantle the quartermaster transport fleet and turn seaborne logistics over to private contractors.[4]

In 1909, just when Aleshire had begun to put his remount project in place, the American army neared the end of the animal transport era. By 1910 reliable internal combustion automobiles and trucks were in production and commercial trucks were replacing animal transport in urban America. Introduction of the new technology, however, posed formidable problems. American roads and bridges were so poor that currently available trucks could not operate effectively over them. West of the Mississippi and along the Mexican border, except for simple dirt tracks, road networks did not exist.

From a hundred years of experience, quartermasters knew the range and carrying capacity of animal transport. They knew how much forage an animal consumed in a year and how much fodder it took to move a ton of supplies a given distance. They knew how long it took to build a fleet of wagons. Parts of the army escort and cargo wagons were interchangeable, and in an emergency the quartermaster general's office had old and trusted suppliers like Studebaker to meet its needs. The premature introduction of motor transport would also complicate maintenance. New requirements for automotive fuel and spare parts would grow, while the need for harness, fodder, and wagon parts would continue. Money was scarce for testing new equipment, and the army moved cautiously until it was certain that trucks and cars could replace animals successfully. By 1908 automotive research and development had moved from the fragile to the volatile phase, but it had not yet become robust and stabilized. At first it was not even clear that the gasoline engine was the best power source. The first army automobiles were electric cars, which the Signal Corps purchased in 1899. Battery failures quickly showed that they were unsuitable for field use and later experiments with steam cars showed that the gasoline engine was the only suitable one for military vehicles.[5] Early trucks were underpowered. Chain-propelled four-wheel drive gave some off-road capacity, but lack of a transfer case meant that there was no way for the same vehicle to operate effectively over both rough country and improved highways. Tests with light vehicles at the 1906 and 1908 maneuvers, though, showed some promise.[6]

The Quartermaster Department did not have exclusive procurement authority. In 1912, when the bureau published its first specifications for a one-and-a-half-ton truck, four other War Department bureaus—Engineers, Ordnance, Signal Corps, and the Office of the Surgeon General—also bought motor trucks, and each bureau pressed for special models to meet its own particular needs. In 1913 the Quartermaster Bureau began an enduring association with the Society of Automotive Engineers (SAE) that a generation later would provide the army with the finest fleet of transport trucks in the world.[7] In 1916, spurred by the large-scale use of trucks on the Mexican border, the SAE and the bureau set out to design a group of standard army trucks. There were no existing organizational connections for the War Department to bring all the using services and the SAE together to implement such a policy except for ad hoc conferences. Commercial truck manufacturers were not interested in building special vehicles, because doing so meant short production runs and little profit. They insisted that the army buy their regular commercial products. In 1916, aside from color, there was no significant standardization of military trucks in the American army.[8] Technology was still imperfect, and it seemed prudent to wait for motor transport to become robust before making the investment involved in shifting completely from mules to motors.

The Quartermaster Bureau also conducted an extensive building and remodeling program that proved very popular with Congress. The increased size of the army, requirements for new construction in Hawaii, the Philippines, and the Canal Zone, and the expansion of existing posts in the United States championed by the War Department brought increased appropriations and provided lucrative work for local contractors. In his report for 1903, Quartermaster General Luddington claimed that "a vastly greater amount of construction work was planned, undertaken and contracted . . . than during any previous year in the history of the army."[9] The Quartermaster Bureau was committed to the "beautiful park" approach to post building, and, in keeping with the spirit of contemporary city planners, army posts, especially ones such as Governor's Island in New York harbor, became models of urban landscaping. Secretary of War Stimson phlegmatically complained in 1912 that they might be nice to look at but they had very little room for the combined arms maneuvers essential for war readiness.[10]

In 1912, more than a decade of agitation finally bore fruit when Aleshire took up the issues raised in the Burnside Committee recommendation of 1878 and secured congressional legislation combining the offices of the paymaster general, the commissary general, and the quartermaster general into the Quartermaster Corps. Luddington and Humphrey had opposed consolidation, and Aleshire was unimpressed when Commissary General Henry G. Sharpe pushed the merger of the Commissary and Quartermaster bureaus. After a tour of European armies in 1907, Sharpe reintroduced the idea of a single department of supply that would also include technical agencies such as the Ordnance Bureau. Consolidation of all the supply bureaus, when proposed in 1878, had received a cold reception, and in 1907 opposition again arose to including Ordnance, the Signal Corps, the Medical Corps, and the Corps of Engineers in a single agency.[11] Four years later, however, Aleshire, encouraged by Secretary Stimson's drive for efficiency and rationalization, persuaded that Sharpe, at least for the present, had no ambition to become quartermaster general, and reassured that no reductions in officer strength or appropriations would occur, agreed to a more modest proposal that turned the Quartermaster Bureau into a militarized logistical and supply branch with a projected enlisted field service corps of more than 6,000 men.

Consolidation of the Paymaster, Commissary, and Quartermaster bureaus were connected indirectly with the Wood-Ainsworth affair. In 1910 Secretary of War Jacob M. Dickinson appointed members to the War Department Board on Business Methods, and in 1911 he directed that each bureau examine its operations and reduce "the unnecessary large amount of intricate and cumbersome paperwork in the Army." Under the direction of Inspector General Ernest A. Garlington, documents from the bureau chiefs were collected and a report was submitted in February 1911. The next month President Taft appointed members to the Federal Commission on Economy and Efficiency in Government. Chaired by Frederick A. Cleveland, the president's financial adviser, it had access to the Garlington report and carried out its investigation during the early stages of the Wood-Ainsworth muster roll affair. The new secretary of war, Henry Stimson, immediately leaped into the reorganization effort and insisted that the Garlington report become part of the Cleveland Commission's recommendations.

Although the commission was not primarily concerned with restructuring the military, it did recommend the consolidation of the Paymaster, Quartermaster, and Commissary bureaus into a single general supply agency. The proposal had foundered earlier in the decade in part because the new supply chief would be a major general and outrank his colleagues in the other bureaus, but, when that idea was rejected in 1912, consolidation was secured without great difficulty. Then everything stopped. Congress paid little attention to the other recommendations of the Cleveland Commission because they proposed reductions in political patronage and the further expansion of the civil-service system. The project got no further funding, and the Taft administration left office before it could be implemented.

What happened next is still opaque. The available information suggests that an informal agreement was struck between Quartermaster General Aleshire and Commissary General Sharpe that Aleshire would become the first chief of the consolidated Quartermaster Corps and that Sharpe would succeed him when he retired. The bargain did not sit well with other members of the quartermaster staff, and in 1916 Sharpe was appointed only after a difficult fight with Brigadier General Carroll A. Devol, who believed he should be Aleshire's successor.[12] In June 1916, the new Quartermaster Corps, with its expanded staff, could support an operation such as that against Spain in 1898 without difficulty. Neither Aleshire nor Sharpe, nor anyone else for that matter, however, was prepared for a war at long range against a first-class power.

☆ ☆ ☆

The Ordnance Department, always a multiproduct manufacturing enterprise, was among the most active and progressive elements in the War Department. Chief of Ordnance William Crozier, whom Hugh Aiken has described as one of the most important organizational innovators in the War Department, was interested in reducing costs and in the specifics of industrial management. Colonel Charles G. Mettle, who would command Watervliet Arsenal during the First World War, and Colonel James Walker Benét, the artillery expert and son of former Chief of Ordnance Stephen Vincent Benét, who would succeed Mettle, were nationally recognized efficiency experts.

On November 22, 1901, Crozier became a brigadier general and the youngest chief of ordnance since George Bomford. He was an inventor with a good reputation in the professional engineering community as well as an experienced diplomat. Born in Carrollton, Ohio, in 1854, Crozier graduated fifth in his class from West Point in 1876. As a young officer he served in the West with the Fourth Field Artillery and participated in campaigns against the Sioux and Bannock Indians. In 1879 he returned to West Point to teach mathematics. In 1881 he transferred from artillery to ordnance and was promoted to first lieutenant. Crozier was interested in heavy guns and disappearing carriages. During the mid-1880s he worked with A. R. Buffington to design a disappearing carriage that was later adopted for the new coastal fortifications system, and in 1890 he was promoted to captain. Crozier was inspector of gulf and Atlantic coast defenses during the Spanish-American War. In 1899, still a captain, he became the military advisor to the American representative to the International

Conference on Peace and Arms Limitation at the Hague. He subsequently served in the Philippines and was chief ordnance officer in the China Relief Expedition. Secretary of War Root and President Roosevelt played important roles in his promotion, which, unfortunately, left resentment among more conventionally trained bureau technicians and ultimately led to a congressional investigation.[13]

Crozier took command at an opportune time. Military small-arms and artillery technology were technologically robust. After two experimental decades, under the direction of gifted designers and inventors; innovative factory managers such as Benét; and field artillery and small-arms experts like Charles B. Wheeler and the virtuoso John M. Thompson, the bureau was prepared to undertake the most far-reaching small-arms and artillery production program up to that time in American peacetime history. Within a decade the Ordnance Bureau developed a new model rifle and a new small-arms cartridge, standardized the Vickers-Maxim machine gun, and designed, developed, and deployed a modern system of quick-firing field artillery with improved fuses and ammunition. Ordnance technicians also insisted that the new field guns be produced with interchangeable parts.

Crozier controlled a rapidly expanding industrial establishment that, over the previous decades, had captured substantial artillery tube, breech, and recuperation production from the private sector and had doubled its small-arms capacity at the Springfield and Rock Island arsenals. It designed and manufactured most of its own ordnance except propellants. The Dick Act and subsequent legislation in 1908, which standardized the weapons and equipment of the National Guard and the regular army, made larger manufacturing runs of small arms and artillery possible. Continued appropriations for seacoast guns and carriages for home defense and colonial fortification and the navy's need for increased capacity to produce guns for the expanding fleet kept the arsenals at Watervliet and Watertown operating at near capacity. At Rock Island, the new rifle plant and the recently completed field carriage and caisson plant were expanded.

Crozier strove to make the bureau a model of arms-making professionalism and efficiency. Like the other bureau chiefs, he was concerned about the impact of the detail system, and it was that issue that led to the creation of a formal postgraduate ordnance school like those of the Engineers, Signal Corps, and Coast Artillery. In December, 1901, shortly after he took command, Crozier detailed Captain Beverley W. Dunn of the Frankford Arsenal, outside of Philadelphia, Pennsylvania, to inspect the best engineering schools in the country and make recommendations for a professional postgraduate ordnance school. His orders were to construct a one-year course to be offered at Sandy Hook proving grounds to train young officers coming into the bureau from line assignments in "all duties in connection with gun construction, carriage construction and their attendant mechanical features." The curriculum would also include "general mechanical engineering, electrical engineering, and the chemistry of explosives and optics."

Dunn inspected the Massachusetts Institute of Technology and Rensselear, Cornell, and Johns Hopkins Universities and reported on his tour in February 1902. Ranging far beyond his instructions, he defined the tensions between ordnance technicians and line soldiers in words reminiscent of those of the early-nineteenth-century chief of ordnance George Bomford and criticized the new detail system, arguing that "manufacturing and soldiering are too radically different to be combined in one successful vocation" and that detailing ordnance officers to the line would "render [them] non-productive in Ordnance work." Dunn labeled the traditional ordnance apprentice system one of "no instruction" and asserted that ordnance officers were "specialists without special education." His own career, he pointed out, was an example of the limitations of the current system. He had been overwhelmed with responsibility very early and never gained real proficiency in his discipline of artillery ammunition design and production. Dunn advised that the army follow the navy's lead. When young naval officers were selected for training as naval construction engineers, they were sent to a special one-year postgraduate course at MIT before taking up their assignments. He suggested that a similar program in mechanical and electrical engineering be offered to young West Pointers. After no more than a year's service in the field, a budding ordnance officer should be required to earn an engineering degree at a school such as MIT. After short familiarization tours at each arsenal of production, the young army officer should select a specialty, devote his career as a lieutenant and captain to perfecting his professional skills under the direction of an expert officer, and take correspondence courses in administration. In Dunn's opinion, the officer should stay at the same assignment for his active specialist career. Upon promotion to major at about age forty-three, he would give up his work in design and construction and move into general administration, thus fitting himself for the general direction of work in all specialties and for the responsibilities of command. The personnel of the Ordnance Bureau should be doubled and all civilian engineers at the arsenals should be replaced with professional soldiers.

Dunn admitted that the scheme was utopian. His practical advice was to regularize the pattern of informal instruction and examination that had emerged a generation earlier under Benét. He recommended a one-year curriculum modeled on the mechanical and electrical engineering theory courses at MIT and the practical shop technique courses offered at the University of Pennsylvania. The machine shops and laboratories at the proving grounds should be expanded and equipped with the latest facilities. Dunn thought that a fine start had already been made at the Sandy Hook proving grounds in providing research equipment. He suggested that formal relationships should be established with the great engineering schools and that their faculties should be invited on a regular basis to the proving grounds to teach. Businessmen, engineers, and managers from the steel and electronics industry should be regular visitors at the school and student officers should visit the private arms makers on a regular basis as part of their training. After a visit to Fort Monroe, Dunn added that ordnance officers should also attend firing and maintenance classes with coast artillerymen. Crozier approved the Dunn report, and by 1907 a formal school of instruction was operating at Sandy Hook, the first class of young officers was working in the arsenals, and ordnance had joined the signal service and the engineers in creating a rational system of instruction that would supplement the older examination method and support their independent professional status in the army.[14]

Compared with the turbulent nineties, connections between the Ordnance Bureau and the private national defense sector were stable. By 1900 a new group of client firms—Bethlehem, Midvale, Carnegie, and Crucible Steel—had replaced the old South Boston–West Point–Allegheny network. They were bigger and less dependent on government contracts but met Crozier's needs for private peacetime production of field and coast artillery and provided surge capacity for emergencies. The Colt Patent Firearms Company continued to manufacture pistols and machine guns under license, while Driggs-Seabury supplied shells to reinforce the production of the Frankford Arsenal. Like his predecessors, Crozier viewed old small-arms rivals such as Remington and Winchester suspiciously, but he was not above occasionally granting them small ammunition contracts to maintain production capacity.[15]

The controversy over armor-plate prices that plagued relations between the navy, Congress, and private producers during the Progressive Era and brought demands for a public armor-plate factory did not touch the army. Crozier had his own facilities and encouraged civilian production of complex weapons to assure a second source in emergencies. He allocated contracts to favored domestic manufacturers such as Warner & Swasey of Cleveland, Ohio, to develop domestic sources of optical glass for rangefinders and binoculars. The bureau continued previous practices of indirect subsidy by buying from

American manufacturers and advancing funds and furnishing machinery to private contractors, but Crozier did not hesitate to buy technology abroad when domestic research and development were too costly.

The new three-inch field gun was a good example. The English historian of field artillery, Ian Hogg, called it an "off the peg" Austrian-designed Erhardt, but that was not exactly the case. It had a modified Franco-British breech mechanism, a modified British recuperator, an American carriage, and modified German sights. The government paid royalties on all non-American features, because the costs of the patent rights were much less than the costs of domestic development. In the surge to reequip the army with new artillery after 1902, requirements for high-quality nickel-steel forgings outran domestic supplies and Crozier persuaded Root to allow him to contract with Rhienmetall, Schneider, and Armstrong to make up the deficit.[16]

There was one exception. Since 1890 the bureau had been investigating the production of the new smokeless powders and building informal relations with American private producers to encourage production. The army had always procured its black powder in the private economy and, during the nineteenth century, developed a special patron-client relationship with the DuPont Company of Wilmington, Delaware. It was the practice, after accepting competitive bids, to divide the annual powder appropriation between DuPont, which consistently bid low, and several other powder makers to maintain a mobilization base. Except for the construction industry, which used dynamite, and producers of sporting arms, smokeless powder and high explosives had only military consumers, and, as smokeless replaced black powder, producers could no longer simply allocate a portion of regular black powder production to military use. They had to buy special equipment and build new facilities, and by 1905 only DuPont and its subsidiary, the International Smokeless Powder Company, had the capacity to manufacture the new explosives. There were several other producers connected indirectly with DuPont, by then called the "Big Company," but they lacked DuPont's ability to supply large quantities of high-quality smokeless powder. The Wilmington firm was the first to establish a separate military explosives division to compete with European producers.[17] During the black-powder era the annual powder makers' bids on government business had been similar, but during the early years of smokeless powder they grew closer, until by 1900 manufacturers were asking the same price for their products.[18] This occurred as DuPont bought into the other smokeless companies and created what the newspapers called the "Powder Trust."[19]

General Crozier was not antibusiness, but he knew from previous experience that DuPont was following the collusive business practices the government already faced among big gun and armor-plate manufacturers. Crozier recommended that Congress create an army powder plant similar to the navy plant established some years earlier at Indian Head, Maryland. In October 1907, after Congressional hearings similar to the armor-plate hearings of the mid-nineties, the army smokeless powder plant at Picatinny in New Jersey opened and began production.

Crozier actually preferred to work with DuPont because the company could guarantee a high-quality product, but DuPont executives interpreted the opening of the government powder plant at Picatinny as a direct attack. "Colonel" Edmund G. Buckner, who headed the DuPont lobby in Washington, stated in 1908 that the Ordnance Department should be considered "a competitive manufacturing organization."[20]

By 1910 Crozier headed a comprehensive, government-owned, multi-product arms corporation and, as the leader of a large-scale enterprise, faced issues of efficient organization and management similar to those encountered by corporate managers in the private sector. He sought to simplify bureau organization, reduce paperwork, and bring down production costs. Unlike his private counterparts, who had more flexibility, Crozier could not invest capital or allocate resources without the consent of Congress. Appropriations for the arsenals and depots depended as much on the activity of local business groups, some of which resented the presence of government plants, and Congressional coalitions, which strove to attract federal money to their own states.

An attempt to innovate in the management of the arsenals of production led to one of the rare political failures of Crozier's prewar career. Like any other business executive, he faced problems of labor-management relations, and in 1910, as part of his program to make his organization more cost-effective, he made an ill-advised attempt to change the methods of shop management at the arsenals. Crozier was an admirer of the efficiency expert Frederick W. Taylor, and he ordered the Taylor time-and-motion-study system introduced at Watertown and Rock Island arsenals. The Taylor plan defined labor as a commodity and threatened a most satisfactory labor-control system introduced in army plants a decade before, which followed a different, more humane course than in private industry. When Crozier attempted to introduce "expertise and efficiency" into the ordnance production system, he was immediately confronted by worker resistance, especially at Watertown Arsenal in upstate New York, and the plan was blocked in Congress in 1912.[21] Even so, under Crozier's leadership, ordnance plants reorganized and expanded to a point where, by 1912, they rivaled the most efficient private industrial enterprises in the country. Testifying before both the House and Senate Appropriations committees in 1913, Crozier argued that his enterprises served as yardsticks to protect the public from exploitation by private arms makers.[22] He was such a successful champion of public production of military equipment that Congress undermined his plans to maintain second civilian suppliers as a war mobilization base by forbidding the Ordnance Bureau to purchase any items from private manufacturers in peacetime that could be made less expensively in publicly owned plants.[23]

☆ ☆ ☆

The Signal Corps achieved its first public recognition in electronic communication during the Progressive Era. According to Chief Signal Officer Adolphus Greely, when General William Shafter sailed for Cuba he rejected Greely's offer of communications troops. "I don't want men with flags," Shafter snorted, "Give me men with guns." Greely claimed Shafter, who departed Tampa "without even a call bell," continued to show what Greely called the characteristic denseness of the field soldier toward military communications; however, James Allen, who succeeded Greely as chief of signals, used wireless intercepts to locate the Spanish fleet in Santiago harbor in May, 1898, and Shafter expressed his appreciation to his signals staff in his after-action report.[24] After the turn of the century the Signal Corps supervised the building of the Alaska Telegraph and the transpacific cable connecting the United States with its new possessions in the Far East. Electronics was the road to advancement, and every chief signal officer before the First World War was either a communications manager or an electronics scientist and technician.

None of the new electronic technologies was specifically developed for military purposes, but all had obvious military uses. The telephone, telegraph, and wireless radio made it possible, potentially, to centralize command and control on the battlefield and apply combined arms doctrine in ways previously considered impossible. Commercial wire telephone, telegraph, and intercontinental cable technologies were robust, and Greely shrewdly positioned the Signal Corps to exploit them. Greely's successors, James Allen and George Scriven, encouraged research-and-development, and by the First World War the Signal Corps, in cooperation with the electronics industry, had developed a singular research-and-development program and had adopted reliable field telephones and field telegraphs. The major electronic suppliers for the Signal Corps were General Electric, formerly the Edison Electric Company, and Westinghouse; and connections between the Signal Corps, Western Electric, and the Bell Company in the area of electronic communication approached symbiosis.[25]

The greatest innovations before the First World War came in wireless communication. Before 1914 the Deforest vacuum tube and the Fessenden and Alexanderson alternators opened possibilities for voice-radio telephony, and the Signal Corps moved quickly to exploit them. In 1909 Signal Corps appropriations for radio research alone was ten times its entire budget before the Spanish-American War.[26] The key figure was George Owen Squier. Unhappy with the available rudimentary commercial wireless equipment, the Signal Corps began to build its own equipment in a small Washington laboratory and distribute it to the army. Squier and his associates expanded the experimental radio telephone operations and made it clear they were willing to share information with the rest of the electronics community. The navy was also interested, as was the Bureau of Standards. In a short time the navy and Signal Corps established experimental laboratories at the Bureau of Standards and began to conduct cooperative tests at the new signal laboratory in Washington, D.C. By the time war began in Europe in 1914, the Signal Corps was a leader in electronic research and was about to build an experimental radio telephone that, though still fragile, had a range of more than a hundred miles and possessed the potential to solve the frustrating communication problems of the early-twentieth-century battlefield.[27]

The communications mission connected the Signal Corps with the new science of aeronautics and the infant aircraft industry. From his days as a weatherman, Greely had been fascinated by balloons. He encouraged experiments with dirigibles and understood the military potential of heavier-than-air technologies. Greely helped persuade the Board of Ordnance and Fortification to channel $125,000 in development money to Samuel Pierpont Langley of the Smithsonian Institution to help build a heavier-than-air machine. Langley had been interested in heavier-than-air technology since the 1880s. When he moved from Pittsburgh's Allegheny Observatory to Washington, he opened a laboratory and began to experiment. In 1894 Massachusetts senator Henry Cabot Lodge unsuccessfully introduced legislation to offer a prize of $100,000 for a heavier-than-air machine. During the Spanish-American War, a joint army-navy board investigated the Langley experiments and secured a development grant from the Board of Ordnance and Fortification.[28] The failure of Langley's "aerodrome," which plunged into the Potomac River in December 1903, subjected the War Department, the Signal Corps, and the Board of Ordnance and Fortification to Congressional ridicule and brought on a more cautious approach to public-supported research and development.

The Signal Corps proceeded cautiously after the Wright brothers flew their airplane nine days after the crash of "Langley's Folly." From the new signal school at Fort Leavenworth, Squier kept a careful eye on their experiments, forwarded information to Washington, and in August 1907 helped persuade the new chief signal officer, James Allen, to establish an aeronautics division in the Signal Corps. A few months later, on December 23, 1907, Allen, who understood that without any immediate commercial application the aircraft industry needed military encouragement, circulated a formal set of performance specifications for an airplane with military capabilities throughout the embryonic aircraft industry. They stipulated that the machine, powered by a motor reliable enough to keep it airborne for more than an hour, should carry two men at speeds in excess of forty miles per hour over a prescribed course. The specifications were also forwarded to Chief of Ordnance Crozier, then serving as president of the Board of Ordnance and Fortification.

The Allen specifications marked a significant change in relationships between users, inventors, and developers. The Signal Corps asked industry to build a device that previously did not exist to meet their specific needs and specifications.[29] On September 3, 1908, the Wright brothers launched their new military flyer at Fort Myer, across the Potomac from Washington, and, during the next few days, met the requirements. The subsequently slow development of American military aviation was caused as much by the greed of the Wrights as by the military. The Wrights tried to hide their secret and prevent others from copying their invention. Historians of the air force, motivated in part by ideology, have argued that the War Department did not encourage aviation. The technology, however, was in its first, fragile phase. Reliable engines were unavailable. The relatively small amount of money the War Department had to encourage new inventions had to be allocated carefully among all newly emerging military technologies. In 1913 Congress appropriated $125,000 for continued work on the airplane, and in 1914 the chief signal officer established a small aviation center at San Diego to experiment with improved aircraft and advanced engines. During the first two years of the First World War, aviation technology moved into a second, volatile phase, and in 1916 Congress made substantial appropriations to expand the Air Service. Early the next year, George Squier, a pioneer in army electronic technology, became chief signal officer.

Squier had been cooperating with C. D. Walcott, the new secretary of the Smithsonian Institution, to establish a research laboratory for military aeronautics similar to the one already in place to develop electronic communications. In 1912, at Squier's suggestion, Walcott proposed that Congress appoint a national advisory committee on aeronautics, but they refused. Temporarily rebuked, he revitalized the Smithsonian committee that had been moribund since the Langley affair and tried to persuade government agencies to participate in the endeavor. Stymied by the comptroller of the treasury, who claimed no government employee could serve on a private committee like the one Walcott proposed without legislative approval, he went back to Congress again. In 1915, sympathizers added a rider to the naval appropriations bill establishing the National Advisory Committee for Aeronautics (NACA).[30]

☆ ☆ ☆

After the Spanish-American War the Corps of Engineers built the Panama Canal. The operation was a large-scale, public, interagency, mutlifunctional enterprise surpassing anything Alfred D. Chandler described in *The Visible Hand*. It created the modern reputation of the Corps of Engineers, and an army engineer, Colonel George W. Goethals, who directed the latter phases of the operation, came to symbolize American power and efficiency as effectively as Theodore Roosevelt. Goethals helped bring the army out of the shadows in the first decade of the twentieth century and gave Americans a representative twentieth-century celebrity, the "soldier administrator and technician."

Goethals was a self-made man. He was born in New York City in 1858, the son of Dutch immigrants who had come to America in 1850. Like many illustrious members of his generation, he worked his way through school, spending three years at the City College of New York before securing an appointment to West Point. Goethals had wanted to become a doctor, but at City College he fell in love with mathematics. At West Point he excelled in engineering and graduated second in his class in 1880. As a young engineer officer, he worked on the Columbia River basin project, explored the Far West, helped improve navigation on the Ohio River, and worked on the Tennessee River and Muscle Shoals projects. He taught at West Point and was serving in the office of the chief of engineers in Washington when the Spanish-American War began. Goethals was chief engineer of the 1st Army Corps when the war ended. He was working on the harbor forts in Narragansett Bay when he was called to serve on the new general staff in Washington and was on duty there when Secretary of War William Howard Taft persuaded Roosevelt to select him for the canal job.[31]

The original executive agency for the work was the Panama Canal Commission, a committee of seven members accountable to Congress and the president, stationed in Washington. Although it was modified in 1905, the commission remained a cumbersome body. The new governor of the Canal Zone, Charles E. Magoon, was a member of the commission, but its chairman, Theodore Perry Shonts, a railroad executive, remained in Washington.[32] The first chief engineer, John H. Wallace, was ineffective and was replaced by

John A. Stevens in 1905, when Wallace, allegedly fearing yellow fever, fled the zone. Stevens, like Goethals, was a self-made man with a reputation as a daring explorer, surveyor, and railroad builder. He had risen from laborer to manager as a protégé of James J. Hill, president of the Northern Pacific. Ironically, it was Hill, an archenemy of Theodore Roosevelt, who recommended Stevens to the president. In Panama Stevens applied railroad-organizational methods to conditions in the Canal Zone. He rebuilt the rail system to ensure that the millions of cubic feet of rock and dirt could be expeditiously removed. He understood the necessity of a firm base of operations and supported the soldier-physician William E. Gorgas in his campaign to eradicate malaria and yellow fever. He improved workers' housing and provided amenities that made the tremendous task of construction endurable. He sought control over supply and procurement and in 1906 secured personal authority over the construction of the canal through a clear chain of command from Roosevelt.

Stevens organized the indispensable grand base for the project, but as the railroad phase ended and the time for "making the dirt fly" approached, he grew restive. Perhaps he sensed trouble. Working with public officials was not his strong suit. He wanted to subcontract construction to large private American firms, whereas the administration in Washington was determined to make it a government operation. Perhaps some underlying insecurity led him to hesitate before the challenge of Culebra Cut and Gatun Dam. Theodore Roosevelt, during his spectacular visit to the Canal Zone in November 1906, made it clear who would get the credit if the project succeeded and who would get the blame if it failed. Possibly Stevens feared what he would reap if the work faltered. The record of his thinking is ambiguous. If the railroader showed no signs of diminished self-confidence before Congress, when he changed his mind in 1906 and supported a "lock-and-lake" system instead of a sea-level canal, he was certainly agitated later in the year when he wrote the president that he was exhausted, under attack by unidentified conspirators, and needed a rest. Why he resigned in 1907 will probably never be known, but the evidence suggests that he was driven by temporary anxiety to write a letter that he was not permitted to retract. Stevens would not be the first self-made man, suffering a personal crisis of confidence and loathing failure, to create a situation that allowed him to escape without retreat.[33]

By 1907 the canal was a public operation. The Panama Canal Corporation was the first government business venture of its kind and served as a model for the Emergency Fleet Corporation in 1917. The only private contracts that would be let in the future would be those to construct the locks and their complex electrical and hydraulic support systems. The final decision to make the canal a "lock-and-lake" rather than a sea level route had been made just a little over a year before Goethals and his associates arrived in Panama. Goethals pushed construction forward, administered the Panama Railroad, and directed the thousands of civilians, black and white, required to complete the task.[34] As director of construction and later as governor of the Canal Zone, he filled two of the most significant civilian posts held by a regular army officer since the Civil War. He coordinated civil and military activity, worked with congressional committees, and developed the long-range, multiorganizational logistical support for the massive civil-military enterprise. Goethals never wore a uniform in Panama, yet he led an expeditionary force. Some called him a martinet—one commentator said he reminded him of Louis XIV—but Goethals could delegate the work and share the glory. He held regular Sunday complaint sessions for the workforce, and the evidence indicates that he listened to them. Goethals loathed councils and committees. He was cold, ruthless, and brutally demanding. His leadership style was paternal, hierarchical, and even at times stereotypically military, but civilians and soldiers alike could see he was committed to the success of the mission.

Goethals said later that his most important challenge was "to seize control of the work." Stevens had seen the canal as a job and bonded the force to himself. Lacking Stevens's charisma, Goethals bonded the force to the mission. As Stevens's entourage resigned, Goethals brought in his own people. He modified the functional railroad organization he had inherited and erected a geographic one with a director in charge of each district. Civilians ran the Pacific division and soldiers ran the Atlantic division. Colonel David D. Gaillard had the responsibility for the Culebra Cut, while Colonel Harry F. Hodges supervised design of the lock system. Major Carroll A. Devol, selected by Secretary of War Taft for his successful emergency work during the 1906 San Francisco earthquake, became chief quartermaster and, assisted by Lieutenant Robert E. Wood, handled labor, general supply, and construction of quarters. Wood, who became general purchasing agent, remarked later, "I was [Goethals's] assistant for seven years, and I might say that everything in my life since has seemed comparatively easy."[35] By 1912 Goethals was in control. Commanding from Panama rather than Washington, he dominated operations, from procurement of general supplies to the allocation of labor on the construction sites.[36]

The most elegant part of the endeavor was the planning, design, and construction of the Gatun and Miraflores locks. The locks symbolized the way American technology and industrial organization had improved since the 1880s, and the army helped midwife the new era. The steel doors, hydraulic valves, concrete reservoirs, and restraining cables formed an integrated system operated by electricity. The locks required vanadium and manganese-alloy steels, and the contracts went to the American plants that had poured many of the castings for the big seacoast guns. The massive industrial shapes were allocated to midwestern structural-steel makers who had grown with the help of contracts for mounts for the new harbor-defense batteries. Familiar with the rigid standards of War Department inspectors, steel men at Wheeling, West Virginia, and Pittsburgh, Pennsylvania, had little trouble supplying the gears, shapes, and plates for the locks.

A most interesting aspect of the story involved the part played by the electrical industry in completing the canal. Colonel Henry Hodges controlled the general process, but engineers from the General Electric Company of Schenectady, New York, designed and deployed the electrical system. GE had previous experience with the army, having provided electric equipment for harbor fortifications. The specialists from GE and the army engineers established parallel research and development laboratories in Schenectady and Panama and moved scientists and engineers between them, building a full research-and-development loop. Communications between the engineers on the site and scientists in the laboratories flowed through wireless, telephone, and telegraph. The complex system of locks and reservoirs, the first ever operated completely by electricity, closed quietly and filled flawlessly on September 26, 1913.

As the work neared completion, Wood recalled, "I really believe that every American employed would have worked that year without pay, if only to see the first ship pass through the completed canal. That spirit went down to all the laborers." By the end workers had excavated more than a quarter billion cubic yards of dirt and rocks, and the canal had cost more than half a billion 1914 dollars. When asked about the secret of his success, Goethals replied laconically, "The pride everyone feels in the work."[37] The "Conqueror of Panama" saw the project as duty well done and closed up shop apparently unaffected by public lionization. He was not given to prophesy and never joined those who saw in technocracy the answer to social problems. There is no evidence that he was strongly interested in the wave of writing on scientific management then engulfing the country. His management methods were authoritarian rather than consultative. Goethals was an innovator, but his was the timeless kind of innovation that raises up leaders in any society. He had the ability to define a mission, see the project in all its parts, and bring others to commit themselves to its completion. President Woodrow Wilson made him the first governor of the Canal Zone, and the army rewarded him with two stars. In 1915 he retired from active service.

Most commentators and journalists complimented Goethals and compared the direction, organization, and construction work at Panama to the action of a great, efficient, well-oiled machine. Others called it a harbinger of future industrial societies, people and machines integrated and coordinated efficiently in large-scale enterprises. For most whites the orderly rows of homes and apartments deftly segregated and assigned by status were part of a comforting vision of an understandable America. Movies, commissaries, YMCAs, and churches provided wholesome food for the body and the spirit, while the grand project gave well-paid, useful work and a reason for being. This was the utopia of the new industrial managers who were going to remake the world. A few commentators, however, were fearful that the Zone was merely a carefully controlled army base or a big company town like Pullman, Illinois, for a time under benign supervision. Nobody owned anything except their clothes and possibly a few tools. Workers did not participate in any political process by right. Goethals was a benevolent despot and philosopher-king, but no one could tell who would come after him. If this nonparticipatory monstrosity was the wave of the future, they wrote, liberty and democracy were at risk.[38]

CHAPTER 4

TECHNOLOGY, DOCTRINE, AND REFORM, 1885–1916

During the generation before the First World War, western military forces introduced technical innovations more quickly than at any previous time. Integrating new weapons and developing new doctrine, while simultaneously modifying field formations to reflect technological change, challenged the best thinking in the War Department.[1] A decade before the Spanish-American War, the army made efforts to formalize the nineteenth-century research and development system by creating permanent equipment boards composed of technicians and field soldiers. After the conflict, Secretaries of War Elihu Root and William Howard Taft, as well as Chief of Staff J. Franklin Bell, himself a former commander of the General Service and Staff College at Fort Leavenworth, encouraged the development of new methods to incorporate ideas and weapons on the battlefield. In 1912 Captain John McAuley Palmer, a young general staff officer and a 1910 graduate of the Army War College, wrote in his influential paper, "The Organization of the Land Forces of the United States," that among the purposes of general staff duty itself was the creation of "common doctrine as to the purposes and ends of training, the means to be employed and the results to be obtained."[2]

The tactical organization of the army during the Progressive Era was not as obsolescent as some historians have suggested. Soldiers recognized that logistical and tactical requirements for mobile operations in the southwestern United States and in northern Mexico, where man-land ratios were low and road and rail networks were thin or nonexistent, required cavalry until internal combustion technology became robust. American infantry had little need of big operational units and the division remained an administrative organization until 1913, when four regular divisions were organized.[3] Heavy with commissioned and noncommissioned officers, its ten-company, three-battalion, three-regiment, three-brigade structure could be divided easily into mobile combat groups to deal with the small campaigns of the era. Small arms and automatic weapons and equipment were robust and light weight. The recently designed field artillery was mobile and lively, with less range but more striking power per weight of gun than comparable European weapons. Sturdy six-mule wagons and pack trains supplied support in the field. Despite these facilities there would be big problems if the country had to fight a war with a major power.

Under the Dick Act, the National Guard became the official organized reserve force, augmenting the regular army and forming a mobilization base of a quarter of a million men. Before 1903 the guard and the regulars did not even have the same tables of organization and equipment, much less a common understanding of doctrine. By 1906 thoughtful soldiers were arguing that the regulars should be organized into a "mobile army" with a standard training year like that of other modern powers. Annual joint maneuvers could then be conducted with the various National Guard units to familiarize them with current doctrine, tactics, and weapons.

In the late nineteenth century, American infantry tactics were thought to be the most advanced in the world. Doctrinal cohesion was assumed rather than formally articulated. The 1892 edition of *Troops in Campaign*, the bible of the field soldier, was only fifty pages long and small enough to fit into a shirt pocket. It dealt primarily with march orders and campsite selection and contained no specific doctrinal statements. During the early 1890s branch field manuals were upgraded, but the tactics used in Cuba and in the Philippines did not prove particularly effective. In 1905 *Troops in Campaign* was rewritten. The name of the new manual, modeled on contemporary German texts, was changed to *Field Service Regulations*, its size leaped to 250 pages, and a new section that promoted the conventional wisdom that infantry was "Queen of Battles" was added. The 1910 edition reinforced the commitment to infantry supremacy. Although the term "combined arms" appeared in the text in 1911, it was 1914 before a statement of combined arms doctrine appeared. The 1914 *Field Service Regulations* designated infantry as the primary arm and cavalry and field artillery as auxiliary arms. The foot soldiers conducted the main work on the battlefield, and their action decided the issue in combat. The 1914 regulations concluded that "the role of the Infantry, whether offensive or defensive, is the role of the entire force and the utilization of that arm gives the entire battle its character. The success of the Infantry is essential to the success of the combined arms."[4]

But what did that mean? Major John F. Morrison and his colleagues at the School of the Line at Fort Leavenworth taught a modified Uptonian doctrine. An infantry attack should be conducted with fire-and-maneuver tactics to thicken the attacking line and concentrate friendly rifle fire. Once enemy fire was suppressed, a final rush with the bayonet would win the day. Morrison's map exercises and student briefing assignments were useful, but they did not emphasize the problems involved in coordinating rifle fire with automatic weapons and artillery fire from various distances and concentrating it at particular points and at particular times. That not only required communication technologies that were not yet available but also was inconsistent with the practice of rapid movement and open warfare favored by the American army.[5]

At the turn of the century, the coast artillery was on the cutting edge of military technology. A separate branch of the service under its own chief after 1907, it received a substantial share of the army budget, and its members were little inclined to listen to criticism of their doctrine or their system. They disputed claims that their big disappearing guns, which were terribly complicated and lacked overhead protection, were vulnerable to gunfire from the sea and worried that plans for a mobile army, championed by the other combat arms after 1906, would replace current coastal defense policy, reduce their budget, and challenge their status in the army hierarchy.[6]

Coast artillerymen understood the need to cooperate with the technical bureaus that handled fire-control electronics, telephone, telegraph and wireless communications, fortification construction, and heavy-artillery design and production. In 1904 Secretary of War Taft was persuaded to appoint a fire control committee, including representatives from the coast artillery, the Ordnance Department, and the Signal Corps, which would meet at the Coast Artillery School at Fort Monroe, Virginia, and bring their best thinking to bear on coast-defense technology and doctrine. It was soon clear that interpersonal and interbranch rivalries were hard to overcome. Johnson Hagood, then a "cosmoliner" (coast artilleryman), recalled what happened. "In 1904 old Fort Monroe was a nest of inventors," he wrote. "All the cranks—you might say—in the Army were collected there to turn out some new thing in connection with the rapidly developing system of seacoast defense." Colonel Isaac Lewis, "the most outstanding man the Army had produced in the last fifty years," and who had developed a range finding system in the early nineties, was the best-known expert and dominated the group, but it included also Melvin Rafferty, an old colleague of Lewis's, James Whistler, an expert on coastal guns, and Albert Davis, who was also interested in rangefinders. "It was thought that all these experts should be collected in one spot, that between them they could work out something to combine the best qualities of all," but instead, "the most intense jealousy" came out and "each man who had a scheme became more determined to put it over." Fort Monroe became a nest of vipers. According to Hagood, the committee accomplished nothing useful, and the first attempt by the army to create a think tank ended in failure.[7]

The Field Artillery, little more than "red-legged infantry" after the Civil War, was the most underdeveloped arm in the service. Light batteries trained with the cavalry during the 1880s, and the war with Spain posed little challenge. In postwar exercises at Fort Riley, Kansas; Fort Sill, Oklahoma; Fort Leavenworth; and in the Philippines, individual field artillery batteries proved competent but were incapable of combining and concentrating fire. After 1906 conditions began to improve. Congress authorized several new artillery regiments, and field artillery was permanently included in the revised divisional tables of organization and equipment. Chief of Ordnance Crozier dispatched John Thompson, Isaac Lewis, and Charles B. Wheeler, the officers who had helped design the new 3-inch and 4.7-inch guns, to explain the improved weapons. Courses on fire control and communications appeared in the field artillery school curriculum, and representatives of the Signal Corps and the Quartermaster Corps attended maneuvers to help with the work. George Squier, originally an artilleryman and among the cofounders of the *Journal of the United States Artillery*, assisted by Lieutenant William Mitchell, worked to coordinate telephones and wireless with field artillery at Fort Leavenworth. Younger field artillery officers such as Oliver L. Spaulding, Marlborough Churchill, and Charles Summerall, all of whom later became editors of the *Journal*, as well as William Westervelt and William Snow, called for more and better equipment, more ammunition, and improved combined-arms coordination.[8] By 1916 field artillery manuals were current, the infantry and the field artillery were training together at Fort Sill, the cavalry and accompanying guns were conducting joint exercises at Fort Riley, and at Fort Leavenworth officers were attempting to bring the new weapons and equipment together in innovative ways to create a modern combined-arms organization. But everything was in the process of becoming and little was formalized and institutionalized.[9]

☆ ☆ ☆

Weapons selection and the coordination of tactical doctrine would have been much more effective if the army had seen fit to take advantage of the possibilities of a War Department agency that had been in place since the 1890s. Few nineteenth-century soldiers thought about the army and the War Department as an integrated system, and the Board of Ordnance and Fortification reflected the emphasis they placed on informal cooperation and community. Yet it also showed significant possibilities for weapons modification in the light of new realities. The board was established in 1885, when Congress ordered an investigation into the locations and equipment of the proposed new coastal-defense system. The members of the board of investigation, headed by Secretary of War William C. Endicott, included Chief of Ordnance Benét and Chief of Engineers John Newton. Captain William T. Sampson represented the navy. Although the Endicott board's recommendations were often outlandish—it recommended the refortification of the Canadian frontier with turreted artillery—they provided the foundation for American coastal-defense planning for the next decade and a half.[10]

By 1888 it was clear that construction and location of the new fortifications required formal coordination of the technical and construction bureaus and the army combat arms as well as close cooperation with the navy. In an unprecedented piece of legislation passed on September 22, 1888, Congress mandated a permanent Board of Ordnance and Fortification chaired by the commanding general of the army and including representatives of the War Department staff as well as an independent civilian representative to integrate the coastal defenses of the United States. The first formal interbureau managerial experiment by the War Department, it brought together engineers, ordnance, signals, and artillery officers to discuss systematic weapons research and development, improve cooperation between themselves and with the navy, and cultivate technical connections with American industry.

The history of the board during the 1890s revealed the power of informal connections in American military affairs and the relative influence of the line, military technicians, civilian designers and producers, and Congress. Its records show the possibilities for reform as well as the weaknesses inherent in the contemporary American system of weapons development. The board investigated, tested, recommended, and, at first, contracted for most of the new equipment adopted by the army. It studied "a great number of devices, ranging from positive absurdity to real merit . . . [and sifting] what was good in these ideas from the worthless, with a view to utilizing everything valuable." Although the board advised the secretary of war, Commanding General John Schofield's prestige as its first president was so great that it was able to set initial requirements and specifications for the new coastal guns and to secure the "Hundred Gun Contract" for Bethlehem Steel. If used with imagination, it could have become an important institution, one of those "vital intersects" that might link new technologies, tactical doctrine, military planning, and national policies.

According to its original charge, the board allocated appropriations among the various bureaus involved in coastal defense and made "all needful and proper purchases, experiments and tests to ascertain, with a view to their utilization by the Government, the most effective guns, small arms, cartridges, projectiles, explosives, torpedoes, armor plates, and other implements and engines of war." It was also "to purchase or cause to be manufactured, under the authority of the Secretary of War, such guns, carriages, armor plate, and other materials and articles as may, in the judgment of the Board, be necessary in the proper discharge of the duty devolved upon it."[11]

Such a unique and innovative experiment in formal organizational cooperation faced great difficulties. The traditions of separate spheres and parallel paths were very strong. The bureau chiefs, suspicious of the commanding general and accustomed to informal methods of interbureau cooperation, protected their turf vigorously. Brigadier General T. L. Casey of the Corps of Engineers and Chief of Ordnance Benét insisted that they control their own contracting, and in 1892 the board's power to act independently was curtailed and fiscal control returned to the bureaus. General Schofield understood that the issue would not interfere with the primary mission of the board to coordinate technical development and, protecting his close relationship with the secretaries of war, moved gracefully to appease the bureau chiefs. As president of the board, he stated in 1893, "In view of the language of the statute [the act of 1888], attention is called to the fact that no contracts are made directly by the Board, but are made by the Ordnance and Engineer Departments, upon the recommendation of the Board, and approved by the Secretary of War."[12] He pointed to complications which had been overcome and relationships which had been improved. "In short," he concluded, "in five years the whole situation has been changed, and, with nearly every problem solved, . . . the work can now go forward at a rate that will give the country a practically complete system of modern defenses and armaments early in the next decade, if the requisite appropriations be forthcoming."[13]

Under Schofield the board made an outstanding record. The general operated indirectly, relying on his personal influence with the bureau chiefs and with the various secretaries of war. Weapons and equipment testing remained in the hands of the bureaus, with general coordination left in the hands of the Board of Ordnance and Fortification. The board standardized 8-, 10-, and 12-inch coastal defense guns with sophisticated carriages and recommended a new system of field guns and carriages. It tested support and communication equipment for the artillery. It adopted and issued a new rifle to the infantry. The board, however, refused to adopt a new machine gun to replace the obsolete mechanical Gatling guns because, it claimed, machine guns were held under private patents and early selections "would naturally advance the price of the article should it become known that the manufacturer practically had a monopoly."[14]

There was much about the board and its research and development work that was organizationally inelegant. By law it established types, but the Ordnance

Bureau and the engineers had their own boards and controlled the contracting process. The commanding general, a threatening presence, presided over the board, and the only center of authority was the secretary of war. So long as the personal relationships of the commanding general, the secretary of war, and the bureau chiefs were cordial, the system worked and the army approached the Congress for appropriations united. Controlling such a profoundly political process was frustrating. Opportunistic inventors with powerful legislative friends were a torment and line officers and bureau chiefs, who were not above circumventing the board themselves, often joined together to oppose outsiders. Congress still exercised the ultimate power.[15]

The successful operation of the Board of Ordnance and Fortification hinged on personal consultation and informal connections. Schofield left the board in effective working order, but in 1896, upon becoming commanding general, Nelson Miles instigated a bureaucratic fight with Chief of Ordnance Daniel Flagler. Miles's difficulties with the Ordnance Department went back, at least, to his unsuccessful attempt to have a repeating rifle adopted in 1878. After he became commanding general, he recommended turret- and barbette-mounted seacoast guns and charged that the new disappearing guns were too complicated and lacked overhead protection. When Miles attempted to assert the power of the board to expend money and make contracts to develop specific weapons independently, he stirred up Flagler. Secretary of War Daniel Lamont attempted to clarify the situation. On January 7, 1896, Lamont wrote Miles a letter very much like the one Robert Todd Lincoln had written to General Sheridan a decade before. Lamont reasserted the reasons for the board's creation, defined the peculiar problems of weapons development that characterized the last decade of the nineteenth century, and categorized the issues, especially the important one involving contracts and finances, that had troubled the relations of the board and the bureaus since 1888. Lamont recommended that Miles avoid battles over status and allow the bureau chiefs to continue to place contracts. Miles could retain control over weapons selection through exercising the board's clear, statutory power to advise the secretary of war.[16]

Miles seemed to agree with Lamont, but he was back again in 1898 recommending to Secretary of War Alger that expenditures be made "by the several bureaus of the War Department heretofore having jurisdiction of the same, or by the Board itself . . . [which] believes it to be for the best interests of the service that it should more directly control the appropriation made for its work, subject always to the approval of the Secretary of War." He concluded that this was the most efficient way to "keep in touch with the best inventive talent of the country in all that pertains to war material, to encourage the development of every suggestion and device of value presented, and to use the funds at its disposal to secure for our service the best products of American genius." The ordnance member of the board, Lieutenant Colonel Frank H. Phipps, refused to sign the report, stating, "I concur in the above, except as to the proposed change in the manner of making disbursements, believing the method prescribed by Congress at the creation of the Board is still for the best interest of the Government."[17]

Miles secured the change through congressional legislation the next fiscal year, but it added a running feud with ordnance and the engineers to his well-known difficulties with Secretary of War Alger and, later, with Secretary of War Root. After the "Embalmed Beef" scandal and the imbroglio with Commissary General Eagan, Miles even lost the support of Congress. Secretary of War Root was determined to be rid of him and was convinced that the efficiency of the army should never again be dependent upon mere personality. In his report of 1899, Root wrote as if the Board of Ordnance and Fortification did not exist.[18]

During the Progressive Era the board was overlooked, ignored, and resisted. As the general staff system went into effect, the reports of the board disappeared from the *War Department Annual Reports*, membership was downgraded, and much of the overall planning went to the War College Division of the General Staff. Weapons and equipment development and standardization fell back into the hands of the technical and supply bureaus or were assigned to the new permanent combined boards that appeared in the years before the First World War. The last chief of staff to preside over the board was John C. Bates, and the last chief to attend a meeting was J. Franklin Bell, who was apparently interested in the possible military uses of the Wright brothers' new airplane. After 1907 the chief of ordnance or his deputy was in the chair. In 1915 Secretary Lindley M. Garrison, rather than use the board to consolidate the new Taft Board recommendations on coastal fortifications with those of the Endicott Board, ordered the bureau chiefs to report changes in plans to a War Department board of review under the chairmanship of Assistant Secretary of War Henry Breckenridge (1913–1916). After Breckenridge resigned there is no evidence that Secretary of War Newton D. Baker or Assistant Secretary of War William Ingraham even knew such a board of review existed.[19] Meanwhile, the Board of Ordnance and Fortification lingered on, conducting tests and making recommendations to little effect. It finally disappeared when its duties were absorbed in August 1918 by a much more narrowly defined Inventions Section of the War Plans Division in Peyton C. March's reorganized general staff.[20]

An example of the failure of the War Department to use the Board of Ordnance and Fortification in a situation that clearly demanded interbranch and interbureau consultation and cooperation involved the Benét-Mercié machine rifle. The "Benny-Mercy affair" became a cause célèbre, revealing traditional interest group concerns, congressional politics, and personal rivalries that dominated the selection of new weapons, especially when more than one branch of the army was involved. Mechanical machine guns had been deployed to the field since 1866, but soldiers had never determined their proper function. Were they artillery or infantry weapons? In the American army the heavy Gatlings were general-purpose weapons issued to combat units on demand or allocated to the artillery. The Gatlings were notoriously unreliable, as were the automatic guns that began to appear after 1890. It was 1904 before the technology was considered robust enough for field service and the Ordnance Department standardized the Vickers-Maxim gun. The Colt Fire Arms Company, which owned the English patent rights for the Vickers-Maxim, won the initial contracts.[21]

By that time it was obvious that the machine gun was a useful weapon for all the combat arms. After the Spanish-American War, hot-headed and ambitious John H. "Gatling Gun" Parker agitated for the creation of a new machine gun branch in the army that he, of course, would command. Despite the initial support of President Roosevelt, Parker was unsuccessful in his quest and it was probably the reports of military observers at the front during the Russo-Japanese war rather than his propagandizing that persuaded the army to deploy the new weapon. By that time the conventional wisdom, championed by most field soldiers and accepted by the Ordnance Department, was that the machine gun was a defensive weapon and should be issued to all combat arms.

The Vickers-Maxim was a heavy, water-cooled, belt-fed weapon weighing more than a hundred pounds with its tripod. It was expensive and beautifully finished, with a polished-brass water jacket. Between 1906 and 1910 the army experimented with various platoon- and company-sized organizations to determine the proper place of the new weapon among the combat arms.[22] The infantry was content with the new machine gun, but it caused the cavalry some problems. It was difficult to transport and bring into action, and it slowed deployment for battle. Even before it was adopted the horse soldiers were grumbling, and within a year they were calling for a lighter, less-complicated weapon. Subsequent experiments at Fort Riley and Fort Leavenworth supported the cavalry, and General Crozier, sensitive to advice from the combat arms, sought a more appropriate gun. His search led to Lawrence Benét, one of the sons of the old chief of ordnance and the American representative of the

French-based Hotchkiss Company. A few years before, Benét, with his associate Andre Mercié had designed a light machine gun, the "Hotchkiss Portative," for use in the desert. In late 1908 Benét offered to sell the patent rights to the Ordnance Department. In 1909, after a series of tests by ordnance experts and the School of Musketry, and with relatively little apparent understanding of the doctrinal impact of his decision, Crozier introduced the Benét-Mercié machine rifle.[23] It was a technician's dream—light (experts disagree; some say twenty-two pounds, and others say twenty-seven pounds), cheap, clip-fed, and air-cooled, with a quick-change barrel and an elegant folding bipod. In 1911 the "Benny-Mercy" replaced the Vickers-Maxims, and the latter were withdrawn into storage.

The "Benny" was an orphan. It was not a heavy defensive gun like the Vickers-Maxim; it was an automatic assault rifle. The infantry hated it. They clamped it on a forty-pound tripod and claimed it was inaccurate because of heat waver and incapable of sustained fire. The cavalry liked its portability but complained that it was too lively and so finely machined that a little dirt jammed it in the field. No one liked the ammunition clips that had to be loaded "upside-down." It was not that some did not see the possibilities of the light gun. Writing in the *Journal of the Military Service Institution*, First Lieutenant William E. Roberts of the Tenth Infantry called it "a wonderful little gun" that, "with a few minor changes," would be "nearly as perfect as we should expect at this time." He claimed the Benny was a light assault rifle that should have an offensive role, but it seems that even the imaginative Roberts did not understand that the troops needed both the Benny and the "Maxim." In fact, no one did until the second year of the Great War.[24]

Meanwhile, other inventors with innovative automatic guns, including Crozier's old rival, Isaac Lewis, believed they had been short-changed by the Ordnance Department. Lewis exploited his powerful civilian connections to persuade Congress to mandate new machine-gun tests. In 1913 Crozier ordered a comprehensive series of automatic weapons tests, which set off an ideological wrangle between the infantry and the cavalry. As a compromise, in mid-1914, the Ordnance Bureau agreed to purchase new, lighter, water-cooled Vickers machine guns for the army and retire the Benét-Merciés as soon as replacements were available. The contracts were let in early 1915, but by that time Colt, which won the Vickers contract, was overloaded with British orders. Delivery of the first of the Vickers guns had not yet begun when the United States entered the First World War.

The Benét-Mercié affair offers an opportunity to examine in detail the connections between individual army officers—in this case General Crozier and Colonel Lewis—private companies in the national defense sector, and the Congress before the Great War. The Crozier-Lewis rivalry, which involved patent rights, charges of conflicts of interest, professional ambition and personal jealousy, dated from the early 1890's. It culminated just before the First World War and reflected badly on both men. Lewis and Crozier had leapfrogged each other during their entire careers. A few years younger than Crozier, Lewis was a part of Miles's entourage and, in 1901, believed that he rather than Crozier should become the new chief of ordnance. Born on October 12, 1858, in New Salem, Pennsylvania, Lewis, like Crozier, entered the Ordnance Bureau from the artillery. In the 1890s, while Crozier was working on his big-gun carriages, Lewis gained a reputation as an electronics and fire-control wizard. It was at that point that he and Crozier crossed swords for the first time. According to War Department records, Crozier refused to make a Lewis fire-control invention standard equipment for coastal-defense guns and called for more tests. Lewis became angry and sold his patent to a private concern to which the War Department paid high prices during the war with Spain. Crozier privately charged Lewis with unethical behavior. In 1901, after returning from a mission to France (during which Johnson Hagood later claimed he stole the plans for the recuperator for the new model 1897 French 75 mm gun), Lewis designed a carriage for the new American 3-inch field gun. An ordnance board picked another carriage designed by Captain Charles B. Wheeler. Lewis sold his carriage design to Bethlehem Steel and it appeared as the Bethlehem model number 2 in subsequent field trials. Lewis's connection with Bethlehem Corporation reinforced Crozier's conviction that he was an opportunist who put private gain ahead of the public interest. Lewis, still brooding about Crozier's appointment as chief of ordnance, insisted he never earned a penny from his fire-control or carriage designs. He spread rumors that there was an "ordnance ring" under Crozier's control that traded in corrupt contracts and practiced insider favoritism. When Leonard Wood, another former member of Miles's circle, became chief of staff in 1910, Lewis thought that his moment had come. He had recently made arrangements to develop an automatic machine gun, a modification of the McClean-Lissak, with the Automatic Arms Company of Buffalo, New York, which held the McClean-Lissak patents.

In 1911 Lewis demanded that his new invention be tested against the recently adopted Benét-Mercié. The colonel was after Crozier and claimed that the Benét-Mercié had been introduced under mysterious conditions as part of a corrupt bargain between the Ordnance Department, Benét, and the Hotchkiss Company. Lewis, who had only recently become a member of the board of directors of the Automatic Arms Company, never questioned the validity of the contract with the Colt Company, which was the second producer of the Benét-Mercié gun and held its American patents. A few months later the Lewis gun was tested and declared inadequate by an ordnance machine gun board. Later, in 1912, Lewis, claiming his light gun had not been given a proper test, took the matter to the House Military Affairs Committee, and started a controversy that lasted through the First World War. He retired a full colonel in early 1913, asserting that he had been done in by the "ordnance ring," and sold production rights to his gun abroad. In Lewis's defense, Crozier does seem to have shunted him off into limbo whenever he could, and Lewis was only one among several officers who continued the nineteenth-century practice of selling patent rights privately until the Army Reorganization Act of 1903 declared that patents with exclusively military applications should be government property. For example, George Squier in the Signal Corps continued to hold patent rights privately with little effect on his career.[25]

The story of the Benét-Mercié ended with an event that tarnished its reputation irretrievably and seriously damaged Crozier's career. Before dawn on the morning of March 9, 1916, Mexican irregulars under Pancho Villa attacked the town of Columbus, New Mexico. Surprised American troops fought back, but their Bennys were difficult to get into action. Later, some troopers claimed that the technology of the gun prevented its use in the dark. The intricate system of loading, they said, caused jams. Newspapermen had a field day, calling the Benét-Mercié the American "daylight gun" and suggesting that the rules of war be changed to require only sunlit battlefields so that Yankee machine gunners could participate. The Ordnance Department, rather than the combat arms, drew the criticism for the alleged failure, and in the spring of 1917 the United States had no standard machine gun. For the first year of the war, the army used a hodgepodge of air-cooled and water-cooled guns. A congressional investigating committee in December 1917 accused General Crozier of incompetence. That was a great injustice. He was no more guilty of such charges brought by old enemies such as Lewis than they were themselves. He was simply part of a weapons development system that made communication between users, designers, and producers difficult if not impossible.[26]

The story of the Board of Ordnance and Fortification is one of a road not taken. Some historians have argued that Chief of Ordnance Crozier gained control of the board in a bureaucratic contest to prevent the combat arms from capturing technology and confirming the primacy they had already gained over military doctrine and policy through the general staff. The field soldiers, however, had always been accorded doctrinal precedent, and everyone wanted to improve weapons, equipment, and communication. The Signal Corps at Fort Leavenworth, the Coast Artillery fire-control committee at Fort Monroe, and the Ordnance Bureau weapons boards all provided state-of-the-art small arms and machine guns, coast artillery, field artillery, and signals. The American army had problems, but they were not ones of simple, one-branch weapons selection. Few saw that doctrine and weapons existed in a volatile technological environment and required the recognition of conceptual connections between ideas and arms if multiple new technologies were to be integrated into a coherent system. If those in power had understood that, they could have used the Board of Ordnance and Fortification for such purposes.

☆ ☆ ☆

The National Defense Act of 1916 was more than a simple reorganization. The debates during the preparedness movement (1915–1916) addressed issues of political, social, and economic reform, reorganization, and modernization that had challenged American assumptions about the role of the state since the final decades of the nineteenth century. It acknowledged that the mission of the army had expanded since the turn of the century and that its organization should be modified to meet the challenges of a new era. The discussions reflected the longstanding ambitions of combat officers, the concerns of bureau technocrats, the interests of representatives of the national defense sector of the economy, and the objectives of certain civilian professional groups that had previously shown little interest in military affairs. It has been described as a campaign against "the specter of a dragon" in which President Woodrow Wilson, playing the extremes against each other, controlled the debate, created a compromise national-security policy, moved the political connections in American organizational life toward a new balance, and achieved the first comprehensive American military reform in almost a hundred years.[27]

The campaign covered every aspect of American military policy. The debate over manpower involved proposals for extensive changes in traditional relationships between the states and the federal government. Army officers, aside from Leonard Wood and his associates, believed the world crisis that began in 1914 offered an occasion to fulfill the dreams of John C. Calhoun and Emory Upton for a national army with its own reserves and to end dependence on the National Guard and unorganized volunteers.[28] They also saw an opportunity, a mere wish under the Morrill Act of 1862, to build a corps of well-trained, college-educated officers for the new national-reserve forces they advocated. Civilian critics had even broader agendas, ranging from modest changes in the National Guard to proposals for universal military service as a means to consolidate the country in anticipation of a possible new round of world competition. Many New Nationalist Republicans called for a citizen reserve raised through volunteering or, if possible, through conscription, which would, to use their contemporary Social Darwinist rhetoric, help build a coherent, efficient, competitive, and modern corporate nation from the ruins of a parochial, fragmented, and outdated America. A few of the new professional managers, such as the efficiency expert Walter S. Gifford, of American Telephone and Telegraph, much to the dismay of their more politically sensitive colleagues, used machine and factory rhetoric to describe people as commodities to be allocated scientifically and efficiently like any other raw material in a contemporary industrial corporation. Defenders of traditional connections, including localists, states' righters, antimilitarists, and pacifists, couched their arguments in the political rhetoric of the nineteenth century. During 1915 their concerns over the changing relations between business and government, citizens and the state, and local and national authority were clearly revealed.

The movement began in early 1910. By that time periodic war crises in Europe had led American army officers, concerned about what they believed was the futility of incremental legislation, to call for measures that would expand the army in peace and sustain it in war.[29] Soon reform-minded congressmen, businessmen, and intellectuals entered the military-policy arena seriously for the first time in more than a generation. In 1911 Secretary of War Stimson confided to his diary that the time had come to assert executive leadership, and in early 1912 he published a blistering attack on congressional policy making. Later in the year, with the enthusiastic support of Chief of Staff Wood and relying on the work of Captain John McAuley Palmer, Stimson proposed a scheme that would solve the problems of local control and state loyalty that had plagued the country since the eighteenth century.[30] *The Organization of the Land Forces of the United States* recommended an alternative to the Uptonian expansible army: a citizen volunteer reserve force of officers and soldiers separate from the National Guard and the regular army and under federal control that would, when connected with the other two organizations, form a twentieth-century "Army of the Nation."[31]

The debates reached a climax during the first Wilson administration. Wilson was, at least at the beginning of his presidency, a military romantic. In 1911, shortly after he had formally declared himself a candidate for the presidency, he had defined war as an instrument of political change. "There are times in the history of nations," he wrote, "when they must take up the crude instruments of bloodshed to vindicate spiritual conceptions. . . . Liberty is a spiritual conception, and when men take up arms to set other men free there is something sacred and holy in the warfare." His first secretary of war, Lindley M. Garrison, became entangled in the debate among professional army officers, and between them and the National Guard and other civilians with an interest in military affairs, about the current field organization and reserve policies of the army. The reserve question, in particular, involved differences among regular army officers. Some officers were Uptonians who wanted an "expansible" long-service professional force with fully integrated reserves. Others were supporters of the "citizen-soldier" proposals of the Palmer Plan and championed short-service forces with large, nationally controlled reserves based on universal compulsory peacetime military service. Both approaches raised conflicts with members of the National Guard, who insisted that they should constitute the first line of defense for the nation. The question threatened to divide the country as had no other political issue since the Civil War era.

Secretary Garrison had neither military experience nor any understanding of the deeper issues involved in the debates about military policy, but he quickly became caught up in the discussions. He supported Chief of Staff Wood's efforts to establish voluntary summer training camps for college youth and pressed for modest increases in the military budget. He reflected President Wilson's views closely and defended existing force levels. In his 1914 *Annual Report*, he contrasted militarism, which he associated with aristocratic values and warlike intent, and the military way, which he equated with effective national defense.[32]

After the European war began in August 1914, Garrison continued to advise merely that existing force levels should be maintained. It was not until May 1915, after the *Lusitania* crisis, that, at the president's request, he began to prepare plans for a larger army. Garrison ordered Major General Hugh Scott, who had become chief of staff in November 1914, to have the War College review the whole scope of American military policy. *A Proper Military Policy for the United States*, which was nearly complete by mid-March 1915, proposed to expand the regular army, relegate the National Guard to traditional home guard and local defense missions, and create a national reserve, or "continental army," of 400,000 volunteers enlisted for six years and trained annually on the European model.[33]

The proposal immediately drew the opposition of the National Guard and those members of Congress who understood that the measure threatened local control of the militia and would change the traditional connections between the states and the federal government. Many citizens' groups, including the members of the Plattsburg Movement, a privately sponsored organization to train reserve army officers and educate the public to the need for a stronger military, endorsed the plan; others, including General Wood, who had moved to command the Eastern Department, based at Governor's Island, New York, after his tour of duty as chief of staff ended, and former President Theodore Roosevelt, who had already moved beyond voluntarism, opposed it apparently because it did not call for universal compulsory military service. The plan for a continental army was attached to proposals for universal peacetime compulsory military service, and in the subsequent national debate, the two ideas became inextricably linked, much to the disadvantage of the continental army plan.

Supporters of universal service had contradictory agendas. Some were romantics like Roosevelt and perhaps Wood, who saw it as embodying a kind of fresh-air experience—a Boy Scout camp out—that, by emphasizing military virtues, could develop a sense of community and build strength and character in youths who they believed were becoming increasingly sedentary and alienated. Others, like Grenville Clark and the writer and founder of the *New Republic*, Herbert Croly, saw it as a way to combine military service, technical training, and citizenship education to integrate and unite an ethnically and socially fragmented society into a modern, cohesive, democratic, industrial state. Less-benign advocates, politically alienated from mainstream Progressivism and crudely Darwinian, feared popular government and saw American society as threatened by a proletariat of anarchistic, nihilistic, urban subhumans who must be tamed by military discipline before they destroyed conventional decency and order. Few were really interested in universal service as a way to build an effective fighting force.[34]

The agitation of Wood, Roosevelt, and the other less attractive and more extreme partisans doomed the continental army. To pass legislation that would impose peacetime conscription or bypass the National Guard to create a national reserve—whether volunteer or conscripted—completely under federal control, such as Garrison proposed, was politically impossible. In early 1916, Representative James Hay of Virginia, a traditional states'-rights Democrat and enemy of the general staff, with the assistance of Wood's old antagonist, former Adjutant General Ainsworth, prepared a bill that strengthened the National Guard, provided for federal control of the state troops in emergencies, and eliminated the continental army. Hay was joined in an incongruous alliance by George Chamberlain of Oregon, chairman of the Senate Military Affairs Committee, who had recently been reelected as a "Bull Moose Democrat" on a nativist platform that played upon West Coast anxieties about Asian minorities. Chamberlain, a champion of universal peacetime military service, had his differences with Garrison and was ideologically closer to Wood and

Roosevelt than he was to the secretary of war, but he was at that time a loyal party man. He was backed by Chief of Staff Scott, who assigned the physically frail but strong-willed and intellectually aggressive judge advocate general, Enoch Crowder, and Captain George Van Horn Moseley from the War College to help draft the legislation. The Chamberlain Bill abandoned the universal military service section rather than lose everything in a quixotic battle for a cause that was not achievable. In the end Chamberlain even proved willing to forsake the separate federal reserve force favored by Crowder and take the partial loaf offered by Hay.[35] President Wilson, who dominated the center of the debate, after testing public opinion, supported Hay and his House of Representatives associates. Garrison, unwilling to abandon the idea of a federal volunteer reserve, resigned on February 10, 1916. Wilson waited for a month and then appointed Newton D. Baker secretary of war. It became Baker's task to deal with the critical issues of army-industry relations.[36]

☆ ☆ ☆

One of the more complex members of the Wilson circle, Baker had spent his life in municipal politics and had just completed a term as mayor of Cleveland, Ohio, when the president called him to Washington. Baker was inclined to suggest, not command, and saw the War Department and the army as a complex urban community—not an industrial machine or a law office—whose problems were little different from those of any city and whose multiple interests could be harmonized through consultation and cooperation. Baker was no champion of centralized national power. "I have long believed," he wrote in 1916 to his friend, Judge John H. Clarke of Cleveland, "that the problems of democracy have to be worked out in experiment stations rather than by universal applications."[37] Shortly after his appointment in March 1916, he authorized a committee chaired by Colonel Francis J. Kernan to study government production of munitions and, after consulting members of his staff and Secretary of the Navy Daniels, had Judge Advocate General Crowder prepare a working paper on industrial preparedness. In early April 1916, using the Crowder memorandum as a basis for discussion, Baker and Daniels submitted a confidential report recommending a "council of executive information" to President Wilson. The report proposed a kind of industrial national guard that could be mobilized in the same way as military reserves. Baker testified later that the object of the proposed legislation was to prepare for an emergency through voluntary cooperation rather than by executive fiat, but the memorandum did not read that way. After analyzing the sources of preparedness agitation, Baker and Daniels called on the president "to lead the emotion for preparedness into definite lines and to make it a national policy." The paper recommended a permanent "council of national strength" composed of cabinet officers and "captains of industry and commerce" that might provide a plan whereby the enumerated, cataloged, and known industrial resources of the nation could be located. Small peacetime contracts for military hardware could then be awarded, which would pay for the labor and material involved in keeping them ready to turn their energies from ordinary industrial production to special programs needed in a national emergency. Then came a most astonishing suggestion. In an emergency, civilian industrial plants should be federalized and militarized and their dividends controlled to deny any possibility of war profits. It was a statement apparently aimed at "taking the profit out of war," but it advocated the full militarization of American industry in wartime.[38] Why Baker supported the proposal is unclear. His own more modest ideas were revealed in the suggestion that government arsenals should become "experimental stations" to keep abreast of research and development and train officers to support civilian managers in an emergency. The public arsenals would be designated as assembly plants for components manufactured throughout the country.[39]

Militarizing industrial production was never a realistic proposal, and Baker never explained what he meant by voluntary compulsion. Southern Democrats, who controlled key congressional committees, and many midwestern representatives opposed any redistribution or expansion of federal authority. There was even less support in the Wilson administration for handing control of industrial mobilization over to business and conscripting labor than there was for drafting soldiers. The president supported a compromise solution. A section of the National Defense Act of 1916 recommended the procurement of military supplies on a large scale but rejected War Department control of industry. The secretary of war was empowered to conduct an industrial inventory of the nation and procure, in peacetime, gauges, jigs, and dies necessary to the production of arms and allot small educational contracts to industry.

The opposing positions on industrial preparedness—that of the army, which was determined to control industrial mobilization, and that of corporate businessmen and engineers, equally convinced that they should direct the industrial effort—were reconciled in a supplement to the Army Appropriations Act of August 29, 1916, which created the Council of National Defense (CND) composed of the secretary of war, the secretary of the navy, and the secretaries of labor, commerce, interior, and agriculture. Congress rejected compulsory military service. It also rejected compulsory industrial or labor policies. The CND had an independent staff with a professional director and secretary and a National

Defense Advisory Commission (NDAC) composed of seven civilian technical experts. The act affirmed, theoretically at least, the cultural perspectives of soldiers and businessmen but also recognized that the new industrialized warfare required the effective coordination of both. In that sense, the rider establishing the CND carried forward the Progressive themes of voluntary national cooperation and organizational efficiency in the public interest, while it avoided the corporatist extremes of monopoly capitalism or state socialism.[40]

By the autumn of 1916, the Wilson administration had created a new balance between the center and the periphery in the debate over American military policy. Only doctrinaire fringe groups like universal training extremists, populist anticorporatists, and antimilitary ideologues advocated further changes. The National Defense Act of 1916 shifted the organizational fulcrum sufficiently to resolve the most outstanding difficulties of the nineteenth-century system. Avoiding extreme ideological solutions, it tailored the army to the expanded role of the nation on the world stage and recognized that in a *materielschlachten* war, such as the one raging in Europe, connections between the military and industry must be clarified. Difficult soldier-politicians like Leonard Wood were contained, while officers of the combat arms secured some of the objectives toward which they had been working for a generation. The dream of a revolutionary army of the nation built on universal conscription was put aside, but in a compromise that ended the nineteenth-century coalition army, the power of the state governors was reduced and the National Guard was brought under federal control, making it possible to surge to half a million men in an emergency. Meanwhile, the Naval Appropriations Act of 1916 expanded the fleet to unprecedented size and the Shipping Act brought merchant marine policy under central guidance and created the Emergency Fleet Corporation to construct government vessels in government yards. The Adamson Act, passed during the spring of 1916, established conditions of labor on the nation's railroads and confirmed the power of the federal government to control the lines in an emergency. The Federal Highway Act of the same year inaugurated the study of an all-weather road network to meet the strategic and logistical needs of the country.

Passage of the legislation marked the end of a decade and a half of administrative turbulence in the War Department. Soldiers were as active and reform-minded as other progressives, and their efforts brought substantial modernization of the War Department. By 1916, the War College had drafted plans to defend the American coast, the Caribbean, and the Philippines; the engineers under George W. Goethals had shown in Panama their expertise in managing big construction; and under its new chief, the gifted Henry Sharpe, the Quartermaster Bureau was routinely moving troops by land and sea and maintaining them over long distances. The new quartermaster field service was beginning to shift from animal-drawn transport to internal-combustion technology. The Signal Corps had laid the Pacific cable and built the Alaska telegraph, and Colonel George Squier, who had recently returned from a tour in London as a military attaché and was soon to become chief signal officer, and his associates in the signal laboratory were in the forefront of the electronic-communications revolution and were moving carefully to examine a volatile new technology, the airplane. The field army had modern armaments, and a board chaired by Brigadier General Charles G. Treat had recently recommended that its artillery component be increased. Chief of Ordnance William Crozier, who had re-equipped and reorganized the arsenals and depots and made them models of contemporary management, was ready to supply the guns within two years if funds became available. Congress seemed willing to appropriate the money to provide a future war reserve for a million men. Other 1916 legislation enabled the construction of government-owned nitrate-and-armor plate plants, but when the Kernan Board reported later that year it counseled that the long-run interests of the nation were best served by continuing traditional mixed-procurement policies. The new CND, with its advisory commission of expert engineers, scientific managers, and administrators, would provide the necessary connections between the army and industry and formalize the nineteenth-century military system of separate spheres and parallel paths to meet the demands of the new corporate age.

It seemed that all conceivable issues had been discussed, and within the limits of political realities, soldiers and civilians had hammered out a modern, orderly, and rational military policy for the United States. In the minds of line officers, however, there was still no clear military command-and-control structure. They loathed the idea that the chief of staff was merely the chairman of the board. The very real power to coordinate War Department affairs, which the chief of staff had exercised since 1903, was not enough for them. In 1912 Leonard Wood, in his effort to recreate the position of commanding general, had alienated key members of the military establishment and the Congress and opened the army to charges of militarism and "Prussianism." His later partisan political activities estranged many members of the Wilson circle. Although Secretary of War Baker saved the general staff system, the bureau chiefs still retained the right of access to his office and to control the design and production of weapons and equipment. In November 1916, General Treat labeled the situation disturbing. He described the bureau chiefs as cantankerous and jealous of their prerogatives. Every dispute or attempt to coordinate their activities required the chief of staff to become a referee in numerous petty jurisdictional disputes. Secretary Baker, he claimed, was constantly asked to resolve conflicts between disgruntled department heads and the chief of staff. Any proposal involved so many endorsements and so much detail work that there was no time left for the secretary of war or the chief of staff to think seriously about issues of strategy and organization. In Treat's view the balance between hierarchy, which seemed to assure that an order would be carried out but engendered resentment and resistance, and consultation, which seemed to assure harmony and cooperation but brought delay and congestion, had still not been resolved.[41] The terms "machine" and "factory" were still anathema to many War Department officials, including Secretary Baker, who, playing his own game, kept his office door open to everyone. But none of that seemed important at the time, and as long as the scale of battle remained within the realm of existing contingency planning, such situations could be met as they arose. The army program would take about eight years to complete. By then the war in Europe would be over and the nation would have sufficient forces to support any new foreign-policy initiatives. It was time to put the issues aside. The War Department needed an interval of stability to allow the modified system to become customary practice. Anyone who stated publicly that within a year the United States would be supporting an army of thirty divisions over a supply line of four thousand miles and fighting in an international coalition for the first time in more than a hundred years would have been labeled a certifiable lunatic.

CHAPTER 5

THE WILSON ADMINISTRATION AT WAR

FOREIGN POLICY, MILITARY STRATEGY, AND ARMY MOBILIZATION

When the United States went to war on April 6, 1917, fantasies that had been so much a part of the preparedness campaign evaporated. German troops were not going to land on Long Island; American troops were going to be deployed in France sometime in the near future. For the next eighteen months, the American army expanded and reorganized relentlessly. Administrative turbulence grew rather than diminished until the end of the conflict and exposed significant questions about connections both within the War Department and between the War Department and the forces operating in the field. The war was an organic entity. What the Wilson administration launched as a limited intervention in April 1917 became, by the spring of 1918, a campaign of "force to the utmost" that committed an independent American army to battle in northern France a year earlier than anyone thought possible. The sheer scale of the war required that issues believed to have been settled during the previous decade be considered anew, while the mobilization and equipment of a mass army confronted President Wilson and his associates with critical questions about connections with other parts of American society. The Wilson administration was reluctant to expand federal power permanently and was concerned that the conflict might be used as an excuse to challenge the political equilibrium of the Progressive Era. But the president had committed the country to a battle that would ultimately become an extended experiment in international political, military, and economic cooperation. By the end of the war the administration had introduced national conscription, underwritten the organization of industrial trade associations along lines previously considered dangerously monopolistic, allocated food and fuel, seized enemy and American ocean-going vessels, dictated their deployment, and even nationalized the railroads.

☆ ☆ ☆

Woodrow Wilson has been described as a pacifist and antimilitarist, an inno-
cent in world affairs, an internationalist, a nationalist, an imperialist, an anti-
imperialist, and an idealistic priest of a peculiar American secular religion,
but he has seldom been cast as a warrior and grand strategist. The president
saw peace as normal and war as abnormal. He had never read a book of military theory. Yet, as many of his opponents failed to realize, he was that most
dangerous of adversaries, a warrior-priest. Like Abraham Lincoln before him
and Lenin (Vladimir Ilyich Ulyanov) in his own day, President Wilson saw
war whole. As one of the creators of the modern liberal tradition, he believed
in a rational world in which a higher realism and self-interest would change
the nature of societies and bring people and their governments—peacefully
by choice, through battle if necessary—to create a voluntary and cooperative
community of nations based on social equity, free-market economic associations, and political liberty. He was remarkably consistent in pursuit of those
objectives. His ideas defined the ideological contest, and copies of his speeches,
especially the Fourteen Points, saturated Germany and Austria-Hungary,
establishing the boundaries of the debate.

The president directed the American war effort toward a single objective: to
secure as early as possible a favorable position from which to negotiate a satisfactory peace treaty. It was essential to his plan that an independent American
army appear in France. Wilson sought to bring the Germans to the table, not
annihilate their country. Indeed, there was a direct linkage between his Peace
without Victory campaign of December 1916 and his Fourteen Points declaration of January 8, 1918. His strategy was to fight and negotiate simultaneously,
and he would have preferred to marshal American forces slowly, using their
growth to encourage the Germans to make peace on honorable terms before
they were faced with military disaster.

Wilson controlled his powerful internal passions only at the cost of great
emotional stress. Illness plagued him at crisis moments in his career, and he
had suffered at least one stroke before he became president. Wilson was aware
of the physical effects of stress and strove to husband his energy. His apparent disinterest in the actual battle stemmed not only from his concentration
on high policy, but also, as he said later, from his fear that awareness of the
human costs of the war would reduce his effectiveness and interfere with the
detachment he felt necessary to pursue his greater purposes. Aware of his own
physical limitations and committed to reason and emotional control, he was
skilled in delegating administrative responsibility. Wilson kept his hand on
events without cluttering his mind with the day-to-day detail that might spell

the end of great plans. He struggled constantly to keep American objectives central in his thinking as he dealt with troop shipments, raw-material shortages, labor and management problems, and the myriad other issues involved in running the war. His command style bothered many soldiers who wanted direct access to the president and believed that the chief of staff should have a cabinet seat. Such a recommendation was made by the War College in December 1917, but it never got beyond Acting Chief of Staff John Biddle's office.[1]

Wilson exercised command through Secretary of War Newton D. Baker or through General Peyton C. March, who became acting chief of staff early in March 1918, or directly himself. March took his orders from Baker unless the president requested that he communicate directly with the White House. Wilson usually contacted General Tasker H. Bliss, who, after November 1917, served as the American military representative on the Allied Supreme War Council (SWC), through Secretary Baker, but if the occasion arose, he used his friend and executive agent, Edward M. House, as a personal conduit.

The war brought out Secretary Baker's worst as well as his best qualities. He was no advocate of "top-down" management and was comfortable in the traditional informal nineteenth-century War Department structure. He tried at first to maintain equality between the general staff and the bureau chiefs, insisting that they all should have equal and direct access to his office. He resisted, at least for a time, efforts of corporatist-minded soldiers who sought to use the war to establish line control of the War Department and the army. He opposed efforts to dislodge authority from the War Department and place it in business-controlled "super-agencies" like Bernard Baruch's War Industries Board (WIB). Baker was a formidable opponent of other civilian war managers, whom he considered mere opportunists and materialists.

The secretary of war could drive people mad with frustration, but he was also able to persuade others to work together for the public good. He would compromise, blandly confuse issues with all the guile of the fine lawyer that he was, buy time, and, on those occasions where he thought real substantive issues of principle were involved, strike hard and ruthlessly. During the winter of 1917–1918 he reluctantly increased the War Department's control over industrial mobilization, strengthened the general staff, and brought in General March to energize the changes. In October 1918 he was still clearly in charge at the War Department. Sitting in his big chair, his leg curled under him, his pipe going and a fresh pansy on his desk, Baker carved out a place as a most effective secretary of war.[2]

Generals March, Pershing, and Bliss were not the simple soldiers they claimed to be. March was a combat veteran and an artilleryman. Tall and slim with a carefully trimmed beard and mustache that gave him a slightly sinister appearance, he was at the peak of his powers during the last spring and summer of the war. During his extensive prewar staff and field service, he had proved ambitious, brave to the point of foolhardiness, a glutton for work, and a first-class administrator. At the same time, he seemed to believe that tact, courtesy, diplomacy, and simple good manners were signs of weakness. He had a nasty temper and a sardonic sense of humor that led some to think that he took too much pleasure in the pain of others. He seldom gave compliments and only rarely revealed his private emotions. Perhaps he was just a simple soldier, but, for all his professional virtues, it was hard not to believe that March was a mean-spirited, arrogant man whom one postwar critic accused of desiring to be "the Ludendorff of the American Army." March's drive for power would cause Secretary Baker to spend much time smoothing relations between him and Pershing and healing unnecessary wounds his chief of staff inflicted at home. It would never have crossed March's mind, however, to question civilian authority. Even if it had, President Wilson and Secretary Baker had no intention of relinquishing any control of national policy to the military.[3]

Like March, Pershing had seen battle and had a reputation as an able organizer and administrator. Although only of average height, his imposing presence made him seem larger than life. Pershing was a cavalryman and, unlike March, a fine companion with a deep capacity for friendship. He had served on the plains during the last days of the Indian wars. In those days of slow promotion, he had, on several occasions, fallen into despair over his future and considered leaving the army. He was saved by the war with Spain. After active service in Cuba and the Philippines, he was promoted in 1906 from captain to brigadier general. Pershing had good connections in the Republican Party. He was well known to Theodore Roosevelt. It was army gossip that he owed his promotion to his father-in-law, Wyoming senator Francis Warren, but Pershing was a conventional soldier—never a political officer like Leonard Wood. In 1916 he commanded the punitive expedition into northern Mexico, where he gained the confidence of Secretary Baker and President Wilson. Still relatively young in 1917, Pershing had recent active duty and could be counted on, or so it was believed, not to rock the political boat.[4]

General Bliss had a special place in Secretary Baker's and the president's affections. Nearing the end of an unconventional military career, portly, often with a dusting of cigarette ashes on his tunic, the balding, bespectacled soldier was the only uniformed officer who Baker and Wilson thought able to appreciate the nuances of American foreign policy. Bliss graduated from West Point in 1872 with a commission in the artillery, but he never held a combat command and was considered a military intellectual. He served as an aide to General John Schofield and was military attaché in Madrid when the Spanish-American War began. Subsequently, he was an administrator in Cuba, a teacher at and president of the Army War College, a provincial governor in the Philippines, and a general-staff planner. In May 1917 he replaced Major General Hugh L. Scott, who was in Russia with the Root mission, and officially became chief of staff in September. In October Bliss sailed for Europe as military adviser to the House mission and played an important part in creating the Allied Supreme War Council (SWC). He remained chief of staff in name until May 1918, when March formally replaced him. The President, on occasion, would listen to Bliss on matters of policy and strategy.[5]

☆ ☆ ☆

Although a member of the coalition, the Americans were never allies. Wilsonian war aims were unique, and the term "Associated Power," which he chose, clearly separated his purposes from those of the British, French, and Italians. Events, as much as policy, however, controlled the scale of American mobilization and the deployment of the American Expeditionary Forces (AEF). In April 1917 neither President Wilson nor any of his advisers was prepared to commit an American army to the struggle. The president hoped it would be unnecessary to send troops to Europe immediately. He made a virtue of necessity, for there seemed no way to deploy well-trained and -equipped forces abroad for at least two years. By first ordering the navy to convoy and antisubmarine duty and then slowly deploying the army, he hoped to exert sufficient pressure on the German government to bring it to the conference table.

Wilson and his colleagues had little interest in destroying the traditional European balance of power. They were almost as afraid of an Anglo-French victory as they were of a German triumph. Although sufficient American forces would ultimately have to be moved to the continent to ensure Wilson the influence he desired at the peace conference, too much power applied too rapidly might tip the balance in the Allies' favor. American troops should not appear on the battlefield in numbers before both sides were nearing exhaustion.[6] In his war message, the president spoke of raising a half million men immediately and more if necessary. Wilson had already rejected the advice of Herbert Hoover and Colonel Edward M. House that Americans should be encouraged to enlist in allied forces. The views of the members of the interallied mission led by Sir Arthur Balfour, which arrived in the United States in mid-April 1917 and argued for the assimilation of American troops in battalion strength into Anglo-French divisions for training and combat, only added to the president's resistance. If British and French advice was followed, Acting Chief of Staff Bliss wrote in late May 1917, "When the war is over it may be a literal fact that the American flag may not have appeared on the line because our organizations will simply be parts of battalions and regiments of the Entente Allies. We might have a million men there and yet no American Army and no American commander." Wilson would not accept such conditions and, already determined that an independent army must appear somewhere at some time in Europe if his policy objectives were to be achieved, made his decision to deploy a force abroad on May 3, 1917. Ten days later Secretary of War Baker signed a formal agreement with Marshal Joseph Joffre to dispatch an expeditionary force to France, followed by other troops "restricted only by transportation difficulties."[7]

The War College had already developed plans to place a large army abroad, but General Bliss preferred to delay its organization until advice arrived from Pershing's headquarters. In late May 1917, a War Department mission headed by Colonel Chauncey B. Baker of the quartermaster corps embarked for Europe to make "such observations as may seem of value for the transportation, operation, supply and administration of our forces in view of their participation in the war." In early July 1917, the mission reached Paris and began conversations with members of Pershing's staff on the size and organization of the force, and on the basis of their recommendations a plan was devised in cooperation with Pershing's staff to place thirty American divisions in France by December 1918. The General Organization Project, or thirty-division program, together with a logistical-support project developed in August 1917, was adopted by the Wilson administration in early October as the official American army program.[8] Neither the president nor American military planners were comfortable with a strategy that seemed to close all options except the Western Front. In late March, General Bliss argued against piecemeal troop movements to France and advised that the army be trained and equipped at home for two years and, sometime in 1919, open a second front with a massive amphibious assault against Heligoland.[9] Even when it became clear that such prospects were beyond American capabilities, Wilson continued to examine theaters of operations other than the Western Front. He badgered Baker with questions about possible operations in Macedonia, Turkey, Italy, and Russia. Baker always replied patiently, pointing out the logistical problems involved anywhere except in France, but the president was undeterred. Finally, on November 11, 1917, after receiving still another request for information from the White House, Secretary Baker wrote the president an exasperated note urging him to quit reading newspaper strategists and understand that "the tonnage question necessarily controls the strategy of the war so far as our participation is concerned whatever conditions there may be on the other side." It was not Baker's recalcitrance, the recently approved thirty-division program, War Department stubbornness, nor even French and British pressure, but events in Europe that closed the Baker-Wilson discussions.[10]

☆ ☆ ☆

There is a myth that Chief of Staff Hugh Scott told John J. Pershing when he left for France, "Now Jack, this is not the Army of the Potomac." In one sense, his statement did not reflect well on his view of the stability of contemporary American society; yet in another sense he was right, but not in the way that he intended. Raising and organizing the wartime army brought a significant transition in traditional manpower policies and ended an era in American military history. It involved three steps, none of which seemed connected at the time, that nevertheless transformed not only the way in which the army was raised but also the way in which it was organized.

The first step was national conscription. In late March 1917, contingency plans, based on those developed during the preparedness debates of the previous year, were made to raise an army of a million men, half of whom were to be volunteers. In April and May 1917, the regular army was increased to war strength, and in July 1917 the National Guard was federalized and ordered into service in accord with the National Defense Act of 1916. The traditional volunteer army, however, did not appear. The Wilson administration for a number of reasons—not all of them associated with the war and manpower issues—introduced legislation adopted by Congress on May 18, 1917, that raised the additional troops through conscription. The Militia Act of 1792 and the Dick Act of 1903 had established the universal obligation of American male citizens to serve, but traditionally such legislation had been executed at the local or state level. Selective service, even though it was implemented at local polling places by civilians selected by state governors, was controlled from the War Department through the office of Judge Advocate General Enoch H. Crowder. Registration was universal, and the draft numbers were drawn in Washington. President Wilson refused to admit publicly that anything had really changed, and his assertion that the system was "in no sense a conscription of the unwilling" but a "selection from a nation which has volunteered in mass" was a convenient rhetorical rationalization covering the shift in administrative power from the periphery toward the center.

On June 5, 1917, men between twenty-one and thirty began to register for the draft. Although blood did not flow in the streets as some critics had predicted, there was considerable opposition. Draft evasion grew more serious during the summer of 1918, when more troops were required for the vastly expanded military program and the registration age was extended to include men from eighteen to forty-five. More than three million eligible men avoided registering during the war and more than two million of those who registered found ways to escape military service. Nevertheless, the opposition was never serious enough to interfere with the war effort.[11]

The next two steps, which began in September 1917, were interconnected and involved the general reorganization of the army. The National Guard was called up in the summer and in early September the first men for the new national army began to assemble. It was then that the massive reorganizations recommended by the Pershing-Baker Board more than doubled the size of American combat divisions, broke up or eliminated historic National Guard units, introduced completely new regimental and divisional organizations, and completely reshaped the army from the light, mobile formations well-suited to operations in the American Southwest to heavy, relatively unwieldy formations organized to fight in northern France. The third step grew directly out of the second. The 1917 reorganizations brought continuous upheaval, and the draftees who arrived in camp in early September 1917 were shipped from pillar to post for months. The majority did not begin training until the last two months of 1917 and the first two months of 1918. Even then equipment, especially automatic weapons and artillery, was in short supply, and the difficult weather during January and February 1918 threw individual instruction, advanced training, and combined-arms maneuvers far behind schedule. Shipment of infantry and machine-gun troops without their artillery and logistical support, which began in April 1918, undermined unit cohesion even further.

Until the early spring of 1918, National Guard divisions going abroad were, wherever possible, brought up to strength with national-army men from their home states or regions. During the spring and summer of 1918, as a result of the rush of troops to France and the manpower expansion required to fulfill the new eighty-division program, however, recently drafted men were transferred from one unit to another and shifted en masse to fill up divisions at ports of embarkation. There is still some question as to whether any of the troops shipped during the late summer of 1918 received any training at all beyond a bit of close-order drill.

In August 1918 it became clear that something had to be done to stop the hemorrhaging of troops from divisions in training to divisions moving toward ports of embarkation. Chief of Staff March, asserting that all personnel were interchangeable, ordered the end of the separation of the army into regular army (divisions 1–25), National Guard (divisions 26–75), and national army (divisions 76 and beyond), and ordered its unification into the United States Army. He also ordered branch replacement camps established in the United States and draftees assigned to them regardless of their state or region of origin.[12] Thus three disconnected decisions—the first, in part political, to adopt national conscription in May 1917; the second, Pershing's demand to double the size and reorganize the American combat division in September 1917; the third, March's crisis-generated decision to reorganize the army and establish replacement training centers in August 1918—shaped the structure of the American army for the next fifty years.

The 82nd Division was a representative national army unit. The division was organized at Camp Gordon, Georgia, under the revised Tables of Organization and Equipment of September 1917. During October and early November its original members were shipped as fillers to newly created units in the United States and to regular-army and National Guard divisions going abroad. The troops who replaced them, many of whom did not speak English, were from all over the country. Short of everything, including junior officers and non-coms, the division trained for weeks without small arms, machine guns, or artillery. Indeed, it received little or no equipment until February 1918, and the troops received no instruction beyond close-order drill and small-arms familiarization. The 82nd arrived in France in June 1918 without undergoing large-unit maneuvers or combined-arms training.[13] If the 82nd Division was an example, the army that Pershing was about to throw into the battle in France was a far cry from George Gordon Meade's Army of the Potomac or "Pecos Bill" Shafter's band of regulars and volunteers that took Santiago in 1898. Whether it would be as fragile as Hugh Scott implied remained to be seen.

☆ ☆ ☆

During the summer of 1917 cooperation between the general staff and the bureaus was arranged through the War College Division. On June 11, 1917, Bliss informed the various chiefs that all issues between the bureaus should be submitted to appropriate committees of the War College division for study. Recommendations would then be passed through the chief of staff to the secretary of war for approval. In July 1917, Bliss, in a move that foreshadowed Peyton C. March's staff reorganizations of the spring of 1918, ordered the War College organized into six committees—recruitment and organization, military operations, equipment, training, legislation and regulations, and intelligence. Recommendations began to stream toward the army, navy, and state building from the War College on the Potomac at the foot of Capitol Hill.[14]

In March 1917, the bureaus began to place contracts for the initial supply of the expanding army. The pathway from program to estimates and requirements to production and distribution was far different for Quartermaster General Sharpe than it was for Chief of Ordnance Crozier or Chief Signal Officer George Squier. Sharpe faced no compelling questions of doctrine and design and had substantial uncommitted civilian plants at his disposal. All he needed, even to handle camp construction, was a target number and a mobilization schedule. Crozier faced complex design and production problems unknown in the quartermaster general's office. Squier, whose Signal Corps was responsible for aircraft selection as well as communications equipment for the first year of the war, had little trouble with signal equipment but lacked a doctrinal framework on which to base decisions on aircraft, and the domestic capacity to produce engines and airframes of a quality and quantity equal to the wartime challenge was quite limited.

Each bureau developed different relationships with the businessmen and civilian war managers with whom they had to deal. Sharpe, who had to house, clothe, and feed the assembling troops, could procure large amounts of well-known materials from a technologically mature industry. A certain amount of conversion was required, but after a relatively short time the capacity of existing plants, except for certain kinds of web equipment, was equal to any challenge. Following plans formulated the previous year, the quartermaster general moved in March 1917, without immediate congressional authorization, to clothe and equip the first million men. Although existing stocks had been drawn down by the demands of the punitive expedition, the Philadelphia and Jeffersonville depots could fill minimum requirements for the regular army within three months.[15] Much of the annual wool clip had already been bought by the Allies, but Sharpe placed emergency orders for nonstandard textiles to meet the immediate needs of the drafted troops who would arrive in camp in September 1917. He hoped that cotton summer uniforms would suffice and that the situation would improve before winter issues were necessary. Thousands of horses and mules were purchased. The bureau let contracts for motor cars and one-and-a-half-ton and three-ton trucks of various makes. With the assistance of the SAE, bureau technicians designed a standard military truck and presented it to the automobile industry for bids. They also placed massive orders for wagons, animal harnesses, web equipment, tentage, and food. Tables of organization and equipment were ready by June 1917, but they had to be extensively revised during August and September after arrival of the thirty-division plan from France.[16]

In late May 1917, Sharpe created an independent Cantonment Construction Division headed by Colonel Charles Littell, an experienced construction man. During the summer the division began to build thirty-two assembly and training camps. Sixteen were temporary tent camps in the South and sixteen were wooden camps, mostly in the North and West. Money and budget were no longer issues. Standard quartermaster contractual procedures were not followed. There were no open bids and for each camp a "cost-plus" prime contract was negotiated, usually with the largest local construction firm. A quartermaster program officer and his staff, accountable for the completion of the project, supervised each camp. Political considerations delayed the selection of the camps until early June.[17] Vexing shortages plagued construction. The railroads were slow to lay spur lines and lumber deliveries were delayed. Disputes arose between troop commanders and construction commanders. There was little empathy between organized labor and the quartermaster officers who supervised construction. The program officers hampered the work by attempting to impose military discipline on the eight to ten thousand civilians toiling to complete the camps on schedule. The July 1917 recommendations of the War Department /AEF Board, which virtually doubled the size of combat divisions and added corps, army, and other support troops, led to extensive remodeling. In spite of the setbacks, and largely through the use of power-driven equipment, the sixteen tent camps for the National Guard were usable by the end of August. The sixteen wooden camps were ready to receive some drafted troops by September 1917 and were generally complete by the spring of 1918.

If conditions had not been so fluid there would have been few clothing and equipment shortages. Sharpe knew the fate that usually befell the man who began a war as quartermaster general. He had been in the bureau during the Dodge investigations and knew how long it took General Luddington to restore his reputation after the Spanish-American War. He remembered the humiliation of Commissary General Eagan and was determined that such a fate should not overtake him.[18] He protected himself and his people with memorandum after memorandum, making clear his position on decisions that might reflect badly on the corps.[19] In early April he wrote that he could equip half a million regular and National Guard troops and another half million draftees within nine months if current requirements were not tampered with.[20] Two weeks later, when the possibilities of expanding initial mobilization began to surface, Sharpe declared that it was impossible to clothe and equip any more troops than were included in the original estimates.[21] When the First Division sailed for France in late May 1917, the troops carried six months' reserve supplies of scarce woolen clothing with them. Engineer and forestry troops who followed during the summer were similarly equipped, and the Second, Twenty-sixth, and Forty-second divisions, which sailed between August and October, took mountains of winter uniforms with them. The reorganization of the army in September made the rerouting of more supplies to the training camps and cantonments in the United States necessary. On July 21, 1917, Sharpe warned Bliss that his office had already equipped more than 130,000 troops not called for in the original War Department plans and that more shortages could be anticipated during August and September.[22] Regulars were supplied first; then in July and early August, Sharpe supplied summer uniforms and other minimum necessities to the National Guard, which was mobilizing in Southern camps. After passage of the Selective Service Act in early May, he planned to provide similar equipment for the first drafted men who were expected to be in camp between late September and mid-October. By August, he was in trouble. Despite his protests, national army men were called to the colors in early September. He immediately wrote Bliss, noting the inadequate communications between his office and the general staff and complaining that it was impossible to meet expanding clothing and equipment requirements.[23]

One of the most important elements in explaining the difficulties of the early quartermaster effort was the absence of adequate storage and warehousing at ports of embarkation. In June, a study committee of the Council of National Defense (CND) was appointed, but it accomplished little. In August, supplies littered the docks and freight cars were being used for emergency storage all along the East Coast. On August 15, 1917, a storage branch of the Supplies Division was established, but the real beginning of the Quartermaster Corps (QMC) storage program seems to have been the result of a lecture by O. D. Street, general manager for distribution at General Electric, who addressed the War College at about the same time. Sharpe, who attended the lecture, was impressed and brought Street into the QMC to head a new warehousing division, but there was still less than three million square feet of storage space available in the fall of 1917.[24] The bureau was also plagued by shortages of personnel. Key men had sailed on the *Baltic* in May and others accompanied the 1st and 2nd divisions later in the summer. Still others were transferred to the new training camps. Sharpe complained that his efforts to secure experienced reserve officers were hampered by the chief of staff and the adjutant general and that officers with long years of merchandising experience were assigned to places from which they later had to be recalled.[25]

During the summer, some of the logistical and supply duties of the quartermaster general were assigned to a new agency. When the first elements of the AEF went abroad, their equipment was shipped to the East Coast by the Transportation Division of the Quartermaster Bureau, but in August 1917 General Bliss, in one of the first transfers of operating power from a bureau to the general staff, organized an embarkation service that put command of each port of embarkation under an officer directly responsible to the chief of staff.[26] Sharpe agreed with the concentration of control, but he thought the port commanders should be quartermaster officers who reported directly to him. His attitude convinced some War Department officers that he was self-serving and narrow in his view of the war effort. When, on December 12, 1917, Sharpe laid his complaints about personnel before the acting chief of staff, John Biddle, they were sent on to the War College Division for comment. Colonel P. D. Lockridge replied on December 31 that Sharpe, especially with regard to appointments, habitually acted without reference to War Department policies and failed to recognize that other bureau chiefs had equally important requirements.[27]

Sharpe made no apologies. He was convinced that, given proper support, his organization was capable of handling the emergency. His organization retained its five prewar sections: administration, finance and accounting, supplies, construction and repair, and transportation. An Estimates, Reserve Supplies, and National Defense Act branch already had been added to the administrative division in late 1916, and Sharpe placed all requirements estimates and contracts in that new agency. In the fall the bureau added an independent remount division and established a conservation branch in the Supply Division. As the war program expanded, Sharpe appointed a board of officers to study the work methods and organization of the bureau and to recommend further modifications that would expedite the handling of quartermaster business.[28] In his view he had acted with dispatch to meet unforeseen conditions. There was no lack of zeal and little evidence of incompetence in the bureau. At the end of October 1917 he predicted that, if there were no more changes in the size of the army or in its schedule of deployment overseas, he could meet its needs on time.

☆ ☆ ☆

General Crozier faced more complex challenges. Between April 2 and October 15, 1917, the Ordnance Department laid down the initial American program. Crozier was informed at the same time as the quartermaster general of the intended size of the expanded army. He had only the existing artillery tables of organization and equipment and the information on standard days of fire compiled by the War College in 1916 for guidance. American army artillery was, by European wartime standards, very light and in 1917 still traded weight for flexibility and mobility in the sparsely populated, arid, and nearly roadless country in which it expected to fight. Since 1901 Crozier had warned three different administrations that equipping a large force with artillery in an emergency would require at least two years. If the American army did not go abroad before the end of 1918, he believed he could supply them with adequate mobile artillery from American sources. Any earlier deployment would make other arrangements necessary. The army arsenals at Watertown and Watervliet would have to be enlarged, and that would take time. The two existing private concerns capable of producing artillery, Bethlehem and Midvale steel, which Crozier had counted on before the war to provide surge capacity, would have to be cleared of Allied orders, and the navy had priority of production for the first year. With the private firms in the national defense sector preempted by the Allies for at least three months, nothing could be gained by commandeering their plants and interrupting the flow of material to forces already at grips with the enemy. In addition, storage and warehousing was inadequate and the railroads had already had trouble the previous year in moving foodstuffs to the East Coast.[29]

In April 1917, the Ordnance Department knew neither what it wanted nor where to procure it. By September it knew both in a rough way. The initial decision was reached with regard to small arms. At the request of Secretary Baker, a small-arms board composed of Crozier, General Bliss, and members of the advisory commission of the CND met in late March 1917 to consider the problem of rifle supply. The Springfield model 1903/06 had completely interchangeable parts. It required extensive machining and was exceedingly hard to mass produce. Over the years half a million of them, with large quantities of ammunition, had been accumulated at federal arsenals. During the war the British government had funded a large extension of the American small-arms industry to produce the modified Lee Enfield .303 rifle. Although the Enfield was not completely interchangeable, it could be produced in large quantities. Its adoption without modifications, however, would render the existing stocks of small arms and ammunition unusable. Crozier and Bliss wanted to produce the Enfield without changes in the interest of immediate availability and simplification of ammunition supply if, by necessity, American troops were integrated with the British. On the advice of Samuel Vauclain of the Baldwin Locomotive Company, however, Secretary Baker decided to modify the Enfield to take American ammunition and to send American troops abroad with their own small arms. The private small-arms plants that had been producing for the British and the Russians were allowed to complete existing contracts and then converted to produce modified Enfields for the American army. The first American Enfield orders were placed with the Winchester and Remington Arms companies in June 1917.[30]

The war finally solved the machine gun controversy that had plagued the Ordnance Bureau since 1911. It brought the cavalry and infantry to see that a single machine gun could not meet their needs for offensive direct fire as well as defensive support and indirect fire. In mid-1916, after the Benét-Mercié imbroglio, Crozier ordered 4,600 Vickers heavy machine guns chambered for American ammunition from the Colt Company to equip the regular army and the National Guard. Colt's commitments to the British, for whom the company was building Vickers guns, and to the Russians, for whom it was building model 1895 Colt guns, however, made it impossible for the manufacturer to meet its delivery schedules. That was the situation when, on October 26, 1916, Secretary Baker ordered a final test to select a new standard gun. Crozier moved with dispatch, and on May 1, 1917, less than a month after the United States entered the war, two decades of controversy came to an end when the board ordered the Browning water-cooled heavy machine gun and the Browning automatic rifle. Colt got the Browning contracts, while the army placed orders for more Vickers guns, Marlin machine guns, and the controversial Lewis light machine gun with other firms. The orphaned Benét-Mercié was relegated to the training camps.[31] Revolvers and automatic pistols of various calibers were secured wherever capacity existed. The basic designs of small arms were not changed for the rest of the war, and within a year after contracts were placed, production of those relatively simple weapons reached substantial levels.

The Americans were at the mercy of the Allies for heavy ordnance. In May 1917, after the arrival of all the members of the Franco-British missions in the United States, General Crozier met with French representatives, including Marshal Joseph Joffre, and secured promises that their plants could provide artillery for the anticipated American reinforcement. On June 9, 1917, after a meeting of an ad hoc artillery board, Crozier received the following memorandum from General Bliss:

> Referring to information conveyed by you to a committee of the War College Division of the General Staff that the French government would be able to deliver to this government five 75mm field guns and carriages daily commencing August 1, and two 155mm howitzers and carriages, commencing October 1, and that ammunition therefore could be provided, the Secretary of War directs that you enter at once into arrangements to procure this material. . . . The limbers, caissons and other vehicles necessary to equip complete units should be obtained from the French or some other sources. . . . The French types of ammunition should be used with the above material and our corresponding types not too near completion should be

chambered and bored to receive the same ammunition. . . . Arrangements should be made to obtain the French ammunition for the service of these cannon in war. . . . The construction of our own types should be continued, with modified chamber and bore because there is no prospect otherwise of obtaining within the necessary time the number of cannon required for the successful prosecution of the war.[32]

The Crozier-Ganne agreement and its successors of the summer of 1917 provided field and heavier guns for the Americans out of Allied stocks for the first year of the war in exchange for raw materials, steel billets, rough forgings, and steel castings, part of which would be shipped as ballast with American forces sailing to France. In mid-June the agreement was linked to the War College plans for an expeditionary force.[33] The thirty-division program, however, increased field artillery requirements by a third and called for large numbers of heavy and super-heavy guns and howitzers for corps and army artillery parks.

Uneasiness about the situation had already been reflected in General Bliss's note to Crozier, which ordered him to continue the production of modified American artillery. Then a cable from Pershing arrived in mid-July, declaring that France was not so rich in supplies as the Joffre mission had claimed and that "nothing should diminish our efforts at home not only to produce those types 155's and 75's but also those of American design, 4.7's and 6" mobile types." Pershing also asked that production of British designed 8-inch and 9.5-inch howitzers then being built at Bethlehem Steel continue. By September 1917, the American artillery program had doubled.[34]

The adoption of foreign artillery precipitated other problems. The national defense sector of the steel industry had always been small and the thirty-division program meant that many new firms had to convert to the production of a different, if not completely unfamiliar, product and learn to work to closer tolerances than had ever before been thought necessary. The machine-tool industry also had to expand, and French metric measurements had to be converted into feet and inches. The whole thing had to be superimposed on plants already committed to Allied orders. But Crozier was confident. The ordnance organization was efficient, and during the summer an effective initial expansion was accomplished. Requirements were developed in the equipment division, while the distribution of ordnance supplies was controlled by the supply division. Inspection, which had been decentralized through officers at the various arsenals, was now centralized in the office of the chief of ordnance. The money to expand government arsenals, which had been appropriated in the National

Defense Act of 1916, was tripled and even more was promised for construction and expansion. As American production came on line, European sources of supply would become unnecessary. In his 1917 report, Crozier claimed that he had found 50 percent of the skilled personnel that he needed and had made suitable arrangements to secure the rest. He reported a substantial expansion of rifle manufacturing and "considerable progress" in machine gun production. He commented on the "very cordial and useful cooperation given by our allies in regard to field artillery material" and concluded that "every possible opportunity" was being taken to manufacture "foreign designs . . . in this country." Crozier was sure that the Franco-American artillery agreement was adequate to equip the AEF during 1918, and he anticipated equipping an additional thirty divisions from American sources by the end of 1919.[35]

The decision to adopt new small arms and machine guns and employ foreign artillery departed from previous American practices. The conventional explanations stress military and political necessity. The army was short of machine guns and artillery, and the Wilson administration was determined that the first troops to arrive in France carry American weapons. The only weapons the War Department had in any numbers were a half million Springfield rifles. Secretary Baker's argument, made at the time, that the decision to rechamber the Enfield rifle simplified ammunition supply was deceptive. The Americans were dependent on the French for machine guns and ammunition for at least the first year of the war, and the decision not to use British calibers meant that three different types of small-arms ammunition were required. The international mix of field and heavy weapons and ammunition made the situation even more complex. There is a supplementary explanation and it reflects unfavorably on the prewar weapons development policies of the Ordnance Department. American small arms and field artillery had interchangeable parts. In their search for perfection, ordnance officers had developed an array of weapons that were so carefully designed and finely machined that they could not be adapted to mass production. Less-complicated arms had to be adopted if the proposed wartime schedules were to be met.

☆ ☆ ☆

The aircraft program required a new and quite different set of connections between the army and industry. Its origins are still unclear. Considered by some mere administrative propaganda to create an illusion of action in the summer of 1917, it has been labeled by others a pioneering organizing experiment that attempted to link theory and practice and connect the men who designed and built airplanes with those who flew and fought in them in the sky over France.[36] The Americans believed the airplane was most useful for reconnaissance and artillery observation. Accordingly, responsibility for the procurement of aircraft rested with the Signal Corps. Brigadier General George Squier, who had only recently become chief signal officer, was well known as a physicist and electronic technician, but he had little knowledge of airplanes and was unfamiliar with the air-power theories emerging from the battles over the Western Front.

The problems of aircraft doctrine, design, and production were substantially different from those in the Quartermaster Corps or the Ordnance Bureau. When the war began, Secretary Baker turned to the CND, which established an aircraft production board to help the army and navy formulate their programs and "consider matters relating to the quantity production of aircraft in the United States." Meanwhile, a board of officers toured the central and western states to locate airfield sites to train the personnel of the new arm. Force planning and the construction of new schools developed apace. The War Department sent requests for information to the American military attaché in England and to the larger attaché group organized late the previous year in France. Major William Mitchell, who was at that time a member of the attaché group in Paris, wrote the group recommendation that 20,000 aircraft be produced in the United States before March 1918, with provisions for expansion at a later date. His recommendations concurred with those of Premier Alexandre Ribot, who arrived from France in early June 1917. The two papers were forwarded to the War College for study. General Squier appointed Major Benjamin Foulois of the Signal Corps Air Service to work with representatives of a War College committee on aviation to coordinate and consolidate the recommendations. Meanwhile, Howard Coffin, president of the Hudson Motor Car Company and head of the Aircraft Production Board of the CND, had his own plan. He recommended that a modest program be adopted to produce five thousand training aircraft and fifty thousand pilots. The Mitchell/Ribot plan and the Foulois/Squier plans were forwarded to Coffin with a covering letter asking whether such an ambitious scheme was possible. Coffin, who had absolute faith in the ability of the American automobile industry to do anything, dropped his scheme and replied, "We firmly believe the aircraft program can be met." On June 23, 1917, a program to produce twenty thousand aircraft in less than one year was approved by the War Department.[37] In the meantime, General Squier made an arrangement similar to the Crozier-Ganne artillery agreement to buy combat aircraft from the French and British. Canadian pilots would be trained in Texas during the winter of 1917–1918 in exchange for the immediate training and equipment of ten squadrons of American pilots in England.[38]

The War Department seemed mesmerized by numbers. Secretary Baker announced that Congress would be asked to appropriate $640,000,000 "to build the greatest air fleet ever devised" and informed President Wilson that he was "thoroughly fascinated by the possibilities of the thing." Colonel Edward M. House wrote the president, "If you give the word and will stand for an appropriation of one billion dollars, the thing is done." Congress, obsessed with visions of clouds of war planes bombing the Germans into defeat instead of waves of young American infantrymen hurling themselves on German machine guns, voted the appropriation with scarcely any debate.[39] On October 4, 1917, the secretary of war announced that the Signal Corps, in conjunction with the Aircraft Production Board of the CND, had placed contracts for twenty thousand aircraft. Baker believed the situation was under control and released a statement to the press that was characteristically progressive and, perhaps, the most optimistic assessment of the power of organized human intelligence to control events made by an American during the First World War. Baker stated, "The work of the aviation section has been thoroughly systematized. The training of aviators, the building of motors and the construction of wings is proceeding uniformly—each keeping pace with the others and with general war plans. The comprehensive plan is that when the motors are ready there will be ready also the planes necessary; and when the motors and planes are ready aviators and machine guns shall be available. Coordination has been developed in every branch of the Aviation Section."[40] By the fall of 1917, however, substantial military, political, and logistical problems were emerging that would make the secretary of war regret his optimism.

☆ ☆ ☆

When General Bliss was ordered to Europe as part of the American mission headed by Edward M. House to attend inter-Allied meetings in late October 1917, he was not without pride in the American accomplishment. In early October 1917, the thirty-division project, agreed to by the War Department's Baker Board and Pershing and his associates, became the official American army program for the next year of the war.[41] Bliss believed the pace had been logical and deliberate and he assumed that it could be carried out during the next eighteen months. Leaders in Washington also believed the country was well on its way to implementing a program that would carry Wilsonian policies into effect deliberately and systematically. But in November the successful Bolshevik seizure of power in Russia, the Italian collapse at Caporetto, and the failure of the British offensive in Flanders signaled a period of extreme danger for the Allied cause and ended the deliberate pace of American mobilization. At home the mobilization program virtually collapsed during the late fall and winter of 1917–1918. Rail transportation ground to a halt, and shipping proved inadequate to meet demands. Meanwhile, the most severe weather in years struck the country. Rivers and canals froze. Autumn gales slowed the passage of both cargo and troopships on the North Atlantic, while trainloads of military supplies continued to pour into the northeastern ports where the army was scheduled to embark. Ships could not find berthing facilities in New York harbor, and the congestion made it almost impossible to provision ships ready to sail. In the heavily industrialized East only enough coke remained by mid-December to keep the blast furnaces going for a few more weeks.

CHAPTER 6

REORGANIZING THE WAR DEPARTMENT AND BUILDING THE AMERICAN EXPEDITIONARY FORCES, 1917–1918

The First World War raised two major institutional and organizational issues for the American army. The first involved internal organization and control within the War Department. The second concerned command and control between the commander of the AEF and the chief of staff in Washington and reached back to the days of Winfield Scott. Difficulties inside the War Department and between the War Department and the AEF made necessary measures previously considered philosophically unwise, organizationally unsound, and politically impossible. The battlefield controlled events. During the winter and spring of 1917–1918, the unexpected turn of allied fortunes brought new requests for reinforcements from General Pershing. If the thirty-division program, the product of parallel planning between the AEF and the War Department, continued into 1919, an American force of fifty-four divisions would be deployed. The crisis of November 1917–March 1918 threw that project into disarray. Massive shipments of American troops in April and May 1918, the continuing battlefield emergency, and pressure from the Allied high command led General Pershing to reconsider his requirements and, in June 1918, he was calling for the deployment of one hundred American divisions to France by the end of 1919.

The War Department began to analyze existing programs in April 1918, and the War College prepared alternative projects of fifty-four, sixty, sixty-six, eighty, and one hundred divisions for President Wilson's consideration. In July 1918, after a review of all the available data from the civilian war agencies as well as the military, Secretary of War Baker informed the president that the most the country could support was an eighty-division effort. Wilson approved the eighty-division program in late July 1918, and his decision was cabled to

Pershing as the official American war program for 1919. The eighty-division program was based more on national capacity than on battlefield realities, and neither the War Department nor the AEF commander, who was still pressing for one hundred divisions, questioned the size of the effort.[1]

☆ ☆ ☆

When the war began, Secretary Baker dealt with affairs through existing agencies, but in the late autumn of 1917 he began to listen to officers such as Acting Chief of Staff John Biddle, only recently returned from France, who called for the reform and reorganization of the War Department. The reform impulse came from three sources: the general staff itself, the bureau chiefs, and civilian experts outside the War Department. The general staff was a planning and consultative body rather than an executive agency, but the chief of staff, like the commanding general before him, could exercise executive power indirectly through the office of the secretary of war. Chief of Staff Wood's victory over Adjutant General Ainsworth in 1912 proved short lived, and, in 1916, it was only Secretary Baker's intervention that saved the general staff from emasculation. In all bureaucratic structures access is the key to power, and when the war began in 1917 all the bureau chiefs still had access to Secretary Baker's office. Chief of Staff Hugh Scott urged the secretary of war to end the practice, and in his final report of September 1917 asserted, like every chief since 1903, that the chief of staff should control access to the secretary of war. The drive to extend general staff control in the War Department grew during the summer and fall of 1917 as War College planners proposed that the entire war program be brought under military control, that supply and logistical agencies be formally subordinated to the chief of staff, and that the bureau chiefs' access to the secretary of war should be ended.

The second source was the bureau chiefs themselves. Judge Advocate General Enoch H. Crowder championed an alternative organization to the one proposed by the War College. Crowder was as much an innovator as March. He was supported by a coterie of younger officers and had made a great success administering the selective-service system. For a time in 1917 it was rumored that he would be the new chief of staff. It was Crowder who, in December 1917, persuaded Secretary Baker to create a war council in the War Department to direct the military effort through the chief of staff who would be its agent. The war council was an alternative to domination by the chief of staff and would control affairs without destroying historical informal, consultative War Department relationships.[2]

The third source involved the Council of National Defense (CND) and its advisory commission, the War Industries Board, and other federal emergency agencies—the Shipping Board, the Food Administration, the War Trade Board, and the Fuel Administration—and the United States Chamber of Commerce. In December 1917, Thomas Nelson Perkins, a representative of the WIB with the House mission in Europe, proposed that all business and industrial functions should be removed from the War Department and lodged in a separate civilian Ministry of Munitions. The Perkins plan generated a great deal of support among the public and in the Congress during the winter of 1917–1918.[3]

☆ ☆ ☆

In December 1917, Secretary Baker, with Acting Chief of Staff John Biddle's help, began to consider recommendations from all three sources. He had already begun to reorganize his own office in mid-November 1917, replacing Assistant Secretary of War William Ingraham with Benedict Crowell, a Cleveland engineer who had been involved in the preparedness campaign. Crowell, who had strong connections with the United States Chamber of Commerce, had been a member of the Kernan Board and had come into the government through the Ordnance Department. He quickly became an effective, if controversial, member of Baker's administrative staff. In late December 1917, Edward R. Stettinius Sr., who before the war had handled allied purchasing for the firm of J. P. Morgan, was named second assistant secretary of war and surveyor general of supply.

Secretary Baker had previously followed Civil War precedents and appointed special assistants to oversee significant issues, but beginning with the Crowell and Stettinius appointments, he began to name the men assistant secretaries of war. In late spring 1918, after Congress authorized further expansion of his staff, Baker made Frederick Keppel, a former dean of Columbia University who had been a special assistant for personnel, assistant secretary of war and director of personnel. In late July 1918, John D. Ryan of Amalgamated Copper became assistant secretary of war and director of the air service. In July 1918, after Stettinius went abroad with a large staff to head the American mission at the inter-Allied supply meetings, Baker, as a result of a complex series of encounters involving Stettinius, Crowell, and Major General George W. Goethals, redefined Crowell's duties and made him director of munitions.[4]

Major General John Biddle, acting chief of staff from October 1917 through February 1918, is one of the neglected figures in War Department history. Biddle was born in Detroit and graduated from West Point in 1881. Like many engineers, he spent most of his career on river and harbor work. He served on the general staff from 1911 through 1914 and was an observer with the Austro-Hungarian army during the first two years of the Great War. He returned to the United States in 1916 to become superintendent of the military academy at West Point. He was in France helping to build the AEF logistical base when he was called home. Biddle was a talented planner but lacked the ruthlessness to transform ideas into new institutions. It was his task, one for which he was temperamentally ill suited, to deal with the wave of War Department reform which began during the fall and winter of 1917–1918. After his relief in late February 1918, he served with distinction as commander of American forces in England, where he played a major role in clearing the congestion at the port of Southampton during the summer and fall of 1918.

Blending the advice of the War College and that of Generals Crowder and Biddle, Baker, in December 1917, appointed General Goethals quartermaster general and director of storage and traffic in the general staff, to straighten out logistics and warehousing. He placed War Department procurement in the hands of Brigadier General Palmer E. Pierce, who became director of purchase and supply. The mission of the general staff to plan and coordinate was reaffirmed and its supervising power was strengthened. A war council composed of the secretary of war, Chief of Staff Biddle, and the bureau chiefs formalized and facilitated interbureau cooperation. Secretary Baker's announcement on December 19, 1917, that the changes he was making in the War Department were not connected with the congressional hearings then in progress did not impress anybody. One editorial writer stated, on the announcement of Crozier's appointment to the war council, "Making General Crozier a scapegoat for the delays, omissions, and futilities of the War Department is the wrong way to reform a bad business." Another charged that General Henry Sharpe, who was also appointed to the war council, was simply being "kicked upstairs."[5] In January 1918 Secretary Baker ordered Major General Peyton C. March home from Europe to become chief of staff. The first phase of the reorganization was made public on January 15, 1918.[6] The second phase further consolidated control of supply, and logistics in the general staff became official in War Department General Order 14, of February 9, 1918. General Biddle coordinated affairs until March took office on March 4, 1918. The chief of staff's later criticism of Biddle in *The Nation at War* was unkind and unjust.[7]

When he took up his duties in Washington, March moved simultaneously to speed troop shipments to France and to impose top-down control in the War Department.[8] He well understood the significance of the war council—chairing a planning, coordinating, and supervising committee was not for him—but, at least for a while, he used it. On March 21, 1918, when the great German offensive opened on the Western Front, March began round-the-clock meetings with the war council to rationalize the shipment of troops to France and provide for their logistical support. During March and April

1918, whole sections of the CND and the WIB were transferred into the War Department, but it was mid-May before the war council, its role assumed by other agencies of the general staff, ceased to meet formally.

From April through August 1918, the War Department was in organizational turmoil and the way in which this occurred reveals much about March and his methods. After the first of the year, Assistant Secretary of War Benedict Crowell promoted a War Department reorganization plan of his own. During January and February 1918, he circulated a scheme that would separate all supply functions from the general staff and place the supply bureaus under his control. Crowell saw himself as a kind of chief of staff for supply, equal in power to March and with direct access to the secretary of war. He opposed any plan that would remove control of procurement from the War Department and place it in the hands of an independent department of munitions and insisted that all communication with civilian war agencies should be through his office. Secretary Baker did not approve of Crowell's plan, but he needed his drive and technical expertise. As long as Baker was in Washington, he kept Crowell on a short lead, but in late March 1918, while Baker was in France, his assistant, as acting secretary of war, attempted to put his own plan into effect. The next month Crowell further alienated Baker and triggered a contest with Chief of Staff March, which left the assistant secretary isolated until the end of the war.

In early April 1918, Crowell appointed a "committee of three," composed of Hugh Johnson, Charles Day of the secretary of war's office, and Thomas N. Perkins of the WIB, who was just back from Europe, to study the supply situation. March immediately intervened, and, on his orders, the committee rejected all Crowell's plans to place supply under his control and submitted one of its own that eliminated the war council and transformed the general staff from a planning and coordinating agency to a command center. It also combined Palmer Pierce's Purchase and Supply Division with the Storage and Traffic Division to create a single Purchase, Storage, and Traffic Division (PS and T) of the general staff, headed by Goethals. As a member of the general staff, Goethals would control general military supply from the point of production to French ports, where responsibility would be assumed by the AEF. On April 16, 1918, after Baker returned from France, the report became official policy. Crowell backed off quickly. Hugh Johnson became director of purchase and supply on Goethals's staff, and March secured, at least temporarily, command of the War Department bureaucracy.[9]

In the Goethals appointment March revealed his best qualities. He was a good judge of character and abilities. He was also decisive and could delegate authority. Although March played a critical part in approving army programs and worked effectively to secure the shipping necessary to get troops and equipment to France, he took little part in the day-to-day work with the civilian war boards, which he left to Goethals and his associates. March wrote later, "We had a meeting once a week . . . of the heads of the principal war boards with Secretary Baker and myself. . . . At these meetings each person responsible for a part of the great war program . . . told us precisely what he was doing and proposing to do in carrying out his part of the general scheme." March wrote later of Goethals's work, "The work he did as the virtual Chief of Supply of the army far transcended in magnitude and certainly equaled in importance . . . the construction of the Panama Canal. Yet he is known only for the latter work while his great work as Chief of Supply is completely unknown to the general public."[10]

March was at his worst when he dealt with Palmer Pierce, who headed Purchase and Supply. March and Goethals thought Pierce was too close to the civilians at the WIB and did not represent the army's views aggressively at its meetings. When March abruptly fired him in mid-April 1918, he said, "Pierce, I have cut off your head and ordered you out of the War Department." He was equally cruel to Adjutant General Henry P. McCain. When McCain's tour was up in August 1918, March, without consultation and despite McCain's protests, simply removed him and sent him away from Washington to command a recently organized infantry division.

March was promoted to the wartime rank of full general and officially became chief of staff in May 1918. The Overman Act of the same month legalized the changes already made in the organization of executive agencies and authorized the president to make any changes in the future that he deemed necessary to prosecute the war.[11] March carried the reorganization forward during the summer of 1918. By General Order 80 of August 26, 1918, the chief of staff was designated as "the immediate adviser of the Secretary of War on all matters relating to military programs." By the same order the general staff was divided into four divisions: War Plans (WPD), Operations (OPD), Purchase, Storage, and Traffic (PS and T), and Military Intelligence (MID). War Plans and Operations were responsible for articulating the military program in consultation with the AEF and other divisions of the staff. Goethals got the program from Operations, developed its supply and logistical dimensions in cooperation with the civilian emergency agencies, and moved troops and supplies to France where the AEF Service of Supply (SOS) took over. In six months March turned the general staff into an executive command-and-control agency linking program planning, administration, and execution. General Order 80, which concentrated control of military supply in Goethals's office, literally disestablished the bureau chiefs. Goethals reported directly to March. By October the general staff was changing from a planning, consultative, and coordinating agency whose chief was "first among equals" to a dynamic operating agency headed by a chief who, in the name of the secretary of war, directed rather than consulted with and coordinated the War Department staff. Opposition had not disappeared, but it had been muffled in part by the demands of the war crisis and in part by the will of Peyton C. March, who drove the American war machine at home furiously until the end of hostilities.[12]

☆ ☆ ☆

If there was an "organizer of victory" during the First World War, it was George W. Goethals. Goethals knew that Secretary Baker had brought him into the War Department to take advantage of his name and reputation. Necessity dictated, Goethals claimed, that the army supply system be brought under central direction. By war's end he had begun the most far-reaching reorganization of military supply in American history.[13]

One of Goethals's great strengths as an administrator was his ability to delegate authority, and in January 1918, within a month of his appointment as quartermaster general and director of storage and traffic, he appointed a civilian railroad executive, Harry M. Adams of the Missouri Pacific Railroad, and Colonel F. B. Wells, a member of the old "Canal Gang," to coordinate transportation and storage. At first both officials merely supervised the activities of the various agencies, but, as Goethals asserted his own influence through the supply system, their roles became increasingly directive until, in October 1918, they assumed operational control of military traffic and storage within the United States.

Goethals reorganized the quartermaster general's office as well. In January 1918, he persuaded Robert J. Thorne, former president of Montgomery Ward and Company of Chicago, to assist him. Although Goethals chose to keep Thorne a civilian rather than give him military rank, the Chicago merchant never lacked executive power. He immediately established in the Quartermaster Bureau a requirements division that began to grapple with future demands for raw and finished materials. He analyzed existing contracts and, by April 1918, could report to Goethals precisely what had been purchased and what was yet to be purchased to fulfill the thirty-division program and prepare for 1919. Thorne also reinforced Goethals in his campaign to convert the quartermaster general's office into a purchasing agency similar to one the latter had created in Panama. Thorne carried the plan forward under Major

General Robert E. Wood, another of Goethals's associates from the old days, who was called home from France in late April 1918 to manage quartermaster affairs after Goethals took control of the PS and T. In October 1918, the title of quartermaster general was abolished, and Wood became director of purchases in the PS and T, with Thorne as his assistant charged with the procurement of all general supplies.[14] Creation of the PS and T brought another important personality to join Thorne, Adams, and Wells in the Goethals coterie. Hugh S. Johnson became director of purchase and supply and served until released for duty in the field in October 1918. It was as Goethals's associate that he gained the experience with industry that attracted Franklin D. Roosevelt's attention in 1933.

The PS and T had its most important connections with the Operations Division of the General Staff and the Supply bureaus. Johnson, as director of purchase and supply, received the military program from operations and transmitted it to the bureaus, the most important of which were ordnance, under Clarence C. Williams, and quartermaster, under Wood. Theoretically, the bureaus would then move in a coordinated way toward the common objective. The general staff could control the process without rousing the enmity of the bureau chiefs or destroying utterly the traditional purchasing practices of the army.[15] As army programs came increasingly to shape the business life of the country, Goethals himself served as the military representative on the vital Priorities Committee of Bernard Baruch's War Industries Board, while Johnson handled routine matters of requirements, clearance, and production.[16]

In late May and early June 1918, Goethals began to shift procurement of standard articles to the Quartermaster Corps while the purchase of specialized technical items remained in the hands of the other bureaus. In mid-June he prevailed upon Gerard Swope of the Western Electric Company to carry the consolidation to fruition.[17] With the help of Johnson and other officers from Goethals's staff and certain bureau representatives, especially Thorne and Wood, Swope developed a plan that would create a central agency to procure all standard articles of army supply, control their movement and storage in the United States, and oversee their shipment to France. As Swope envisioned it, the director of the PS and T would assume full responsibility for the general supplies program, thus incorporating into the general staff the functions formerly exercised by the bureau chiefs. The bureaus would be absorbed administratively into the general staff, and their supply and logistical functions would be distributed among branches of the PS and T.[18]

The Swope plan encountered considerable opposition, especially from Chief of Ordnance C. C. Williams, Chief of Engineers William M. Black, and Surgeon General William C. Gorgas, who considered it a bureaucratic monstrosity, an insult to the consultative tradition, and a blow to their not inconsiderable accomplishments thus far in the war. It also roused the ire of Assistant Secretary of War Crowell, who still hoped to concentrate control of supply in his own office.[19] Goethals had worked well with Assistant Secretary of War Stettinius, who oversaw the procurement of general supplies, because the latter was willing to treat him as a colleague rather than a subordinate. Goethals, however, could not abide Crowell. He warned the Clevelander to stay out of the way until the Swope plan was given a fair trial. March hesitated to accept such a revolutionary proposal, and Goethals fretted and fumed for more than a month and pestered the chief of staff daily for a decision. Nothing was forthcoming until General Order 80 was published on August 28, 1918. A victory for Goethals, it disestablished the bureaus and concentrated general supply authority in his hands. He reported directly to March instead of Stettinius, who was in France. Transfer of functions began in late September 1918, and the major part of the project was completed by the armistice. On paper at least, the traditional bureaus virtually disappeared, replaced by a highly centralized supply and logistical directorate within the general staff. Although the Goethals reorganization dealt the tradition of "separate spheres and parallel paths" important blows, organizational turbulence persisted. The contest was too deeply rooted in past War Department and army history to be ended so quickly, and at the armistice fierce bureau resistance continued, showing that the ancient debate remained unresolved.[20]

☆ ☆ ☆

The chain of command between the War Department in Washington and the headquarters of the AEF in France was always more complicated than it appeared. Secretary Baker's connections with his three most-important uniformed subordinates—March, Pershing, and Bliss—were built more on consultation than on formal hierarchy. The American army had never fought a war with a corporate staff system and the nineteenth-century tradition of command, with its war councils built on informal personal connections and informal communication, offered few clear precedents. As a result, two separate American military establishments appeared—one in France and the other in the United States—and it was not clear who commanded where or what.

In May 1917, General Bliss and Secretary Baker, with the best intentions, set the stage for a struggle for supremacy between the general staff in Washington and the AEF at Chaumont. Bliss rejected the idea that the chief of staff was the Wilson administration's agent of military command and sought to reestablish the command structure that had proved so effective during the Civil War. He would play Baker's Halleck to Pershing's Grant. Like Halleck, he described himself as the personal adviser to the secretary of war and the AEF commander's subordinate and military representative in the War Department.[21]

Secretary Baker at first reasoned from similar Civil War precedents. When Pershing went to France in May 1917, he carried two letters of instruction. One was drafted by Pershing and his chief of staff, James G. Harbord, and signed by General Bliss; the other was drafted by Brigadier General Francis Kernan and signed by Secretary Baker. Both letters reinforced the traditional view of the relationship between the staff in Washington and the general commanding in the field. The Baker letter, which took precedence, carried forward President Wilson's prime directive to keep the AEF independent and instructed Pershing, except in exceptional circumstances, to keep the American forces intact and, at a time of his own choosing, commit them to battle. The letter invested Pershing with all necessary authority "to carry the war on vigorously . . . toward a victorious conclusion."[22] It was easy for Pershing to take the traditional view that his authority in France, which seemed to combine that which Grant wielded in the last years of the Civil War with that of an American colonial proconsul, extended across the Atlantic to the War Department. Pershing had direct access to Baker and he was able, at least for the first year of the war, to make organizational plans from Chaumont the basis of the American program; however, when Peyton March returned to the United States and began to consolidate power in his office, a contest began with Pershing for control of the army.[23]

March was among that group of American army officers whose careers spanned the institutional transition from a nineteenth-century system with a commanding general who, in theory, directed the army in the field and was supported by a subordinate War Department staff, to a twentieth-century one with command and control vested in a corporate general staff headed by a chief of staff, which, again in theory, integrated and coordinated war making through one central military agency. Looking as much to past American experience as to current models of command and control, March strove to be commanding general as well as chief of staff. He might later describe himself as a chairman of the board or chief executive officer, but at the time his views were more in keeping with those of William T. Sherman than with those of any contemporary corporate organizer.[24] March considered Pershing a subordinate, and it was easy enough for the traditional view of the commanding general's power to resurface. But there simply could not be two commanding generals. The nineteenth-century command tradition, with its ambiguities and dependence on personality and informal organization, inclined in Pershing's favor because there was only one active theater of operations. General Bliss held the traditional view that the commander in the field was also the commander of the American military establishment, including the staff in Washington. After March returned from France, the conflict became one between two assertive men who had grown up in the "old army," with its institutional memory of powerful commanding generals like Grant and Sherman, and revealed March and Pershing's ambivalence about the new corporate-staff model of command and control. Both men agreed that only soldiers of the line should serve as chief of staff and that all administrative and technical services must be subordinate to the line. But March insisted that Pershing was directly under his command. Conflicts between the chief of staff and the AEF commander ranged from questions of promotion, to a scheme to turn Pershing's supply and logistics over to George Goethals, to a critical argument over the ultimate size and order of battle of the American army. The situation was more like a bad toothache than a life-threatening illness, but it was an invitation to administrative dissension.[25]

The two American military establishments had different production, procurement, and logistical agencies and conducted separate business affairs with the French, British, Italian, and other European governments. In July 1917, shortly after he established his headquarters at Chaumont, Pershing anticipated that the thirty-division project then taking shape would create enormous supply problems and place a great strain on available shipping.[26] He saw that every pound of material that could be purchased in Europe would reduce his dependence on transatlantic shipping. Although Andre Tardieu, the French high commissioner, made solemn agreements in Washington, Pershing, in France, was soon frustrated and complained that "the failure of the French to realize the necessity of hearty cooperation became evident very early in our relations with them. The higher authorities apparently understood, and promises of assistance were readily given [in Washington] but when we got down to actual details we encountered difficulties."[27]

The American command in France strove to bring War Department agencies in Washington under AEF control. In mid-July 1917, Pershing organized his staff functionally along the French "G" system and placed the chiefs of his supply and logistical agencies under his personal command. On August 13, 1917, as part of the expansion of the AEF staff organization, he established the line of communications (LOC) under Major General Robert M. Blatchford and assigned control of rail transport to William W. Atterbury, former general manager of the Pennsylvania Railroad. In a move characteristic of the command turbulence during the first six months of the war, Blatchford was replaced in October 1917 by Mason B. Patrick, who was in turn followed by Major General Francis J. Kernan, who was then touring France as commander of the Thirty-first Division and had a good reputation as a staff planner and engineer.[28]

Pershing was especially concerned about the War Department bureau chiefs who insisted that he was merely another field commander and did not control their representatives in Europe. He complained that they contracted for equipment in Europe without informing his headquarters and issued directives to their people in Chaumont along their own chains of command. At the end of August, Pershing ordered all communication between the bureau chiefs in Washington and their people in France to pass through the appropriate sections of his headquarters in Chaumont. He still had trouble, though, and later wrote, "So independent of control or suggestion had some bureaus of our War Department become that it was a long time before their chiefs would consent to leave such matters to their representatives at my headquarters acting under my authority."

The AEF supply organization was militarized, whereas the key actors in the War Department were civilians. Johnson Hagood, later chief of staff of the SOS in France, defended the action of his chief and helped create a postwar myth that the War Department had collapsed completely. He wrote, "The whole General Staff and War Department, generally, fell like a house of cards and a new organization had to be created during the process of the war. The old system failed and individuals had to be pressed in to serve whenever they could be found. In France we had to do the same thing and in the scramble to establish a working machine the organization in France did not match up with the one back in the states."[29]

In August 1917, Pershing established a single purchasing agency through which the various military bureaus in his command could deal with their European suppliers. Pershing's old friend from Nebraska days, Charles G. Dawes, had arrived in France in July and Pershing asked him to bring together the AEF supply chiefs, the Red Cross, and the YMCA in a unified purchasing board. Dawes resisted. As Pershing wrote in his diary, "He tried to beg off, but when its importance was explained, he gracefully accepted."[30] Pershing made Dawes a colonel—later brigadier general—and ordered him to unite all the purchasing bureaus in the AEF, approve all purchases made in Europe, procure the transport necessary to bring them to the front, and establish liaison with Allied authorities. He told him to consolidate interbureau ordering to gain the lowest prices and attract the attention of the greatest European wholesalers. Dawes was also to handle all transfers of equipment from the Allies to the AEF.

Dawes paid most of his own expenses and his headquarters in Paris at the Hotel Mediterranee, up the Seine toward Notre Dame, were close enough to the Ritz Hotel on the Place de Vendôme to allow the enterprising Chicagoan to conduct much of his business from its bar and restaurant. A less military headquarters was impossible to imagine. Dawes's unsoldierly demeanor was famous throughout the AEF. On one occasion he purposely saluted with the wrong hand and on another neither rose nor removed his cigar from his mouth when Pershing entered his office. Pershing had more forbearance with his old friend than with other members of his staff and suggested that it was appropriate when the commander of the AEF entered a room that Dawes "at least shift the cigar from one side of [his] mouth to the other." Pershing finally said to him, "Charlie, as a soldier you're a poor sight indeed, but as a banker you're just what I need."[31]

When he was not dining at the Ritz or attending the *Comédie Française*, Dawes oversaw massive expenditures of money. Although it did no direct purchasing, his office, which included Democratic businessmen like the younger August Belmont, approved the orders of the AEF bureaus and had veto power over inappropriate contracts. The Chicago banker had more power in the fall of 1917 than any single War Department administrator, except possibly Secretary Baker himself. Every ton of supplies secured abroad saved at least two tons of precious shipping and months of time. By the end of the war Dawes had overseen the purchase of more than ten million tons of supplies for the AEF, three million tons more than were shipped from the United States.[32]

By September 1917, Pershing's people were competing with the War Department and with the Allies. The AEF drove up prices, robbed French civilians of necessities, duplicated orders, and wasted scarce resources.[33] For example, Spain was a potential source of supplies and Dawes sought to purchase lumber, blankets, mules, and foodstuffs on the peninsula. The Spanish were at first uncooperative and sought guarantees that American embargoes on strategic materials to Spain would be lifted. Dawes, frustrated by the recalcitrant Spaniards, requested in late September 1917 that Ambassador William G. Sharp ask the State Department to apply pressure on the Spanish government to release the goods. Meanwhile, John R. Christie, Dawes's colleague, told Dawes that he could do nothing with the Spaniards alone and that "the situation there is such that [the] want can only be supplied with some sort of reciprocal arrangement by our government." News of Dawes's activity had already reached Washington, rousing the State Department and the Export Control Board, which the Wilson administration had appointed in August 1917. In mid-October, Pershing suddenly was informed that all transactions between the Allies and the AEF had to be undertaken at the intergovernmental level and that all purchases had to be first cleared at home.[34] The order from Washington revealed what had been going on during the previous months. Anxieties over equipping the gathering American land forces, the relationship of the army's programs to the requirements of the navy, and awareness of the needs of Allied forces already in battle with the Germans brought the first steps to rationalize War Department procurement and also the first substantial efforts toward interallied logistical cooperation.

Even after the great German spring drive on the Western Front began on March 21, 1918, the situation between the AEF and the War Department remained unclarified. In the midst of the crisis, Pershing's staff, without consulting Washington, developed a plan to increase the size of the AEF to one hundred divisions or four million men by the end of 1919.[35] Equipment and supply cables from France oscillated wildly week by week, creating administrative havoc in the War Department. Work lagged on port facilities and inland bases at home, whereas French railroads lacked the capacity to support even the current American program. Port facilities in France were so congested that more ships would simply make the situation worse. If troops and supplies could not clear the ports, more shipping would be locked up waiting to unload. On the other hand, if the ports could be cleared, turn around times for the cargo and transport fleet could be cut down and more tonnage made available to ship American troops and supplies.[36] All the ships in the world, however, would not help if Pershing's supply and logistical planning did not improve.

AEF combat and support agencies were concentrated in Chaumont and their leaders were beginning to step on each other's toes. Dawes was doing good work as general purchasing agent for the army, but Brigadier General William W. Atterbury, the director of transportation, was ill disposed to taking orders from army officers. Indeed, Atterbury had resisted a commission and believed the entire supply and logistics business should be taken out of the army's hands and placed "in the hands of a big business man who would reorganize it and operate it in the principles of big business back in the United States."[37]

In early February 1918, Pershing assembled a board chaired by Major General Johnson Hagood that recommended the separation of supply and logistics from the general staff and their organization with a separate military staff in Tours and Paris, far distant from Chaumont. Dawes and Atterbury were members of the board and their altercations revealed the differences over organization among American businessmen during the First World War. Dawes confronted the railroad man directly. It was the job of big business to do as it was told and support the army, not argue with it. Businessmen could give advice, but they had to abide by the decisions of the military when their advice was not heeded. It was the height of folly to propose any scheme by which a businessman, no matter how brilliant, should dictate methods to the military, whether it be methods of conducting combat operations at the front or methods of supplying troops from the rear. Compared to the army, the industrial corporation was a newcomer, Dawes asserted. The function of an industrial corporation was to make a product as cheaply as possible, sell it as dearly as possible, and make a big profit. The function of the army was to win a war as cheaply and quickly as possible. War was not a matter of personal profit and every part of the military organization had to function automatically and get the right thing to the right place at the right time in order to win the battle.[38] Atterbury did not have a chance. On February 13, 1918, the line of communication was abolished and the supply and logistical functions of the AEF were turned over to Francis Kernan, who was named commanding general, services of supply. Atterbury retained his post but reported to Kernan. Dawes, as general purchasing agent, was the link between the AEF, SOS, and the continental and Allied economies.[39]

Meanwhile, Pershing was willing to pool everything except soldiers. He opposed amalgamation of the armies but supported amalgamation, at least for the time being, of supplies. In mid-April 1918 he advised General Foch that the American army favored a general arrangement to pool all allied supplies in France. Dawes reflected later, "To give common sense in inter-Allied military cooperation the supremacy over human pride and jealousy, only a great emergency and the instinct of self preservation as a rule will suffice."[40] On April 27, 1918, Pershing cabled Washington that the questions of tonnage and supply pooling were intimately connected and "both should be under military control as far as possible" from his side of the ocean.[41] The first meeting of the Military Board of Allied Supply took place on June 28, 1918. It was to take the necessary measures to place under common control, "so far as possible, all the depots in which are brought together the different supplies destined for the different Armies, bases, permanent warehouses for food and medical supplies, depots of ammunition, engineer depots, regulating stations etc."[42]

Pershing's proposals were self-serving. Dawes went on placing orders in Europe without consulting Washington and contradictory cables continued to flow from Chaumont. Representatives of the AEF insisted they were in command and, as the only people who understood the situation, should be obeyed without hesitation. By implication, and often by direct assertion, they insisted they were the equals and possibly the superiors of representatives of the War Department and other government agencies. In early June 1918, the

British, who wanted a more flexible civilian to replace Pershing in diplomatic negotiations over the possible amalgamation of the American army, began to call for restriction of General Pershing's authority and the transfer of logistical, supply, and diplomatic functions into other hands. They contacted Edward M. House, who advised Wilson that all inter-Allied relations ought to be conducted by General Bliss's staff at the supreme war council. House suggested that equipping and maintaining the AEF should be removed from Pershing's control and his duties confined to "training and fighting our troops."

The president sent the letter to Secretary Baker, who consulted March. Both saw the House suggestion as an opportunity to bring AEF supply and logistics under War Department control. The chief of staff recommended that Goethals place a subordinate, possibly his assistant, Hugh Johnson, in charge of supply in Washington and go to France, where he would take over supply matters from Kernan. Baker wrote Pershing for his opinion. Pershing, who had already heard about the plan, exploded. He had rejected Goethals for service in France earlier in the war and was adamant that all theater military activity remain under his own command. On July 27, 1918, he cabled Secretary Baker, rejecting Goethals and insisting that he must control the AEF line of supply. To quiet criticism, Pershing expediently relieved Kernan and appointed James G. Harbord as commanding general, SOS. Baker and the president were pleased when the military effort seemed to improve, but questions of command relationships between Washington and Chaumont remained unresolved. Pershing was still calling for a hundred divisions and continued to maneuver during August and September 1918 to get his way. He acted as if the secretary of war had not been told what General March was doing and would put a stop to it if he knew how he was being manipulated by War Department bureaucrats. That was not the case, and when he arrived in France for his second visit in early September 1918, Baker was shocked to find Pershing still pressing the larger program. Baker sidestepped a confrontation and cabled March to inform Pershing that the eighty-division program was official policy. Just before Baker left for home in early October 1918, however, Pershing wrote him an astonishing letter, insisting that "the General Staff and every supply department in Washington should strive to supply us promptly with the necessary personnel and material in the order called for . . . to be coordinated by your General Staff." To Pershing, March was a mere quartermaster, and the AEF commander made that even more clear in early November 1918 when he audaciously submitted a Goethals plan in reverse, suggesting that his quartermaster general, Harry Rogers, return home to run the supply program in the United States.

Baker could no longer run his two bickering generals in tandem. He ordered Rogers to stay in France and moved to support his chief of staff as the senior and commanding general of the American military establishment.[43]

☆☆☆

When the American First Army opened its headquarters on August 10, 1918, the AEF numbered more than one and a half million men. That was a great triumph. In sixteen months Pershing had created the independent American army that President Wilson had ordered. But the men he was about to throw into battle against the tired, reduced, but still deadly Germans were hardly parts of a well-oiled machine. The force Pershing committed to battle in September 1918 at Saint Mihiel and at the Meuse-Argonne was composed for the most part of soldiers who had been in service for less than a year. It was poorly trained, indifferently organized, and badly equipped. It succeeded at Saint Mihiel, but it was in trouble in the Meuse-Argonne from the first day. Between September 26, 1918, and October 14, 1918, Pershing drove the AEF forward in a bitter slugging match with the Germans, and the issue was very much in doubt. On October 10, he extended the battle to the east and created a new Second Army under Robert L. Bullard. He named Hunter Liggett to command First Army and assumed the role of army group commander. Under Liggett and Bullard the Americans moved a bit better, and by October 14 they had finally secured the objectives that were supposed to have been taken on September 27. The grinding attacks brought small gains at great cost. Although two depot divisions were skeletonized and two recently arrived infantry divisions were broken up, the First and Second armies were still short eighty thousand combat troops.

American operations were closely observed by the Allies, and they did not hesitate to complain if the Americans flagged. Marshal Haig did not think the Americans were sufficiently organized for offensive operations, and in early October French premier Clemenceau, after an interview with Marshal Ferdinand Foch, threatened to request that President Wilson relieve Pershing of command. Foch dissuaded Clemenceau, arguing that he would "nibble" troops away from Pershing for use elsewhere, thus meeting the premier's desires without alienating the American commander. Meanwhile, the stress of the contest began to tell on Pershing. He became short tempered, according to his aide, Colonel John G. Quackemeyer, and broke down emotionally for a short time after the initial American assault was blunted. Calling his dead wife's name, he exclaimed, "Frankie . . . Frankie . . . my God, sometimes I don't know how I can go on."[44]

Some have argued that the reason for the poor performance of American combat units was that they suffered from inappropriate fighting doctrine and might have done better with a different training system or a more open-minded commander. Pershing had entered the war convinced that prewar doctrine based on fire and maneuver and the supremacy of the well-trained rifleman, embodied in field regulations worked out between 1908 and 1916 at the schools at Fort Riley, Fort Sill, and Fort Leavenworth, was still viable. Under the rubric "open warfare," the AEF commander at first argued that there was no reason to rethink basic doctrine, but conditions in the West had changed. The Anglo-French armies and the armies of the Central Powers were in a volatile tactical state. Doctrines of fire and maneuver, similar to those championed by the Americans, had failed. During the first two years of the war, the infantry of all the armies was massacred to no decisive end, and in France siege warfare had become the rule. During 1917, tactics and doctrine began to change. The British began to combine artillery with new weapons—poison gas, mobile armor, air power—linked by wireless, telephone, and telegraphic communications, into improved battlefield tactics. The Germans responded with defense in depth and the linear trench warfare, fixed later in the public mind by films such as *All Quiet on the Western Front* (1930), disappeared, replaced by systems of strong points shielded by deep fields of barbed wire and covered by interlocking automatic weapons and well-positioned artillery.

In August 1917, Pershing's staff, assuming that there would be time to implement their recommendations, proposed a systematic development and training program for the AEF. The basic American unit of organization would be a corps. It would include six divisions. Four of them would be combat organizations that would be assigned specific training areas. They would alternate battalion and regimental units in the battle line brigaded with French and British troops to gain experience and then return to help train the rest of the division. One of the two other divisions in the corps would train replacements and move them to the depot division, which would allocate the troops to the combat forces once they had been committed to battle. The program would move incrementally until an entire division entered the fighting front, first in a quiet sector and then in a more active one. Organization at the corps level would follow; eventually an independent American army headquarters would be opened, and the AEF would hold its own sector of the front. Ultimately, an American army group would join the allies as an equal partner in the battle against the Germans. The staff also recommended that a complete set of schools for weapons specialists, junior officers, regimental and division commanders, and general-staff officers be established to inculcate what Pershing called "pure American" fighting doctrine.[45]

The project was overtaken by events, and, in light of the compression of the American military effort, Pershing's training philosophy or doctrinal pre-conceptions had little influence on American performance. He never had time to put anything in place. At first, troops appeared more slowly than expected and the first six divisions for the First Corps were still not in France when the massive German offensive erupted in March 1918. When the troops arrived with a rush, any systematic doctrinal instruction and training was out of the question. Organizational turbulence wrought havoc. At the AEF schools, train-ing personnel were always in short supply, and unit commanders complained continuously when commissioned and noncommissioned officers and troops were kept on as cadres. Training cycles were shortened and then shortened again. Only the First Division finished the prescribed course. It was not until late summer 1918, after the German offensive had been contained and turned back and more than a million American troops were in France, that the AEF staff began to get any control of affairs. Even then, during the brutal fighting in the Argonne Forest, no particular doctrine or training method substituted for experience.[46] In his June 1919 report, Brigadier General H. B. Fiske, Pershing's chief of training (G-5), wrote that even at the end of the Meuse-Argonne battle the Americans were still paying a terrible price in lives for their lack of skill. AEF combined arms practices were the most primitive on the Western Front. Artillery support for the attacking forces was often ineffective, tank-infantry cooperation was virtually nonexistent, and air-ground coordination was atro-cious. The general concluded, "The truth must be recognized. . . . [T]his war has not reversed all the lessons of the past by proving that tacticians can be made in a few months training or service at the front; or that handy, flexible, resourceful divisions can be made by a few maneuvers or by a few months association of their elements. To conclude that such has been proven would be to go far indeed from the truth and would be fatal to the adoption of a logical military policy for the future of our country."[47]

☆ ☆ ☆

In early November, the war ended on a sour note for the Americans. Dur-ing October, the Germans had given the AEF a ghastly training course in advanced combined arms, and if the war had ended on October 25, 1918, the main American military effort in France could have been labeled a failure. For seventy-two hours, during the last week in October and in direct contradic-tion to orders from home, Pershing called for unconditional German surren-der and tried to prolong the armistice negotiations until the stalemate in the Meuse-Argonne could be broken.[48] Secretary of War Baker must take some of the blame for the situation. He had never decisively defined the connections between March and Pershing, and, in not doing so, he had failed to solve the command problem in the American army. In the past he had treated Pershing as a colleague rather than as a subordinate and had given the AEF commander reason to believe that he could play fast and loose with War Department instructions and just wait things out. Pershing would seem to agree with his colleagues and simply go ahead with his own plans. Pershing did not actually prolong the war. He did not really confound President Wilson's peace efforts. There were many others who were trying to do that, and other issues, especially those involving reparations and freedom of the seas, made it difficult to end hostilities any earlier. Wilson and his colleagues thought the general had presidential ambitions, but they were political creatures and Pershing, though an able military politician, was not particularly interested in holding a civilian office. Perhaps illness and the strain of command temporarily distorted his judgment. Perhaps, as he wrote in his memoirs, he had always believed unconditional surrender would deter the Germans from future aggression. But he never said anything like that before October 30, 1918. Yet Pershing took a big chance for some reason; something far more important to him than the presidency was at stake. The AEF was his creation, and if an armistice had been granted at any time before November 5, 1918, his great enterprise could have been compromised. On that day, at the end of October 1918, Pershing could see only the few remaining miles of German strong points that lay before the Americans and open country. In his mind the honor of the army was at stake, and he tried to buy some time to put in the attack that would vindicate all his efforts. We will never know for sure. Secretary Baker wisely let the matter drop. He wrote Pershing on November 8, "I am writing this note in the tense hours during which the representatives of the German Government are supposed to be in consultation with Marshal Foch. . . . Our army has done a splendid and historic service. . . . Americans can have a full cup of happiness and pride from the effort our nation has made and the success which has crowned the chivalrous gallantry of our Army."[49]

CHAPTER 7

COORDINATING INDUSTRY AND TRANSPORTATION

THE VIEW FROM THE WAR DEPARTMENT, 1917–1918

In 1917 the Wilson administration undertook a program to raise, supply, and equip an army of more than a million men and move it to France in eighteen months. During 1918 the army program virtually tripled, growing to eighty divisions, more than three million men. The Americans had to provide initial supplies for this army and at the same time prepare for the future. As a short-run expedient, they secured artillery, machine guns, airplanes, and some sea-lifts from the British and French, but ultimately they would have to develop their own resources. Government arsenals and production depots had to be expanded. Civilian factories had to be converted, expanded, or constructed. The inland transportation system had to supply the industrial needs of the country at the same time it carried the army and its supplies to the East Coast. The Wilsonians then had to secure shipping to move American forces from ports of embarkation to the fighting front. The endeavor, which involved moving from a free market toward a command economy, lasted just a little over eighteen months. It required that the leaders of traditionally competitive, even hostile, sectors of the American economy at first be persuaded and later, reluctantly, compelled to view the war effort as an overriding imperative that transcended individual and corporate ambitions. Activities on all levels moved concurrently. Thus, the question of time compression poses one of the more difficult problems involved in analyzing the American war effort.[1]

☆☆☆

The Wilsonians were reluctant to expand federal power. Since 1913, progressive reformers, at least those associated with the president and his programs, had argued that they were modernizing the country's economic affairs through voluntary cooperation and self-regulation, thereby avoiding the political stagnation and degeneration they associated with command economies directed through formal centralized bureaucracies. President Wilson, ignoring the precedent already created with the Selective Service Act and resisting popular calls to draft industry and wealth as well as the country's young men, declared that he did not intend to expand formal national authority in any permanent way during the war. Nor did he propose to repeat the Civil War experience when, for the first two years, the states had run their own mobilization programs, often in competition with each other and with the federal government. At a meeting of state and local Councils of National Defense on May 2, 1917, Secretary Baker made it clear that the administration would coordinate the critical economic, political, and military dimensions of the war and local authorities should work along voluntary and consultative lines to encourage popular participation in the war effort. What Wilson would do, if state governors tried to take mobilization into their own hands, was revealed in the early autumn of 1917. When Governor James Cox of Ohio attempted to allocate fuel and industrial facilities, the Wilson administration ordered him to end his efforts immediately and allow federal fuel and industrial authorities to mobilize the state's resources.[2]

The Council of National Defense (CND), chaired by Secretary Baker, with its advisory commission of business experts, had been created the previous year to bring the military into contact with industry. Baker might have built the CND into a powerful agency to direct economic mobilization, but he was not so inclined. He aggressively protected War Department prerogatives and neither used all the power that he possessed nor allowed anyone else to use it.[3] He was convinced that the War Department must control the industrial effort and have final authority to determine type, amount, and production priority of military equipment. General Hugh L. Scott, then chief of staff, agreed with Baker, as did the bureau chiefs.[4] Civilians on the advisory commission were largely overruled by the army on policy questions. During the first three months of the war, the CND spawned consultative committees and boards. A Munitions Standards Board was formed in late April to expedite ordnance work, but the pleas of its chairman, industrialist Frank A. Scott, for decision-making power were ignored. A supply committee, chaired by Julius Rosenwald, president of Sears Roebuck, assisted by Vice Chairman Charles Eisenman, a Cleveland merchandiser, worked closely with Quartermaster Sharpe, acting as his agents, to place contracts for clothing and equipment.[5] By the end of June 1917, more than 150 CND committees were associated with various army bureaus.[6]

Not all in the administration were as worried about the dangers of a command economy as the president. Near the end of May 1917, Secretary of the

Treasury William G. McAdoo expressed concern about the organizational complexity of the CND committee system as well as about the way the War Department was dominating industrial mobilization planning. Worried about financing the anticipated military effort, he wanted a stable, predictable program. McAdoo was also concerned about conflicts of interest among members of the advisory commission and possible violations of law involved when committee members, acting as government agents, made contracts with their own companies. McAdoo insisted that one man, independent of the War Department, should be given control of industrial mobilization with the power to establish priority of production and delivery among the military and between them and the civilian economy. The secretary of the treasury was closely associated with Bernard M. Baruch, who at that time was chairman of the raw materials committee of the advisory commission of the CND. In May 1917, on Baruch's recommendation, McAdoo advised Wilson that, as a first step, one person should be appointed with full power to control and direct purchasing by the American military and for the Allies.[7]

Baruch had been appointed to the advisory commission because of his politics rather than his grasp of organizational affairs. A South Carolinian by birth, a Jew and the son of a Confederate army surgeon, he was, like many in the Wilson circle, a "carpetbagger in reverse." Baruch had made his money as a Wall Street speculator in the halcyon days of market manipulation before the Great War. He had no formal corporate connections, but, like August Belmont and Thomas Fortune Ryan, he was a wealthy traditional Democrat and that made him suspect among some progressives.[8] But McAdoo admired and trusted him and Secretary of the Navy Josephus Daniels, in part because of Baruch's Southern connections, found him safe and sound politically.

When President Wilson asked Baker about the desirability of having a single director of purchases, Baker suggested a more limited advisory council, which would include members of Scott's Munitions Standards Board, Rosenwald's Supply Committee, and State Department and Treasury Department officials, to advise regular executive agencies on both American and inter-Allied purchasing.[9] On June 13, 1917, Baker boldly sent the president a proposal that he suggested would make the CND more effective in meeting the needs of the government through the creation of a War Industries Board (WIB). The plan was the brainchild of Walter Gifford, the AT&T efficiency expert, who apparently suggested the name and contemplated "an immediate subordination of all committees to the Council of National Defense with the Advisory Commission acting in a purely advisory capacity." The WIB would take the place of the Munitions Standards Board and would consist "of a civilian chairman, with Army and Navy representatives . . . with such additions to its membership as might be appropriate for the consideration of special subjects." The WIB chairman would be one of five "official representatives of the government." The others would be a chief of raw materials, a chief of priorities, a chief of finished products, and a purchasing agent for the Allies, all of whom would report to the CND chaired by Secretary Baker.

The president did not respond immediately. During July 1917 he continued to listen to everyone. Baruch continued to suggest that one person be appointed to control all purchasing. On July 11 he wrote the president, "Yesterday the Advisory Commission was shown for the first time the plan of reorganization as proposed by the Council of National Defense. I do not agree with the reorganization as being a wise one or an improvement on the present plan." Doubt about its effectiveness was widespread within the commission and among members of the CND. Rosenwald, McAdoo, and Daniels believed that it did not provide the central control necessary to make the industrial effort effective, but Baker was unswayed. Writing to the president on July 14, he stated, "Mr. Baruch and Mr. Rosenwald did not believe the plan effective. . . . Mr. [David F.] Houston, Mr. [Daniel] Willard, Mr. [William C.] Redfield, Mr. [Franklin K.] Lane, and I all took the other view and we had an earnest discussion." Baker added, "I understand what Mr. Baruch's feeling about it is, although I do not share his feeling and I do not know what remedy he would suggest if any." Wilson replied that he had a plan of his own to bring industrial mobilization under control. The president's solution brought supervision of the more important aspects of the industrial effort together in one committee yet kept the War Department in control and the new WIB in a consultative relationship. It associated the supply committees of the CND with the WIB. On July 28, McAdoo wrote the president that he was "genuinely discouraged that such a complicated piece of machinery had been set up" and again advised that executive authority be invested in one man rather than in a board. Wilson, however, had no intention of accepting the McAdoo-Baruch plan, which would literally give one man control of industrial mobilization, and on July 28, 1917, he moved to implement the War Department–CND initiative. A short time later, in early August, he introduced legislation into Congress to create two new executive bodies, the Food Administration, and the Fuel Administration. He appointed Herbert Hoover and Harry Garfield, president of Williams College, to head the new agencies. Secretary Baker, his defense of the War Department supply program successful, wrote to Wilson that he was confident and happy about the new board and sure that in a very little while its harmony would be complete.

The new WIB organization represented a victory for Baker and the War Department, which desired a consultative board to coordinate rather than to direct the industrial effort. Although Baker immediately appointed Colonel Palmer E. Pierce of the general staff to the WIB, the War Department continued to pursue its own course with the business community. War service committees of the United States Chamber of Commerce, composed of key members of trade associations rather than state and local political authorities, were the preferred contacts. They formed the core of the CND committee system and after the July reorganizations they became informal War Department agents. Although associated with the WIB, they continued to work with the bureau chiefs as if the WIB did not exist.[10]

The organizational momentum of the first five months of the war favored the War Department and worked against the transfer of coordinating power to an outside agency. Even within the WIB the loyalties of many committee members were to their new associates in the War Department. Frank Scott, a personal friend of Baker who Wilson had moved from the Munitions Standards Board to chair the WIB, was forced into a struggle for domination with the War Department, which he would have preferred to avoid. In mid-September, ambivalent about his obligations, harassed by lack of authority, and his health broken by strain, he submitted his resignation.

The president was immediately under pressure from McAdoo to name Baruch as WIB chairman. Baker disliked Baruch and considered him little more than a daring speculator. Many members of the board felt the same way. On September 18, "Judge" Robert S. Lovett (chairman of the executive committee of the Union Pacific Railroad), who many believed was an anti-Semite, told Wilson that he would resign if Baruch were named. To avoid trouble Wilson suggested that Baker select Lovett to replace Scott. Baker replied that he was aware that "the Judge had some feeling of the kind suggested" but added that he was not willing to appoint Lovett immediately and that Scott had promised not to resign until "a suitable person could be found." Nevertheless, no businessman was interested in the post unless he was assured an immediate grant of independent power. Baker later named Lovett to serve unofficially until he could find a permanent replacement for Scott. On November 6, 1917, Baker met with Homer L. Ferguson of the Newport News shipyards and begged him to assume the task. Secretary Daniels, who accompanied Baker, wrote in his diary that Baker exclaimed, "You cannot leave until you accept," but Ferguson refused unless given clear authority.[11] In early November 1917, Baker turned to Daniel Willard, president of the Baltimore and Ohio Railroad and chairman of the transportation advisory commission of the CND, who reluctantly agreed to serve as interim chairman. Baker guilelessly wrote to Wilson that, because the WIB had been established "with the idea of all of us cooperating through it," Willard certainly should have no concern over the matter of power.[12]

☆☆☆

Between December 1917 and March 1918, the reorganizations in the War Department were paralleled by a struggle within the Wilson administration and between it, Congress, and the expanding national-defense sector for control of the war effort. During the summer of 1917, efforts in the Senate led by Henry Cabot Lodge of Massachusetts to create a committee on the conduct of the war, like the one that had often complicated matters for the Lincoln administration, had been blocked by Wilson, but as the winter emergency deepened, the Senate Military Affairs Committee, chaired by George Chamberlain, began to examine the connections between the War Department, the CND, and the WIB. In early January 1918, Chamberlain introduced a bill to create a war cabinet of "three distinguished citizens of demonstrated executive ability," something like the ministry of munitions recently established under David Lloyd-George in England, which would include no members of the official cabinet, would be superior to the secretary of war and the secretary of the navy, and would be responsible only to the president. The measure received bipartisan support in both houses of Congress.[13] Republican James W. Wadsworth Jr. stated, "This is no time for partisanship. We need men of vision, ability, and courage to handle our war problems," while Democrat Gilbert M. Hitchcock explained that the bill was "not to embarrass the Administration, but to help it."[14] Willard's resignation as chairman of the WIB on January 15, 1918, only added to the general uneasiness.

President Wilson opposed a cabinet-level munitions ministry, especially if it meant being saddled with Republicans Theodore Roosevelt, Elihu Root, or Leonard Wood, but he knew that it would be politically disastrous to continue along in the way the administration had been going. Around the first of the year, Secretary McAdoo began to push Baruch forward again, this time as a possible replacement for Secretary Baker.[15] When Wilson made it clear he would not sacrifice Baker, McAdoo renewed his earlier campaign to have Baruch made chairman of the WIB. The struggle between McAdoo and Baker began on January 24, 1918, when the CND met to consider a replacement for Willard. On January 24, 1918, Baker submitted a report to Wilson that contained his recollection of what had occurred at the meeting and his own ideas about a chairman. He indicated that Daniels favored Baruch but emphasized that Secretary of Agriculture David Houston, Secretary of Commerce William Redfield, and Vance McCormick of the War Trade Board believed that Baruch did not possess the executive ability to fill the post. Baker favored John D. Ryan, president of Amalgamated Copper, suggesting that his appointment "would be more acceptable in the eastern part of the country, and perhaps would carry the greatest assurance of strong business, executive capacity." He dodged the Baruch issue. Although he admitted that the Wall Streeter was "the most absolutely loyal man in sight," he claimed that he did not "know enough about his executive capacity to recommend him." McAdoo immediately wrote the president condemning not only Ryan but also many of Baker's other War Department appointments. McAdoo argued that Edward R. Stettinius, Baker's new surveyor general of supplies, was not loyal to the administration and warned Wilson, "As I have been going over the country I have been impressed with the suspicion of and feeling against the big interests—and J. P. Morgan and Co.—as they are believed (and justly I think) to have made enormous sums through financing and purchasing for the Allies prior to our entrance into the war." He continued to recommend Baruch, who he insisted was the "ablest man for the place. . . . Absolutely loyal and dependable," while the only reason Baker had for opposing him was Baruch's "reputation as a Wall Street speculator." McAdoo concluded, "I do not believe it wise or sound policy to put ourselves too fully in the hands of our enemies and the 'interests' and take the unnecessary risk of losing the confidence of the masses of the people as well." Daniels, who, like McAdoo, favored Baruch, thought that Baker was inclined to agree that Baruch would be a good choice, but Baker was merely avoiding an argument.[16]

Wilson decided to strengthen the WIB while Baker was still juggling the organization of the War Department. The president consulted Justice Louis D. Brandeis who, like Baruch, was Jewish. Brandeis advised him that only by redefining Baker's responsibilities could the country get the "full benefit of his great ability and fine qualities." For a short time the president considered Stettinius for the WIB chairmanship, but Colonel Edward M. House, who was probably counseled by McAdoo, wrote, "I hear that Stetinius [sic] is being thought of as head of the War Industries Board. McAdoo and [Joseph P.] Tumulty think it would be a mistake and I am inclined to agree with them. I am afraid it will look too much like the Morgans are running things."[17]

On February 1, 1918, Wilson requested that Baker and Baruch meet and agree to some mutually acceptable arrangement to make the WIB an effective agency to coordinate industrial support for the War Department. Baker continued to insist that the power to set program must rest with the army and suggested that the WIB ought to continue as a coordinating rather than a directing agency. Baruch convinced Baker that congressional criticism could only be quieted by forthright reform of the civilian sector of the war effort. Baker agreed that the WIB should become a "legal, authoritative, responsible, centralized agency" to expedite the military program. Moreover, it should have power, subject to the approval of the president, "to commandeer plants, products, equipment, manufacturing facilities, mines and materials" and the additional power of "distributing materials thus commandeered." It was agreed further that the board should procure military supplies, control the industry of the country, and determine prices and compensation, thus assuring that "single representatives of War, Navy, Allied, and Shipping Boards could meet, clear their difficulties, coordinate their needs, and in consultation with the chairman of the War Industries Board submit their program for his [the chairman's] final allocation, distribution, and judgment."

Baker sent Wilson the results of the conference the following day. It is not clear just when Wilson decided on Baruch, but when McAdoo wrote him asking that Baruch become his assistant in the railroad administration, Wilson replied that he had decided to appoint Baruch chairman of the WIB as soon as he could do so "without risking new issues on the Hill." When the presidential letter announcing Baruch's selection and calling for "the fullest possible co-operation of your department" arrived, Baker had left Washington on a tour of the fighting front in France. He never revealed what he thought about the appointment.[18]

In March 1918, Baruch became chairman of the WIB with power to coordinate war manufacturing in support of the armed forces, but he was no "czar." He often had to act without the support of Secretary Baker. His efforts were hampered by the obnoxious anti-Semitism of wartime associates such as Lovett and Judge Edwin B. Parker. Baruch did not originate the famous WIB commodity committees. The United States Chamber of Commerce, through its war service committees, had already organized the existing trade associations and was busily creating more. War Department administrators had already linked the war service committees and army supply agencies. Baruch had nothing to do with the Overman Act of May 1918, which was drafted by Judge Advocate General Crowder in February 1918, and that legislation had legalized all previous changes in the emergency war agencies and authorized the president to prosecute the war by executive order if necessary. During the summer of 1918 he was as much out of touch with political and military realities as everybody else in the Wilson war government.[19] Baruch never questioned the industrial measures proposed to support the eighty-division program.[20]

President Wilson expected Baruch to be his traffic manager. The Wall Streeter, who had abandoned his earlier clamor for sole control, operated with a small staff of three executive assistants. "I was never one for paper work or administrative routine," he later wrote. "With the help of these three men I was able to free myself from detail and keep myself mobile. Each man knew that he had free rein to carry out his job, that he had authority equal to his responsibilities." It would have been easier if Baruch really had the power he later claimed to possess. In early March 1918, he accidentally ran into Surveyor General of Supplies Stettinius at the War Department. "Mr. Stettinius," Baruch said, "I am going to rely on you for many things." Stettinius replied, "Mr. Baruch you can't rely on me for a thing."[21]

Baruch was charged with determining, with the advice of the Priorities Board, the order of production of scarce materials and considering, with the cooperation of the other emergency boards, priorities of delivery. In determining prices he was to act with the assistance of the raw material and manufacturing experts of the Priorities Board and representatives of the Federal Trade Commission, the Tariff Commission, and Garfield, the fuel administrator. He was to assist the government in allocating contracts and locating materials where they had been preempted or were in short supply. He was to adjudicate cases where government departments were competing for supplies and develop an effective follow-up system for contracts and deliveries. Finally, he was to anticipate the needs of government departments as far in advance as possible so that industry could be provided a definite war program. In deliberate phrases the president told Baruch to "let alone what is being successfully done and interfere as little as possible with the present normal processes of purchase and delivery in the several Departments" and "in brief, to act as the general eye of all supply departments in the field of industry." The president warned him to stay out of the army's way and facilitate and coordinate the American industrial effort with as little friction as possible.[22]

It was inevitable that administrative difficulties would plague so complex an operation. Stettinius's warning to Baruch was no accident. The army resented the WIB and Hugh Johnson termed it an "obnoxious" organization.[23] Johnson was frustrated by periodic short circuiting of his own administrative procedures by the WIB, which insisted on dealing directly with the various bureau chiefs rather than going through Johnson's office.[24] The WIB had its own complaints about the army, especially its neglect of the Requirements Division and the Priority Board. Pope Yeatman, chairman of the Non-Ferrous Metals Section who earned Johnson's wrath by contacting the Chief Signal Officer on a matter of copper wire, insisted that he did so because he could not get the 1919 requirements from the Purchase and Supply Division.[25] Parker was of the same opinion. "If the government agencies should find that they cannot readily procure material," he stated, "there will be no one to blame but themselves."[26] Johnson recognized that there was justice in those complaints when he issued a memorandum to the Purchase and Supply Division on July 24, 1918, taking his subordinates to task for "not making the maximum use of other governmental agencies." The memo concluded, "It is desired to work in very close relation and team-play with the WIB and to make every use of their great powers and facilities."[27] In August Johnson lent a group headed by H. L. Hatfield, director of the Planning and Statistics Section of the PS and T, to Alexander Legge, head of the requirement division of the WIB, to compile statistical lists of material requirements for 1919. In September 1918 a special requirements committee was formed to hurry information from the army to the WIB.[28] Nevertheless, at war's end cooperation was still only tentative.[29]

During the summer of 1918 the country was organized into twenty-one production zones and the WIB reached out to locate unused plants, develop new facilities, and bring uncommitted industry into more effective cooperation with the government. The industrial inventory section of the CND had been working on such a project since the previous year, and in March 1918 the army joined forces with it and the WIB to make a census of American industry and seek out all available resources. The task was carried forward by the new resources and conversion section of the WIB and its chairman, Charles Otis, of Cleveland, an old acquaintance of Secretary Baker and Assistant Secretary Crowell, who organized the businessmen in each of the new production zones into resource advisory committees. In July 1918 Otis told Baker, "You are providing the soldiers. Tell business what you want to supply these men, and let someone be in authority to see that these supplies are going forward in a proper way." Much was accomplished through informal consultation between soldiers, War Department bureaucrats, and businessmen. Comfortable relations with Crowell, whom Otis called Ben, Stettinius, and director of finished products George Peek helped Otis tremendously.

Critical to Otis's work were the war service committees of the chamber of commerce. With key members in the War Department as well as in the WIB, chamber leaders named regional central committees, which in turn created subordinate committees in the manufacturing centers in their zones. These committees advised army supply agencies on available plants and also provided the WIB with information about conversion and new construction. As regional resource committees they developed a dynamism of their own, lobbying in some cases to secure government contracts. Franklin D. Crabb, chairman of the regional advisory committee in Kansas City, wrote Edwin C. Gibbs, his opposite number in Cincinnati, "We find from experience that it will be absolutely necessary for us [to have a regional representative in Washington], in order for us to secure any business for our manufacturers." By the end of the war, most of the important manufacturing regions of the country had agents in Washington to protect their interests.

Otis left a reminiscence of the way the system worked. During the summer of 1918, he cultivated Hugh Johnson, the director of purchase and supply, and Clarence C. Williams, the chief of ordnance. The Cleveland industrialist knew almost everybody, and, if he did not, one of his regional managers did. As he described it, he formed "little War Industries Boards" in each production zone and connected them with his office by telephone and telegraph. With a phone call he could find out what production facilities were available in a particular city and whether its management was able to produce results. On one occasion a company in Kansas City wanted to make wagons. "I called Crabb who told me the company could not deliver in less than six months. . . . I want the business for Kansas City," Crabb told Otis, "but I must tell you that this plant cannot produce."[30] Thus, formal organizations, linked through informal consultation with agencies like those created by Otis with access to the WIB and the War Department as well as direct connections in Washington, were beginning to bring some order into the organizational turbulence.[31]

☆ ☆ ☆

During 1918, the constantly expanding and unpredictable requirements of the army made systematic planning virtually impossible. The need for steel for guns, tanks, and ships, and coal to make the steel, run the railroads, and fuel the troop and cargo ships was at the heart of the war program. The steel requirements for the Railroad Administration, the Shipping Board, the army, the navy, and the Allies grew from ten million, to seventeen million, to twenty million, and finally, during the summer of 1918, to twenty-seven million tons, from a national capacity of thirty-five million tons. Steel had been one of the first commodities to be brought under partial government control. Prices were fixed for the first time in mid-September 1917. Even the notorious "Pittsburgh Plus" pricing system was eliminated for the duration of the war and a common Chicago-Pittsburgh base price substituted for it. The transportation tie-ups of the winter and spring of 1917–1918 cut deliveries of coal to the coking mills and resulted in immediate decline in steel production.[32]

In the spring of 1918, Leonard Replogle was made director of the Steel Division of the WIB and given potential power to run the industry as a government operation. Replogle, president of Vanadium Steel, however, was not enamored of that prospect and sought in every way to secure voluntary cooperation from the steel men. On May 17, 1918, Replogle, Baruch, and Parker met with representatives of the steel industry. The steel men and H. H. Barbour, a member of the iron and steel section of the Priorities Board, insisted that there was no serious steel shortage and that further government coordination was unnecessary. Barbour agreed to have Replogle's representative sit on the rating committee so that some sort of common assessment might be had.[33] On June 3 the group met again and the discussion continued with the same result. Finally, Replogle reluctantly concluded that the new government programs would consume the entire capacity of the steel mills for their direct and indirect requirements.[34]

In February 1918 reports to the CND indicated that production of artillery and aircraft were far behind schedule, while deliveries of basic commodities such as coal and steel were below their prewar levels.[35] By April 1918, *Iron Age*, the spokesman for the nation's more important steel manufacturers, which had shortly before seen no reason for massive national regulation, began to call for the organization of the entire nation in support of the war effort.[36]

In July 1918 steel production was still below 1917 figures, and in September the WIB moved toward compulsion. Steel rationing to less essential industries began that month.[37] Civilian production ranging from automobiles to baby carriages was curtailed. Passenger-car production was cut to 25 percent of 1917 levels, while farm-implement production was cut to 75 percent of 1917 levels, but there was still not enough steel. On September 5 Baruch wrote to Assistant Secretary of War Crowell about the persistent shortage. Crowell contacted Chief of Staff March, and on September 18 the War Department published General Order 86, which commanded all bureaus to economize drastically on steel articles that had no combat value.[38] Conditions were little better when the war ended.

Coal deliveries were at the center of the steel problem.[39] After the January industrial shutdowns, fuel administrator Garfield moved to utilize the inland waterways and coastal shipping as much as possible to move coal, but the lack of terminals made it impossible to take up all the slack. If a better showing was to be made later in 1918, the coal shortage had to be attacked all along the line. Absenteeism, the short week, and frequent, informal holidays—problems familiar to those with knowledge of the ways of the coal industry with its seasonal peaks and frequently unsteady demand—had to be dealt with immediately. Mine shutdowns, whether because of mechanical failure or cave-ins, had to be reduced. Industrial strife, long common in that unhappy industry, had to be limited, and miners and managers had to be united to support the war effort.

The key to obtaining more coal was to make better use of the railroads. In April Edward N. Hurley, chairman of the Shipping Board, wrote to Charles R. Tower, of the Tower-Major Candy Company, "Contrary to widely held opinions, the fuel difficulty lies not at the mines or at the coke ovens; it lies in the railroads' inability to handle the business."[40] An August report of the Geological Survey, the best source for mining statistics during the war period, supported Hurley, showing that car shortages, mine disability caused for the most part by owner neglect, strikes, and worker absenteeism had caused the slowdowns, the first two by far the most important. Garfield struck hard at the coal distribution problem. He divided the country into coal production districts and ordered that industry within each district should be supplied with fuel only from mines within that district. That freed up cars by ending a substantial amount of cross-hauling and competition among the railroads. The fuel director appealed to mine owners and workers to increase supplies, and on July 4, 1918, coal production remained steady rather than falling off as it had the year before. In cooperation with the WIB, Garfield allocated coal, shifting substantial amounts to essential industries, and confined nonessential plants to a supply barely sufficient to prevent total shutdown. Industrialists were urged to buy and stockpile their winter coal supply early, and the Wilson administration began to subsidize the construction of new coking ovens. Such activities were uncommon in a nation devoted to the doctrine of individual enterprise, and the effects of the latter program in particular would not be felt until late 1919. Secretary James Inglis of the WIB wrote, "The more you get into it the more hopeless the situation becomes. Simply shifting the present output of coal from one point to another is mighty unsatisfactory business."[41] The coal fields, he added, might have to be seized like the railroads.

In July 1918, representatives of the fuel administration met with the mine owners to find a solution for the country's coal troubles. Nationalizing the mines was the one measure the owners wanted to avoid, and, in cooperation with Garfield's office, they worked out an alternative plan. Each of the new coal production districts was headed by an experienced coal man. To secure the support of the mine workers, each large mine in each district appointed a standing committee representing the owners and workers to suggest policies that would improve safety, reduce absenteeism, and step up production. Such cooperation had been an objective of the United Mine Workers for years, and William Hard, a Washington reporter for the *New Republic* and longtime critic of the mine owners, could not pass up the opportunity to point out that "the muse of history still stands, unlovely among her symmetrical sisters, with her tongue in her cheek. Why this advance toward a higher manhood? To get more bituminous. And we shall indeed get more of it thereby."[42] A few months later, Hard noticed that production was up and that, though there there was still a shortage, cooperation between the owners and the men seemed to be working.[43]

☆☆☆

War Department connections with the steel, coal, and railroad businesses had traditionally been contractual and often adversarial. Before the war the quartermaster general negotiated annually with various American railroad corporations to move troops and supplies in the United States and, over the opposition of private shippers, operated a small fleet of river boats, troop transports, and cargo vessels to support the forces deployed on foreign and colonial stations. During the debates over the National Defense Act of 1916, War Department officials, very much aware of difficulties during the Spanish-American War, had denied that any voluntary arrangements with railroad or shipping corporations would be effective and had called for the seizure and militarization of land and sea transportation in a national emergency. Those recommendations had fallen on deaf ears, and when the war began voluntary cooperation continued to govern the connections between the army and civilian transportation agencies.

The railroads felt the pressure immediately. The American railroad business was seasonal, and the lines had previously encountered car and locomotive shortages at peak movement periods. They suffered from industry-wide attitudes, as well as federal regulations that required competition and made equipment pooling and interline cooperation difficult, if not illegal.[44] In 1916 the lines east of Pittsburgh already were congested, and storage facilities proved inadequate to handle the American harvest and Allied war orders. In April 1917, when the United States entered the war, the CND authorized a voluntary Railroad War Board consisting of the chief executive officers of the major trunk lines to coordinate the movement of troops and building materials to the mobilization camps. They accomplished the task successfully, but cars that ordinarily would have carried fuel to eastern industries and seaports were transferred to other work, and freight accumulated at ports of embarkation faster than the available ocean tonnage could carry it to Europe.[45] The military effort was directed toward only the French theater, and troops and supplies streamed toward Boston, Philadelphia, and New York, choking off the delivery of essential industrial supplies—especially iron ore, coal, and coke. On December 28, 1917, President Wilson authorized the seizure of the railroads and turned operations over to William G. McAdoo, who, in addition to his duties at the Treasury Department, became director general of the United States Railroad Administration. McAdoo pitched in with a will, but during the first two months of 1918 troop shipments to France remained slow and transportation difficulties in the United States continued to obstruct the war effort. The railroad difficulties were not simply the result of car and locomotive shortages or the failure of the Railroad War Board to stop inter-road competition. The country lacked terminal facilities all along the railroad rights of way and at ports of embarkation that made it necessary to use cars for storage when they were desperately needed to move supplies.[46] Although Acting Chief of Staff Bliss had transferred control of ports of embarkation to the army in August 1917 and Quartermaster General Sharpe had begun to expand storage facilities, conditions had not improved much by December 1917, when George W. Goethals became quartermaster general and director of storage and traffic.

During 1918 Goethals struggled with the storage and rail transport problems. After the creation of the PS and T in April 1918, he began a massive terminal and warehouse construction and acquisition program. It was a headache for the WIB, but it played an important part in reducing eastern rail congestion, and McAdoo cooperated effectively with Goethals. Operating the rail system as a single unit, the director general allocated cars and engines with little regard for private railroad interest. McAdoo virtually halted civilian traffic during January and February 1918 until congestion was cleared and fuel, troops, and supplies were forwarded to eastern factories and ports.

During the spring of 1918 the amount of freight moved increased substantially, while the miles of track actually in use declined.[47] From Chicago to the Atlantic coast, however, railroads were still jammed, and from Pittsburgh eastward the nation's industry was choked with war orders. In April McAdoo wrote a memorandum to the president. He called attention to the expansion of industrial plants in the already congested eastern districts. "It seems to me," he wrote, "there ought to be a definite policy on the part of the government to discourage such development in the eastern territory and to throw all possible additional industrial development south of the Potomac and Ohio Rivers." The railroads could not haul the raw material eastward "without additional facilities which it may be impossible to provide quickly," whereas northeastern ports were already overburdened with war shipping. "It seems suicidal," he continued, "to permit this demand to keep on steadily increasing through the establishment of war industries." McAdoo wanted a government effort to decentralize industry in the interest of logistical efficiency.[48]

The memorandum was circulated during April and May 1918 and seems to have received some support from the WIB. Writing to Charles W. Hodell in June, Secretary Inglis lamented the disorganized state of war contracting. Eastern firms were jammed with contracts, he wrote, while many other businesses were so underworked that they faced closure. "We are unalterably opposed to the creation of new facilities and the expansion of plants, especially in the congested eastern district, where there is such a shortage of coal, power, and transportation." A large amount of business, he concluded, was being diverted to the Midwest, "where this overtaxing of facilities is not so great or does not exist."[49] Ordnance plants and textile finishing mills were scarce except in the East, however, and the McAdoo plan hindered the PS and T warehouse and terminal-building program on the East Coast, which Goethals was pushing during the spring and summer of 1918. Goethals's attitude frustrated Inglis.[50] Nevertheless, by September 1918, Goethals came to understand the situation and "expressed himself as being in favor of making analyses of the various districts within the congested district beginning with the Philadelphia district."[51] The investigation convinced Goethals that a real effort to decentralize war production and establish regional storage facilities away from the congested Northeast was necessary. In mid-October he ordered a supply bulletin circulated directing that purchasing be shifted wherever possible to the South and West. The bulletin stated in part, "It is much desired that the facilities of these districts be definitely ascertained and that every effort be made, even at some inconvenience to procurement, production, and inspection, to place orders in these districts."[52]

Cooperation between the Railroad Administration and the Inland Traffic Division of Goethals's office developed apace, but it was clear by late spring 1918 that the navy, the Allied Purchasing Commission, and the Shipping-Control Committee would have to be brought in also if rail traffic was to be fully coordinated.[53] It appears that, at the suggestion of McAdoo, an exports control committee, including representatives of the army, navy, Railroad Administration, Shipping-Control Committee, and the Allied purchasing missions, was appointed in early June 1918 to expedite the movement of men and goods. The duties of the committee were to inform its members on how much freight would have to be exported to prosecute the war, how the freight could best be routed through the various ports, and how much other essential export traffic would have to be handled by the railroads. The committee also investigated the amount of local traffic necessary at each port to determine how freight could best be distributed among the ports to facilitate handling and avoid congestion at any one port. The Exports-Control Committee selected the ports where specific freight would be sent. To make its work effective, goods were not allowed to come forward from the interior without a permit, and the permits were issued "only when there was a practical certainty, barring the exigencies of war, that shipping would be available to handle the shipments at the arrival at the port."[54] The committee was not uniformly successful, but at least its work, together with improved storage facilities located inland as well as at the ports themselves, deterred a recurrence of the difficult conditions of the previous winter.[55]

☆☆☆

In May 1917, General Bliss told Secretary Baker that shipping was the key to any successful American military participation in the war. With insufficient tonnage, he stated, troops and equipment would simply pile up in the Atlantic ports and involve the country in a work of extreme folly.[56] During the summer of 1917 the War Department was hampered by both the navy and the Allies. Because of the distances involved and the alleged "submarine threat," the navy refused to convoy troopships below Chesapeake Bay. The Allies even requested that a number of American vessels be released for their exclusive use. In light of those difficulties, in September 1917 Baker and Navy Secretary Daniels called upon Edward N. Hurley, chairman of the United States Shipping Board, to exert every effort to secure the ships to support the recently adopted thirty-division program.[57]

The Shipping Board had been formed in September 1916. Its subsidiary corporation, the American Emergency Fleet Corporation (EFC), was created in mid-April 1917 to expedite the construction of new ships in government yards. The so-called "Wooden Ship" controversy, which began immediately between William Denman, who originally headed both organizations and supported a wooden ship–building program, and Goethals, who was at the time general manager of the EFC and a supporter of steel-ship construction, resulted in the resignation of both men in July 1917. In the aftermath, President Wilson named Hurley, a former chairman of the Federal Trade Commission, to head the Shipping Board. Hurley appointed industrialist Charles Piez to head the EFC. Knowing that new construction could not be delivered for at least a year, Hurley seized the German vessels interned in American ports and commandeered all American vessels larger than 2,500 tons for war work. In November 1917, he helped form a War Board for the Port of New York to cooperate with the army embarkation service. In mid-October, however, Hurley had to inform the War Department that there was still insufficient tonnage available for the thirty-division program unless it could be taken from essential commercial trade routes.[58] In January 1918 Hurley again warned that "transport does not appear to be provided in sufficient quantities to insure getting animals and general supplies to France at a rate proportionate to that of arrival of troops."[59] In early February 1918 Goethals was so concerned that he advised that troop movements abroad be suspended until supplies were accumulated for them in France. He predicted that shipment of troops and supplies abroad for the rest of 1918 would raise even more difficulties.[60]

There were only three ways to acquire more ships: by construction at home and in foreign yards, by commandeering and allocating existing domestic and foreign tonnage, and by negotiating the acquisition of more Allied tonnage. Home construction of troop and cargo ships was the most highly publicized effort and one of the great failures of the war. Chairman Hurley was aware that the EFC had never recovered from the fight between Goethals and Denman and still faced at least nine months before Hog Island, on the Delaware River outside of Philadelphia, and other government yards could achieve quantity production of fabricated ships. Steel shape and plate requirements were an important factor in forcing steel director Replogle to ration the nation's steel supply. Despite the fact that the navy gave turbine engine and boiler priority to the EFC in early July 1918, it was clear that production of those essential items could not keep up with hull launchings even if the minimum goals of the EFC were the only ones met.[61] Foreign construction, especially in Japanese yards, could not provide more than a few ships. As the army program grew from thirty to eighty divisions, the ship construction program expanded as well, first from six million tons to twelve million tons, and then to an utterly unrealistic seventeen million tons, to support the enormous 1919 program.

In April 1918, Hurley, hoping to speed production, demoted Piez and named Charles Schwab, president of Bethlehem Steel, to chair the EFC. Schwab, born in 1862, was a prodigy in the steel industry. He had started as a dollar-a-day engineer's helper in the Carnegie Steel Works and risen rapidly. At twenty-five he was superintendent of the J. Edgar Thompson plant of the Carnegie works; at twenty-nine, after helping Henry Clay Frick break the Homestead Strike, he was made general manager of the whole Carnegie steel empire. He handled, some say initiated, the negotiations that created the United States Steel Corporation. Schwab was a consummate egoist. After a disagreement with Elbert Gary, then president of U. S. Steel, Schwab left to become president of the Bethlehem Steel Company, which specialized in armor plate construction and warship building. Schwab was in bad odor with the Wilson administration for his work with the British in producing submarines before the United States entered the war, but the steel man, with his copious memory, grasp of detail, and penchant for grand visions, was the logical choice to salvage the shipbuilding program.[62]

The EFC suffered from a chronic sense of embattlement stemming in part from the Denman-Goethals affair and in part from subsequent public and congressional charges of corruption and mismanagement. Anxious to give the impression that he was sweeping away inefficiency, Schwab gave broad publicity to the new production goals while privately he and his colleagues became increasingly security conscious and sensitive to criticism. Writing to Inglis in June, Legge stated that the EFC was by far the most difficult of the war agencies to work with and concluded, "I notice that the fleet representative brought in a little information regarding boilers this morning. Let us hope they acquire the habit."[63] The EFC was equally deceptive in its contacts with the army and proved incapable of implementing any of its promises. In June, Piez assured Goethals that the EFC would deliver more than three million tons of shipping to the army by December 1918, eighty thousand tons above expected deliveries for the year. "The total deliveries for the remaining months will cover 362 steel ships of 2,389,189 tons," he stated, and, though wooden ship deliveries were "somewhat less certain," it seemed there would be 200 more wooden vessels of some 750,000 tons ready to replace steel ships in safe trades and free up vessels for army service. Should there be any changes or departures from the program," he concluded, "we shall make it our duty to notify you as promptly as possible."[64]

Piez's figures were reassuring, but in less than a month they proved incorrect. Goethals went to Secretary Baker, who wrote Hurley, "Unless these are reasonably certain dates, a very serious situation with reference to our supplies is apt to result." The ships that were coming into service, Baker continued, suffered from construction faults that could not readily be corrected and were thus lost to the army for months. What the army wanted was not propaganda but "definite and reliable information."[65] In October 1918 shipping was still critically short and 61 percent of the material shipped by the Inland Traffic Division to Atlantic ports was still sitting on the docks.[66] In early November a correspondent friendly to Piez wrote that the shipbuilding program was chaotic and filled with corruption and graft.[67] No doubt there was mismanagement, but there was little graft, at least not in high places.[68] After the war, Hurley blamed the army and the fog of war for the shortcoming of the shipping program.[69]

☆ ☆ ☆

The American war program was sound politically, for it gave the Central Powers cause to seek an early peace. It was unsound industrially and logistically because it committed the country to a massive overmobilization. The thirty-division program could have been achieved.[70] The eighty-division program was another matter entirely. The illusions of voluntary cooperation evaporated. By the late summer of 1918, the expectations that the war could be supported without affecting traditional relationships between government and industry could no longer be sustained. The 1919 program would expand national administrative capacity, change organizational connections within the war government and between it and the national defense sector, and create a command economy that the president and his advisers had previously considered unwise or unnecessary. Army requirements had to be accurately forecast, priorities established all along the line, the industrial plant of the nation canvassed, and contracts let, not only to achieve quantity production and delivery at the proper time, but also to avoid, if possible, the terrible congestion that had virtually halted the war effort the previous winter. In addition, the navy, the Food Administration, the Fuel Administration, the United States Railroad Administration, and the Shipping Board with its adjunct, the EFC, vied with the War Department for scarce war supplies, transportation, and services. The WIB language of voluntary cooperation still reflected a certain reality in mid-July 1918, but it was doubtful that the agency could continue much longer to be a mere traffic controller chaired by a genial industrial facilitator. Like the new army munitions building, the structure of the war government was unfinished. The temporary offices of the War Department, WIB, shipping, fuel, food, and other emergency agencies sprawled everywhere in Washington. Even after a year of expansion and with the Germans on the Marne, Johnson later claimed he had difficulty getting anything done. He compared the War Department to a feuding family, called it an "old chambered nautilus," and labeled everybody except the people in his own department ineffective. The War Department was a "headless riot," and the rest of the war organization was as wobbly as the jerry-rigged, warping, green lumber shacks in which they worked.[71]

During the late summer of 1918 the realities of a command economy emerged. As the demands of the 1919 program began to bite, those industries that were not involved closely with the war effort were cut off from fuel and raw materials and their leaders began to complain that massive governmental interference was unnecessary and that the army program was unrealistic. Domestic producers also had been whining for months that every contract let in Europe robbed American manufacturers of legitimate profits and took food from the mouths of American workingmen and their wives and children. Why, representatives of the wool industry asked, commandeer the entire wool supply of the country and allocate it only to the 40 to 50 percent of the industry capable of meeting army requirements, only to find the soldiers who wore the uniforms stranded in the United States without ships to take them to France. They insisted the program would set textile manufacturing back a generation.[72] Auto manufacturers raised the same question, and soon it reached the press, forcing Hugh Johnson to write to Peyton March on August 1, 1918, to express his concern about the situation.[73] Shipping Board chairman Hurley had already written Schwab on July 18 that businesses were being shut down without reason.[74] Samuel Vauclain, chairman of the Locomotive Committee of the WIB, who had been a part of the war government from the beginning, responded to such criticism bluntly: "The Secretary of War says 'We want these locomotives, now you get them,' by George, we will have to get them whether the domestic business stops or not, because the first business today is to fight this war. It does not make any difference what else there is. I notice in all these scraps we have down here the Secretary of War usually walks off with his dope. Whatsoever he want he gets."[75]

Charges that the eighty-division program was logistically unrealistic and interfered unnecessarily with traditional business life soon reached the House and Senate Military Affairs committees. From there it was a short journey to the president's desk. Wilson sought information to refute such claims and on July 24, 1918, addressed a letter to all the agencies involved in the war effort. The president pointed out that steel requirements for the next six months would be at least 3,500,000 tons above the capacity of the country and noted that the army required the total domestic wool clip for 1918 and 1919 for the eighty-division program. The president urged that something had to be done about conditions that were growing more dangerous politically every day.[76]

☆ ☆ ☆

William McNeill has described modern planning as paradoxical and ironic, often linking "the irrationality and dissonance of the whole with the closer harmony and superior organization of its separate parts."[77] Nowhere was that more clear than in American planning during the Great War. Conventional management strategy in large organizations of the day involved five consecutive steps, all of which depended on reliable statistics: creation of a general plan, isolation of its component parts, assignment of appropriate organizations to carry them out, integration of the individual parts, and systematic execution of the program. Progress was measured by a central statistical organization that would provide executives with quantitative information, define the status of current projects, and help forecast future plans and requirements.

American war managers never admitted that they had limited resources and capacity. They believed that their goals were achievable if they could only get the war program stabilized. They could then project estimates and requirements and schedule production. The components of finished products could be translated into raw materials for the commodity committees of the WIB. The needs of the army for imported materials could be made known so that shipping schedules might be set and merchant tonnage, always in short supply, provided. Finally, reliable data would enable the army to approach an increasingly skeptical Congress with its budget requirements to fight the war. Information was all they needed, or so they thought, and that was the one thing that was almost impossible to get. The disorder in the bureaus, the general staff, the secretary of war's office, and the civilian war agencies during the first year of the war was a nightmare. The thirty-division program doubled, then tripled, during the first six months of 1918. The result was, among many other distressing outcomes, a most exasperating absence of reliable statistics.[78] Every agency had its own statistical division. At the Shipping Board, Edwin F. Gay, dean of the Harvard Business School, was already installed as the director of statistics. Government statistics came from the Bureau of Standards, the Department of Commerce, the Department of Labor, and the Bureau of the Census, whose data on manufacturing and production were invaluable. Finally, the data provided by the trade associations and their house research and publicity organs were important sources of information. As mobilization progressed, all of the major American war agencies developed their own statistical divisions, each of which generated its own self-serving data. By January 1918, the War Department bureaus, the navy, the WIB, the Food and Fuel Administrations, the War Trade Board, the Emergency Fleet Corporation, the Shipping Board, and the Railroad Administration all had independent statistical capacity. Although individual statistical agencies were often well organized, coordination was underdeveloped.

In late 1916 the CND had recommended formation of a central statistical agency and Director Walter Gifford had named Leonard Porter Ayres, an education expert from the Russell Sage Foundation, head of the operation. Gifford himself was a distinguished statistician. Indeed, one of the reasons for his appointment had been his experience in gathering and interpreting quantitative data. Gifford thought that Ayres's office could provide the government with a central source of hard data with which to measure the progress of the war effort, but nobody would report to Ayres. Even the information he collected was incomplete, and, in cases like the Emergency Fleet Corporation and the Aircraft Production Board, data were deceptively optimistic. In March 1918, Ayres and most of his statistical people were transferred from the CND to the War Department, where Ayres became a colonel in the reorganizing general staff.[79]

In the spring of 1918, Thomas N. Perkins returned from Europe profoundly impressed by British statistical methods. In a report to the WIB he wrote that the British had a most effective statistical organization. He claimed Americans needed just such a centralized graphic and quantitative capacity to describe the national resources the war managers would need to deal with their French and British associates.[80] In late May 1918, at the request of Secretary Baker,

President Wilson asked Bernard Baruch to construct just such a central statistical office. In early June the Central Bureau of Planning and Statistics (CBPS) was established under Dean Gay, who left his duties at the WIB, the Shipping Board, and the War Trade Board to undertake the task. When he took over the CBPS, Gay immediately found that poor reporting practices and duplication of effort made it difficult to consolidate, clarify, and verify information on the American war program. That was the situation in July when President Wilson's letter arrived and explains in part Secretary Baker's subsequent embarrassment during his meetings with European leaders.

If national statistics were good, international statistics were even better. In the late spring of 1918, the Supreme War Council proposed to create an inter-Allied bureau of statistics to provide the Inter-Allied Munitions Council "with all necessary data and statistics [from all the Allied and Associated Powers] in connection with the production and possibilities of production of munitions." It could, in combination with the statistical staffs of the other inter-Allied executives and boards, develop a quantitative and graphic projection of the entire current and projected efforts of the associated governments. No one was thinking small, but when the representatives of the powers met in Paris in the summer of 1918, everybody brought their own statisticians, their own numbers, and their own graphics. Their disagreements over numbers not only helped shape inter-Allied relations but also affected American interagency politics during the last three months of the war.[81]

CHAPTER 8

COALITION WAR-MAKING, 1917–1918

There is a myth that Sir Douglas Haig, commanding the British armies in France, offered up a prayer before the great British offensive of 1917 opened in Flanders: "Oh God of Battles, give us victory before the Americans arrive." The Allies feared Wilson almost as much as they feared the Germans. Prime Minister David Lloyd George understood that British and American economic competition in Latin America continued unabated and that Americans were as opposed to plastering the world with the Union Jack as ever. Premier Georges Clemenceau, who once described Wilson as "a hungry wolf," feared an American peace would rob his country of the territorial fruits of victory promised in secret Allied agreements. Thus, it was to the advantage of the Allies to reduce American political participation in the war while maximizing their own control of American military and economic resources. Wilson understood this very well, and it was among the reasons he had for ordering Secretary Baker to get an independent American army under its own leaders onto the battlefield.[1]

As the leader of an "Associated Power," Wilson would have preferred to move the political center of the struggle to the new world and to conduct business in Washington rather than in Europe.[2] In September 1917, British Ambassador Cecil Spring-Rice revealed President Wilson's views in a letter to Lord Balfour: "He wants to keep his situation of aloofness with a view to the peace negotiations, he wants to convince the American people that he has not entered into any entangling alliance."[3] But that was not to be. During the summer of 1917, Secretary of the Treasury McAdoo began to urge the president to call for an inter-Allied financial council to govern the allocation of the large American loans that were flowing to the allied governments. He insisted that accountability and predictability were essential if his program of war finance were to succeed. He was joined in early September 1917 by the director of the new Food Administration, Herbert Hoover, who had recently completed negotiations for the purchase of the 1918 cereal crop, and Harry Garfield, the new fuel administrator, who also advised the president to form similar agencies to coordinate the acquisition of critical resources. In September, the Wilson administration established an Allied purchasing commission, based in New York and linked formally with the American war government through the WIB, to coordinate French and British procurement in the United States.[4]

The War Department also knew that agreements would have to be negotiated to meet the growing shipping requirements of the American army. On September 12, 1917, Lieutenant Colonel T. Bentley Mott prepared a memorandum for General Bliss that expressed the War Department's concern and anticipated accurately the events of the next few months. After analyzing the work of the inter-Allied organizations that had already been established during the first three years of the war, Mott stated that, in light of the implications of the Crozier-Ganne agreement, a supreme political-economic council should be formed and that, "once it has the list of supplies of all kinds agreed upon to be furnished by or to each country, it can act as a permanent body for the execution of this program and above all for the apportionment of tonnage in order of necessity and importance for the transport of supplies." Mott continued, "[T]he matter of tonnage presents the greatest difficulty. Since Great Britain controls the vast majority of tonnage, she has [previously] merely apportioned it to her allies. In deciding new apportionments it is important that the United States be represented on any executive board formed." He then concluded that such a "London Board . . . should be formed at once, and suggested that the American representative should be a "military officer" or "a first rate businessman."[5] Bliss sent the memorandum to Secretary Baker, who replied cautiously, "As I understand it, the President is personally dealing with the tonnage question and this suggestion would be embarrassing. I prefer not to raise it at this time."[6] The secretary of war did not reveal that events were already converging to bring the Americans into closer connection with their European associates.

☆ ☆ ☆

The impetus for the first American mission came from Prime Minister Lloyd George, who hoped to persuade President Wilson to support his scheme to open a second front in Eastern Europe, but the president was in no hurry to entangle the United States in Allied politics. Little in American prewar thinking had prepared them for international coalition operations, and it was late September before Wilson ordered a delegation abroad. The group which sailed for England in mid-October 1917 was headed by the president's friend and personal emissary, Edward M. House. It included Chief of Staff Bliss; Admiral William S. Benson; Assistant Secretary of the Treasury Oscar T. Crosby; Vance McCormick, head of the War Trade Board; Bainbridge Colby of the Shipping Board; Dr. Alonzo Taylor, representing Herbert Hoover and the Food Administration; and Thomas N. Perkins of the WIB. Supporting the mission was Charles Day, a statistician and engineer, and his staff, who would later help establish the first coordinated planning and statistical organization in the history of the American War Department.

The Americans stopped first in London, then moved to Paris and spent the last weeks of November and the first week in December at Versailles at the first session of the Supreme War Council (SWC), which had just been established to coordinate Entente strategy. President Wilson had ordered House to insist upon "unity of plan and control between all the Allies and the United States," but, as the European powers soon discovered, Wilson meant that unity of plan and control should be accepted only if it forwarded American interests. The president insisted on American participation in all the meetings but kept his own distance. His military representative was General Bliss. His political observer, Arthur Hugh Frazier of the State Department, was essentially a conduit through which information flowed to Washington when House was not in Europe. Membership on the SWC secured American equality in the war effort while Wilson's personal unavailability emphasized the political separation between the Americans and the Allies. The coordination of the military and political sphere, where the Americans were gaining strength, and the economic sphere, where they were powerful from the very beginning of the war, created the first transnational political-economic organizations of modern times.[7] Americans were suspicious of the Allies, and representatives of the Treasury, the War Trade Board, and the Food Administration analyzed Allied requests coolly and retained the distance from their associates that had been so characteristic earlier in 1917.

When the SWC convened, all the American war priorities had to be drastically revised. Defeat of the Italian army at Caporetto, with great losses of men and equipment, caused dismay. The Bolshevik seizure of power in St. Petersburg put an end to any fantasies that the Russians would continue in the war. The need to reinforce the Italian front, combined with the reverses suffered by Franco-British arms in the West during 1917, ensured that they would face the Germans the next spring with reduced forces. Indeed, Pershing's intelligence staff predicted that the Germans would have a three-to-two manpower advantage in France after they had transferred troops from the Eastern and Southern fronts.

The SWC cast the United States in the role of financier and raw-material and manpower supplier. In early December, the Americans met with their opposite numbers from the British and French ministries of munitions, who declared to Thomas Perkins and his WIB colleagues that Allied artillery production exceeded demand. Even after resupplying the Italians, they alleged, Franco-British arms factories could provide all field, medium, and heavy artillery required by the American army.[8] The Allies wanted American manpower as quickly as possible, and the suggestions of the previous spring became the demands of the autumn. They declared that the bottom of the Anglo-French manpower pool had been reached and no new French and British formations could be deployed in 1918. Indeed, the number of organizations in the field would decline during the next three months. Shipping remained the controlling factor. Submarine sinkings, despite the introduction of convoying, were still outrunning new construction, and the SWC recommended to Colby that the United States supply British yards with as much ship and boiler plate as possible and increase their ship-building program from six to nine million deadweight tons.

The conferees proposed a functional international division of labor to produce tanks, aircraft, artillery, and ammunition. The Italians would build aircraft engines, the British and French would build airframes, and the United States would furnish the raw materials. The Americans, the British, and the French agreed to build heavy Mark VIII tanks jointly. The Americans would furnish liberty engines and drivetrains for the thirty-ton monsters, while the British furnished frames, armor, and guns. The French would build an assembly plant for the Mark VIIIs and continue to produce the light six-ton Renault tank.[9] The Allies would furnish the Americans with artillery while American sources would furnish semifinished castings and forgings. As American forces entered the battle, expenditure of artillery ammunition would outrun supply and the Allied representatives recommended that the United States increase its production and delivery of smokeless powder, shells, and fuses. In essence, the Allies recommended that the Crozier-Ganne agreement of June 1917 be extended into 1919.[10]

The meetings in early December 1917 established certain principles. First, shipping would determine the size of the American war program. The larger the program the more difficult the problem. Second, everything possible must be done to increase the cargo tonnage available for 1918, and nothing should be produced in or shipped from the United States to its troops in Europe that could be produced in England or France. Third, joint inter-Allied committees should be formed as quickly as possible to rationalize munitions production, expedite raw materials procurement, and establish shipping priorities. Finally, all nations were to open their shipping requirements and production records, establish joint committees to coordinate munitions production and procurement plans, and create a common pool of shipping to meet allied needs for 1918. The capstone report was prepared by General Bliss and reiterated the need for a deliberate program with predictable schedules.

Subsequent reports revealed other American concerns. L. P. Sheldon, the Food Administration representative in London, complained that the Allies had failed to impose cereal rationing on their populations to cut down the tonnage needed for the importation of grain during 1918. Colby, of the Shipping Board, believed that real cooperation between the powers, if it came at all, would be "the result of compelling circumstances, or of conditions which have in them certain potential and coercive elements not yet present in the situation." Colby foresaw the emergence of a "Corsican figure" among the allies or of a single strongest nation and claimed that was the only way "the coordination that amounts to authority plus obedience will come about." Perkins of the WIB insisted that "there is no time for the United States to prepare what seems to it an ideal program for its army, which program will materialize at some more-or-less distant date. Our efforts must be immediate and effective. To accomplish this it is necessary that there be intelligent cooperation with the efforts of the Allies so that the greatest possible supplies of men and materials shall be available early in the spring of 1918." General Bliss concluded that everything was in the hands of the British and the Americans, "who must furnish the necessary tonnage." The inter-Allied conference at its final session adopted a resolution that proposed "to create an inter-allied organization . . . to liberate the greatest amount of tonnage possible for the transport of American troops."[11] After all the calls for cooperation and the pledges of support were over, after all the formal recommendations of the council were approved, Colby still questioned whether coordination would ever really be possible.[12]

☆ ☆ ☆

By the time the sobered delegates returned to the United States, a substantial reorganization had occurred in the War Department. In December 1917, Secretary Baker created a formal war council and brought in George W. Goethals to head the military logistical effort. A month later portions of the CND were incorporated into the War Department and a number of top civilian business-

men, the most important of whom was the new surveyor general of supply
and second assistant secretary of war, Edward R. Stettinius, joined Secretary
Baker's staff to coordinate supply matters. The reorganizations culminated in
the appointment of Peyton C. March as chief of staff. The March appointment
soon connected issues of inter-Allied cooperation with questions of command
and control between the War Department and the AEF. Secretary Baker at
first acquiesced in Pershing's view of his authority, but toward the end of 1917
his attitude began to change as he came to see that building and supplying
the AEF was only one part of a very complex war effort. Altered perceptions
catalyzed intrinsic conflicts among the Americans over command and control,
revealed fundamental disagreements between Washington and the AEF about
the 1919 military program, and launched disconcerting arguments about production priorities that, in turn, set the stage for a series of inter-Allied supply
and logistical meetings later in 1918.

It was already clear that there was not enough shipping to carry out the
original American thirty-division program in the time previously thought possible. After meetings between General Bliss and the British, the program was
reduced to twenty-four divisions and revised downward again when the American mission arrived home. CND statisticians cast a gloomy picture when, on
December 17, 1917, they projected that the entire American merchant marine
would be required to transport and support even twenty-four American divisions and that the effort would extinguish all American foreign trade for the
duration of the war. They advised that it was essential to secure more tonnage
from the Allies, especially the British, and seize all neutral vessels in American
ports. Shipping Board statisticians reinforced those pessimistic conclusions
in January 1918, when they predicted that "the rate of arrival of our troops in
France will be much slower than our authorities in Washington have figured
on."[13] Secretary Baker turned the figures over to Goethals, who prepared the
official army response. Goethals labeled the whole situation a disaster and
recommended that troop shipments be discontinued until adequate tonnage
was actually in American hands.[14] When the British were not forthcoming
with the ships, the Wilson government became stubbornly independent and
slow to cooperate.

In early 1918 the United States was represented on only the most critical
inter-Allied councils. Bliss was the military representative on the Supreme War
Council, and Oscar Crosby, who had been abroad since October 1917, served on
the inter-Allied Purchasing and Finance Council. Hoover's Food Administration
had continuous but informal connections with the wheat executive. George
Rublee and Raymond Stevens were at first only observers on the Inter-Allied

Maritime Council. The Wilsonians avoided linking their interests with those of the other powers in the coalition, and many Americans serving abroad were discouraged by what they believed were the administration's wrong-headed and unwise attitudes. Jerome Green, Rublee and Stevens's colleague on the Inter-Allied Maritime Council, wrote Edwin Gay that the British were really quite forthright people and worthy allies despite the arguments over troop tonnage. Rublee was of the same mind and expressed greater fear of his own government's parochialism than he did of any British machinations.[15]

It took the catastrophic German attack of March 1918 to bring the British to release sufficient shipping and for the Americans to cooperate seriously with their associates. As it became clear that a major German offensive would begin in the spring, the British offered to release tonnage if the troops transported in British bottoms were attached to the British army. In early February 1918, Pershing, Bliss, and the British hammered out an agreement to transport six additional American divisions to France. They would train with the British and then be reunited with the American army. The promised British tonnage restored the original American thirty-division program, and during March and April, when Allied calls for American manpower exploded, they were dealt with in a series of conferences in Europe with Pershing, Bliss, who by that time had been appointed permanent American military representative to the SWC, and Secretary Baker, who was in France when the German drive began on March 21, 1918. On March 1, 1918, there were fewer than three hundred thousand American soldiers in France. By July 4, 1918, the force reached a million. In early April 1918 the War Department began a study that culminated, in July 1918, with a plan to place three million American soldiers organized into eighty combat divisions in France by the end of 1919.[16]

The military crisis flung all procurement programs into disorder. Even the modifications that had been wrought by the inter-Allied agreements of December 1917 were put aside. Nobody could tell what would be needed in a month, much less a year.[17] There were repercussions in London, Paris, Washington, and New York. Every American or Allied agency connected with ocean tonnage felt the burdens of the new programs. After the German spring offensive began, the British were ready to consider additional transfers of ships to the American war effort. But even then they were interested only in manpower—infantry and machine gunners to supplement their exhausted troops in Flanders—and gave little heed to the problems of supplying the Americans once they were in France. From mid-April to the end of the war, the more successful the troop transport program became, the more pressing was the need for more ocean tonnage for logistical support. American decision makers could not secure reliable information about material needs and shipping tonnage to transmit to their wartime associates. The situation was confounded in the spring of 1918, when it became clear that the EFC would not be able to meet its launching schedules for at least two years and that rigorous allocation of existing tonnage would be necessary. Such allocations would adversely affect the American civilian import and export trades, involve the preparation of lists of essential imports, and compel the assignment of shipping to meet civilian, as well as military, needs.

The Americans brought part of the problem on themselves. In September 1917, when the Wilson administration commandeered all ocean tonnage more than 2,500 tons, vessels were permanently assigned to the army, the navy, the Food Administration, the Fuel Administration, and the Shipping Board itself. It was impossible to transfer ships between agencies and match them with available cargoes. In November 1917, when congestion developed in New York harbor, in part because of this arbitrary arrangement, the War Department and the Shipping Board cooperated to form a Shipping-Control Committee (SCC) for the Port of New York. On February 11, 1918, the idea was expanded and an SCC was formed under the leadership of P. A. S. Franklin, president of the International Merchant Marine Corporation, a Morgan subsidiary, to control all American-flagged vessels in all American ports. Franklin promptly contacted the WIB, the Railroad Administration, and the food and fuel people to ensure that civilian needs would not be entirely neglected in the division of tonnage. The SCC persuaded the War Trade Board and the treasury to use their licensing and inspecting power to bring the shipping industry to conform to the committee's rulings. They pooled vessels and allocated them to various agencies on the basis of temporary need. Sailing ships and older, slower steamers were sent into the "safe" Pacific trades to free newer and faster steel vessels for the dangerous North Atlantic run. There remained, however, substantial tonnage in the civilian export trades, and it was there that a situation developed that reflected not only upon long-range commercial concerns and internal politics in the United States, but also the interests of America's associates, especially the British. The exports issue also brought Franklin's motives into question. The Wilson administration suspected that he was manipulating the SCC in the interests of the Morgan shipping combine and was reluctant to withdraw American shipping from the profitable South American trades. The British, who had captured the German portion of the trade for themselves, were not going to turn over their shipping to the Yankees only to make them commercially dominant. The situation brought a number of tense diplomatic exchanges and played an important role in the meetings of the Inter-Allied Maritime Council until the end of the war.

The spring crisis, meanwhile, put incredible burdens on shipping. The shipping board seized Dutch tonnage in March 1918 and put Scandinavian vessels under American control later in the year. About half of the foreign shipping was moved into the Pacific to replace American vessels, but there was still simply not enough to go around. Other pressures were building as well. In 1917 a considerable part of American production went to the Allies, but, as the American army took more 1918 industrial production and the 1919 program developed, problems of inter-Allied supply in the United States emerged that could not be met by simply referring them to the WIB's Priorities Committee. The Allies had never cooperated with the WIB, and the French and British high commissioners had on many occasions ignored the Inter-Allied Purchasing Commission and continued to use their own agents to place contracts with American industry. Until March 1918, the United States government had no idea of the amount of raw and semifinished materials that it owed the Allies in return for the ammunition, automatic weapons, and field and siege artillery it had secured under the Crozier-Ganne agreement. The enlarged American program required coordination all along the line. Raw materials, explosives, ordnance, and food were all in short supply, and broad international supply and shipping agreements were necessary if the new program was to have any chance of success.[18]

Intense negotiations brought the creation of a number of inter-Allied economic and supply committees to establish priorities, allocate resources, and coordinate a joint war program for 1919 and 1920. The Allies were aware that American production at home and purchasing abroad were uncoordinated. The Americans talked of cooperation in December 1917 but proved recalcitrant when critical issues of troop amalgamation arose in the spring of 1918. As the various councils and committees recommended by the inter-Allied conference were formed, a stream of cables from abroad reached Washington urging closer cooperation. Many were not even acknowledged. Finally, on June 8, 1918, a formal memorandum from the newly formed Inter-Allied Munitions Council was sent to Washington demanding that the Americans appoint official representatives to the inter-Allied committees and station them permanently in Paris.[19] It took another month and a further flurry of cables before the American government agreed to dispatch a mission. When it did leave, it was not accidental that its departure coincided with the dispute over command and control that had erupted between Chaumont and Washington. As Secretary Baker forwarded the eighty-division program to the president, he also addressed a memorandum to Lord Reading, the British Ambassador and chief of mission in the United States, agreeing to participate in the inter-Allied meetings.[20]

In late July 1918, the American mission left for Europe. Headed by Stettinius, it included representatives of all the emergency war agencies. Stettinius's orders were, first, to assure that there would be sufficient cargo tonnage to support the American army in France; second, to secure enough reliable information from the associated powers about their future requirements to allow the Wilson administration to plan its 1919 program; and, third, to bring the financial and procurement activities of the AEF under War Department control. The Stettinius mission met with their allied colleagues for two weeks and accomplished little. Stettinius also had difficulty getting any cooperation from the AEF, the WIB, and the other American emergency boards. Everybody had trouble with the British and French, and the Americans found the British cool and suspicious. The Americans did little to warm the atmosphere. When the WIB mission arrived, for example, it found the Allies not disposed to consult with them, especially regarding chairmanships of the conference committees. This was most disconcerting to American steel men. Leland L. Summers, the WIB mission leader, simply took the chair at the steel committee organizational meeting, stated the purpose of the meeting, and declared that, inasmuch as the Americans were furnishing the Allies with more steel that the former's combined annual production, an American should be the permanent chairman of the committee. He nominated Paul Mackall of Bethlehem Steel for the post and announced that, because there were no further nominations, Mackall was elected. Later, Andrew Bonar-Law (a member of the British "War Cabinet"), on being introduced to Summers, remarked, "So you are Mr. Summers. Well, you have been the most talked about man in the British cabinet for the past two weeks."[21] After the German battlefield reverses of early August, the British began to think again about their postwar interests. Stevens and Rublee of the Inter-Allied Maritime Council cabled Edward N. Hurley, chairman of the Shipping Board, on August 31, 1918, that it seemed they could no longer depend on the British for anything.

The inter-Allied committees had been in session for a month before the Americans finally appeared. By September 1918, each war agency had a representative abroad. Stettinius, who was supposed to head the mission, seemed unwilling to make decisions. He would not give the army's steel requirements to the inter-Allied steel committee and insisted that all such requirements had to be reviewed by Washington. He would not even share information with his own colleagues and told Summers that a steel council was of little use to the War Department and that he would share no information with him and just might withhold his cooperation. The WIB got the information from the Allies, and Summers later commented that it was harder to deal with the War Department than it was with the French.

It was not until Secretary Baker arrived in early September and assumed the duties of chief of the American mission that things began to move. On September 13, 1918, Baker indicated that the War Department would submit its production programs to the Inter-Allied Munitions Council. His first objective, however, was to secure shipping for the eighty-division program and bring Pershing to heel. His task was complicated by the fact that the tonnage figures he received from AEF headquarters were substantially larger than those he had brought with him from the United States. Baker used the War Department figures when he talked to the British. They insisted that they could make no agreements that threatened their own food supply unless they were assured that the Americans were doing everything possible on their side of the ocean.[22] Baker talked with Pershing about the 1919 program and believed he had made the War Department position clear to his recalcitrant general. He also met with the British shipping authorities. On September 23, 1918, after initial conversations failed to bring forth a shipping agreement, Baker cabled the president for permission to make an agreement that would meet all the British objections.[23]

While awaiting Wilson's reply, Baker continued his conferences with Pershing and his staff and attended sessions of the new Munitions Council and the Maritime Council. There the problem, as it had been all along, was that the Associated Powers were reluctant to reveal production capacity and import and export programs to each other. Self-interest dictated that postwar economic and commercial positions must be protected. The terrible destruction of the war made such action absolutely imperative for the Europeans. The Americans and British had benefited from the German commercial withdrawal from Latin America and were determined to retain shares of that trade after the war. Characteristic of American ambiguity about the situation was a cable from Summers to Baruch on September 30, 1918, that counseled full American cooperation with the Allies and then damned the British for maneuvering in such a way as to secure a substantial financial return for handling inter-Allied supplies, this time Australian wool. "If we were to propose a similar charge against wheat and cotton furnished the Allies, you can appreciate what it would mean." On the same day, Summers, who was then in Italy, complained in another cable to Baruch that the British had rendered further negotiations on leather, wool, and flax impracticable without complete submission to their wishes, and that they would continue to resist any kind of pricing agreements or equitable distribution of raw textile. He concluded that "commodities of Raw Materials Department are not pooled in Allied interest but used directly to benefit British trade during and after war and avowedly to employ Belfast . . . labor."[24] Some progress was made the same day, however, when a resolution was adopted committing the British and French "to supply the requirements of artillery ammunition to the American Expeditionary Forces until the output of American plants is available in France" and, for the next two months, to give "priority [to the Allies] over the American shell manufacturing program to as great an extent as possible without interfering with the continued manufacture of shells in American plants."[25]

The president's reply to Baker's cable of September 23 must have arrived about October 1, for on October 2 the secretary of war announced that President Wilson had ordered that the United States mission should "fully disclose its shipping programme, its import programme and its programmes of all kinds." Baker apparently thought Pershing agreed with him on the 1919 program and wrote the general that he had accomplished everything he had set out to do. Baker was in for a great shock and it was not only that Pershing was still pressing for one hundred divisions. Marshall Foch, who had demanded one hundred American divisions in the spring of 1918 and was still making similar requests in July and August, told Baker in late September, to the latter's stupefaction, that he would win the war with the American divisions which were already in France.[26]

Meanwhile, the inter-Allied meetings made some progress. Four boards for shipping, munitions, food, and finance were created to sit permanently in Paris to supervise pooling of supplies and to prevent duplication of effort.[27] On October 6, 1918, Baker cabled the president optimistically that "Army has renewed attack and is progressing. Tonnage situation favorably cleared up," and he prepared to return to the United States. As it became clear that the German army was collapsing, however, the agreements began to unravel. The British refused to turn over any shipping other than the 200,000 tons they had promised. On October 26, 1918, Baker addressed a cable through State Department channels to Lord Reading, asking him to explain why the promised tonnage was not forthcoming and asking for the "maximum assignment possible for the month of November." Lord Reading's office replied that they were withholding more ships because they had WIB figures showing that there were still two million tons of American-controlled shipping in excess of minimum needs employed in the American import-export trades. That brought on heated debates in the United States between the War Department, the Shipping Board, the WIB, and the War Trade Board that were still in progress when the armistice was signed and that were symptomatic of the interagency conflict and dislocation present in the American war government even at the end of the war.

For some weeks suspicion had been growing in the Wilson administration that Franklin and his colleagues on the SCC were not doing everything possible to draw ships from nonessential trades. The British had secured their figures from WIB sources after a conference on October 18, 1918, between Franklin, Hurley, and McCormick that was sufficiently important to reconstruct in some detail. The War Trade Board, where suspicion of Franklin was most acute, had just ordered a massive culling of shipping in the South American export trade to meet the needs of the army. Donald Scott, who represented the War Trade Board, reported that Franklin claimed that there was no more shipping to be had from those sources and that he had already met all army requirements. The problem, he argued, was shortage of cargo to move rather than shortage of ships to move it. Such an idea was beyond Scott's comprehension, and he cited figures from Gay's Division of Central Planning and Statistics indicating that army tonnage was piling up on the docks and that substantial shipping was still in the "nonessential" trades. Franklin scoffed at his figures and claimed, "If we could be at one of the Wednesday morning conferences and see how everyone smiled when reference was made to the figures of Mr. Gay we would see how lightly they were held." The meeting ended on that note. Subsequent investigation showed that Gay's figures were accurate. A resolution of the Shipping Board of November 1, 1918, revoked part of the power to allocate tonnage granted to the SCC the previous February and returned allocation of shipping in the import-export trades to the Shipping Board. The resolution stated further that Gay's Division of Planning and Statistics, rather than any other organization associated with the SCC, would be the source of information for the Shipping Board and that "tonnage available for the commercial needs of the United States is necessarily subordinate to . . . military and naval requirements."[28] Matters ended badly. On October 14, 1918, General Bliss wrote Chief of Staff March: "Yesterday afternoon Mr. Stettinius called on me and we had a long talk on the subject of the Munitions Program. It seems to me somewhat evident that the European allies will attempt to minimize the American effort as much as possible. They think they have got the Germans on the run and that they now do not need as much help as a little while ago they were crying for."[29]

☆ ☆ ☆

On one late October night in 1918, George Goethals gloomily looked at the lights of Foggy Bottom from his office in the half-finished munitions building. In France Pershing was still calling for one hundred divisions, and Dawes was still running his own operation. The Allies were being difficult about shipping, and he wrote his son Tom, "We're in bad shape here in shipping, not having the requisite bottoms to carry what Pershing says are his minimum requirements. We are hustling men over while the cargo end gets worse and worse. I shouldn't be surprised to see the whole shipping situation collapse." On November 10 he wrote Tom that he thought Americans would have to depend on their own resources in the future and confided, "Our shipping situation is bad and I see no hope of making up the deficiency, so that if we are to continue with the war, we will have to reduce the number of men we send over to the number of men we can supply."[30] Almost a year before, Colonel House had made a similar assessment: "[W]hat discourages one most in the whole situation is the lack of unity and control and of action. There is but little coordination anywhere between the Allies. Jealousies are everywhere rife. None of them at heart likes one another, and I doubt whether any of them likes us. It is the idea of 'hanging together or separately' that keeps them going."[31]

CHAPTER 9

GENERAL SUPPLIES, ARTILLERY, AND SMOKELESS POWDER

As the expanding demands of the AEF and the Allies for men and equipment reached Washington after the Supreme War Council meetings of December 1917, War Department design, development, and procurement systems were tested as never before. Quartermaster, ordnance, and signal-supply and technical experts recognized that there was a relationship that could be defined formally between ideas and weapons. Before the war the bureau chiefs had modified their equipment and weapons-testing systems to give representatives of using services a consultative voice in equipment selection. Nevertheless, the difficulties inherent in the traditional producer-dominated selection process, with its many competing interest groups inside and outside the War Department, were hard to overcome. In August 1918, Chief of Staff March abolished the Board of Ordnance and Fortification and made research and invention, training, and tactics separate sections of the War Plans Division of the general staff. Even after these reorganizations, the complex relationships between the AEF and Washington still complicated his efforts and the organizations he approved often worked at cross-purposes, proving just how difficult it was to build, often for the first time, formal interagency and even intergovernmental organizations that linked military doctrine, weapons design, industrial production, and battlefield performance.[1]

☆ ☆ ☆

General equipment requirements were not difficult to meet. Quartermaster and engineering demands were filled with commercially available products. Small arms, automatic weapons, artillery, ammunition, explosives, and propellant technologies were robust, but constantly expanding programs posed significant time, scale, production, and quality-control problems. General Sharpe's promotion to the War Council in December 1917 cleared the way for appointment of Goethals as quartermaster general and director of storage and traffic. His international reputation gave credibility to the substantial changes he was about to make in the structure of supply and logistics. Goethals's centralization of policy making, which began in December 1917 and matured during the spring and summer of 1918, brought at least a modicum of coordination to the general supply program.[2] Robert Thorne, president of Montgomery Ward, aided by members of the supply committee of the CND who were transferred to the Quartermaster Corps in early 1918, brought imposing civilian mercantile expertise into the bureau. Thorne quickly gained control of the clothing and subsistence program and made the Quartermaster Corps an enormous purchasing agency. Clothing, equipment, and subsistence procurement were conducted as much as possible by regional and zone quartermasters. Only general policy matters received attention in Washington.[3]

Subsistence and clothing posed few problems. In January 1918, after a careful investigation by Goethals's office, emergency purchases of nonstandard cotton and wool textiles ended. The quantum leaps in military requirements during the first half of 1918, once they were known, were handled effectively. By September 1918, quartermaster shops at Philadelphia and Jeffersonville, Indiana, alone could outfit a third of the army as well as provide standards of acceptance for uniforms and equipment from the private sector.[4] In June 1918, Goethals told Secretary Baker that, though there might be some minor shortages of wool uniforms in the fall, he could house, clothe, and feed all the troops who might be called up. Camp construction was virtually complete, the supply depots were full, and a vast storage- and warehouse-building program was underway. Any future shortages that might occur, Goethals claimed, would be caused by the failure of the Railroad Administration or the Shipping Board to deliver the goods.[5] On June 22, 1918, the secretary of war wrote to Thomas Nelson Page, American ambassador to Italy, that "our preparation in material is at last beginning to bear abundant fruit. In . . . clothing and food we are out of the reach of want and have enough adequately to equip all the troops we can send.[6] During the summer of 1918 the Quartermaster Bureau placed further contracts to support the eighty-division program. The end of the war found it overwhelmed with food and clothing supplies that required a large-scale disposal effort in 1919 and plagued the army with surplus uniforms and other quartermaster supplies for the next decade.

☆ ☆ ☆

The American artillery and munitions programs were never integrated with those of the Allies. Despite British and French assurances that they could supply the AEF with guns and ammunition of all calibers, General Pershing in November

1917 cabled that they had not fulfilled their obligations and demanded a full American artillery production program at home. On December 15, 1917, General Bliss sent a contradictory recommendation that the United States concentrate on production of smokeless powder and artillery shells rather than develop a balanced artillery-production program.[7] No one questioned Pershing's November request, and Washington either misread, misunderstand, or ignored the Bliss memorandum. The War Department imposed the Pershing proposals and the December inter-Allied munitions report on existing programs in the United States.

The Americans resented their dependence on British and French production. It not only challenged national pride but also compromised the Wilson administration diplomatically with Allied policy makers. In January 1918, the War Department was planning to have a maximum of sixty-six divisions in France in 1919, with thirty in place by the fall of 1918. In late February 1918, Acting Chief of Staff John Biddle announced that the new artillery program required production of materials to equip as many as ninety divisions with American-made artillery and ammunition by the end of 1919.[8]

No one at the time asked how the guns and shells could be produced and, once produced, how they could be shipped to France. No one asked whether they would be needed if the Allies prevailed in the forthcoming battles or whether they could be used at all if the worst happened and the French and British collapsed. Meanwhile, organization of the War Council in December 1917 removed Chief of Ordnance William Crozier from the day-to-day operations of the department. Crozier's ordeal in the Ordnance Department roused far less sympathy than that of Quartermaster General Sharpe. When he reminded George Chamberlain, chairman of the Senate Military Affairs Committee, of the failures of the Congress to support the prewar expansion of ordnance procurement programs, he only made matters worse. On December 19, 1917, Crozier joined the War Council and the chief of the ordnance supply division, Brigadier General Charles B. Wheeler, became acting chief of ordnance.[9] Wheeler found that a rudimentary technical communication system already connected Washington and Chaumont but that Pershing's headquarters could not specify clearly the types and numbers of weapons it wanted, making it impossible for ordnance officers at home to translate the changing requests from Chaumont into effective weapons-procurement programs.

General Wheeler did not hesitate to use civilian management and production experts. Benedict Crowell had only recently left ordnance to become assistant secretary of war, and, possibly on his recommendation, Wheeler called upon Colonel (later Brigadier General) Guy E. Tripp, president and chairman of the board of Westinghouse Electric and Manufacturing Company, to install an effective production command-and-control system in the Ordnance Department. Tripp's plan involved the functional reorganization of the bureau. The old Cannon, Carriage, and Small Arms divisions had been modified by General Crozier during the summer of 1917, when he established the Supply Division and the Nitrates Division as separate entities, and Tripp's functional reorganization carried the momentum forward. A new administration division conducted the paperwork of the bureau, accounted for all funds and property, and oversaw the recruitment, examination, and assignment of military and civilian personnel. The Engineering Division recommended equipment adoptions, produced and distributed blueprints and operating manuals, and conducted the testing, experimentation, and research required to improve American arms. The Procurement Division placed all orders with the government arsenals, contracted with private producers, and became the contact point between ordnance, the general staff, and the civilian emergency war agencies. The Production Division expedited deliveries from arsenals and civilian plants by placing at their disposal "every known means to aid, stimulate and accelerate production to the end that constantly increasing requirements may be promptly met." The Inspection Division assured the quality of ordnance materials, especially those from civilian plants. The Supply Division stored, shipped, and issued ordnance materials to the troops. The Nitrate Division established and operated the government plants that were coming on line to meet the enormous smokeless-powder and shell requirements of the 1919 program. The Office of the Director of Arsenals completed the structure.[10]

The Tripp plan went into effect on January 14, 1918, and it was soon clear that the new organization had as many deficiencies as the one it supplanted. The most important problem lay in Washington, where the Supply Control Bureau established in the administration division did not work and there was no clear chain of command or formal subordination between the functional chiefs and their various representatives in the field. The problem is best understood through examining Tripp's administrative ordeal. Using the Federal Reserve System as a model, he established a number of production districts, each with its own manager who reported directly to Washington. Tripp's intent was to create a unique kind of civil/military organization. "The district offices were under civilian chiefs who took their orders from an army officer in Washington and gave orders to army officers stationed in their districts." The arrangement was intended to secure "a measure of elasticity and a degree of discretion" for the district production managers that "they could not obtain if they were under military discipline." It was also intended "to inspire among manufacturers the sense of cooperation and reciprocal understanding that the presence of a civilian chief was calculated to arouse; and to give the whole undertaking in the districts and the shops the sanction and authority which properly go with the uniform of the country."[11] Each division chief in the Ordnance Department appointed his own district manager. As chief of the Production Division, Tripp came immediately into conflict with the chief of the Inspection Division, who was concerned with quality control. Soon even minor administrative conflicts were being referred directly to the Ordnance Department by district managers for adjudication between their division bosses. By April 1918 Tripp was in despair.

Later that month General Wheeler was ordered to France, and Brigadier General W. S. Pierce became interim chief of ordnance. Wheeler's relief is puzzling. The reassignment occurred without consultation with Secretary Baker, who was in France. Assistant Secretary of War Crowell made no reference to the matter in his own story of the munitions effort. General March wrote later that it conformed to a rotation policy he put in place, with the consent of Assistant Secretary Stettinius and the concurrence of General Pershing, to have as chief of ordnance at home a man who "had been largely instrumental in securing our artillery for us in France and knew at first hand what the problems of the AEF were as regards ordnance." Wheeler became AEF chief of ordnance and General Clarence C. Williams was ordered home to take Wheeler's place.[12]

Williams had a different philosophy than Crozier or Wheeler. He insisted that ordnance should serve the soldiers in the field. "If the fighting men want elephants, we get them elephants," he is reported to have declared.[13] The new chief immediately consulted Tripp and made a number of significant changes. Tripp got the credit, but it was Williams who implemented them and he later described his approach:

> As the ordnance program of the government gathered volume and got underway and the consequences of new conditions indicated themselves, it became apparent that Washington would become a national choke point unless radical steps were taken. The circumstances called for a system which, while retaining the general control in Washington, would yet set up intermediary organizations at other points that should relieve the central ordnance authority of the overwhelming mass of routine, segregate the essential from the non-essential for reference to Washington, and stimulate production in the only way that it could be stimulated—by close range attention.[14]

In May 1918 district production managers began to make all nonpolicy decisions locally. According to Ordnance historians, the effects were immediate:

> [C]ontractors got prompt payment for completed items, enabling them to turn the money back into new work, and relieving the Finance Division in Washington of an intolerable burden. The district production men exerted themselves to remove obstacles and stimulate output by seeing that manufacturers were provided with shipping orders, priorities, raw materials, coal power, and lubricants, gages and machinery; that engineering changes were expedited; that freight matters were quickly handled; and that requisite information of all kinds was available. The district engineering managers accelerated operations by interpreting specifications and handling minor changes.[15]

Ultimately, the Ordnance Department formed thirteen production districts. The Baltimore/Washington district specialized in ammunition production, especially shrapnel, 37 mm guns, and ammunition and ammonium nitrate, and included the big Seven Pines powder-bag-loading plant outside Richmond, Virginia. The Boston district specialized in leather and textile equipment, boosters and adapters for shells, and time fuses. It also handled the largest orders for 155 mm howitzer carriages and produced hand grenades. The Bridgeport Ordnance District contained the largest government and private small-arms production plants and produced rifles, machine guns, shotguns, revolvers, bayonets, and trench knives. All privately manufactured small-arms ammunition came from the Connecticut Valley.[16] The Chicago District was the most important subcontracting area in the country. It produced everything from railroad artillery mounts, artillery ammunition, and gun carriages to recuperators. The Cincinnati Ordnance District produced machine tools and held the larger part of the production contract for the Renault tank. It also produced ammunition and provided inspection and control for the big government powder plant at Old Hickory, Tennessee, the picric-acid facility at Brunswick, Georgia, and the two nitrogen fixation plants at Muscle Shoals, Alabama, and Ancor, Ohio. The Cleveland District produced big guns, tanks, all twelve-inch railroad mounts, gun carriages, and various types of shell bodies. The Detroit District produced all kinds of gun carriages, vehicles, tractors, recuperators, the Ford three-ton tank, and various types of shell bodies. New York was the largest district in terms of contracts, and the largest amount of industrial conversion in the country occurred there. The New York District made military pyrotechnics, war gases, TNT, and gun carriages. It loaded fixed ammunition, bagged powder, and provided a mass of miscellaneous material from needles to saddle soap. The Philadelphia District made forgings for the big guns, produced Enfield rifles at the Remington/Midvale plant at Eddystone, made explosives, and loaded artillery ammunition. It assembled all the helmets shipped abroad. The Pittsburgh District provided all kinds of forgings for guns and recuperators. At Neville Island six miles below Pittsburgh, the United States Steel Corporation began what was to be the largest big-gun plant in the world. It was to have covered 573 acres and employ 20,000 workers, turn out fifteen fourteen-inch guns a month, and cast 40,000 fourteen- and sixteen-inch shell bodies a month, but it was never completed. The Rochester District made optical equipment, Lewis machine guns, and light artillery, and included a government training school for precision-optical workers. The Saint Louis District, which covered most of the Far West, produced walnut rifle stocks and controlled the government toluol and picric-acid facilities at Los Angeles, San Francisco, and Picron, Arkansas. The Toronto Ordnance District, which included all of Canada, produced both heavy- and field-artillery ammunition, as well as powder and high explosives.[17]

The district system strengthened relations with business in two ways. First, the district chiefs were members of local business communities and had wide and deep contacts. Second, local groups of manufacturers formed associations in each line of ordnance work and established contact with the district offices and later with local advisory committees of the WIB, which served as facilitators. Thus, the organizational relationships between American businessmen and the government grew more intimate. The Ordnance Bureau itself, however, maintained only indirect contact with the WIB and its chairman, Bernard Baruch. The WIB was unable to curb even the army's most outrageous demands, and wartime connections between the War Department, its civilian experts such as Guy Tripp, Robert Thorne, and Gerard Swope, and the WIB were always ambiguous.

Placing the power in the hands of the production managers raised all kinds of other issues. Before Williams arrived, the Supply Control Division in Washington had difficulties coordinating the production of component parts and their shipment to assembly plants. In mid-May Williams established the Estimates and Requirements Division, to take the place of the Supply Control Division, and began weekly meetings with Ordnance Division heads to establish internal administrative control and some measure of coordination with the PS and T and the WIB. Status of contracts and production could be ascertained, but at the end of the war effective control of the ordnance program had not yet been achieved.

☆ ☆ ☆

Administrative organization and reorganization had very little effect on what became known as the "Ordnance Problem." Production of rifles, automatic weapons, and small-arms ammunition supplies reached adequate levels by the fall of 1918, but field and heavy-artillery production could not surmount inexperience, overconfidence, faulty shop practices, and the escalating demands of the AEF.[18] As late as January 1918, public and private gun plants were working for the navy in compliance with the "Navy First" agreement of April 1917 or for the Allies. Ordnance lacked trained commissioned and enlisted personnel, and the hurried recruitment of civilians failed to secure the experienced people necessary to carry out the production program. Ordnance historians have pointed out that the program was also plagued by conflicts with "Big Steel" over prices during the summer and fall of 1917.[19]

Expansion of the government arsenals at Springfield, Rock Island, Watervliet, Watertown, Frankford, and Picatinny began in the summer of 1917. Rock Island manufactured or procured regionally everything from infantry equipment to cavalry accouterments. Employment at the big complex grew from 2,263 in 1916 to 15,000 by November 1918. Deficiencies in machine tools were hard to remedy and the "model 03" rifle line, shut down in 1913 but reopened in the fall of 1916 in response to the requirements projected in the National Defense Act, was slow getting into quantity production. Production of 4.7- and 3-inch gun carriages expanded, and at Rock Island experimental work finally solved the problem of mass producing the French 75 mm recuperators. The labor forces at Springfield and Frankford doubled as the rifle works and small-arms ammunition plants went on round-the-clock shifts. Watertown tripled in size. It doubled its forging capacity and, by the end of 1918, employed more than five thousand workers at the carriage- and shell-making facilities alone. At Watervliet the work force expanded to more than five thousand employees and a systematic change took place as the arsenal tooled up for the first time for mass production. Colonel John E. Monroe, who commanded the gun plant during the most hectic days of expansion, wrote of the year from June 1917 to July 1918: "The salient feature of the past year's history of the Arsenal has been the change in the manufacturing plant from what was virtually a jobbing shop to a works designed for quantity production. . . . [T]he year has been on the whole, one of preparation for larger service rather than of actual accomplishment." The new construction at Watervliet included a modernized gun shop for 240 mm howitzers and a breech-mechanism shop. Colonel James Walker Benét admitted in his report for 1919 that the majority of the light and heavy guns were completed after the armistice: "Prior to the period covered by this report, cannon production at the Arsenal was much hampered by want of proper machine tools. Beginning in March 1917, a program of installation of up-to-date machine tools began and during the period covered by this report, has been completed to the point where the cost of production has been reduced by, in many cases, as much as two hundred percent."[20]

Building new civilian plants involved years not months, so the conversion of existing plants and subcontracting were the keys to success. Still, plants had to be located, machine tools redesigned or rebuilt, and the labor force expanded. Contracts for artillery and ammunition were divided among numerous firms, mostly located east of Pittsburgh, which had little or no experience with government work.[21] The work was so concentrated that the Niagara power grid failed in the winter of 1917–1918 and the eastern industrial region experienced the first electrical "brownout" in American history.[22] By early 1918, the zone was referred to as the "congested area" and Washington was looking elsewhere in the country for unused plant and power sources. The industrial base for a war of such magnitude was inadequate, and conversion and retooling was only beginning when the war ended.

No administrative reorganization could solve the technical problems faced by American industry as it attempted to produce unfamiliar foreign equipment.[23] The automobile and steel-rail businesses were unaccustomed to working to close tolerances and had great difficulty adjusting to the metric system. Jigs, dies, standard gages, and machine tools were in short supply. Component parts were badly made and not interchangeable. Shell fuses often would not explode. *Iron Age* reported in early January 1918 that "Improperly designed gages with improper tolerances already have caused American manufacturers and the Allies the loss of millions of dollars." In the summer of 1918, machine tools were still scarce and General Williams pointed out that it was silly to try to commandeer what did not exist.

The only foreign artillery produced successfully by private industry during the conflict was the model 1917 75 mm gun and the 8-inch howitzer. Both were rechambered or modified British models that were already in production at Bethlehem Steel. The production of French equipment was a nightmare. French parts were not interchangeable, and their shop practices allowed for considerable filing and fitting. Screw threads were not standard. Blueprints were incomplete and often wrong. The oil-gauge rod on the 75 mm recuperators, for example, was longer than the blueprints showed, and the firing shock of the first dozen models produced at Rock Island Arsenal tore the carriages to pieces.[24] Conversion of metric measurements to feet and inches was harder than American factory managers believed, while specifications kept changing as new calls for more and different equipment rolled in from Pershing's headquarters in France.

As late as February 1918, some business and industry spokesmen remained optimistic. In an editorial, "War Contracts for the Little Plant," the editor of *Iron Age* wrote, "Our war program does not appear large enough to tax the country's production capacity . . . even with the increasing numbers being taken into the army by the draft." During the spring of 1918 the Ordnance Department undertook "probably the largest single inquiry for machine tools that has ever been issued" and made a public appeal through the Iron and Steel Institute for unused and underutilized equipment. By June 1918, however, optimism had evaporated and *Iron Age* admitted that the future looked bleak.

One of the most difficult and frustrating problems was the lack of a list of reliable bidders. In the rapid expansion of ordnance production no one knew for sure which manufacturers were capable of fulfilling their contract obligations. In Hamilton, Ohio, for example, the Mosler Safe Company, a firm known for a generation as one of the most reliable manufacturers in the country, bid for a contract to produce carriages for the 155 mm howitzer. An officer who followed the contract through to its miserable denouement left the following account: "This company had a very excellent reputation as manufacturers of steel safes and bank vaults. It had grown from a very modest beginning to one of the first of its kind in the country over a period of forty years under the management of two brothers, William and Moses Mosler. These two men were very affable gentlemen and gave the impression of being thoroughly confident of the ability of their very conservative organization. . . . Their representative, who came to Washington and secured their contract, was one of the most accomplished salesmen I have ever seen." In a short time it became clear that the Moslers had no idea of how to get on with their task. They lacked machinery and personnel, and the contract amounted to ten times its annual business. The brothers subcontracted the planning to a company of efficiency experts who botched the job. After six months, under protest and at the insistence of the Ordnance Department, the brothers Mosler placed a shop superintendent and general manager chosen by Tripp in charge of the work. Matters did not improve, and finally the War Department commandeered the plant and turned operations over to a business rival, the American Rolling Mill Company of Middletown, Ohio. The ARMCO people literally tore the Mosler Safe Company to pieces. The officer concluded, "By the time they had completed all the rearrangements the Armistice . . . fortunately put an end to the war."[25]

The Tripp-Williams organization marked a triumph of quantity over quality. During the spring of 1918, for example, the Dodge 155 mm recuperators plant in Detroit, Michigan, fell behind on its contract. To increase output the plant manager approached the local ordnance-production manager for advice. The finished machining on the outside of the recuperator sleighs for the 155 mm howitzers was done by a large form cutter on an Ingersoll milling machine. When the cutter became dull, considerable time was required to resharpen it. If tolerances could be relaxed just a bit, the plant manager said, the cutters could be used for a longer period without sharpening and production would increase. The production manager agreed. The inspection manager opposed the decision but went along with the production manager in the interest of meeting the deadline. When the sleighs were completed, attached to the rest of the recuperators, and assembled with the gun cradles at the proving grounds at Aberdeen, Maryland, for firing tests, it was found that they interfered with the rivet heads at the bottom of the cradles, and the recuperators would not return the guns to battery after firing. The rivets had to be chipped off with air hammers and the interiors of the cradles remachined.[26]

Production of artillery ammunition faced similar difficulties. The department subcontracted shell components and the completed rounds were assembled and loaded at special plants. The problem with the 75 mm shell program was the boosters. The shell was a French design. The American three-inch shell had no booster, and the French booster was drawn steel and had to be precisely constructed. American production of complete rounds fell as assembly shops waited for boosters.[27]

One of the few cases of technological innovation in the Ordnance Department during the war resulted in what Ian Hogg later incorrectly called the "Crime of 1916."[28] Even before the Treat Board met in 1916, the Ordnance Bureau had been experimenting with a new carriage for the 3-inch field gun. Conventional single-trail mounts had little elevation and virtually no traverse, and in 1913 ordnance technicians designed a split-trail carriage. When the war began, although the model 1916 field gun and carriage was still a prototype, General Crozier made a daring decision. The Americans would use existing American 3-inch guns for training; order the model 1897 75 mm gun from French sources; accept the British eighteen-pounders built by Bethlehem Steel, rechambered to take 75 mm ammunition, and labeled U.S. model 1917; and commit the Ordnance Bureau to produce the model 1916 split-trail 75 mm gun as a replacement for all light field artillery in 1919.

The American tube-and-breech mechanism was the usual sturdy, finely machined ordnance design, but during the summer and fall of 1917 the model 1916 carriage and recoil mechanism suffered significant teething troubles. In February 1918, shortly after Crozier's relief, most of the model 1916 gun program was canceled. That month Willis-Overland, which had the contract for the carriages, shifted production from the model 1916 split-trail to the French

Model 1897 carriage and recuperators. Production of the French model foundered on the recuperators. The French hydraulic-pneumatic recoil mechanism was a problem throughout the war. The system was allegedly secret, and it was hard to get reliable blueprints, but the only thing secret about it, one commentator later wrote, "was the immense difficulty in constructing it."[29] Watervliet and Watertown continued production of the 1916 split-trail carriages during the summer of 1918, and, when the first improved models were completed, ordnance experts in the United States pronounced the American carriage superior. Pershing's headquarters, after testing it in France, requested that mass production of the split-trail carriage begin. General Williams replied that no further changes in 75 mm material would be tolerated. None of the model 1916 75s with the new split-trail carriage ever fired a round in anger.[30]

☆ ☆ ☆

Relations between the War Department and I. E. DuPont de Nemours, the smokeless-powder giant, provide a case study of the political complications that strained the relationships between the War Department and large American corporate enterprises during the war. Pierre DuPont was an assertive businessman and a champion of the gospel of corporate efficiency. He had matured in the rough and tumble of late-nineteenth-century American enterprise and, ironically, at one time had been a business partner of Secretary of War Baker's own mentor, the single taxer and future mayor of Cleveland, Tom L. Johnson. Pierre DuPont, often against the determined opposition of other members of his family, reorganized and modernized the DuPont business empire along modern corporate lines and was the creator of the "Big Company." He was not particularly prone to self-examination, and it was a long time before he saw himself as anything but a simple entrepreneur who often had to face the oppressive power of outside authority intent on subverting his family's interests.

The European war fostered the expansion of civilian powder and propellant production enormously while it soured relations between DuPont and the Wilson administration. Secretary of the Navy Daniels, who considered DuPont profits obscene, was particularly wearing to the powder makers. When Secretary of War Garrison was replaced by the progressive Baker, DuPont's cup of bile overflowed. DuPont was particularly vexed by the "Munitions Tax," part of the preparedness program of 1916, which placed a flat tax of 12.5 percent on DuPont's net profits. By late summer 1916, DuPont estimated that the powder company and the two other smokeless powder concerns with which the family was associated, Hercules and Atlas, paid well over 90 percent of all the taxes the government collected under the new ammunition law. Ruly Carpenter, director of the development department at DuPont, was so annoyed that he recommended that "we write off this year every pound of military powder capacity we have and consider that we will secure no more of their business." The Wilson administration drew further wrath when, later in 1916, it began to build a government nitrate-fixation plant to remedy the country's dependence on Chilean supplies and refused to allow DuPont to develop a separate private nitrate-fixation plant at Muscle Shoals. Small wonder the smokeless powder magnate opposed Wilson's reelection in 1916.[31]

When the United States entered the Great War, Chief of Ordnance Crozier worked to secure the munitions necessary to support the anticipated American reinforcement. There were no great technological secrets involved in the production of smokeless powder, and Crozier anticipated few difficulties in securing an adequate supply.[32] But conditions changed radically during the summer and fall, and by late November 1917 there was concern in the United States that Franco-British commitments were not going to be met and growing awareness that the Americans might have to shoulder far more of the material burden of the war than they had believed necessary six months before.

The increased demand for smokeless powder was brought on by two virtually simultaneous events. First, under the thirty-division program, the structure of the American combat forces was transformed and the number of field and heavier guns assigned to the newly reorganized army was doubled. Pershing's headquarters concurrently doubled the number of "days of fire" for artillery ammunition and thus automatically doubled the smokeless powder program. Second, British and French artillery doctrines changed during 1917. General Pétain's policy after the mutinies of the spring of that year was to restore confidence in the French army by launching limited offensives supported with massive artillery preparation. This placed heavy demands on French industry, especially for large-caliber shells, and increased its need for raw materials from abroad. The British made the same judgment after the Somme offensive, and they increased their expenditure of heavy-artillery ammunition by 200 percent for their anticipated 1917 attack in Flanders.[33] On December 14, 1917, General Bliss cabled from London, "The French and to a lesser extent the British require as soon as possible large supplies of propellants and high explosives. They ask that the American efforts shall be immediately directed to the production of propellants and high explosives on the greatest scale."

The reasons for that request became evident soon after the Crozier-Ganne agreement was signed in June 1917. In late July the French revealed that they lacked the capacity to provide all the ammunition that was needed for the proposed American thirty-division program. French picric acid was also in short supply, and they asked that the United States make up the shortfall. Although nitrates and picric acid were in short supply in the United States, experiments by German chemist Fritz Haber had shown that nitrates could be produced from the air. In 1916 Congress had provided funds to construct a nitrate-fixation plant at Muscle Shoals using the cyanamide process, and one at Sheffield, Alabama, using the Haber process. General Crozier expanded these plants and TNT, picric acid, shell-loading, and powder-bagging plants were rushed to completion. The chief source of nitrates was Chile, and among the first attempts at inter-Allied cooperation was one to bring the Chilean government to allocate its full nitrate production to the Allies and the Americans. By early July 1917, smokeless-powder contracts aggregating some sixty-seven million pounds had been placed, but requirements were skyrocketing. In October 1917, however, General Crozier still believed the situation was manageable. In his *Annual Report* he stated, "The present capacity of the country for the production of both smokeless powder and military explosives is so large that . . . war requirements will necessitate only a comparatively small percentage of increase."

Unlike Crozier, Pershing understood the situation. On August 23, 1917, in another cable, he informed the administration that the smokeless-powder question had become an international issue requiring close consultation with French and British authorities. "In order to avoid calamity," he argued, the United States must supply not only its own forces with explosives and propellants, but also "about one half of the French requirements." In the same message Pershing stated that the Allies had reached the "absolute limit of manpower and any further augmentation of their military forces" could not be expected. It was therefore recommended, "that the United States furnish all powders and explosives needed for the present contracts with the French government" and that "the United States government prepare to furnish by December three hundred tons per day of powder for French consumption." Alerted by the Pershing cable, Secretary of War Baker requested that the WIB begin a study of the explosives situation. On November 22, 1917, the board announced that, as of October 1, 1917, the United States Army had placed orders for 67 million pounds of smokeless powder and the navy had contracted for 56 million, for a total of 123 million pounds for the first year of the war. Since September 1, 1917, the smokeless-powder requirements for 1918 for the United States and the Allies had grown to 1,016,748,000 pounds. The capacity of the plants in the United States had been expanded to 472 million pounds a year. If only American requirements were considered, capacity was sufficient, but if those of the Allies had to be met as well, there was a 50 percent shortfall. The report concluded, "It is not alone an Army or a Navy problem but a matter that affects the whole Allied cause, and we are of the opinion that we should take steps to double the output of every factory in the country."[34] What had been a controlled and rational program in April 1917 became by early 1918 an open-ended call for unlimited production of smokeless powder and high explosives. On July 16, 1918, Chief of Ordnance C. C. Williams announced that the American eighty-division program for 1919 would require 470 million pounds of smokeless powder over existing capacity, which was projected to be 1.1 billion pounds a year.[35]

In April 1917 the Wilson administration needed DuPont's capacity but had no use for its management. Secretary Baker was determined to keep control of industrial mobilization in the hands of the War Department, and his suspicion of DuPont at times bordered on paranoia. The feeling was reciprocated. Pierre DuPont writhed under charges that his patriotism was shaped by his profit margins, but there was no immediate political confrontation. Sufficient plant capacity was available to meet the relatively modest initial requirements of the AEF as forecast in June 1917, and DuPont assured the government that it could supply the anticipated requirements of both the army and the navy for the foreseeable future.

General Crozier favored some government capacity to act as a yardstick in dealing with private suppliers, and on his recommendation the army appropriations of 1916 had provided for expansion of Picatinny's capacity, funded construction of a new government powder plant, and proposed a public artificial-nitrate-generation facility. When the war began, the army plant at Picatinny immediately increased production to more than a million pounds of smokeless powder and other propellants a year, while the navy plant at Indian Head, Maryland, expanded in a similar way. Thus, when the United States entered the war, annual smokeless-powder production, including that of DuPont, was approximately 384 million pounds a year.

It seemed to be enough. In April 1917, General Crozier, responding to Secretary Baker's orders to prepare to supply an army of a million men to be deployed abroad at some indefinite time in the future and basing his estimates on the findings of the Treat and Kernan boards, ordered artillery rounds and small-arms ammunition on the basis of estimates of days of fire from the first two years of the European war. Neither the Ordnance Bureau nor the DuPont Company found the estimates beyond the capacity of American industry, but both assumed that the American effort would escalate incrementally, reaching its peak in two years. When the troops were ready, the guns and ammunition would be ready. At a meeting on April 15, 1917, Irénée DuPont told Frank Scott of the General Munitions Board that the DuPont Company "had carefully considered the government's forecast of their requirements and [was] prepared to meet them without interfering with our contracts with the Allies." Five days later, on April 20, Buckner and H. F. Brown of the DuPont Explosives Division declared that they were willing to accept contracts to ensure the initial smokeless-powder supply for the entire American army and navy. The Wilson administration, reassured that the nation could produce enough smokeless, announced that it had no intention of building new plants "where existing capacity [was] in excess of requirements." They were also assured by Scott that DuPont's prices were "lower than the present cost of manufacturing this powder at the army powder factory."[36]

By October 1917, however, April's optimism had evaporated. Maximum production in existing powder plants had been achieved and the changing military situation seemed to require rapid plant construction. General Crozier, acting without direct orders, told DuPont executives to be prepared for expansion and on his own initiative asked Pierre DuPont to build a new powder plant that could produce a million pounds of smokeless powder. Crozier's request posed a sticky problem. Acquiring smokeless powder was not simply a matter of going into the economy to purchase it, because there was no peacetime civilian demand for the product on such an enormous scale. Who would pay for an enterprise whose usefulness would only last for the duration of the war? Traditionally, the American government had expanded public capacity and relied on market forces to provide emergency supplies. Government subsidies were not unknown, and negotiated, sole-source contracts had been a part of previous procurement procedures. Advance payments had normally been used to help defray start-up costs, but the give and take of the contracting negotiations themselves had been counted on to provide protection for private stockholders and amortization for private resources committed to public production.

The DuPonts had little use for such traditional contracting procedures. An unfriendly administration could bring disaster on the company. To rely on arbitration by a government board or redress of grievances through a petition to Congress would tie the company up in litigation for years. That had been the unhappy fate of many small-arms companies after the Civil War. Only recently the board of directors had been informed that the Winchester and Remington firms had been badly hurt by following similar naive practices with their British and Russian small-arms and machine-gun contracts. DuPont was determined not make the same mistake. The company had been astute in its smokeless-powder contracts with the Allies, and it was going to be just as careful with the Wilson administration, which only months earlier had labeled them war profiteers. The resulting contract was not unique in the history of the connections between federal authorities and American industry. It can be argued that all that happened was that the practice of subsidizing private munitions plants and using government-owned machinery in those plants, which was not uncommon in the nineteenth century, was simply extended incrementally.[37]

There were to be two new facilities that would be government owned. The DuPont Company would operate the plants as the agents for the government. A profit of 15 percent was allowed for the construction and the overhead connected with that work. The company would manufacture the powder and the government would pay all costs of operation plus five cents per pound for all powder delivered and accepted. After all expenses were calculated, if costs were less than 44.5 cents a pound, the government would pay, in addition to the five cents a pound, 50 percent of the difference between that amount and the base price of 44.5 cents a pound. Thus, an incentive was given to the company to lower costs by sharing in the savings.[38] The clause that caused the most trouble was one that created a separate organization, the DuPont Engineering Company, which would limit DuPont liability and avoid the possibility of financial loss. The new company, not DuPont itself, would build the plants. The contract was signed in Washington on October 25, 1917, and DuPont took up options on land outside Nashville, Tennessee, and Charleston, West Virginia, and purchased the Betts Machine Company of Wilmington, Delaware, to produce the machinery for the new factories. Within a week, the DuPont Company spent or committed more than $3 million to smokeless-powder plant expansion.

In late October General Crozier, in a routine way, brought the DuPont contract to Secretary Baker for his signature. Crozier was no enemy of the DuPonts. Baker was. Indeed, he would soon launch a vendetta against Pierre DuPont that would affect the production of smokeless powder until the end of the war. Baker told Crozier that he would like to look further into the matter before he signed the DuPont contract and consulted Bernard Baruch and Daniel Willard of the WIB. The WIB was in some disarray at the time because of the recent resignation of its chairman, Frank Scott, and the two executives told Baker that a committee they had working on the powder situation was not yet ready to report. They indicated that they thought the DuPonts were charging too much for construction costs and for powder as well. They also complained that General Crozier had not bothered to consult them when negotiating the contract. Baker, as was his custom in such situations, consulted President Wilson, who told him to suspend negotiations until the WIB report was finished. On October 31, 1917, Baker wired Pierre DuPont: "I have just had presented to me the details of the proposed contract with regard to increased capacity for powder production. The matter is large, intricate and important. Do nothing about it until you hear further from me. Stay all actions under the order until I can acquaint myself thoroughly with all features of the matter."[39]

Baker already had the army cost figures from Picatinny, and Robert Brookings of the WIB went to the navy powder plant at Indian Head to get more figures on the costs of production. When, on November 7, 1917, Pierre DuPont went to Washington to talk directly with the secretary of war, Baker apparently told him that he believed the DuPont Engineering Company would make too much money out of the construction contract and that DuPont itself was overcharging the government for powder. The secretary of war was unimpressed by DuPont's attempt to explain the intricacies of corporate overhead to him and claimed, as did many other Wilsonian progressives, that a private firm working in the public interest should exercise "civic virtue" and make no profit of any kind out of the war. DuPont was deeply hurt and claimed Baker questioned his patriotism. This was not true, but Baker *did* question the powder maker's philosophy and values. The next day DuPont offered to turn all the construction plans over to the government and get out of the construction end of the contract completely. On November 14, 1917, he met with Baruch, Brookings, and ordnance officials. Although he offered to take a cut to 8 percent for the production contract and a reduced profit per pound for the powder contract, neither Baruch nor Brookings would agree. Crozier dolefully commented that, regardless of the argument, the government needed the powder and the only reliable source for construction and production was DuPont.

Baker was already seeking another solution. He began negotiations with the Thompson-Starrett Construction Company to build the powder plants for the government and called upon the WIB to give him some alternative to DuPont to make the powder. He received cold comfort from Willard, who was just about to accept the WIB chairmanship after two months of dillydallying, and wrote Baker on November 26, 1917, that DuPont was the only source available. Willard recommended that a new construction contract be negotiated with DuPont and suggested that it be a straight-cost plus fixed-fee contract, which would guarantee the company a profit of at least a million dollars. The cost of the powder itself could be periodically renegotiated and binding arbitration established to settle accounts at the end of the war. Baker, however, had talked to the president again and was adamant. He wrote to Louis J. Horowitz, with whom he was personally negotiating the Thompson-Starrett contract: "I have just come from the White House [and] I may tell you that we have made up our minds that we are going to win this war without DuPont."[40] Baker still had to deal with Willard and General Crozier, who persuaded him to meet DuPont one more time. On November 27, 1917, Baker presented the WIB contract to the angry powder maker who huffed off to Wilmington, where the DuPont board of directors turned it down. By this time the affair had become a matter of mutual trust, not money. After a last effort on December 10, 1917, Baker announced to the DuPont Company that the War Department had closed the smokeless-powder question: "It will not be reopened and . . . the Government [will] proceed directly in the matter."[41] The War Department pressed on with the Thompson-Starrett contract, and on December 15, 1917, Baker brought Daniel Cowan Jackling, a well-known mining engineer, into the War Department as director of explosives to run the smokeless-powder program under the oversight of Assistant Secretary of War Crowell.

The next month was a tangle of false starts and political complications. Jackling quickly saw that he needed DuPont experts to meet his goals. The capacities of the plants at Nitro, West Virginia, and Old Hickory, outside Nashville, whose construction he supervised, were only half a million pounds. He needed more capacity if he were to meet the requirements set down in the Bliss cablegram of December 14, 1917. Jackling persuaded Crowell to let him talk to DuPont again. By that time on the defensive and driven to distraction by congressional critics, Baker acquiesced to get some kind of construction going. On January 24, 1918, the Jackling contract with DuPont was concluded.

The provisions of the contract cannot be understood outside the congressional investigations of the War Department that were then taking place. Pierre DuPont, who had come to believe Baker was deranged, had been passing information about the powder contract to Senator George Chamberlain, who had been leading the charge against the secretary of war for more than a month. Baker was aware of the correspondence between DuPont and Chamberlain and in his testimony before the special Senate investigation committee labeled the DuPont Company profiteers. It took all the persuasive power of Elihu Root, who convinced DuPont that his political meddling was playing into the hands of the Wilson administration by creating "a feeling that the War Department [was] championing the cause of the plain people against big business," to quiet the powder king. The Jackling contract reflected the concerns of the company that Baker's accusations about price gouging might be actionable as well as the desperation of the administration that needed powder fast. Thompson-Starrett would continue to build the Nitro plant, while DuPont agreed to take over construction of the Old Hickory plant at cost plus half a million dollars and 3.5 percent of the final cost of the plant, not to exceed $1.5 million. The government would bear all costs of operation and pay DuPont 3.5 cents a pound for all powder accepted. The DuPont Company would receive a bonus of 50 percent of the savings if the overall costs of powder production fell below 44.5 cents a pound.[42] The whole program would continue to be under the supervision of the director of explosives.

Work got underway immediately and the government team at Nitro and the DuPont team at Old Hickory raced to get their plants into production. Friction between DuPont engineers and Jackling's supervisors at Old Hickory slowed construction and winter weather interfered. To complicate matters further, in mid-February 1918, just after Baker left for France on a fact-finding tour, War Department planners informed Jackling that powder production had to be expanded by another third, which meant that existing plants had to double their production and an additional half million–pound plant had to be built. Jackling, near despair, wrote Irénée DuPont on the February 24, 1918, soliciting his advice. The company's answer of March 1, 1918, revealed both the management's frustration with the government and its desire to find a way to end the insinuations about profiteering that had plagued the powder program for nine months. The letter read in part,

> You have explained to me the urgency of this work as well as the necessity of its undertaking by E. I. Du Pont de Nemours and Company. It is only this necessity that warrants our considering the burden. The latter is so great that the question of compensation is of less importance than the question of the saving of manpower, especially that of the administrative end of the business. I therefore urge upon you to arrange that the carrying out of this work may be placed in the hands of our company entirely without hindrance as to supervision and approvals. In return for this concession, we are prepared to place the question of compensation beyond possibility of criticism.

The contract would probably never have been signed if Secretary Baker had remained in Washington, but he was in France during March 1918, and assistant secretaries of war Crowell and Stettinius, assisted by Colonel Samuel McRoberts, formerly of the City Bank of New York, and Jackling conducted negotiations. The DuPonts had been operating on their own at Old Hickory since early February anyway, and the suggestion that they be given carte blanche merely formalized what had already happened. With Jackling's approval, the DuPont Engineering Company subcontracted railroad, motor road, housing, street-sidewalk, and sewer-line construction and pressed ahead. At the end of the first week in March, over more than three thousand men were at work at the Old Hickory plant. On March 23, 1918, after three weeks of negotiation with the War Department and after approval from the comptroller's office, the famous "Cost Plus One Dollar" contract between the government and DuPont was approved. The Old Hickory plant would be expanded to produce nine hundred thousand pounds of powder. The DuPont Engineering Company would be placed in absolute control of that operation, while the Thompson-Starrett group would build the plant at Nitro, West Virginia. The government would advance $18.75 million to pay all costs of construction and DuPont would receive one dollar for building the Old Hickory plant. All other parts of the contract were the same as the one negotiated on January 24, 1918. When Baker returned to Washington in mid-April 1918, the contract was a fact of life.[43]

Ground was broken for the Old Hickory factory on March 8, 1918, and the first powder was manufactured on July 2, 1918, three months ahead of schedule and two months ahead of the government-sponsored Thompson-Starrett plant at Nitro.[44] Immediate results were anticlimactic. The smokeless powder was not needed. DuPont did make substantial profits, but the fact that those profits were made, for the most part, before America entered the war passed unnoticed. The Wilson administration remained skeptical about DuPont. In 1930, during the War Policies Commission hearings, charges were made that DuPont had made exorbitant profits from the war. They erupted full blown in 1934 during the Nye Committee hearings when partisans, calling for public ownership of the munitions industry, testified that dupont was a "merchant of death," part of a vast international conspiracy of munitions makers that threatened world peace. Such charges against American business corporations, often in more subtle forms, have never disappeared from the political landscape.[45]

☆ ☆ ☆

By the end of the war, it was clear that General Crozier had been right. So had the members of the Treat and Kernan boards. Even under the best of circumstances, it would take between eighteen months and two years to achieve substantial artillery production. Less than 3 percent of contracts entered into by the Ordnance Department before mid-December 1917 were completed. Only the English model 1917 75 mm field gun and 8-inch howitzer programs made any real progress. French 75 and 155 mm carriages, limbers, and gun tubes lay about waiting for recuperators that would not be available for months. Production of spare parts kits was behind schedule. The 75 mm shell program was still unbalanced. There were 30,600,000 primers; 26,800,000 shell cases; 12,000,000 fuses; 13,900,000 shell castings; and only 10,900,000 boosters. Millions of pounds of unshipped, deteriorating, smokeless powder crowded the storage sheds at the new emergency production facilities. And once the guns and explosives were ready, no one knew where the shipping would come from to move them to France. At the end of the war there was little connection between ordnance production programs and military reality. Ordnance personnel agonized as the American army fought with foreign artillery and ammunition.[46]

CHAPTER 10

MOTOR TRANSPORT, TANKS, AIRCRAFT, AND COMMUNICATION EQUIPMENT

The belligerents fought the Great War with much equipment that was in either the first, fragile phase or in the second, volatile phase of development. Truck technology was volatile and had to be incorporated into a combat support system that remained dependent on animal power. Tanks were not technologically robust and were committed to battle before design and doctrine were fully developed. Aircraft, which were initially fragile, developed rapidly throughout the war, and doctrine changed as their technology became volatile and their military potential grew. Telephone communication was robust before the war, and the conflict catalyzed work on wireless radio telephones. Novel weapons and new technological developments, as usual, brought demands for exclusive branches of the service. During the war a chemical warfare service, a tank corps, a division of military aeronautics, and a motor transportation branch of the Operations Division of the general staff appeared. The war generated new connections within existing organizations and with emerging industrial enterprises.

☆ ☆ ☆

The Quartermaster Corps undertook its only real technological innovation during the war when it attempted to design and produce a group of standardized military trucks. Originally, five separate War Department agencies contracted with the automobile industry for trucks, and the only standard thing about them was their color.[1] All makes and kinds of trucks were hastily procured for the Mexican Punitive Expedition in 1916, and maintenance and spare parts problems plagued the enterprise. In 1917 there was simply no time to make other arrangements, and the supply bureaus placed orders for motor trucks wherever productive capacity existed. Simultaneously, work began on standard vehicles. There were to be as few categories as possible with as many interchangeable parts as feasible to minimize spare-parts problems.

The Quartermaster Bureau had worked since 1916 with the Society of Automotive Engineers (SAE) and the National Automobile Chamber of Commerce to develop a group of standard trucks. The relationship was a new cooperative one rather than the traditional one, which involved competitive bidding. A War Department board selected a development team that included representatives of the Quartermaster and Ordnance Departments and the automobile industry. During the summer of 1917, the team designed standard models for all military trucks, but only the Standard B three-ton "Liberty" truck ever went into production. It was a rear-wheel-drive noncommercial vehicle. All told, 164 separate contractors built the chassis and unit assemblies and the trucks were assembled at fourteen different plants. The assemblies and, to a limited extent, the parts of units of different makes were to be interchangeable. Quartermaster General Sharpe expected great things, but the project was plagued with difficulties from the start. Manufacturers, already loaded with contracts, preferred to build their own models. Parts and subunits from different companies would not interchange. Inspection was lax at assembly plants. Production was just getting underway at the armistice.

The United States Army used 274,000 vehicles, including 216 makes and models of cars, trucks, and tractors, in France during the war, and still AEF transport virtually collapsed during the Meuse-Argonne battle. Between 40 and 50 percent of the trucks were generally unavailable because of lack of spare parts. One noncommissioned officer testified after the war that "fields as large as five or six acres were stacked as high as buildings with spare parts. . . . We were trying to segregate them: in other words put Packard parts in one place, Ford parts in another, Dodge in another and Cadillac parts and so on. . . . There were so many parts that no one really knew what was there; there was no way of finding out." Another testified that he used boxes of magnetos to pave walks around a supply dump because nobody knew what else to do with them.

In the spring of 1919, there were just forty-one Standard B trucks in the whole First Army area in France. There were, however, many more in the United States, and they were causing all kinds of trouble. All Standard B truck contracts were canceled after the armistice and no civilian producers were interested in bidding on new ones. They wanted to sell the army their own commercial models. Nobody wanted to make spare parts either. There was no reliable source for any of the 7,500 parts that made up the truck. They had to be scavenged, and the Standard B plagued the War Department and the army until the Great Depression.[2]

☆ ☆ ☆

The tank was a product of the war. The British and French were building both light and heavy tanks and their uses were wedded to the challenge and response of the changing battlefield. By the end of 1916, more sophisticated battle tactics had replaced simple trench warfare. The Germans changed their dispositions after the battle of the Somme to create a defensive zone organized in depth. The new dispositions minimized German casualties and freed infantry for use elsewhere. The problem was how to break through the new defense in depth and bring about a return to open warfare. German tactics did give Allied forces some room for maneuver. Small units armed with improved weapons—grenades, automatic rifles, submachine guns, mortars, very light artillery—might combine with conventional artillery, tanks, and aircraft to cross the battle zone without prohibitive losses. The conventional wisdom was that the tank was a piece of mobile artillery to shoot infantry through the German defensive zone. More adventuresome thinkers insisted that it could become a vehicle of exploitation once the defensive zone was penetrated.[3]

Conditions were very much in flux when the Americans entered the war. The Ordnance Department had experimented with armored vehicles before April 1917, but, aside from some experiments with Holt and Caterpillar tractors to pull heavy artillery and conventional field tests of armored cars, little had been accomplished. General Pershing was no tank lover and considered it "simply an armored caterpillar-traction motor car." Although in November 1916 the American military attaché's office in Paris completed a study of armored vehicles, the report of the tank section on Allied designs and doctrine did not arrive in Washington until early May 1917. Meanwhile, the first AEF tank committee, composed of Colonel Fox Conner, Colonel Frank Parker, and Colonel Clarence C. Williams, wrote a report that reflected current Allied doctrine. They concluded that "the tank is considered a factor which is destined to become an important element in this war" and recommended that the AEF create a separate armored headquarters and acquire 1,500 light tanks and 375 heavy tanks.[4] The tank headquarters was established under the command of Colonel Samuel D. Rockenbach, and the AEF adopted Allied doctrine.[5]

In mid-August 1917, General Pershing ordered Colonel James A. Drain, a reserve ordnance officer and tank enthusiast with prewar manufacturing experience, and Colonel Herbert A. Alden, an engineer and former official of the Timken Axle Company of Detroit, Michigan, to discuss tank procurement with the British. There had been a running battle in the British war cabinet for months over the effectiveness of tanks, or, to be more precise, the effectiveness of Winston S. Churchill as minister of munitions. The controversy between the War Office and Churchill erupted at about the time the Americans arrived in London. Tanks, the War Office claimed, had failed on the Somme the previous year, and all the money spent on them had been wasted. It would be better to spend the money on guns and shells. Discussions continued during the desperate days following Caporetto and the Bolshevik coup. In November 1917 Drain and Alden joined the American delegation to the inter-Allied conference and were assigned, along with A. C. Stern, Churchill's tank expert, and Colonel E. O. Swinton, the father of the British tank program, to an Anglo-American technical committee to advise their civilian superiors on a proper program. The Americans were joined later by Rockenbach and his assistants, Lieutenant Colonel George S. Patton and Captain Elgin Braine. In the midst of the talks, British armored forces scored their first significant success at Cambrai and opposition to tanks suddenly evaporated in London. The question became not whether there would be more tanks, but how fast as many as possible could be procured. The American technical committee subsequently recommended that the United States continue to order the French Renault light tanks and the improved British Mark VIII heavy tanks.

The search for European production facilities began at once. Neither the British nor the French were willing to shift priorities from their artillery and airplane programs to tank production. They insisted that they could not provide tanks to the Americans, who would have to depend on their own factories for armored vehicles. In early December the technical committee recommended that a joint Anglo-American program be undertaken to produce the Mark VIII tank. General Bliss, after assurances from Thomas N. Perkins that American production of semifinished materials and engines was expanding at record speed, supported the idea and recommended to Secretary Baker that the project be attempted.[6] Secretary Baker approved and the Anglo-American Tank Agreement was signed by Ambassador Walter Hines Page and Arthur James Balfour on January 22, 1918. It was a singular document and took the form of an executive agreement. The parts of the Mark VIII tank were to be interchangeable and built by multiple contractors in the two countries. The Americans were to produce the engines, the starters, the clutches and transmissions, all the running gear, and all the electrical equipment. The British were to produce the armor plate, the structural members, track shoes and rollers, guns, machine guns, ammunition, and storage racks. The United States would replace all steel used by the British in the program with ship plate, ton for ton, on or about the same date the armor was delivered. The components were to be shipped to Chateauroux, France, where they would be assembled by workmen secured by the French. The assembly plant would be capable of delivering at least fifteen hundred tanks in 1918 and thirty-six hundred in 1919. In an emergency it should be able to assemble twelve thousand tanks a year.[7]

By the first month of the new year, the United States Army had a tank corps, a body of doctrine, and a production schedule for its armored equipment. Since August 1917 the American government had committed itself to a joint effort to produce at least fifteen hundred Mark VIII heavy tanks. It had also agreed to build forty-five hundred Renault "Six Tonners" by the end of 1918. That spring, fearful of British collapse, General Wheeler introduced a parallel Mark VIII tank program in the United States. He announced that the 1919 program made it necessary to build an additional fourteen hundred "All American" Mark VIII tanks in addition to those provided by the Anglo-American Tank Agreement. He did not add that not a single contract for tanks had been placed.[8]

Work on the tanks in the United States went forward under a cloak of secrecy. Alden, who returned to the United States in March 1918 to run the Mark VIII program, would not talk in public about his plans. Captain Braine, who had returned at the same time to head the Renault program, was equally uncommunicative. In September 1918, the director of the tank corps, Ira C. Welborn, a former infantryman, stated in his *Annual Report*, "[A]ll information relating to tank production is of a strictly secret nature [and] no statement bearing on this subject can be made at this time."[9] His reticence concealed a number of mistakes. Even as the Ordnance people promised the AEF that the first hundred Renault tanks would be delivered in April 1918, they had not received all the blueprints and had not even translated the French metric measurements on the ones they had. AEF planners did not understand the effects of design modifications on production. When Captain Braine returned from France with a list of modifications for the Renault tank, he expressed astonishment that his plan to change the turret system was greeted with dismay in the Ordnance Department.[10] There were few plants with room for new orders. Contracts had to be spread among firms that had done no army business, an entirely new source had to found for armor plate, and manufacturers were reluctant to take on such complicated propositions as the French Renault design. In addition, the Buta engine, which powered the American Renault, had never been mass produced anywhere. In March and April 1918, contracts were placed among twenty American manufacturers who claimed they had unused capacity. Manufacture and assembly of the Buta engine was turned over to the Maxwell Motor Car Company of Dayton, Ohio, while the C. L. Best Company of the same city and the Van Dorn Iron Works of Cleveland assembled the component parts.

Mark VIII production faced similar problems. More than seventy plants worked on the Anglo-American tank. The major problems were shortages of critical metals and Liberty engines. As the needs of the aircraft program soared, the tank project received a lower and lower priority. Finally, the whole program simply went sour.[11] An ordnance officer wrote after the war that, during the summer of 1918, ordnance inspectors were passing anything that even looked like a tank.[12] At an August 16 meeting of Washington division chiefs called by General Williams, the general mused, "Perhaps we have been slow in getting along in our tank program. We have been unfortunate in getting Liberty engines for the big tank. But the small tank has not come along as it should. [There is] not even yet a complete set of drawings of that small tank." When an officer remarked that there were no complete drawings for the Mark VIII either, Williams asked, "That means that not even a procurement order has been placed?" He was correct. Another officer claimed the Liberty engine was inappropriate for the "International Tank." Williams immediately exclaimed, "It is too late to change now even if we wanted to" and ordered the participants to "take up the matter of tanks and see that they are shoved along."[13]

The tank program was further complicated by the machinations of the Ford Motor Company. In the spring of 1918, Henry Ford faced a dilemma. Some of his resources were committed to the production of "Eagle Boat" submarine chasers for the Navy.[14] The company was building Liberty engines and Ford motor cars and trucks for the military as well as cars and trucks for civilian consumption. In May 1918, the WIB began to talk about formally curtailing civilian production and Ford, to avoid interference from Washington, sought a contract for a Ford tank to maintain full production. It is not clear whether the Ford design was to be a tracked cargo tractor or an armored combat vehicle. It weighed two tons and used mass-produced Ford components, including the Model T engine and the Ford planetary transmission. Using the Eagle Boat analogy, Ford argued that his company could use existing machine tools and production lines to build a combat vehicle from commercial parts at a price far below that of the Renault tank. The company guaranteed production in three months.

Ford apparently consulted no one in the military on design, doctrine, or production, but the situation in the spring of 1918 was desperate and the

Ordnance Department signed a contract for fifteen thousand of the untested machines. It was early August 1918 before Pershing's headquarters received the specifications for the Ford light tank. Several reached France in early October 1918, and after tests, AEF ordnance experts and the Tank Corps labeled them death traps. An ordnance committee reported that they were unsuitable for combat. They might have some use as tractors to pull 75 mm artillery, but they could not be used in combat "unless absolutely necessary." The news reached the United States shortly before the armistice and the contract was canceled. Of the 23,405 tanks on order in the United States on November 11, 1918, 16,015 were the Ford two- and three-man tanks that the AEF had declared useless.[15]

Reports on tank production were optimistic until September 1918. In May 1918 the Ordnance Department cabled that more than forty-four hundred light tanks had been ordered and delivery could be expected soon. In June, Williams promised twelve light tanks in September, one hundred in October, and monthly increments of as many as five hundred Renaults by early 1919. It was clear to Americans in France by June 1918, though, that they could expect very little armor from the United States. The inter-Allied tank committee reported that no significant deliveries could be expected from the United States until the summer of 1919. The AEF secured two battalions of heavy tanks from the British and two battalions of Renaults from the French for use in the battle raging on the Western Front. By autumn, even Washington admitted that no American tanks could be expected in France in the near future. General Rockenbach reported in 1920 that the plant for assembling Mark VIII tanks was not ready and that no Mark VIIIs had been delivered from the United States. A few Renaults arrived in October, but testing revealed that they were constructed of mild steel. One soldier put a pick axe through the front glacis of one and another fired a thirty-caliber round through another. Rockenbach, who had returned to the United States to become the new chief of the Tank Corps, labeled the equipment atrocious. "[The Renault] machines were so defective that it required an average of 225 hours per machine to put them into battle condition," he wrote. "It is an index of what might be expected of wartime production."[16]

☆☆☆

When they dealt with the airplane and its uses, the Signal Corps, the War Department, and the American industrial community faced entirely new problems of doctrine, design, and technology. The Americans knew neither what they wanted nor how to build or use it. When Secretary Baker announced in

October 1917 that the aircraft program was on schedule and that every contingency had been anticipated and provided for, he was already aware that the project was in trouble.[17] He began to understand just how deep that trouble was in early November, when accusations appeared that members of the CND and the Aircraft Production Board were taking kickbacks on aircraft engine contracts and that the members of the board were "a bunch of crooks."[18] A little later the sculptor John Gutzon Borglum, one of the early members of the American Aero Club, an organization of air enthusiasts, who had the ear of President Wilson, claimed he had discovered a conspiracy. In January and February 1918, Borglum, armed with a letter Wilson had given him in a lapse of good judgment, scurried about Washington insisting that the aircraft program was in trouble because of a corrupt bargain between the aircraft board and the American automobile industry. The objective, he claimed, was to concentrate control of the new product in the hands of a few car makers. Naming Colonel Edward A. Deeds of the Signal Corps one of the implementors of the Liberty engine program and Howard Coffin as coconspirators, Borglum demanded a congressional investigation. Although Borglum was quickly discredited, his charges precipitated a chain of events that brought on an investigation of the aircraft program by a congressionally authorized committee headed by Charles Evans Hughes.[19]

That the air program should first be described as a criminal conspiracy was understandable. What was difficult to believe at the time was that the experience with standardization and mass production of the leaders of the American automobile industry, who dominated the aircraft-production program, could really impede the production of sophisticated and effective aircraft. But it did. In an era of turbulent doctrinal and design change, attempts to use existing practices brought the delivery of obsolete, virtually useless aircraft to the American army in France.

The American program suffered from fragmented and ill-defined command, control, and procurement systems at home and abroad. Major General George Squier, who became chief signal officer in February 1917, presided over the program until the late spring of 1918. The aviation section of the Signal Corps controlled selection and design of military aircraft. Two civilian agencies, the National Advisory Committee for Aeronautics (NACA) and the Aircraft Production Board (APB) of the CND, headed by Howard Coffin, controlled production. It was on Coffin's advice that a joint army-navy technical board was created in May 1917 to rationalize aircraft production in the United States. The Joint Technical Board reported directly to the service secretaries rather than to their specific bureau or branch chiefs. In October 1917, Congress separated the APB from the CND but did not link it to the aviation section of the Signal Corps, where design authority rested.

To complicate matters further, in France Pershing separated the AEF air arm from the Signal Corps immediately and made its commander director of Air Service. It was not until the late spring of 1918, when aviation became a separate branch of the army, that a parallel organization emerged in the United States. Conditions were made worse by competition between Colonel William C. Mitchell, who was among the original members of Pershing's staff, and newcomers from the United States such as Benjamin Foulois and Colonel R. C. Bolling, who headed a special mission that arrived in France later in 1917 to make recommendations on aircraft selection. Many of the changes in numbers and types of aircraft coming from France resulted from the dithering between Mitchell, who wanted to substitute bombers for observation aircraft, Foulois, who wanted a balanced force, and Bolling, who was fascinated by long-range bombers. The equipment division in the aviation section of the Signal Corps at home exacerbated internal difficulties between design and production engineers and made decisions on types even more difficult to achieve.

The emerging civilian aircraft industry consisted of little more than a few jobbing shops like Curtis in Buffalo, New York, the Standard Aircraft Corporation of Elizabeth, New Jersey, the Thomas-Morse Company of Ithaca, New York, and the Wright-Martin Company of Los Angeles. None had manufactured more than ten airplanes a year before the war. Thus, by necessity, the airplane production effort was dominated by the automobile industry.[20] The automobile men were unaccustomed to working to the close tolerances required of aircraft manufacturers and were ignorant of the research, design, and development effort required to produce high-performance aircraft. Raw material shortages plagued the program. Spruce, airplane linen, and castor oil for engine lubrication had to be dragged out of an already overburdened economy. In the fall of 1917, all available machine-tool shops east of the Mississippi were commandeered to build the jigs and dies necessary to place the Liberty engine in production, incidentally setting the artillery production program back three months.

Obtaining training aircraft and engines was never a problem. Designs for the Curtis "Jenny" and the Standard trainer were frozen and the low-powered Curtis OX-4 engine was available in quantity. Combat aircraft, however, were a different story. The mania for standardization characteristic of American large-scale business enterprise and the peculiarities of functional industrial organization pressed by Taylorite managers delayed the program. By separating production and operations and placing design in the hands of production specialists, the War Department and, inadvertently, Congress made model modification and improvement virtually impossible. There was no organizational theory or experience available in the United States that incorporated the need for continuous qualitative changes with the requirement for quantity production. By the spring of 1918, the procurement program, which Baker had declared in place in October 1917, had become virtually incomprehensible. Meanwhile, Pershing's headquarters had even less understanding of the problems of aircraft production than they had of tank and artillery production. The AEF claimed that its responsibility ended with requisition, and filling its orders was a War Department responsibility.[21] Pershing's planners never understood the engineering changes their demands placed on industry at home. They ordered fighters, bombers, and observation planes in certain quantities one month only to cancel the order the next month. A month later the same planes would be reordered in completely different numbers. In the fall of 1917, the Bolling mission recommended production of the SPAD single-seat fighter, the Bristol two-place fighter, the DH-4 bomber/observation aircraft, and the Caproni heavy bomber. Then, in December, an AEF cable arrived in Washington indicating that the United States should rely on the Allies for single-seat fighters. The SPAD contract with the Curtis Company was canceled, and the company was told to concentrate on the Bristol fighter. In March 1918, the Bristol fighter contract was canceled. In February 1918, AEF planners again ordered SPAD single seaters. In April 1918, the military canceled that order and replaced it with one for SE-5As. First the DH-4 was ordered and then the DH-9 was substituted. Later the DH-4 was reintroduced and DH-9 production stopped. In January 1918 the Handley-Page two-engine bomber was ordered to supplement the Caproni. The air program was still chaotic and undefined at the end of the conflict.

The story of the Liberty engine—indeed, the story of aircraft-engine development in the United States during the war—can also be told from the perspective of the automobile industry. Howard Coffin was an automobile man first. Wedded to the mass-production techniques of an industry in which he was a pioneer and convinced of the effectiveness of the shop-management processes that he had helped create, Coffin believed that American car makers could produce an aircraft engine the same way they could produce an auto engine. It was not that he was unaware of the differences between the two—he was simply unimpressed by the difficulties that others claimed existed. The Liberty was designed by a team of engineers from the auto industry and the infant aircraft industry. Assistance came from the Bureau of Standards, while the working drawings were prepared by automobile engineers. Production was a team effort undertaken by the auto makers, with components made in various parts of the country and shipped to Packard for assembly. Later, the Ford Motor Company and the Lincoln Company undertook contracts to produce the engine. The shortcomings of the American mass-production system immediately became apparent. After the war, Benedict Crowell blamed them on sabotage, but they appeared too often elsewhere to make that charge credible. Crowell finally admitted that the American automobile industry was not equipped to produce complex aircraft engines.[22]

The Liberty was a good, contemporary engine—not as good, perhaps, as the Rolls Royce 360-horsepower Eagle, but a big, solid, conventional power plant. An amalgam of Packard and Hall-Scott experience, it was designed in the early summer of 1917 to meet the need for a 225-horsepower engine to fill 1918 requirements. By fall it was clear that more horsepower would be necessary, and the program was modified. The original engine had eight cylinders. In October it was redesigned as a twelve-cylinder engine and the horsepower increased to 425. It had a high power-to-weight ratio (it weighed 844 pounds—2.44 pounds to one horsepower) and displaced 1,649 cubic inches. The cylinders of the Liberty were set at a 45-degree angle, rather than the usual 60-degree angle, to reduce head resistance, give greater strength to the crank case, and eliminate vibration. The engine had coil ignition rather than the unreliable American magneto.

The Liberty, designated the standard engine for the American program, was long and narrow, which shifted the weight distribution and reduced maneuverability. Its long stroke and low revolutions were adequate for bombers and observation planes but could not provide the bursts of power necessary for effective fighter performance. Because it was assembled in several plants with parts from the entire auto industry, individual engines varied in reliability. Those assembled by Lincoln were the best, those from Ford were in the middle, and those from Packard were the worst. The engines required a great deal of maintenance and were expensive to operate. By using the Liberty instead of the original Rolls Royce engines in the DH-4, the Americans turned an exceptional airplane into a mediocre one.[23] The attempt by the automobile men to make the Liberty an all-purpose mass-produced engine with interchangeable parts was as much a cause for American fighter-production failures as the conflicting orders from the AEF. It was early 1918 before Signal Corps engineers ended their attempt to adapt the Liberty to the SPAD fighter and April 1918 before orders went to the Curtis Company to place the SE-5A, powered by a Wright-Martin–built Hispano-Suiza engine, into production.

Meanwhile, the effort to power the Bristol Fighter with a Liberty engine went on. The Bristol was considered the great hope for the 1918 campaign, and in December 1917 AEF planners called for the substitution of the Bristol for all single-seat fighters.[24] The first Bristol arrived in the United States in August 1917, and the Signal Corps designers began to rework the airframe to accept the American engine. The Liberty was heavier than the Rolls Royce Falcon III engine that powered the original Bristol and developed more than a hundred additional horsepower. The aircraft division completed the initial redesigning work in November 1917, and the aircraft board signed contracts with the Curtis Company for two thousand American "Brisfits." The first Liberty-powered aircraft crashed in January 1918, but the Signal Corps and Curtis refused to give up. The craft became less and less airworthy and every one of the twenty-six Curtis-built planes crashed during testing. In July 1918, after the expenditure of more than $6 million, the Bristol program was canceled. By powering the Bristol with the Liberty engine, the Americans had hoped to create a high-performance machine rather than a simple copy of another foreign design, and their gambit failed. At the end of the war, not one fighter aircraft built in the United States was in service.

It was not the Liberty engine, or any other technical issue, that caused delays in the heavy-bomber program. It failed for political reasons. The Italian government promised that it could supply adequate numbers of the three-engine Caproni Ca 42 triplanes to the Americans from their factories during 1917 and 1918, but Italian manufacturers failed to deliver. The Italians were reluctant to send blueprints and design experts to the United States and delayed discussions over patent rights for months. As a result, the Americans began a parallel program to produce a Liberty-powered Handley Page. It was July 1918 before the factories in the United States produced the first Liberty-powered test models of both airplanes, and none were delivered before the end of hostilities.

The history of the DH-4 was one of political expediency. The Dehaviland was a day bomber and observation aircraft. It was already obsolete in September 1917, and Colonel V. E. Clark, a member of the Bolling mission, recommended that the Americans produce the improved DH-9 instead. Rather than cancel the DH-4 program, authorities at home produced both airplanes until February 1918, when the DH-9 program was canceled to allow maximum production of the DH-4. Replacing the Rolls Royce Eagle engine with the Liberty proceeded with little difficulty, and mass production began. When the airplane reached France in August 1918, it was outclassed and its crews were massacred by roaming German fighter *Staffels*. Nevertheless, against the specific protests of the AEF Air Service, shiploads of DH-4s continued to arrive in France until the armistice.

There was a final irony to the story. The American decision to end production of the DH-9 proved ill advised. The British had great difficulty with the DH-9. The new Siddeley Puma engine was unsatisfactory and the DH-9 was inadequate in battle. Near the end of the war, however, the British installed several dozen 425-horsepower Liberty engines pilfered from the AEF in their DH-9s and the airplane immediately began to perform superbly. Arrived at completely by accident, the wedding between the Liberty motor and the DH-9 was made in aviation heaven. As the DH-9A, the plane served effectively for the rest of the war and remained in many national air forces until the end of the 1920s.

By the spring of 1918, it was clear that producing effective aircraft posed complex problems. NACA had played a critical role during the early months of the war, conducting practical research on design and screening inventions for usefulness. In October 1917, however, the National Research Council (NRC), which had broad obligations in other work, took the NACA under its administrative wing and downgraded the air research program. Meanwhile, major efforts in research and development were under way in the aviation division of the Signal Corps. In February 1918 the aviation people from the NACA were transferred to the science-and-research division of the Signal Corps, where their work was fused with that of other scientists working for the agency.

By October 1917, the Signal Corps had built an experimental factory at McCook Field, in Dayton, Ohio, and had established the Production Engineering Department (PED) in Washington. Lieutenant Colonel Clark, late of the Bolling mission, tested new domestic designs at the Ohio field while the PED expedited production of established types of aircraft. There was immediate conflict between the PED, the experimental factory, the science-and-research division, and the engineering division. By March 1918, three different organizations—the Signal Corps Division of Aviation, the NRC, and the APB, with only the most tenuous connections, were working on the same problems. Procurement of combat airplanes was in disarray, designers and production engineers were at loggerheads, and Congress, the public, and their superiors in the War Department were demanding results. Continuous changes in requirements from the AEF added more turbulence to plans that had been unstable from their inception. Control had to be established over production at home and requests from abroad.

The first move, one championed by Assistant Secretary Crowell, was to separate the Air Service from the Signal Corps. This would bring organization at home in line with organization in the AEF. Crowell really wanted an independent air force, but he succeeded only with the help of General William L. Kenly, formerly chief of the AEF Air Service, who had recently returned from France, in establishing a separate War Department Division of Military Aeronautics (DMA). Design and production problems were confronted in May with the creation of the Bureau of Aircraft Production (BAP) in the War Department, which absorbed personnel from the APB, elements of the joint technical committee and all the research and development people from the Signal Corps. By the summer of 1918, the BAP engineers were running things, and research and development was subordinate to production until the end of hostilities.

In August 1918, Secretary Baker appointed John D. Ryan of Amalgamated (Anaconda) Copper assistant secretary of war for air. Baker, who had previously supported Ryan for the chairmanship of the WIB, told reporters that the copper king now had "the responsibility of procuring and furnishing to the Army in the field all materials and personnel required for the Air Service and . . . supervision, control and direction over the Bureaus of Aircraft Production and Military Aeronautics with full power completely to coordinate their activities and carry out the air program." At the end of the month Ryan, under great pressure to make a production record, froze all aircraft designs until better information was available and left with Secretary Baker for an inspection tour to France.

During the summer of 1918, missions from the United States hounded the AEF. War Department groups were badly coordinated with scientific missions already abroad, with the technical section of the AEF Air Service by then commanded by Major General Mason Patrick, and with another board of AEF officers headed by General Foulois. Ryan was appointed too late to influence operations. By the time he had familiarized himself with the overall situation, the war was over and all that remained to be done was to count up the losses.[25] The system he inherited made the development of improved aircraft virtually impossible and the fact that a few American designs were about to enter production at the end of the war was remarkable.[26]

☆ ☆ ☆

General Squier may not have known much about airplanes, but he knew exactly the kind of electronic and communication equipment he wanted and how to get it. For years the chief signal officer had cultivated relations with the giants of the electronic industry. He was a friend and colleague to academics working on the cutting edge of research in the field. Communications technology was robust, and the existing scale of industrial operations was large enough that

Squier could provide modified American commercial equipment of adequate if not superior performance without the delays involved in producing unfamiliar equipment. The managerial and production skills were available and had only to be tapped, and the radio and telephone sections of the wartime Signal Corps looked like old-home week at Western Electric, General Electric, and the American Telephone and Telegraph Company.

The chief of signals was an apostle for electronics. After the war he rhapsodized about the role of communications and predicted that radio "lighthouses" would span the world, connecting ships, airplanes, and airships through a sophisticated system of "radio-telephony and telegraphy." He concluded that "such a perfect system will be the cheapest and most certain adjunct to effectively carry out the provisions of the League [of Nations] and will contribute to a better understanding between nations as will no other agency or instrumentality."[27] Perhaps Squier never thought of the airplane as anything but a vehicle to take a radio set into the air; this might explain how he managed to retain two different research-and-development systems in the Signal Corps, and why he never grasped that the same methods that effectively developed wireless, radio-telephones, rockets, unmanned aircraft, and ciphering machines could also be applied to airplanes.

Well-developed research-and-development laboratories had been a mark of Squier's tenure in the Signal Corps, and when the war began, he established similar American facilities in France. Colonel Edgar Russell accompanied Pershing to France aboard the *Baltic* and immediately determined that a Signal Corps research, development, and inspection organization should be established with the closest connections with the combat operations of the AFE. On advice from Russell, General Squier turned the selection of personnel over to J. J. Carty, of the American Telephone and Telegraph Company, who had only recently been commissioned a major in the Signal Corps. Carty scoured the country and brought together "a body of men . . . such [as] had never been gathered together. Inventors, professors, engineers, specialists in all forms of the art of signaling." From the moment the group reached France in the autumn of 1917 under the leadership of H. H. Shreeve, a former executive of the research division of the Western Electric Company, it was an effective operating unit. More than half of its enlisted men were university graduates, and its research operations were headed by physicist O. E. Buckley, who had been engaged in radiotelephone research at Western Electric before the war. Liaison with the British and French was consistently effective, and the research-and-inspection division and laboratory in Paris became the center of signal information for the AEF. Communication was maintained with the technical information section, service of supply in tours. "Finally," as Squier reported, "liaison with the War Department in Washington" moved smoothly "by means of officers who took with them working models of newly developed apparatus or up to date manufacturing information."[28]

The research-and-inspection division was dominated by Western Electric. Lieutenant Colonel H. E. Shreeve, a pioneer in radiotelephone technology, became the American representative on the Inter-Allied Board on Inventions, which began to meet in Paris in the summer of 1918. Unlike other AEF organizations that, until late in the war, were determined to run their business with little concern for the War Department, Signal Corps representatives in France created a reliable research-and-development loop between Paris and Washington that was reminiscent of the one built by Goethals between Panama and the General Electric laboratories in Schenectady during the canal-building days before the war.

Electronic production, invention, and technological innovation moved simultaneously. Through systematic testing and improvement, American wireless senders, radiotelephone, and land-line phone systems became the envy of the Allied powers. At Squier's direction the Signal Corps experimented with pilotless bombers and gave the first official encouragement to Robert Goddard in his work with rocket propulsion.[29] Squier was fascinated by code breaking and supported efforts to apply electronics to that age-old craft. Among the inventions investigated at his request was an electric typewriter of "the type wheel" model. A key disk was inserted into the machine that turned a message into "a miscellaneous lot of letters" that could be deciphered on another machine with a similar disc. A series of plugs connected to the disks could be changed "at will." The invention was in an embryonic stage, the chief of signals reported in 1919, and the single-disk system was inadequate. Despite all electrical changes, "there was a certain sequence to the letters and there was but little trouble in breaking the cipher if an expert was supplied with a number of messages written with the same key disk."[30]

It was shipping shortages, not production difficulties, that explained why so little American telephone and telegraph equipment got to France. In June 1917, as part of the general decision to rely on the French for support for the first year of the war, Squier announced that standard telephone and telegraph equipment would be provided by the French and only experimental equipment would be built in the United States. French supplies fell far below demand, and in the spring of 1918 large orders were placed in the United States for immediate shipment and delivery of standard American telephones to the AEF. Relations between the Signal Corps and the manufacturers were so good that, once clearances were secured from the WIB and the priorities board, production moved fast; however, when two merchantmen loaded with Signal Corps equipment were torpedoed and sunk with the loss of all stores in May 1918, the supply program was set back many months. Increased shipment of troops and the demands of the eighty-division program increased signal requirements by more than 300 percent, but Squier argued in 1919 that the connections between the Signal Corps and its suppliers were so good that the increases posed few problems. "Every available telephone manufacturing concern in America [was] given an order for the telephone equipment he was best able to produce," and by the end of the war the Americans had replaced French equipment from American sources. France and Belgium—and, later, the invaded territories of Alsace-Lorraine and Germany—were covered by a "network of American telephones, American in manufacture, in installation and operation. . . . The telephonic communications . . . supplied by the Signal Corps was one of the influential factors in the winning of the war."[31]

Squier understood that electronic research and development had to be separated from production. The chief of signals farmed out development contracts among a number of companies for problem solving and, after a time, let the production contracts to quantity producers. There was a general agreement among the scientists and manufacturers on the objectives to be attained. Research specialists in and out of uniform already knew each other and spoke the same language, and wartime developments had practical postwar applications that were understood by all involved. Scientists from Western Electric and the Army Signal Laboratory in Washington cooperated to develop the first inexpensive, mass-producible vacuum tube, which, in turn, made possible other developments in radio technology and laid the foundations for the postwar American radio broadcasting industry. The prospect of cash concentrated business minds wonderfully and substantial gains were made in radio-direction equipment as well as in radiotelegraph instruments.

The great communications breakthrough of the war came with the advancements in wireless telephone technology. The Signal Corps was responsible for the development of such devices for both tanks and aircraft and research-and-development breakthrough in one meant progress in the other. Work on the aircraft radiotelephone began in the Western Electric laboratories before the war, and in August 1917 a Western Electric man went to Paris and contacted the newly established Signal Research and Inspection Division of the AEF. Using the newly improved but still-experimental vacuum tubes, they demonstrated the possibilities of aircraft voice radio to skeptical field officers. Meanwhile, at Dayton, Ohio, the army tested Western Electric experimental sets and demonstrated them for representatives of the War Department and the Allies. It was there that the famous message, "Hello, ground station! This is plane number one speaking. Do you get me alright?" was heard and skepticism turned to enthusiasm. Two days later the airplane radiotelephone was used to direct an artillery shoot at Fort Monroe, Virginia, with notable success.

The Western Electric radiotelephone went into production at the company plant in Chicago. The equipment was standardized and various equipment problems, including the design of a lightweight, streamlined dynamo, were solved. In February 1918, quantity production began, and on June 1, 1918, Major General Kenly, the chief of the newly created Air Service, attended an aircraft review that was entirely directed by voice wireless radio. Development continued during the summer of 1918 at Lake Charles, Louisiana, and in October airmen trained in voice radio began to arrive in France. None, however, was destined to test his training in combat. It was mid-November 1918 before the first mass flight of two hundred training aircraft directed by radiotelephone occurred in San Diego.

In 1922, John J. Pershing, by then chief of staff of the army, named Major General George Squier one of the great technicians and inventors in the United States Army. He also called him the least effective administrator in the War Department. Yet this eccentric man brought able people in the scientific and engineering communities together in a successful technological organizational effort and set the agenda of the American electrical industry for the next twenty years. Squier's successful communications programs could have become models for many postwar research-and-development projects in the army.[32]

CHAPTER 11

DIGESTING THE WAR EXPERIENCE, 1919–1940

The Wilson administration can be forgiven for overstating the American achievement in the Great War. Triumphalism was the language of the hour, and, on one level, the War Department had done well. From just a little more than five thousand officers and a hundred thousand enlisted men in 1916, the army expanded twentyfold. The National Guard was reorganized and more than 1,500,000 conscripts absorbed without any radical loss of military cohesion. In the late summer of 1918, the army included more than 130,000 officers and roughly 2,500,000 men. Between June 1917 and November 1918, in excess of 2,000,000 men with their small arms sailed to France, making it possible for President Wilson to bring the Allies to accept the United States as an equal partner in the war against Germany and accord it equal status in the peace negotiations about to begin. The Americans made up their deficiencies in automatic weapons, artillery, tanks, aircraft, and other equipment by forging international agreements with the French and British governments, and they participated in an unprecedented effort to combine the military and economic resources of the Allied and Associated Powers in a joint war program, creating an incipient North Atlantic economic organization. Battlefield events drove inter-Allied cooperation. As the military situation darkened in 1917 and early 1918, cooperation grew. As it improved during the last summer and autumn of the war, it deteriorated. The experiment was very much in the process of becoming when the war ended.

Secretary Baker proved an adroit manager and an able representative of President Wilson and his policies. Chief of Staff Peyton C. March consolidated power temporarily in the general staff, and, by the autumn of 1918, the autocratic George W. Goethals at the PS and T had secured a measure of cooperation from the bureau chiefs, but continuous organizational turbulence still made accomplishing the simplest administrative tasks difficult. The War Department with its prewar organization could have managed the original thirty-division program, but the vast military expansion undertaken during the late autumn and early winter of 1917–1918 and the requirements of the eighty-division program of the summer of 1918 unhinged the groundwork laid the previous year. By November 1918, supply and procurement programs were piled one upon another. Warehouses and docks were crammed with equipment and subsistence. Plants were filled with half-finished trucks, tanks, airplanes, and artillery. Depots and arsenals were heaped with millions of rounds of deteriorating ammunition. Shipping was still short, and the Americans stuffed the vessels they had with incomplete artillery, unfinished trucks, and machine guns without tripods just to fill cargo space, while the army camps at home and the troop transports that sailed for France were packed with newly drafted, influenza-racked soldiers. Brigadier General Hugh Johnson stated later, "It is my firm conviction, supported by accurate information and by the opinions of other men, that had the war continued two months longer there would have been a serious disaster in the supply of our Army. I think it was the finger of God that saved this government from the most terrible cataclysm that ever overtook the nation."[1]

At the armistice connections within the army and between the War Department and industry were still disjointed and often ineffective. Those relationships that could have been cemented and even possibly integrated into a reorganized system had not yet had time to appear. There was great reluctance in the administration to accept all the implications of the emergency, and the War Department, unwilling to lose control to the civilian wartime agencies and suspicious of the business community, was still resisting the creation of any kind of formal coordinating and policy-planning agencies. In any case, the Wilsonians refused to tip the fulcrum of power any further than was absolutely necessary. President Wilson and Secretary Baker still resisted changes that might modify in unforeseeable ways prevailing domestic American social and governmental conventions; as a result, the army, the navy, the State Department, the Treasury, the Food Administration, the Railroad Administration, the WIB, the WTB, and the Shipping Board conducted the war through temporary joint committees. The coercive power of the federal government had expanded, though, and illusions of voluntarism were eroding. If the war had continued into 1919, the WIB might have become something more than an agency to manage traffic, and President Wilson's war cabinet might have extended its power. Very much a nineteenth-century consultative vehicle at the time, it had been begun to meet in the spring of 1918 "to keep together and obtain a 'birds eye view' of the [war] situation."[2] It included the heads of independent emergency agencies, the secretary of state, and representatives from the War and Navy departments. It could have become a kind of national security council, absorbed the CND advisory staff, curbed the unrealistic demands of the army, and restrained the massive overmobilization then in progress. The War Cabinet had neither prescribed powers nor a separate staff, and by December 1918 the emergency government was beginning to decompress and dissolve.[3] In February 1919 the Emergency Fleet Corporation submitted a report that described the situation at war's end: "If we had in the War Industries Board a Director of Production, charged with the responsibility of seeing that all industries producing war materials for the Government were producing in proper quantities and at equal speed to suit the needs of the General Staff, . . . some real results would have been achieved. As it was the several departments of the government arrived at some form of casual cooperation that most imperfectly met the needs of the situation."[4]

☆ ☆ ☆

In 1919, without the pressure of a national crisis and with no consensus about the postwar role the United States should play in the world, debate began over the postwar organization of the military forces of the republic. Peyton C. March and John J. Pershing, both of whom retained traditional perceptions of themselves as commanding general, still held forth in their separate headquarters in Washington and at Chaumont, and most of the other wartime actors were still in place. All the concerned pressure groups—the National Guard, Congress, antimilitary and pacifist organizations, interested business and labor groups, scientific management experts—exerted their influence on army legislation. Inside the War Department, political brawling between the bureaus and the general staff intensified. Unresolved military-bureaucratic conflicts, controversies of the war period, personal jealousies, and battered feelings fueled the anger that was often directed exclusively at General March. What dedicated men would endure in war, they would not tolerate in peace, and March, who always insisted that he had no time for personal feelings or even courtesy, simply did not understand Napoleon's maxim, "War, like government, is a matter of tact."[5] With little agreement inside the War Department or among leading civilians who had participated in the war emergency, the tendency was to reject radical change and merely to modify traditional policies in the light of recent experience.

For more than a year Washington was a veritable tower of Babel. The debates began with March's proposals for a postwar reorganization of the army and the War Department. He had begun to think about permanent military policy during the summer of 1918 and had ordered the War Plans Division to prepare appropriate proposals for his consideration. After radical revision by War Department advisers and the addition of a modified form of universal peacetime military training suggested by Colonel John M. Palmer Jr., an army reorganization plan was introduced in Congress in the spring of 1919 as the March-Baker Bill. It proposed a revolution in American military policy. The power of the chief of staff was clarified, supply was permanently concentrated in the PS and T, and the bureaus were brought under the control of the general staff. The proposed legislation called for an expansible regular army of a half million men supported by federally controlled reserves. Although March insisted that the National Guard would continue to play an important military role and that the universal military training provided in the bill was only to familiarize potential soldiers with army life, the legislation raised the hackles of guardsmen as well as those who believed a citizen army was a surer defense for the republic than a large standing force.

The March-Baker Bill never had a chance. Congress was fed up with "the damned Army" in general and Peyton March in particular. Pershing, still in France, was unhelpful and waited quietly to make his views known. The bureau chiefs were in rebellion. With some justification, they labeled the PS and T a grotesque, inefficient, overcentralized monstrosity. Colonel Palmer accused March of betraying the idea of a citizen army with his Uptonian emphasis on a large standing army. National guardsmen refused even to listen to any plan that threatened their position as the official reserve force.

The connections between the combat arms and the War Department supply, technical, and logistical agencies were also examined. Benedict Crowell, who was the most influential of the wartime associates of Secretary Baker, insisted that all supply matters should be separated from the general staff and turned over to an assistant secretary of war. George Goethals wanted a separate militarized supply staff with its own permanent cadre of uniformed specialists in design, production, and procurement. Businessmen like Bernard Baruch and soldiers like Hugh Johnson insisted that an independent civilian agency similar to the WIB should control national emergency-mobilization policy and participate in war planning. The conflict had been brewing since the 1880s, but the issues were catalyzed by the war. For a year, members of Congress debated whether a hundred years of military policy should be cast aside and a new course based on conditions brought on, in part, by World War I should be adopted. Some reformers, demanding root and branch reorganization, insisted that the remaining parts of the nineteenth-century military system be abolished and a new model corporate "American War Machine" be created. Others insisted that the war had been a mere episode rather than a harbinger of the future. Very few really believed world conditions had changed so completely that extreme reconstruction was required. The National Defense Act of 1920 reflected traditional military and civilian attitudes and resembled the March-Baker-Goethals proposals as closely as the Washington Conference Treaties of 1922 did the Covenant of the League of Nations.

The new legislation amended the basic act of 1916. It rejected a large expansible army and compulsory peacetime military training. It limited the army to 280,000 men and affirmed the National Guard as the primary reserve of the republic. It continued the Reserve Officers Training Corps and strengthened the federal volunteer enlisted- and officer-reserve system established in 1916.[6] The legislation put an end to one major nineteenth-century conflict by making it clear that the president commanded the army through the secretary of war and that the chief of staff took his orders from them.[7] In a startling change, Congress relinquished its power to micromanage the peacetime structure of the army and gave the War Department, within the constraints established by the new Bureau of the Budget, control over its own financial priorities. In 1921, on General Pershing's order, a board headed by General James G. Harbord reorganized the general staff. There were five divisions: G-1 (personnel), G-2 (intelligence), G-3 (operations and training), G-4 (supply), and a War Plans Division (WPD). Finally, in a move that seemed to meld the offices of chief of staff and commanding general, the Harbord reorganization reestablished the Civil War Grant-Halleck connection. The chief of staff would take the field as commanding general in an emergency with the WPD acting as his general headquarters staff (GHQ), while a deputy chief of staff would stay behind in Washington to provide all necessary support. The reorganization pleased Pershing. As long as the commanding general of the armies of the United States and his comrades remained on active duty and there was only one front, it might even work.[8]

The bill reinforced the drive for professional and cultural homogeneity by retaining a single promotion list, asserting, at least legally, that all army officers, regardless of speciality, were soldiers of the republic. It assigned branch chiefs to the infantry, the field artillery, and the cavalry, giving the combat arms equal access, with the other bureau chiefs, to the centers of power in the War Department. It was a good idea in theory; however, traditional branch competition, in large part because of faulty personnel selection, made critical doctrinal communities of interest hard to develop, and in practice it proved ineffective. A comprehensive training-and-doctrine directorate in the new operations and training division (G-3) of the general staff could have brought the various interest groups together and compensated for branch parochialism, but that never seemed to have crossed anyone's mind. A war council like the one abolished by General March in the spring of 1918 reappeared in the 1920 legislation and might also have been a useful connecting agency, but there is no evidence that anyone was interested in exploring its possibilities.[9]

The debates over the future organization of the War Department supply system raised issues about relations with the business community, which were still resonating at the end of the century. General March, General Goethals, and their associates, including, at least at first, Hugh Johnson, were convinced that the PS and T should replace the supply and technical bureaus with a single, functionally organized agency. March believed that the military should supervise civilian economic mobilization and should be under the exclusive control of the general staff. Goethals thought that such an organization, though under the command of a military man, should be separate from the general staff and have its own experts in procurement and production. Assistant Secretary Crowell had a quite different agenda. He wanted to separate the business and military functions of the War Department and turn the direction of all supply matters over to a new civilian undersecretary of war with broad corporate experience.[10] When asked whether he believed the bureaus had really broken down during the war, however, Crowell replied, "No, I do not. I feel quite strongly the other way." Speaking of the work of the Quartermaster Department and Quartermaster General Henry Sharpe, Crowell continued, "I was very close to that and there was no breakdown in that department. . . . But there would have been . . . because the work of the Quartermaster's Department as it was organized when we went into the war was too great for any one man to administer."[11]

Secretary of War Baker was ambivalent about the future. He understood the cultural complexity of the War Department and had never been happy with the militarized command-and-control system favored by March and Goethals. He continued to distrust Crowell. Baker's management style simply did not fit the contemporary managerial wisdom. When he testified on army reorganization in 1919 before the Senate Military Affairs Committee, he stated,

> That is the way it always is in life. In the War Department, which is a coordinative War Department under one supreme head, you have a Chief of Staff acting under the Secretary of War, who controls all the branches, and yet the rivalries and class feelings between the Cavalry and the Infantry and the Artillery are as old as military affairs, and you will find them disposed to

smuggle their secrets away from each other and to improve their arm and to press the advantages of their particular mode of fighting. It is perfectly true and in the Air Service and between the Army and Navy, it is human.[12]

In organizations, he continued, people had to see that their special interest lay in cooperation and in assuring the success of the mission. The prewar system had its flaws, but Baker preferred such a consultative model with the possible permanent addition of a war council, similar to the one created in December 1917, to a hierarchical corporate organization such as March proposed. It was also apparent that Secretary Baker was unenthusiastic about Crowell's plan to place an industrialist in charge of supply and procurement. Although he was not opposed to creating an undersecretary of war, he was opposed to assigning statutory duties to the position. Baker wanted the utmost flexibility for the secretary of war and claimed Crowell's idea was "inelastic" and interfered with the power of the secretary of war to design missions and assign duties as he saw fit.[13] Baker was also concerned about the complex nature of the contemporary professional military. When questioned about the status of the Ordnance Bureau and the effectiveness of the short detail system that had caused so much trouble before the war, Secretary Baker recalled that the Ordnance Department

makes what the other soldiers use and you have a controversy in the Army all the time between the user of the weapon and the maker of the weapon. The user says that "The man that makes it is a manufacturer and he knows nothing about what I am going to do with it and therefore he must make it the way I want it." The manufacturer on the other hand says, "These fellows in the field have no technical knowledge; they do not know a good weapon; my duty is to give them a good weapon." That was the controversy between General Crozier and General Wood. It is a controversy as old as my researches into the history of the War Department. As an actual fact it is not a personal controversy; but General Crozier says I know a good machine gun: that is my business. I am a technical mechanical expert and I know a good machine gun. Gen. Wood says, "The guns you send me may be ideal from a mechanical point of view, and theoretically, but they do not work. I want a gun that will work."[14]

Things were not going to get any better, he concluded. The army was going to have more men in all the scientific corps "who are scientists and technicians and nothing else, . . . men who design 16-inch guns and who cannot fire a rifle."[15] Cooperation would be the key to the future success of the army, and that could be secured only by sensitive consultation and careful coordination. The chiefs of the supply and technical bureaus supported Baker and requested that control be restored to traditional authorities. They were willing to redistribute production and procurement among themselves to rationalize the expanded technological, logistical, and supply requirements of modern war. They were even prepared to redefine specifications for items of general issue to the army and reassign their exclusive procurement to single agencies in the interest of economy and efficiency, but they vigorously attacked any proposals that turned control over to businessmen or made statutory changes that reduced their power and position.

The 1920 legislation clarified and strengthened the position of the chief of staff, abolished the PS and T, and restored the power of the bureau chiefs. On Crowell's advice, however, the coordinating power of the secretary of war's office was expanded and responsibility for industrial planning was placed in the office of an assistant secretary of war. Congress preferred to jerry-build temporary agencies like the WIB if another emergency arose. The joint army-navy planning board was reinvigorated, and a new army-navy munitions board was created in an optimistic move to secure some coherence in any future industrial mobilization. A section of the National Defense Act formally encouraged the assignment of young officers to universities for advanced study and the Army Industrial College was established in 1923. Under the direct authority of the assistant secretary of war, the mission of the Industrial College was to improve communication between the military, the corporate, and the academic communities. An important formal organizational connection that replaced previous informal relationships, it was the first institution of its kind in the world and offered "a unique opportunity for full time study and investigation of the basic industrial, economic, political, administrative and other aspects of harnessing national resources in modern war."[16]

Many military men were unimpressed by the new legislation. They criticized all the plans, whether they came from civilians like Crowell, soldiers like March, or bureau heads like Goethals. They had grave doubts about what they perceived as the artificial separation of industrial mobilization from the planning and conduct of war. They claimed that the military must control industrial mobilization and that the coordinating agencies within the War Department, as well as those connecting the army with the navy and the civilian economy, would prove inadequate. In a lecture at the Army War College in 1922, Colonel William D. Conner, who had been Pershing's G-4 in France, claimed that the control of supply should be centralized and its operations decentralized. Procurement should be rationalized so that one agency purchased all particular items for the army. Control should be in the hands of army officers.[17] A little later another disgruntled ordnance officer wrote that the failures and difficulties of the war were being covered up by special interest groups intent on advertising their own achievements.[18] In 1919, more than a year before the compromise of 1920, James R. Douglas, a young Ph.D. in political science from the University of California at Berkeley who had been a member of the PS and T during the war, wrote,

> It is vital to the efficient organization of the army and its proper preparation for wartime burdens that some sort of supply directing agency be continued [to] direct, supervise, and coordinate under the Chief of Staff and the Secretary of War, the activities connected with the supply of the army. It is essential that this fact be recognized by Congress when it takes up the task of military reorganization. All prejudices should be laid aside. The principle of centralized control and supervision and decentralized administration and operation is coming to be accepted as unassailable even by the chiefs of the supply bureaus themselves no matter what disagreements they may have as to its manner and methods of execution. The United States will be facing many problems during the next few years. No one knows how great a part the army will be called upon to play in meeting these problems. The size of the army, no matter what world conditions may augur to the contrary, will be small. Small in size, it should be organized in such a way most approaching perfection, on a line capable of immediate expansion when war shall come. Experience, one of the few factors capable of salvage from the wreckage of the present war, points unquestionably to a centralized system of control of army supply.[19]

By 1930, however, whether, as March counseled, supply should be controlled exclusively by the general staff or, as Goethals and Crowell believed, it should be separated from the general staff and controlled by a special cadre of War Department procurement and production experts, most soldiers believed that supply was too important a matter to leave to businessmen and industrial managers. Command must rest with the military. In 1936, General James G. Harbord clearly defined what he believed was the cultural divide between soldiers and industrialists and spoke for many in the military when he wrote about the connections between the War Department and the corporate business community:

> The impelling force behind a civilian corporation is to make something for as little money as possible, and to sell it for as much money as possible, thereby leaving a margin of profit for the shareholders. The impelling force

behind a military corporation [is] to get a certain thing to a certain place at a certain time. Money [is] of no consideration except as it might be a means to that end. . . . [It is] the function of Big Business to offer its services to the military to do what it [is] told by the military, to give advice when requested, but to abide by the decision in case its advice [is] not accepted. [It is] the height of folly to propose any scheme by which a civilian business man, no matter how brilliant, should dictate methods to the military, whether it be methods of conducting combat operations at the front or methods of supplying troops from the rear.[20]

But everyone seemed to agree that the days of separate spheres and parallel paths were over and that modern organizational relationships were emerging in the War Department, which would be able to meet any challenges the country would face in the future.

☆ ☆ ☆

Interwar chiefs of staff, who were all combat officers, were loath to give up nineteenth-century command perspectives. After all, Pershing was the general of the armies of the United States as well as chief of staff. John Hines, Charles Summerall, and Douglas MacArthur harbored similar attitudes and, holding military managers and technicians in low esteem, treated them more like expert civilian advisors than fellow soldiers actively engaged in military affairs.[21] Retiring in 1930, Summerall stated that the failure to consolidate command and control of supply and logistics under the chief of staff in the 1920 legislation would bring difficulties similar to those encountered in 1917 and 1918.[22] General Summerall could only see one way to achieve his purposes. Like March and Pershing, he insisted on a single hierarchical command system with supply under a uniformed assistant chief of staff.

The Harbord Board created a complex division of labor between the supply section of the general staff (G-4) and the using arms, each of which had its own chief who was responsible for weapons and doctrine in his own branch and, in cooperation with other branch and bureau chiefs, controlled the development of army combined-arms doctrine. The general staff set requirements while the supply and logistical bureaus designed, tested, and issued equipment in conjunction with the office of the assistant secretary of war, which handled the business aspects of military procurement. The new Industrial College brought top leaders in the army and industry together to consult and to familiarize supply officers with procurement and distribution problems, enhance awareness of common problems, and clarify in the minds of soldiers what the civilian economy could and could not do in an emergency. The problems lay in implementation in the face of reduced funding. There was no ten-year rule as existed in Great Britain, but, as far as allocation of resources was concerned, there might as well have been one. The engineers, who were in the best financial condition, continued their prewar connections with the civilian sector through their coast-defense mission and their separate river and harbor budgets. The Ordnance Department and the Quartermaster Corps retained their arsenals and depots of production, but the disposal of surplus equipment and clothing, much it obsolete and of inferior quality, plagued both departments for more than a decade. Clothing production at the Philadelphia quartermaster depot temporarily ended. The gun factory and the small-arms facilities at Springfield and Rock Island again became mere jobbing shops. The Signal Corps, designated a combat arm in the 1920 legislation, maintained its laboratory for research and development and continued its connections with the civilian telephone, telegraph, and radio industries. And all the bureaus benefited when a number of civilian business executives, many of them highly placed, chose to accept commissions in the Officers Reserve Corps.[23]

The National Defense Act placed responsibility for procurement planning and industrial mobilization in the office of the assistant secretary of war and responsibility for military planning in the office of the chief of staff. Connections rested on a system of interbranch consultative committees in the office of the assistant secretary of war, which included representatives of all concerned bureau and combat arms, and the office of the chief of staff. In each case provisions were in place to add representatives from industry when appropriate. Designation of types of equipment, priority of development, adoption, and issue rested with the using arms and services. Each of the bureaus organized war-plans sections, but, without any immediate outside threat, they were hindered by public inattention and congressional underfunding. Formal connections with the using arms were time consuming and fraught with administrative pitfalls, but they formalized the nineteenth-century system, connecting consumers, designers, and producers far more intimately than they had been before 1917. Although procurement still rested with the individual supply bureaus, the assistant secretary's office cleared all purchases.

A most innovative approach to problems of research and development and consultation was made through the creation of technical committees in each supply bureau composed of representatives of the chief of staff's office, the assistant secretary of war's office, and all concerned bureaus, services, and combat branches, with provision for representatives from the industrial sector when appropriate. A War Department technical committee resolved any differences that could not be ironed out formally in those bureau committees or informally between the chief of staff and the assistant secretary of war. All requests for new or improved equipment went first to the appropriate bureau technical committee. If the request was considered worth pursuing by the members of the technical committee, it was referred to the chief of staff for a statement of need. Upon favorable action by the chief of staff, the item was placed on the design-and-development list of the branch of service responsible for its issue to the army. Under the supervision of the branch technical committee it moved from design to development to field testing. Representatives from concerned industries were formally consulted regarding the feasibility of production. If the reports were favorable, a recommendation for adoption as standard equipment went forward from the issuing branch to the secretary of war, who placed it on the War Department procurement-priority list pending availability of funds. A War Department coordinating committee resolved differences that could not be ironed out formally or informally between the chief of staff and the assistant secretary of war. The technical committee system, though cumbersome, was a real improvement over prewar practices.[24]

Nevertheless, the technical committees lacked a center where issues involving ideas and weapons could be resolved and new technology integrated into fighting doctrine. If there was doctrinal agreement, results were good; if there was disagreement, results were mixed and often ineffective. The artillery program, based on the recommendations of the 1919 Ordnance Department Calibers Board, the Westervelt Board, and characterized by robust technology and relatively stable doctrine, was a qualified success, whereas tank development, carried on in the midst of volatile technological change and divisive doctrinal debates, left much to be desired.[25] A most significant success for the new system was the creation of a fleet of standardized trucks by the Quartermaster Corps. The truck program also revealed that, although the traditional players from the days of separate spheres and parallel paths—using arms, technical bureaus, civilian manufacturers, and their congressional friends—were still very much in the game, they could find ways to consult effectively and achieve critical connections when a well-understood community of interest existed.[26]

Another significant innovation occurred after 1926, when the new Army Air Corps developed its own unique system of research, development, and procurement, and singular connections with the aircraft industry. Historically, both the army and the navy secured their arms and equipment from a mixed system of public and private production facilities. Aside from the short-lived naval aircraft factory, such a public-private mix of producers never developed for aircraft. In an understandable thrust to encourage civil aviation, the authors of the national-defense legislation of the early 1920s decreed that no public aircraft-production plants paralleling army armories and naval shipyards would be created. The uniformed military would establish doctrine and set performance requirements. Design and development to meet those standards would be carried out primarily by private industry.[27]

Many of the top aircraft industry executives during the interwar era were former pilots and, as in the nineteenth century, it seemed easier for army officers to become business executives than for businessmen to become regular officers.[28] Quickly, a set of close, even symbiotic, connections grew up between the officers of the Army Air Corps and the civilian aviation executives who had been their former comrades. Not until the early 1930s, when the feasibility of civilian air transportation was established, was there sufficient outside demand for aircraft to free producers from their reliance on military orders. Contracts were not always awarded on a competitive basis but were spread around, as they had previously been during the nineteenth century, when artillery-tube and powder manufacturing were controlled by private firms, to keep a "warm mobilization base" and ensure that a number of aircraft suppliers were available for any emergency. The national industrial policy for the aircraft industry that emerged during the 1920s became a harbinger, after the partial deconstruction of national arms production in the Department of Defense reorganizations of the later 1950s and early 1960s, of expanded industrial-government connections in the national defense sector of the economy.[29]

☆ ☆ ☆

It seemed that, between the wars, managers and technicians gained an equal place in the military hierarchy. Making war required the integration of multiple military and nonmilitary agencies. Matters of supply, technical development, and administration, declared a staff text in 1926, "cannot be separated from tactics and strategy. [They are] a major factor in the execution of strategic and tactical conceptions, so inextricably interwoven that [they are] a part of each."[30] Until the middle 1930s, however, strategic planning, procurement, and supply remained separate spheres. Ordnance officers, in particular, complained that mobilization planning did not take into account the resources that were likely to be available at the beginning of hostilities and that there was little thought given to the connections between military requirements and material resources. It was not until Malin Craig, who was much more willing to give bureau technicians and logisticians recognition than his predecessors, became chief of staff (1935–1939) that any attempt was made to coordinate strategy and resources. The Protective Mobilization Plan (PMP) of 1937, undertaken at his request and reflecting the deteriorating diplomatic situation in Europe and in the Far

East, was the first to link the military needs of the nation with its industrial capacity. That was the situation in September 1939, when George C. Marshall succeeded Craig as chief of staff and war again broke out in Europe.[31]

In the meantime, the isolationist political environment of the twenties and thirties and the remembered logistical and supply failures, which had put them at the mercy of the British and French, left an abhorrence of inter-Allied cooperation among American soldiers. Until 1938, planners assumed the United States would fight its next war without allies. The curriculum of the Industrial College devoted much time to industrial mobilization and material acquisition, but it gave no attention to inter-Allied cooperation, transportation, and distribution of supplies. The "Color Plans" concentrated on colonial defense, defense of the continental United States, and defense of the Western Hemisphere. The M-Day plans assumed that the United States would enter any future conflict in a traditional manner: a period of tension would be followed by a declaration of war by the Congress.[32] The military had learned the importance of lead time to tool up for production and fill the supply lines and warned that the nation could not hope to field large, efficient, well-equipped forces for eighteen months after hostilities began.

But affairs did not move in anticipated ways, and the nation drifted rather than plunged into war. During the decade before Pearl Harbor, Franklin D. Roosevelt, who was in many ways a late-Victorian man, kept control of national-security affairs in his own hands. To foreign observers, American military organizations seemed to lack connections with each other and with the executive branch. Appearances were deceiving. Like his predecessors, the president relied on multiple channels of communication. He operated through informal ad hoc committees of soldiers, sailors, and civilians to keep up to date and made use of numerous outside private contacts. Often his orders to the military, especially those involving force structure and procurement, provoked resentment from those who were not informed of their relationship to his overall foreign-policy objectives. President Roosevelt's administrative "open door" opened only one way, and that proved to be unfortunate when it became clear that the chief executive did not share all the information he had even with those who had a need to know. Secretary of the Interior Harold Ickes complained that Roosevelt would not talk frankly even with loyal supporters. By the spring of 1941, however, the president had created, through informal and personal means, a joint national-security staff, which he labeled, his "War Council."[33]

During the New Era and New Deal years, War Department organization shifted toward an innovative balance between line and bureau technicians, resolving, some contemporary commentators claimed, the traditional contests

for power between the chief of staff and the bureau chiefs. Changes in administrative structure seemed to support such claims. The new "technical committees" included all interested weapons and doctrine lobbies, bureau technicians,
private manufacturers, and, often, representatives of the army-school system,
many of whom reflected the perspectives of "New Era" corporatist modernizers. The conventional managerial wisdom was that the army had become
a giant technological-industrial machine like any other modern corporation.
Soldiers were interchangeable machine tenders, noncommissioned officers
were foremen, and officers were middle managers. The whole system would
soon be run by a board of directors.[34] But when the War Department and
the army were reorganized and the country prepared for war in 1941, it was in
ways that neither soldiers nor businessmen anticipated or desired. They were
to learn, and not for the last time, that war was not simply another business
operation and organizing it was not merely a matter of industrial management.
Harbord had been right about at least one thing. The officers and noncommissioned officers who commanded the armies were not CEOs and factory
foremen. The soldiers were not machine tenders.[35]

☆ ☆ ☆

In his *Kindergarten Chats*, published in the last decade of the nineteenth century, the architect Louis Sullivan wrote that form must follow function. The War
Department, the Navy Department, and the State Department were originally
housed in one building near the White House. After the War of 1812, the older
structure was given to the navy, and between 1818 and 1820, new buildings for
the War Department and the State Department were completed. Still close to
the White House, they were separate two-story structures built in the classic
manner of brick with stone porticos and window trimming. The "War Office"
was heated by individual fireplaces. There was no inside plumbing and each
bureau had its own privy. Drinking water came from a spring in Franklin Park.
It was not until the late 1830s that inside amenities and gaslights were added.
When it outgrew its new home during the 1840s, the army rented quarters away
from the administrative center around the president's quarters. Before 1861,
"Old War" had at the most thirty-four rooms connected by relatively narrow
corridors and no common meeting rooms. The walkways between the White
House and the administrative buildings gave the president easy access to his
cabinet advisers, but there were no interconnecting paths to give the cabinet
members similar access to each other. As the Civil War opened in 1861, the War
Department building itself symbolized the system within which the officers
of the army and their civilian superiors carried out their duties.[36]

By 1890 the War Department had been in its new home in the recently completed Army, Navy, State Building, still located beside the White House, for less than a decade. A contemporary architectural masterwork, the Victorian pile was fireproof and had a skeleton of iron and a fine slate roof. Its granite stonework was the best quality, and its expensive interior woodwork and marble floors gleamed softly under the electric chandeliers newly installed in the public rooms, offices, and corridors, while the well-lighted and luxurious offices of the civilian secretaries, with their high ceilings and splendid appointments, symbolized the new governmental affluence of the Gilded Age. The magnificently equipped libraries created settings for careful study of the issues of the day and unhurried consideration of high policy. By contrast, the rest of the building was a warren of smaller rooms. Internal traffic patterns were complex. Although there were some overlaps, each executive department had its own wing and there were no great rooms dedicated to joint meetings and conferences. In 1882, even while the construction was underway, Secretary of State Frederick T. Frelinghuysen proposed that the building partitions put in place during construction be retained to prevent access to the State Department from the army and navy wings of the building. Only the complaints of Secretary of War Robert Todd Lincoln that the partitions cut off ventilation and fouled the air brought Congress to order the partitions removed.[37]

In 1940, a half century later, construction on a modern, stark, factorylike home for the military services was about to begin. Perhaps the new building would mark a transition from the traditional military organizations of the nineteenth century to the new organizational realities that had emerged from the challenges of the first four decades of the twentieth century. Most of the officers who had come of age in the old blue-shirted, Indian-fighting army and held high command during the First World War had died or retired. A new generation of officers who had entered the army during the Progressive Era and served in France were moving into positions of power and the "stars were about to fall" on the West Point class of 1915. Despite the organizational changes of the previous decades, when the war came and the soldiers moved into their new home across the Potomac River, a bridge and a world away from the rest of the government, they brought with them the cultural loyalties, antagonisms, habits of mind, and routines that had posed such powerful dilemmas for War Department and army leaders for more than a century. Possibly, the architecture of the new building, with its baffling system of inclined planes and concentric circles, represented traditional army institutions and attitudes more accurately than its designers realized. Although the War Department would avoid many of the organizational and programmatic miscalculations of the First World War, the shades of John Schofield and Nelson Miles still stalked the halls of the Pentagon. Officers of the line still championed the warrior virtues and patronized those they considered mere uniformed "machinists," "bean-counters," and "quill drivers." Technicians and logisticians still wanted to be consulted and recognized as soldiers of the republic. Outside the War Department, soldiers expected the corporate establishment to follow their lead uncritically, while corporate executives sought to control affairs and found it hard to understand that soldiers were not simply uniformed replicas of themselves. Congress still determined the budget and required appropriate deference. And the president commanded in any way he chose. Character and personality still counted. Cultural and professional patterns from the era of "separate spheres and parallel paths" persisted. Those historical institutional complexities, incongruities, and contradictions—unresolved past imperatives—could only be endured and, at times, if treated with sensitivity, transcended.

☆ ☆ ☆

The beginning of the Cold War and the concurrent decisions made between 1948 and 1954 to maintain large peacetime armed forces dramatically changed the scale and scope of American military affairs and seemed to mark the end of an era. Forty years later some observers claimed the vision of the early-twentieth-century modernizers and progressive reformers had finally come to pass. But history confounds analysis. The War Department and the army, with all their myriad historical parts, still retained a persistent institutional life, purpose, and body of received truths beyond contemporary managerial modes. "And so it goes," wrote Kurt Vonnegut in *Slaughterhouse Five*. Soldiers and corporate executives still viewed each other with suspicion. Critical issues between the combat-arms communities and their support organizations from the days of Grant, Sherman, and Pershing remained and were reflected in the words of an anonymous colonel of armor as another campaign, this time in the Persian Gulf, began. "That whole crowd of bastards can go to war with us any time they want, so long as they remember who's driving the bus."[38]

NOTES

1. Separate Spheres and Parallel Paths

1. James A. Huston, *The Sinews of War: Army Logistics, 1775–1953* (Washington, D.C.: Center of Military History, 1966); James R. Jacobs, *The Beginnings of the United States Army, 1783–1812* (Princeton, N.J.: Princeton Univ. Press, 1947); and Erna Risch, *Quartermaster Support of the Army: A History of the Corps* (Washington, D.C.: Office of the Quartermaster General, 1962).

2. Leonard W. White, *The Jeffersonians: A Study in Administrative History, 1801–1829* (New York: Free Press, 1951), 215.

3. Charles M. Wiltse's *John C. Calhoun,* 3 vols. (Indianapolis, Ind.: Bobbs-Merrill, 1944–51), is the best study of the great nineteenth-century administrator. Russell F. Weigley's *History of the United States Army* (Bloomington: Indiana Univ. Press, 1984), 141–42, includes a discussion of the expansible army plan.

4. Even the wily McComb argued in 1831 that "it is the province of the War Department with the approval of the President to make such rules and regulations as shall be proper and necessary for the Govt. of the Army, but I presume it was never contemplated to make regulations which could render the several Depts. so separated and disconnected from the Commander of the Army as to leave him the troops without the power to control, support or conduct them." Major General Alexander McComb to Secretary of War John Eaton, July 25, 1831. Quoted in appendix 6 of Robert F. Stohlman Jr., *The Powerless Position: The Commanding General of the Army of the United States, 1864–1903* (Manhattan: Kansas State Univ. in conjunction with *Military Affairs,* 1975), 144.

5. Chief of Ordnance George Bomford wrote in 1827, "The qualifications requisite for a judicious performance in this branch of service, involving as it does a familiar acquaintance with many of the mechanical arts together with a knowledge of exact science, are to be attained only by long experience and application, joined with an aptitude for such pursuits. Ordnance service . . . differs so essentially from all other branches and is of a character so peculiar to itself, that a separate . . . provision for it is believed to be indispensable . . . and to be required by the best interests of the public." Francis B. Heitman, *Official Register and Dictionary of the United States Army, 1789–1903* (Washington, D.C.: GPO, 1903; reprinted

by the Univ. of Illinois Press, 1966), 44. For more than a decade after the end of the War of 1812, the Ordnance Department was attached to the artillery. In 1832 the first ordnance officers were commissioned in the regular army. For the ordnance manufacturing experience during the first half of the nineteenth century, see Merritt Roe Smith, *Harpers Ferry and the New Technology* (Ithaca, N.Y.: Cornell Univ. Press, 1977).

6. Leonard W. White, *The Jacksonians: A Study in Administrative History, 1829–1861* (New York: Free Press, 1954), 190–93.

7. William Skelton, "The Commanding General and the Problem of Command in the United States Army, 1821–1841," *Military Affairs* (Dec. 1970). For the period after the Civil War, see Stohlman, *Powerless Position.*

8. Edward M. Coffman, *The Old Army: A Portrait of the American Army in Peacetime, 1784–1898* (New York: Oxford Univ. Press, 1986), 211.

9. Charles F. O'Donnell, "The United States Army and the Origins of Modern Management, 1818–1860" (Ph.D. diss., Ohio State Univ. 1982).

10. The "Iron Triangle" is nothing new. Although I prefer to call the sets of connections the "national defense sector" of the economy, the current "military industrial complex" differs only in scale from the academic/government/business connections of the nineteenth century. One must admit, however, that scale does matter. The most recent discussion of the connections between the military and industry before the twentieth century is Paul Koistinen, *Beating Plowshares into Swords: The Political Economy of American Warfare, 1606–1865* (Lawrence: Univ. Press of Kansas, 1996). For the best discussion of the tradition of civilian supremacy, see Richard H. Kohn, *Eagle and Sword: The Federalists and the Creation of the Military Establishment* (New York: Free Press, 1975); and Weigley, *History of the United States Army.* The best study of the relations between staff and line in the nineteenth-century War Department is William R. Roberts, "Loyalty and Expertise: The Transformation of the Nineteenth-Century American General Staff and the Creation of the Modern Military Establishment" (Ph.D. diss., Johns Hopkins Univ. 1979). For other views on command and management issues, see Skelton, "The United States Army, 1821–1842: An Institutional History," (Ph.D. diss., Northwestern Univ. 1968); and O'Donnell, "The United States Army and the Origins of Modern Management, 1818–1860."

11. Alfred D. Chandler, *The Visible Hand: The Managerial Revolution in American Business* (Cambridge, Mass.: Harvard Univ. Press, 1977), 7; Charles G. Sellers, *The Market Revolution: Jacksonian America, 1815–1846* (New York: Oxford Univ. Press, 1991), 3–33.

12. The conventional definition of military professionalism is found in Samuel Huntington, *The Soldier and the State: The Theory and Politics of Civil-Military Relations* (Cambridge, Mass.: Harvard Univ. Press, 1957), which describes military culture as an exclusive one that rejects middle-class business life and values. For a more insightful analysis that takes into account the careers of "unconventional" soldiers with significant connections with civilian life, see Morris Janowitz, *The Professional Soldier: A Social and Political Study* (New York: Free Press, 1960).

13. The role of state and local politicians in selecting military technology needs further investigation. See Lieutenant Colonel George Talcott to Secretary of War William Wilkins, Jan. 16, 1845; and Secretary of War William Wilkins to Lieutenant Colonel George Talcott, Jan. 17, 1845, in *Ordnance Reports and Other Important Papers Relating to the Ordnance Department,* 4 vols. (Washington, D.C.: GPO, 1882–92), 2:6.

14. Marcus Cunliffe, *Soldiers and Civilians: The Martial Spirit in America, 1775–1865* (Boston: Little, Brown, 1968), contains a good discussion of the role of the militia before the Civil War; and John Mahon, *History of the Militia and National Guard* (New York: MacMillan, 1983), includes a fine bibliography on the history of the militia and National Guard. Richard B. Winders, *Mr. Polk's Army: The American Military Experience in the Mexican War* (College Station: Texas A&M Press, 1997), describes the nineteenth-century American military establishment—regulars, militia, and volunteers—in all its contentious, multifaceted splendor.

15. Robert Wiebe, *The Segmented Society: An Introduction to the Meaning of America* (New York: Oxford Univ. Press, 1975); and *The Opening of American Society: From the Adoption of the Constitution to the Eve of Disunion* (New York: Alfred A. Knopf, 1984). The British called it "separate tables." See Sheldon Bidwell and Dominick Graham, *Firepower: British Army Weapons and Theories of War, 1904–1945* (London: Allen and Unwin, 1982), 15.

16. Allan Nevins, *The War for the Union,* 4 vols. (New York: Charles Scribner's Sons, 1959–1971), is the most useful survey of Civil War institutional growth. See also Fred D. Shannon, *Organization and Administration of the Union Army, 1861–1865,* 2 vols. (Cleveland, Ohio: Clark, 1928); and Alexander H. Meneely, *The United States War Department, 1861: A Study in Mobilization and Administration* (New York: Columbia Univ. Press, 1928). For the development of the Union command system, the best book is T. Harry Williams, *Lincoln and His Generals* (New York: Alfred A. Knopf, 1952). Harold M. Hyman, *Stanton: The Life of Lincoln's Secretary of War* (New York: Alfred A. Knopf, 1962), is the best biography of Lincoln's controversial secretary of war. Several books on Civil War command-and-control issues also contain important information on staff consultation and cooperation. See Herman Hattaway and Archer Jones, *How the North Won: A Military History of the Civil War* (Urbana: Univ. of Illinois Press, 1983); and Richard E. Beringer, Herman Hattaway, Archer Jones, and William N. Still Jr., *Why the South Lost the Civil War* (Athens: Univ. of Georgia Press, 1986). Nineteenth-century staff officers have been neglected or relegated to roles as "obstructionists" or "traditionalists." For more favorable assessments, see K. Jack Bauer, *The Mexican War, 1846–1848* (New York: Macmillan, 1974); Winders, *Mr. Polk's Army;* Huston, *Sinews of War;* Risch, *Quartermaster Support of the Army;* Chester L. Kieffer, *Maligned General* (San Rafael, Calif.: Presidio, 1979), a biography of Thomas Jesup; and Russell F. Weigley, *Quartermaster General of the Union Army: A Biography of Montgomery C. Meigs* (New York: Columbia Univ. Press, 1959).

17. Hyman, *Stanton,* 186.

18. Williams, *Lincoln and His Generals.* For Henry Halleck see Stephen E. Ambrose, *Halleck: Lincoln's Chief of Staff* (Baton Rouge: Louisiana State Univ. Press, 1962).

19. Albert B. Moore, *Conscription and Conflict in the Confederacy* (New York: Macmillan, 1924); and Eugene C. Murdock, *One Million Men: The Civil War Draft in the North* (Madison: State Historical Society of Wisconsin, 1971), are the best studies of the Civil War draft.

20. *Official Records of the Union and Confederate Armies in the War of the Rebellion,* 128 vols. (Washington, D.C.: GPO, 1880–1901), series 3, vol 1: 676. The production figures and the description of the condition of the federal army after Gettysburg are from Huston, *Sinews of War.*

21. We know very little about the actual process of Civil War industrial mobilization. There is some work on the railroads and river boats during the Civil War (see the essay on sources). The best general studies are Nevins, *War for the Union;* Louis Hacker, *The Triumph*

of American Capitalism: The Development of Economic Forces in American History to the End of the Nineteenth Century (New York: Simon and Schuster, 1940), 339–73; and V. S. Clark's older *History of Manufactures in the United States,* 3 vols. (New York: McGraw-Hill, 1929). For the economic impact of the war see Thomas Corcoran, "Did the Civil War Retard Industrialization," *Mississippi Valley Historical Review* 48 (1961): 197–210; and Ralph Andreano, ed., *The Economic Impact of the American Civil War,* 2nd ed. (Cambridge, Mass: Schenkman, 1967).

22. For general studies of government contracting during the war, see Huston, *The Sinews of War;* and Risch, *Quartermaster Support of the Army.* For a revisionist account that treats government contracting sympathetically and questions the traditional wisdom that Civil War business profits were excessive, see Stuart D. Brandes, *Warhogs: A History of War Profits in America* (Lexington: Univ. of Kentucky Press, 1997), 67–107.

23. Thomas Weber, *The Northern Railroads in the Civil War* (New York: King's Crown Press, 1952). For military railroads, see James A. Ward, *That Man Haupt: A Biography of Herman Haupt* (Baton Rouge: Louisiana State Univ. Press, 1973).

24. Hattaway and Jones, *How the North Won,* stress logistics. James M. McPherson, *Battle Cry of Freedom: The Civil War Era* (New York: Oxford Univ. Press, 1988), is the best one-volume general history of the war effort.

25. Stephen W. Sears, *George B. McClellan: The Young Napoleon* (New York: Ticknor and Fields, 1988), 46–49.

26. Stephen E. Ambrose, *Upton and the Army* (Baton Rouge: Louisiana State Univ. Press, 1964).

27. The best source for Civil War artillery, design, numbers, and places of production is James C. Hazlett, Edwin Olmstead, and M. Hume Parks, *Field Artillery Weapons of the Civil War* (Newark: Univ. of Delaware Press, 1983). The best work on Union small arms during the Civil War is Carl L. Davis, *Arming the Union: Small Arms in the Civil War* (Port Washington, N.Y.: Kennikat, 1973); but see also Robert V. Bruce, *Lincoln and the Tools of War* (Indianapolis, Ind.: Bobbs-Merrill, 1956). In 1877, after he became chief of ordnance, Benét wrote, "The present equipments were recommended by infantry and cavalry boards . . . of experienced officers of the respective arms. [T]his Department is, of course, only responsible for the quality of the material and the character of the workmanship. "Benét concluded that, in light of the state of the technology and the issues involved during the Civil War, a decision to go to a new weapon at any time before 1865 would have been a daring gamble. See A. B. Dyer to Belnap, Nov. 27, 1869, for the Roberts story; for the Ward-Burton, see Steven V. Benét to Belnap, Nov. 8, 1873; Benét to McCrary, Oct. 22, 1877; and Sherman to McCrary, Jan. 16, 1878, in *Ordnance Reports,* 4:905–7, 913–14, 910–11.

28. The best study of the difficulties encountered by the Confederacy and its ultimate downfall is Beringer, Hattaway, Jones, and Stills, *Why the South Lost the Civil War.* See also Harold S. Wilson, *Confederate Industry: Manufactures and Quartermasters in the Civil War* (Jackson: Univ. of Mississippi Press, 2002).

29. David F. Noble, *America by Design: Science, Technology, and the Rise of Corporate Capitalism* (New York: Alfred A. Knopf, 1977); Thomas C. Corcoran and William Miller, *The Age of Enterprise: A Social History of Industrial America* (New York: Harpers, 1961). Chandler, in *Visible Hand* and *Strategy and Structure: Chapters in the History of the Industrial Enterprise* (Cambridge, Mass., MIT Press, 1962), develops the thesis in a comprehensive manner.

30. For the charges against Chief of Ordnance Alexander B. Dyer and the subsequent history of the War Department and the arms trade, see Lieutenant Colonel Lowell G. Wenger, "The United States Army and the International Traffic in Small Arms, 1870–1914" (paper delivered at the Ohio Academy of History, Apr. 1979; in the author's possession). For the issue of public and private production of small arms during the 1870s, see *Costs of Manufactures at the National Armory, 1872–77* (Washington, D.C.: GPO, 1878), republished by the Springfield Armory Museum, including "A Memorial in Relation to the Manufacture of Arms and Munitions for Supplying the Army and Militia."

31. For the adoption of steel artillery, see Benét to Secretary of War Robert Todd Lincoln, Apr. 19, 1883, in *Ordnance Reports,* 3:335–36; and Judge Advocate General G. Norman Lieber to Secretary of War Endicott, Apr. 2, 1887; Benét to Endicott, Apr. 14, 1887; Lieber to Endicott, Apr. 19, 1887; Attorney General A. H. Garland to Endicott, June 7, 1887; Richard R. McMahon, Acting Comptroller of the Treasury, to Endicott, June 28, 1887; and Benét to Endicott, Feb. 2, 1889; *Ordnance Reports,* 3:161–66. See also William E. Berkheimer, *Historical Sketch of the Organization, Administration, Matériel, and Tactics of the Artillery, United States Army* (Washington, D.C.: James Chapman, 1884), 682; and Vardell E. Nesmith Jr., "The Quiet Paradigm Change: The Evolution of the Field Artillery Doctrine of the United States Army" (Ph.D. diss., Duke Univ. 1977), 202–5.

32. Paul W. Clark, "Major General George Owen Squier, Military Scientist" (Ph.D. diss., Case Western Reserve Univ. 1974), 8–9; Father Donald Smythe, *Guerrilla Warrior: The Early Life of John J. Pershing* (New York: Scribner's, 1973).

33. William B. Skelton, "The Commanding General and the Problem of Command in the United States Army, 1821–1841," and *An American Profession of Arms: The Army Officer Corps, 1784–1861* (Lawrence: Univ. Press of Kansas, 1992). For the latter part of the nineteenth century, see Stohlman, *Powerless Position.* See also Weigley, *History of the United States Army,* 286; and Maurice Matloff, ed., *American Military History* (Washington, D.C.: Office of the Chief of Military History, 1969), 292.

34. Donna Marie Eleanor Thomas, "Army Reform in America: The Crucial Years, 1876–1881" (Ph.D. diss., Univ. of Florida, 1980), 66–67.

35. Ambrose's *Upton and the Army* is the best biography of that controversial officer. See also Graham A. Cosmas, *An Army for Empire: The United States Army in the Spanish-American War* (Columbia: Univ. of Missouri Press, 1971), 25; and C. Joseph Bernardo and Eugene H. Bacon, *American Military Policy: Its Development since 1775* (Harrisburg, Pa.: Military Service Publishing, 1955), 290–91.

36. According to Walter Millis, in 1885, "the Army stood on the threshold of what might be called the managerial revolution in war." Walter Millis, *Arms and Men: A Study of American Military History* (New York: G. P. Putnam, 1956), 122–23.

2. The War Department, 1885–1916

1. Edmund Wilson, *Patriotic Gore: Studies in the Literature of the American Civil War* (New York: Oxford Univ. Press, 1962); Gerald F. Linderman, *The Mirror of War: American Society and the Spanish-American War* (Ann Arbor: Univ. of Michigan Press, 1974), and *Embattled Courage: The Experience of Combat in the American Civil War* (New York, Free Press, 1987), examine the continuities in American life and thought before and after Appomattox. Leo

Marx, *The Machine in the Garden* (New York: Oxford Univ. Press, 1964), describes the general fear and concern about the introduction of technology into American culture during the late nineteenth century.

2. Secretary of War Robert Todd Lincoln to Commanding General Philip H. Sheridan, Jan. 17, 1885. The complete letter is in appendix 6 of Stohlman, *the Powerless Position,* 157–64.

3. For Schofield's administrative style, see John Schofield, *Forty-six Years in the Army* (New York: Century, 1897), 447.

4. See chapter 4 (below) for the significance of the board during the years when Schofield and Miles were commanding generals and for its decline during the Progressive Era before the First World War.

5. *War Department Annual Reports, 1893: Annual Report of the Secretary of War; Report of the Commanding General* (Washington, D.C.: GPO, 1893), 1:50.

6. For War Department organizations other than the Ordnance Bureau, see Walter Griffin, "George W. Goethals and the Panama Canal" (Ph.D. diss., Univ. of Cincinnati, 1988), 1–67. For the increase in appropriations for internal improvements in the nineties, see *War Department Annual Reports, 1899: Annual Report of the Secretary of War,* reproduced in *Five Years of the War Department following the War with Spain, 1899–1903* (Washington, D.C.: GPO, 1904), 53–54.

7. *War Department Annual Reports, 1890: Annual Report of the Secretary of War,* 1:13; *Report of the Chief of Ordnance* (Washington, D.C.: GPO, 1890), 3:37.

8. Schofield, *Forty-Six Years in the Army,* 422, 480, 483.

9. The newest full biography of Nelson Miles is Robert Wooster, *Nelson A. Miles and the Twilight of the Frontier Army* (Lincoln: Univ. of Nebraska Press, 1996); but see also Virginia W. Johnson, *The Unregimented General: A Biography of Nelson A. Miles* (Boston: Houghton Mifflin, 1962). For his own version of affairs, see Nelson A. Miles, *Serving the Republic: Memoirs of the Civil and Military Life of Nelson A. Miles* (New York: Harper & Row, 1911).

10. The idea of linking the size of the army to the population was popular with the officer corps. Secretary of War Lamont and Secretary of War Russell A. Alger submitted annual requests to Congress for legislation reorganizing the combat arms. For Miles's recommendations on troop strength and national wealth, see *War Department Annual Reports, 1895: Annual Report of the Secretary of War* (Washington, D.C.: GPO, 1895), 1:69. For the reduction of military posts from 120 in 1888 to 83 in 1895, see *War Department Annual Reports, 1895: Report of the Inspector General,* 123–24. For an understanding of the developing relationship between Secretary Lamont and General Miles, see *War Department Annual Reports, 1895: Annual Report of the Secretary of War,* 1:3–71; and *War Department Annual Reports, 1896: Annual Report of the Secretary of War* (Washington, D.C.: GPO, 1896), 1:3–79.

11. Rebecca R. Raines, *Getting the Message Through: A Branch History of the Signal Corps* (Washington, D.C.: Center for Military History, 1996), 91–92.

12. The best histories of the American army in the Spanish American war are David Trask, *The War with Spain in 1898* (New York: Macmillan, 1981); and Graham Cosmas, *An Army for Empire.*

13. For Alger's career, see Trask, *The War with Spain;* Cosmas, *Army for Empire;* Margaret Leach, *In the Days of McKinley* (New York: Harpers, 1959); and Roberts, "Loyalty and Expertise."

14. *War Department Annual Reports, 1898: Report of the Chief Signal Officer* (Washington, D.C.: GPO, 1898).

15. The search for artillery abroad turned up only four Armstrong 4.7-inch guns that could be delivered in any acceptable time. See Harvey Deweerd, "Production Lag in the American Ordnance Program, 1917–1918" (Ph.D. diss., Univ. of Michigan, 1939).

16. *War Department Annual Reports, 1899: Report of the Chief of Ordnance* (Washington, D.C.: GPO, 1899), vol. 2, appendix 34, 383.

17. The Report of the Ordnance Equipment Board—the Blunt Board—is appendix 19, 235–40, of *War Department Annual Reports, 1898: Report of the Chief of Ordnance* (Washington, D.C.: GPO, 1898). In 1899 an army-navy board approved standardization of the 30-caliber round for small arms in all services.

18. *War Department Annual Reports, 1898: Annual Report of the Chief of Ordnance*, 2:6–10.

19. Regular and volunteer units going to Cuba carried thirty days of rations with them, and in July General Shafter requested that the order be suspended. Risch, *Quartermaster Support of the Army,* 530.

20. For the Clem Studebaker story, see Emmett M. Essin, *Shavetails and Bell Sharps* (Lincoln: Univ. of Nebraska Press, 1997), 124. A permanent equipment board composed of quartermaster officers had begun meeting regularly in 1883. When Samuel Holabird succeeded Rufus Ingalls as quartermaster general, he found that there was no central repository where all current specifications could be found. In 1889 Holabird published the first complete quartermaster's specification book, which provided guidelines for private bidders and strict instructions to quartermaster inspectors who accepted the products. The specifications book referred to in Holabird's *Annual Report* in 1890 was his last contribution to the army before he retired. See Samuel B. Holabird, *U.S. Army Uniforms and Equipment, 1889,* foreword by Jerome A. Greene (Lincoln: Univ. of Nebraska Press, 1986).

21. Risch, *Quartermaster Support of the Army,* 550; *War Department Annual Reports, 1898: Annual Report of the Quartermaster General,* 1:57.

22. American historians have tended to treat the Spanish-American War as either a farce or an organizational debacle. For a traditional account, see Walter Millis, *The Martial Spirit: A Study of Our War with Spain* (Boston: Houghton Mifflin, 1931). Cosmas, however, shows in *Army for Empire* and "Military Reform after the Spanish American War: The Army Reorganization Fight of 1898–1899," *Military Affairs* 35 (1972): 12–18, that the members of the Dodge Commission considered the job done by the War Department as at least adequate. Cosmas is especially strong on the work of Secretary of War Alger and gives a clear explanation of why McKinley refused to sack Alger immediately. See also Risch, *Quartermaster Support of the Army,* 556; A. Hunter Dupree, *Science in the Federal Government: A History of Policies and Activities* (Baltimore, Md.: Johns Hopkins Univ. Press, 1986), 271–301; Stohlman, *Powerless Position;* William Skelton, "The Commanding General and the Problem of Command" and *An American Profession of Arms.*

23. *War Department Annual Reports 1903: Annual Report of the Secretary of War,* 1:46, quoted in Philip C. Jessup, *Elihu Root,* 2 vols. (New York: Dodd, Mead, 1939), 1:251–52. The best analysis of the 1903 reorganizations is James A. Hewes, *From Root to McNamara: Army Organization and Administration, 1900–1963* (Washington, D.C.: Center of Military History, 1975), 3–56, but Hewes, perhaps, underestimate the importance of the politics of personality, which played

an important role in the affair. The peculiar nature of the new general staff system that Root proposed and the elimination of the office of commanding general, which could have been modified to fit the popular corporate model, reflected matters of personality, first that of Miles and later that of Arthur MacArthur, rather than any contemporary theories of management.

24. Weigley, *History of the United States Army,* 316–17.

25. For the work of the joint army-navy board on strategic planning, especially the development of the color plans, see Richard Challener, *Admirals, Generals, and American Foreign Policy, 1898–1914* (Princeton, N.J.: Princeton Univ. Press, 1973).

26. Otto Nelson, *National Security and the General Staff* (Washington, D.C.: Infantry Journal Press, 1946); Paul Hammond, *Organizing for Defense: The American Military Establishment in the Twentieth Century* (Princeton, N.J.: Princeton Univ. Press, 1961); and the best of them all, James Hewes, *From Root to McNamara,* introduce a conflict thesis that argues that after 1903 a partnership between the new chief of staff and the secretary of war replaced the alliance of the secretary of war and the bureau chiefs against the commanding general that had been characteristic of the nineteenth-century system. Hewes, who had no sympathy for the bureaus, describes a perpetual conflict between "rationalizers" and "traditionalists" in the War Department. Hewes, however, neglects Schofield, who had already established cooperative connections during the early 1890s. Even before 1903, rather than antagonize one group or the other, the secretaries of war worked to encourage internal cooperation that would harmonize the interests of the multiple War Department agencies while maintaining civilian supremacy in carrying out national policy. Nelson Miles was the problem and Root was determined that no one like Miles would be able to hamstring the War Department again. The most recent work on the issue, Ronald J. Barr, *The Progressive Army: U.S. Command and Administration, 1870–1914* (New York: St. Martin's, 1998), adopts Huntington's "Neo-Hamiltonian–Neo-Jeffersonian" model and pays little attention to War Department reformers other than those involved in introducing the general staff system.

27. *Creation of the American General Staff: The Personal Narrative of Major General William Harding Carter,* in *The National Defense: Hearings before the Committee on Military Affairs, House of Representatives, 69th Congress, Second Session, Part I* (Washington, D.C.: GPO, 1927), 503–53. In his discussion of the Root reforms, Carter used both the analogy of the board of directors and the human body to describe the workings of the staff system; however, he most frequently referred to Root's belief that the primary mission of the general staff involved war planning.

28. Richard B. Crossland and James T. Currie, *Twice the Citizen: A History of the United States Army Reserve, 1908–1983* (Washington, D.C.: Office of the Chief, Army Reserve, 1984), 13–14, including notes 46 and 47. Barr's *Progressive Army* pays scant attention to the significance of the Dick Act.

29. Bell's letter was in response to an article on military supply written by Lieutenant Hugh S. Johnson. See Hugh S. Johnson, "The Lamb Rampant," *Everybody's Magazine* (Mar. 1908); and J. Franklin Bell to Theodore Roosevelt, May 24, 1908, "The Correctness of the Statements Made by Lieutenant Hugh Johnson," War College Division Correspondence, 1903–1916, WCD 1387, RG 165, National Archives. For a discussion of Bell's career, see Edgar Raines, "J. Franklin Bell and the American Army" (Ph.D. diss., Univ. of Wisconsin, 1981).

30. Leo S. Rowe, "The Reorganization of Local Government in Cuba," *Annals of the American Academy of Political and Social Science* 100 (May 1905), quoted in Jack C. Lane, *Armed Progressive: General Leonard Wood* (San Rafael, Calif.: Presidio, 1978), 101.

31. This discussion of "corporatism" builds upon the scholarship of Samuel Hayes, *Conservation and the Gospel of Efficiency: The Progressive Conservation Movement* (Cambridge, Mass.: MIT Press, 1959); Samuel Haber, *Efficiency and Uplift: Scientific Management in the Progressive Era, 1890–1920* (Chicago: Univ. of Chicago Press, 1964); Robert Wiebe, *The Search for Order, 1877–1920* (New York: Hill and Wang, 1967); Ellis Hawley, *The Great War and the Search for a Modern Order: A History of the American People and Their Institutions, 1917–1933* (New York: Saint Martin's, 1979); James Weinstein, *The Corporate Ideal in the Liberal State, 1900–1918* (Boston: Beacon Press, 1968); and Stephen Skowronek, *Building a New American State: The Expansion of National Administrative Capacities, 1877–1920* (New York: Cambridge Univ. Press, 1982). In two papers, "The Corporate Process in Progressive America," delivered at the War and Society seminar at Princeton University (academic year 1983–84), and "The Corporate Component of the American Quest for National Efficiency," delivered at the annual meeting of the Organization of American Historians in New York in 1986, Ellis Hawley described corporatism as involving the "forging of new social machinery" to "bridge the gaps between social groups, assist them to see their true interests, and generate social action programs in which each group did its part." State and society would thus be "intertwined through deep interpenetrations," and the former would act "chiefly as midwife and partner rather than director or regulator." For an introduction to corporatist thinking, see Daniel Nelson, *Managers and Workers: Origins of the New Factory System in the United States* (Madison: Univ. of Wisconsin Press, 1975); and *Frederick W. Taylor and the Rise of Scientific Management* (Madison: Univ. of Wisconsin Press, 1980). For another view, see Sanford M. Jacoby, *Employing Bureaucracy: Managers, Unions, and the Transformation of Work in American Industry, 1900–1945* (New York: Columbia Univ. Press, 1985). For more on modernizing, see Noble, *America by Design.* For a discussion of general administrative practices and for the persistence of nineteenth-century professional and cultural attitudes during the first two decades of the twentieth century, consult Wiebe, Hawley, and Skowronek.

32. William R. Roberts, *Loyalty and Expertise,* 253. The best biography of Root is Jessup, *Elihu Root;* but see also Richard W. Leopold, *Elihu Root and the Conservative Tradition* (Boston: Little, Brown, 1954).

33. Edgar F. Raines, "Major General Leonard Wood, U.S.A." (paper delivered at the Cosmos Club, Washington, D.C., Dec. 1986). Mabel E. Deutrich, *Struggle for Supremacy: The Career of Fred C. Ainsworth* (Washington, D.C.: Public Affairs Press, 1962), deals with part of the Ainsworth story.

34. See Jessup, *Elihu Root;* and Elting E. Morison, *Turmoil and Tradition: A Study of the Life and Times of Henry L. Stimson* (Boston: Houghton Mifflin, 1960). For the comment in the text, see Morison, *Turmoil and Tradition,* 146. The best biography of Leonard Wood is Lane's *Armed Progressive;* but see also Hermann Hagedorn, *Leonard Wood: A Biography,* 2 vols. (New York: Harpers, 1931).

35. Henry Stimson (with McGeorge Bundy), *On Active Service in Peace and War* (New York: Harpers, 1948), 36; and Lane, *Armed Progressive,* 166. For the story of the 1912 fight,

see Hagedorn, *Leonard Wood;* Deutrich, *Struggle for Supremacy;* Lane, *Armed Progressive;* and Hammond, *Organizing for Defense.* See also Morison, *Turmoil and Tradition;* Stimson, *On Active Service in Peace and War;* and Weigley, *History of the United States Army,* 332. For Wood and the Wilson administration, see Daniel R. Beaver, *Newton D. Baker and the American War Effort, 1917–1919* (Lincoln: Univ. of Nebraska Press, 1966).

36. Tasker H. Bliss to Enoch H. Crowder, Nov. 3, 1913, quoted in Lane, *Armed Progressive,* 166.

3. The War Department, 1900–1916

1. Between 1895 and 1914, the army expanded from 2,154 officers and 25,341 men to 5,033 officers and 93,511 men and the military budget increased from $51,805,000 to $208,350,000 (unadjusted for inflation). The figures are not significantly different from those cited by Brandes in *Warhogs,* 116, if National Guard numbers and funding are included. See *Historical Abstract of the United States,* cited in Weigley, *History of the United States Army,* appendix, 561–68.

2. The best concise history of the early general staff is in Hewes, *From Root to McNamara,* 3–56. See also Huston, *Sinews of War,* 293–307.

3. *Annual Reports of the War Department, 1906: Annual Report of the Quartermaster General: Armament, Transport, and Supply* (Washington, D.C.: GPO, 1906), 2:54.

4. Edgar Raines, "James Buchanan Aleshire," in Roger Spiller, ed., *Dictionary of American Military Biography* (Westport, Conn: Greenwood, 1984).

5. Andrew Villalon, in an excellent paper, "Walker's War Car: A Study of American Military Response to Technological Innovation, 1900–1902" (in the author's possession), analyzes the problems of testing motor vehicles in the early, volatile phase of automotive technology.

6. In 1911 Captain J. C. McArthur of the 28th Infantry published a scathing article pointing out the achievements of the Europeans and calling for study and experimentation "until animal traction shall be entirely supplanted in the transport service." See Captain J. C. McArthur, "Auto Trucks for the Army," *Journal of the American Military Service Institute* 18 (1911): 248–56.

7. Edwin T. Layton Jr., *The Revolt of the Engineers: Social Responsibility and the American Engineering Profession* (Baltimore, Md.: Johns Hopkins Univ. Press, 1986), 42. The leader of the SAE was Howard Coffin, then vice president of the Hudson Motor Car Company. Even in 1910, Coffin was an evangelist for technical standardization. He would later serve on the Naval Consulting Board, champion a national industrial inventory, and, during the First World War, press the army to standardize motor transport.

8. Daniel R. Beaver, "Politics and Policy: The War Department Motorization and Standardization Program for Wheeled Transport Vehicles, 1920–1940," *Military Affairs* 47 (Oct. 1983): 101–8. The best studies of the early years of the military truck program are Norman M. Cary Jr., "The Use of the Motor Vehicle in the United States Army, 1899–1939" (Ph.D. diss., Univ. of Georgia, 1980); and Mark K. Blackburn, *The United States Army and the Motor Truck: A Case Study in Standardization* (Westport, Conn.: Greenwood, 1996). Huston's summary of quartermaster activity in *The Sinews of War,* 298–99, is less friendly.

9. *War Department Annual Reports, 1903: Annual Report of the Quartermaster General,* 2:21, as quoted in Risch, *Quartermaster Support of the Army,* 581. According to Brandes, *Warhogs,* 116–17, War Department spending increased by 900 percent between 1885 and 1916.

10. *War Department Annual Reports, 1912: Annual Report of the Secretary of War,* 1:164.

11. Memorandum for the Acting Secretary of War from Major General William P. Duvall, Acting Chief of Staff, Nov. 21, 1907 (returned from the Secretary's office Jan. 17, 1908), records of the War Department General Staff, RG 165, National Archives. Duvall wrote, "The better opinion is that measures like the consolidation suggested by the Commissary General should wait until much more vital bills have had their day."

12. Stimson and Bundy, *On Active Service in Peace and War;* and Morison, *Turmoil and Tradition.* See also David A. Clary and Joseph Whitehorn, *The Inspector General of the United States* (Washington, D.C.: Office of the Inspector General and the Center of Military History). Volume 1, published in 1987, covers the years 1777–1903; volume 2, published in 1998, covers the period 1903–1939. This citation is from 2:7–10 of the unpublished manuscript. Events showed it was a mistake to absorb the paymaster general's office into the Quartermaster Corps. Although it had never been a central budgeting and financial planning agency, Aleshire relegated the office of paymaster general to mere accounting and bookkeeping. When the First World War required correlation of War Department budgeting and procurement, a separate finance organization had to be recreated.

13. Hugh G. J. Aitken, "William Crozier," *The Dictionary of American Biography* (Cambridge, Mass.: Harvard Univ. Press, 1930), 3:204–5. *War Department Annual Reports, 1902: Annual Report of the Chief of Ordnance* (Washington, D.C.: GPO, 1902), 3:2–706.

14. "Report of Captain Beverley W. Dunn, Ordnance Department, upon the Establishment of a Course of Instruction for Ordnance Officers," in *War Department Annual Reports, 1902: Annual Report of the Chief of Ordnance,* vol. 3, appendix 3, 101–25. Captain Dunn was a well-regarded ordnance intellectual.

15. *War Department Annual Reports, 1907: Annual Report of the Chief of Ordnance* (Washington, D.C.: GPO, 1907), 9:7–67.

16. *War Department Annual Report, 1902: Annual Report of the Chief of Ordnance,* vol. 7, appendix 4, *Competitive Tests of Field Artillery Material,* 129–79. For the Hogg comment see John Batchelor and Ian Hogg, *Artillery* (New York: Ballantine, 1972), 15. Shortly after the turn of the century, Krupp, who controlled a substantial share of Skoda, secured the Erhardt patents.

17. For a discussion of the development of international markets for smokeless powder, see Alfred D. Chandler Jr. and Stephen Salsbury, with the assistance of Adeline Cook Strange, *Pierre S. Du Pont and the Making of the Modern Corporation* (New York: Harper & Row, 1971), 169–200.

18. Chandler and Salsbury, *Pierre S. Du Pont* is the best source for the study of the powder industry. The price of black powder had been fixed and the contracts carefully divided among the associates for years by the Gun Powder Trade Association, which was dominated by DuPont.

19. *War Department Annual Reports, 1912: Report of the Chief of Ordnance,* 1:1916. For examples of collusive bidding, see "Publically Advertised Bids for Smokeless Powder," July 9, 1904. Ordnance Smokeless Powder Document File in Ordnance Department Records, Box 58, RG 156. The DuPont Corporation was found guilty of conspiracy in restraint of trade in 1911 and was ostensibly broken up by federal authorities.

20. *The History of Picatinny Arsenal* (Picatinny, N.J.: War Plans Division, Plant Engineering Plant, n.d.), 32–37, in United States Army Military History Institute Library, Carlisle Barracks, Pennsylvania; Chandler and Salsbury, *Pierre S. Du Pont,* 248.

21. Crozier should have known better. There had been labor-management trouble in the arsenals even before the Civil War. As full-time employment replaced seasonal factory work during the early days of the industrial revolution, arsenal managers had been forced to reduce the work force and stretch out production to keep the factories open. See Pat Harrahan, "Worker Resistance to Managerial Control of Production at Rock Island Arsenal, 1898–1918," 1–10 (copy in author's possession); *War Department Annual Report 1900; Annual Report of the Chief of Ordnance,* appendix 4: *Report of the Commanding Officer, Watervliet Arsenal* (Washington, D.C.: GPO, 1900), 1:65–66. See also David Montgomery, "Worker Control of Machine Production in the Nineteenth Century," *Labor History* (Fall 1976): 485–509. For General Crozier and scientific management, see Hugh Aitken, *Taylorism at Watertown Arsenal: Scientific Management in Action* (Cambridge, Mass.: MIT Press, 1960). See also N. J. Nadworny, *Scientific Management and the Unions, 1900–1932* (Cambridge, Mass.: Harvard Univ. Press, 1955), 28–103.

22. "Statement of Brigadier General William Crozier, United States Army, Chief of Ordnance," *Committee on Military Affairs: House of Representatives, Hearing on Army Appropriations Bill for Fiscal Year 1911–12* (Washington, D.C.: GPO, 1910), 310–34.

23. *War Department Annual Reports, 1912: Report of the Chief of Ordnance,* 1:885–942. This was a blow to the traditional patron-client relationship upon which the War Department depended for surge capacity.

24. Raines, *Getting the Message Through,* 88–103. See also *War Department Annual Reports, 1898: Annual Report of the Secretary of War,* 1:891–95.

25. Raines, *Getting the Message Through,* 119–64. See also Huston, *Sinews of War;* and Clark, "George Owen Squier."

26. Clark, "George Owen Squier," 177.

27. Susan J. Douglas, "The Navy Adopts the Radio, 1899–1919," in Merritt Roe Smith, ed., *Military Enterprise and Technological Change: Perspectives on the American Experience* (Cambridge, Mass.: MIT Press, 1985), 117–74.

28. Dupree, *Science in the Federal Government,* 284–87.

29. Clark in "George Owen Squier," 128–70, shows that it was not Theodore Roosevelt and private aviation enthusiasts who pushed the Signal Corps into aircraft research but a convergence of forces inside and outside the War Department.

30. For the creation of the National Advisory Committee for Aeronautics, see Raines, *Getting the Message Through,* 192–94. See also Dupree, *Science in the Federal Government;* Huston, *The Sinews of War;* and Clark, "George Owen Squier."

31. Joseph B. Bishop and Farnham Bishop published *Goethals, Genius of the Panama Canal* (New York: Harpers) in 1930. Bishop also memorialized the general in "George Washington Goethals" in *The Dictionary of American Biography.* Griffin, "George W. Goethals and the Panama Canal," is the definitive study of Goethals and the Canal. See also David McCullough, *Path between the Seas: The Creation of the Panama Canal, 1870–1914* (New York: Simon and Schuster, 1977).

32. For a discussion of Charles E. Magoon, see David A. Lockmiller, *Magoon in Cuba: A History of the Second Intervention, 1906–1909* (Chapel Hill: Univ. of North Carolina Press, 1938).

33. McCullough, *Path between the Seas,* 453–89.

34. For the work of John F. Wallace and John F. Stevens, see the *Annual Report of the Panama Canal Commission, 1903–1907* (Washington, D.C.: GPO, 1907). The massive, multivolume *Annual Report of the War Department,* through 1914, gives a general view of the progress of construction.

35. McCullough, *Path between the Seas,* 535.

36. Griffin, "George W. Goethals and the Panama Canal," 438–597.

37. Ibid., 593–97; McCullough, *Path between the Seas,* 590–607. The project, with its effective development and testing loop, was an early example of what, during the Second World War, was called "operational research."

38. The final chapters of McCullough's *Path between the Seas* contain a number of comments on the historical and institutional significance of the canal project.

4. Technology, Doctrine, and Reform, 1885–1916

1. By 1914 the telephone and the recently developed wireless radio had improved operational communication, and the automobile, the airship, and the airplane had revealed their potential to revolutionize the conduct of war. Magazine small arms, machine guns, quick-firing field artillery, smokeless powder, improved fuses, and electrical fire control systems were adopted, raising questions about traditional relationships between weapons and fighting doctrine and creating a volatile environment that challenged War Department technicians, as well as soldiers, in the combat arms. Before 1890 the development of weapons and equipment was dominated by design and production experts. Representatives of the combat arms often complained that they lacked control, but there were few conflicts as long as the weapons were only used by a single branch. There could even be agreements among branches, such as those reached by the army and navy on uniform calibers for small arms in 1899 and by the cavalry and infantry in 1906 to shorten the Springfield rifle and eliminate the carbine. Ordnance officers were willing to consult but resisted efforts to give field soldiers the final decision on the introduction of weapons and equipment. They remained perfectionists, insisting that equipment must be finely finished and weapons produced to very close tolerances. They also retained the tradition of positive yet passive receptivity toward new technology, and bureau technocrats often waited for an inventor to walk through the door before they took any interest in his work. Personality quirks and traditional connections with congressional allies and associates in private industry continued to influence weapons development. For an introduction to the impact of those issues in the American army, see Huston, *Sinews of War,* 296–300.

2. The best book on Palmer and his work on the 1912 proposals is I. B. Holley, *General John M. Palmer, Citizen Soldiers, and the Army of a Democracy* (Westport, Conn: Greenwood, 1982). Weigley has discussed the development of the idea of doctrine in his excellent *The American Way of War: A History of United States Military Policy* (New York: MacMillan, 1973), 192–222, and especially in the note on 511–12, but he does not deal with the relationships between new weapon technologies and contemporary tactical doctrine. For the history of army maneuvers see Charles D. McKenna, "The Forgotten Reform: Field Maneuvers in the Development of the United States Army, 1902–1920" (Ph.D. diss., Duke Univ., 1981).

3. Hewes, *From Root to McNamara,* 15.

4. Perry D. Jamieson, *Crossing the Deadly Ground: United States Army Tactics, 1865–1899* (Tuscaloosa: Univ. of Alabama Press, 1994), 114–54. For an excellent recent critique of American tactics in Cuba and especially the failure of artillery support in combined arms operations at Santiago, see T. R. Brereton, "First Lessons in Modern War: Arthur Wagner, the 1898 Santiago Campaign, and U.S. Army Lesson-Learning," *Journal of Military History* 64 (Jan. 2000): 79–96. For the status of contemporary combined-arms thinking, see *Field Service Regulations, 1914, Articles 123 and 124* (Washington, D.C.: GPO, 1914).

5. Not everyone agreed. See Captain E. D. Scott, "Cavalry, Field Artillery and Infantry: A Proposed Organization for Regiments," *Journal of the Military Service Institution of the United States* 68 (1911): 372. The first year of the course of study at Leavenworth, which was attended by selected company-grade officers, dealt with operations, doctrine, and tactics. The second year, which was even more selective, was devoted to higher-staff training. The course culminated with a staff ride to one of the major Civil War battlefields. The best study of the Leavenworth school system is Timothy K. Nenninger, *The Leavenworth Schools and the Old Army: Education, Professionalism, and the Officer Corps of the United States Army* (Westport, Conn: Greenwood, 1978); but see also Carol Reardon, *Soldiers and Scholars: The U.S. Army and the Uses of Military History* (Lawrence: Univ. Press of Kansas, 1990). Forrest Pogue tells the story of Major Morrison and the School of the Line at Fort Leavenworth in *George C. Marshall: Education of a General, 1880–1939* (New York: Viking, 1963), 93–108.

6. Although coast artillery did not become a separate arm until 1907, it functioned, politically at least, as one after the artillery was divided into field and coast artillery in 1901.

7. Hagood, "Autobiography" (Mss, United States Army Military History Institute, Carlisle Barracks, Pennsylvania), 94–97.

8. The Americans were impressed by the reports of army observers during the Russo-Japanese war, and those views were reflected in the literature. For a representative article, see Captain Oliver L. Spaulding Jr., "The Use of Field Artillery," *Journal of the United States Artillery* 37 (1912): 321–39.

9. For field artillery organizational innovation during the Progressive Era, see chap. 4 of Janice McKenney, "History of United States Field Artillery" (unpublished manuscript in the author's possession).

10. *War Department Annual Reports, 1893; Report of the Board of Ordnance and Fortification,* 1:787; *War Department Annual Reports, 1895: Report of the Board of Ordnance and Fortification,* 1:851. The best study of the work of the Board of Ordnance and Fortification is Robert S. Browning III, "Shielding the Republic: American Coastal Defense Policy in the Nineteenth Century" (Ph.D. diss., Univ. of Wisconsin, 1981), esp. 203–72. Browning later published the dissertation as part of *Two If by Sea: The Development of American Coastal Defense Policy* (Westport, Conn: Greenwood, 1983).

11. *War Department Annual Reports, 1889: Report of the Board of Ordnance and Fortification,* 1:430–31.

12. *War Department Annual Reports, 1893: Report of the Board of Ordnance and Fortification,* 1:787; *War Department Annual Reports, 1895: Report of the Board of Ordnance and Fortification,* 1:851.

13. *War Department Annual Reports, 1893: Report of the Board of Ordnance and Fortification,* 1:811.

14. *War Department Annual Reports, 1896: Report of the Board of Ordnance and Fortification,* (Washington, D.C.: GPO, 1896), 1:922.

15. The checkered history of the Emery elevating gun carriage reveals the political forces that could become involved in the system. The story can be followed in James Stokesbury, "The Army and the Development of Technology," in Robin Higham and Carol Brandt, eds., *The United States Army in Peacetime, Essays in Honor of the Bicentennial, 1775–1975* (Manhattan, Kans.: *Military Affairs/Aerospace Historian,* 1975): 153–55; Berkheimer, *Artillery,* 292–93; Nesmith, *The Quiet Paradigm Change,* 202–205; and in the following government documents: *War Department Annual Reports, 1900: Annual Report of the Chief of Ordnance,* vol. 23, appendix 34, 349–99; *War Department Annual Reports, 1911: Annual Report of the Chief of Ordnance,* 1:696; *War Department Annual Reports, 1915: Annual Report of the Chief of Ordnance,* 1:706.

16. Lamont to Nelson Miles, Jan. 7, 1896; and Miles to Lamont (Jan. 11, 1896), *War Department Annual Reports, 1896: Report of the Board of Ordnance and Fortification,* 1:920–22.

17. *War Department Annual Reports, 1898: Report of the Board of Ordnance and Fortification,* 1:1099.

18. *War Department Annual Reports, 1899: Annual Report of the Secretary of War,* 1:48.

19. For the legal foundations of the War Department Board of Review, see *War Department General Order 91, December 16, 1914; War Department General Order 9, February 20,* 1915; and *War Department General Order 62, November 13, 1915.* See also *Army Regulations, 1913: Corrected to April 15, 1917 (Changes, nos. 1 to 55, Article 1512 1/2),* 308. For comments of the bureau chiefs on the board, see *War Department Annual Reports, 1915: Report of the Chief of Ordnance,* 706; and *Report of the Chief of Coast Artillery,* 795.

20. Hewes, *From Root to McNamara* (table of organization of Aug. 26, 1918), 46.

21. *War Department Annual Reports, 1899–1907: Annual Report of the Chief of Ordnance* (Washington, D.C.: GPO, 1907). Crozier's reports from 1900 to 1912, especially those from 1901 to 1908, are rewarding reading. He showed little of the "not-invented here" attitude that field soldiers and inventors ascribed to the Ordnance Department.

22. David A. Armstrong, *Bullets and Bureaucrats: The Machine Gun and the United States Army, 1861–1916* (Westport, Conn: Greenwood, 1982), 172–85; George M. Chinn, *The Machine Gun: History, Evolution, and Development of Manuel, Automatic and Airborne Repeating Weapons,* 3 vols. (Washington, D.C.: Bureau of Ordnance, Department of the Navy, 1951), 1:203–8. In 1909 the army deployed the Vickers-Maxim in experimental six-gun machine-gun companies on the German model. Unlike the Germans, however, the Americans did not make provision for a division and corps machine-gun reserve that could be deployed offensively. In 1912, for temporary budgetary reasons, the American machine-gun company was reduced to four guns.

23. Even John H. "Machine Gun" Parker, the acknowledged American expert on automatic weapons, seemed to lack understanding of the tactical implications of using a light, air-cooled machine gun in place of a heavy, water-cooled one.

24. First Lieutenant William E. Roberts, "The Benét-Mercié Automatic Machine Rifle," *Journal of the Military Service Institution of the United States* 66 (1911): 451–62.

25. Squier's inventions were not as connected with military uses as were those developed by Lewis. For Squier's career as an inventor, see Clark, "George Owen Squier." There is a set of documents titled "Miscellaneous Correspondence: The Lewis Machine Gun in World War I" in the Records of the Office of the Chief of Ordnance, RG 156, National Archives,

Washington, D.C. For the story of Lewis and the "theft" of the "75 mm" recuperator, see Johnson Hagood, "Autobiography" (United States Army Military History Institute, Carlisle Barracks, Pennsylvania).

26. *War Department Annual Reports, 1916: Annual Report of the Chief of Ordnance,* 1:824–27. The British cavalry and Allied tank forces used the Benét-Mercié or Light Hotchkiss throughout the First World War.

27. There is abundant literature on the preparedness campaign and the National Defense Act of 1916. Among the best books are John P. Finnegan, *Against the Specter of a Dragon: The Campaign for American Military Preparedness, 1914–1917* (Westport, Conn: Greenwood, 1974); John Garry Clifford, *The Citizen Soldiers: The Plattsburg Training Camp Movement, 1913–1920* (Lexington: Univ. of Kentucky Press, 1972); John C. Edwards, *Patriots in Pinstripes: Men of the National Security League* (Washington, D.C.: Univ. Press of America, 1982); and Michael Pearlman, *To Make Democracy Safe for America: Patricians and Preparedness in the Progressive Era* (Urbana: Univ. of Illinois Press, 1984). See also Dupree, *Science in the Federal Government,* 271–301; and Hawley, "The Corporate Process in Progressive America."

28. Finnegan, *Against the Specter of a Dragon,* 42–56. There was a real problem with the National Guard. In 1912 Attorney General George Wickersham expressed doubts about whether National Guardsmen could constitutionally be deployed outside United States borders. Although provision was made for National Guardsmen to volunteer for overseas service in 1914, that was no answer to the reserve problem The War Department and the new chief of staff, Hugh Scott, held traditional views about force structures and wanted to increase the number of regular regiments rather than fight about reserves. Scott was not doctrinaire about conscription, but he knew from experience that any big increases in the regular force, or in the reserves for that matter, could not be secured by voluntary enlistment.

29. Morison, *Turmoil and Tradition,* 144–69.

30. Henry Stimson, *What Is the Matter with Our Army?* (Washington, D.C.: GPO, 1912). Articles by a number of Army officers, as well as Stimson, caused a stir when they were first published in the *Independent* between Feb. and Apr. 1912. Stimson made the decision to bring the essays together and publish them as a government document.

31. Holley, in *John M. Palmer,* provides an excellent discussion of Palmer's early life. For Wood and the 1912 reforms, see Lane, *Armed Progressive,* 168–83. A significant part of the Palmer Plan proposed short enlistments in the regular army and the enlistment of former soldiers in an organized federal reserve separate from the National Guard.

32. *War Department Annual Reports, 1914: Annual Report of the Secretary of War* (Washington, D.C.: GPO, 1914), 4–6.

33. *A Proper Military Policy for the United States* (Washington, D.C.: GPO, 1915). For more background on the War College study, see John Votaw's outstanding dissertation, "The Military Attaché" (Philadelphia, Pa.: Temple Univ., 1992). Garrison relied heavily on information from American attachés and observers in Europe. Although the Americans at first had some difficulty gaining access to information, by 1915 they were sending reports of considerable significance back to Washington that reinforced the arguments of preparedness advocates that modern war was a material struggle swallowing up men, treasure, and supplies on a scale unprecedented in history and required a coordinated national effort. The most important American observers

were George Squier, soon to become chief of the signal corps, who had been military attaché in London since 1913, and Captain William Mitchell, the military attaché in France. By the fall of 1916, the American officers in France were organized into an observer group that sent back consolidated reports to the War Department and the chief of staff. Assertions by some historians that the military attachés' reports simply gathered dust in the War College library are founded on comments from opponents of the bureaus, self-serving line officers, members of the emergency civilian-mobilization agencies, and political opponents of the administration. There are similar remarks in the postwar books of Assistant Secretary of War Benedict Crowell, Bernard Baruch, Peyton C. March, James G. Harbord, and John J. Pershing, all of whom commented unfavorably on prewar plans and policies. All, however, also asserted that the National Defense Act of 1916 was intended to prepare the United States for participation in the Great War and that was simply not the case.

34. For the compulsory universal training movement, see Finnegan, *Against the Specter of a Dragon;* and Pearlman, *To Make Democracy Safe for America.*

35. For the role of Congressman Hay, see George C. Herring Jr., "James Hay and the Preparedness Controversy, 1915–1916," *Journal of Southern History* 30 (Nov. 1964): 383–404. For a detailed discussion of Chamberlain's part in the affair, see Clifford, *Citizen Soldiers,* 117–51.

36. The most recent and most ambitious account of civilian corporate-industrial connections during the Progressive Era and the Great War is Paul A. C. Koistinen, *Mobilizing for Modern War: The Political Economy of American Warfare, 1865–1919* (Lawrence: Univ. Press of Kansas, 1997).

37. Newton D. Baker to John H. Clarke, Mar. 13, 1916, Papers of Newton D. Baker, Library of Congress, Washington, D.C. For a discussion of Baker's early career, see Clarence H. Cramer, *Newton D. Baker: A Biography* (Cleveland, Ohio: World Publishing, 1961), 13–63.

38. Harold J. Tobin and Percy W. Bidwell, *Mobilizing Civilian America* (New York: Council on Foreign Relations, 1940), 12–13.

39. Memorandum, Newton D. Baker to President Woodrow Wilson, Apr. 7, 1916, copy in Council of National Defense file, Papers of Bernard Baruch, Firestone Library, Princeton University; "Extract of Statement of the Secretary of War," June 3, 1916; The Papers of Newton D. Baker, Library of Congress.

40. Tobin and Bidwell, *Mobilizing Civilian America,* 12–13. The best discussion of the background to the Council of National Defense is in Robert Cuff, "The Cooperative Impulse and War: The Origins of the Council of National Defense and Its Advisory Commission," in Jerry Israel, ed., *Building the Organizational Society, Essays in Associational Activities in Modern America* (New York: Free Press, 1972), 233–46. Cuff either overlooked or disregarded the Baker memorandum, which was a bizarre combination of Bakerism, Danielsism, and Giffordism.

41. Brigadier General Charles G. Treat, acting chief of the War College Division, general staff, "Changes in Army Regulations Relating to the General Staff Corps," WCD 639–136, Nov. 20, 1916, RG 165, National Archives. A glance at any "buck slip" that circulated among the bureaus in the War Department during 1916 brings one to understand Treat's concern. He resisted Baker's close involvement in bureaucratic politics, which had been a way for the secretary of war to gain information and maintain control of internal affairs since the days of John C. Calhoun. See also Huston, *Sinews of War,* 292–307.

5. The Wilson Administration at War

1. The scholarly community has benefited tremendously from Arthur S. Link's superb editing of the Wilson papers. See *The Papers of Woodrow Wilson* (Princeton, N.J.: Princeton Univ. Press, 1982–1986), vols. 48–52. Link's *Wilson the Diplomatist: A Look at His Major Foreign Policies* (Baltimore, Md.: Johns Hopkins Univ. Press, 1957) reflects his thinking on the president's wartime diplomacy. For a comparison of Wilson and Lenin, see Arno Mayer, *Wilson and Lenin: The Political Origins of the New Diplomacy, 1917–1918* (New Haven, Conn.: Yale Univ. Press, 1959). John M. Cooper Jr., building on ideas introduced by Robert E. Osgood in *Ideals and Self-Interest in America's Foreign Relations* (Chicago: Univ. of Chicago Press, 1953), has written a comparative account of Wilson as a politician in *The Warrior and the Priest: Woodrow Wilson and Theodore Roosevelt* (Cambridge, Mass.: Harvard Univ. Press, 1983). For the president's personality and its effect on his physical condition, see Edwin A. Weinstein, *Woodrow Wilson: A Medical and Psychological Biography* (Princeton, N.J.: Princeton Univ. Press, 1981). The best recent studies of Wilson's role as commander in chief are Robert Ferrell, *Woodrow Wilson and World War I, 1917–1921* (New York: Harper & Row, 1985), in the *New American Nation* series; Frederick S. Calhoun, *Power and Principle: Armed Intervention in Wilsonian Foreign Policy* (Kent, Ohio: Kent State Univ. Press, 1986); and Lloyd E. Ambrosius, *Woodrow Wilson and the American Diplomatic Tradition: The Treaty Fight in Perspective* (New York: Cambridge Univ. Press, 1987). One should not overlook Thomas A. Bailey's classics, *Woodrow Wilson and the Lost Peace* (New York: MacMillan, 1944) and *Woodrow Wilson and the Great Betrayal* (New York: MacMillan, 1945). For a traditional view of Wilson as commander in chief, see Ernest R. May, *The Ultimate Decision: The President as Commander in Chief* (New York: Braziller, 1960). For another perspective, see Beaver, *Baker;* and David F. Trask, *The United States in the Supreme War Council: American War Aims and Inter-Allied Strategy, 1917–1918* (Middletown, Conn.: Wesleyan Univ. Press, 1961).

2. For Baker's wartime career, see Beaver, *Baker;* Frederick Palmer, *Newton D. Baker: America at War,* 2 vols. (New York: Dodd, Mead, 1931); and Trask, *United States in the Supreme War Council.*

3. Beaver, *Baker,* 179–211.

4. For Pershing's Mexican experience, see Jeff Jore, "Pershing's Mission in Mexico: Logistics and Preparation for the War in Europe," *Military Affairs* 52 (July 1988): 117–21. The best study of Pershing as commander of the American Expeditionary Forces is by Father Donald Smythe, S.J., *Pershing: General of the armies* (Bloomington: Indiana Univ. Press, 1986); but see also the general's own memoir, *My Experiences in the World War,* 2 vols. (New York: Frederick Stokes, 1931); and Frank E. Vandiver, *Black Jack: The Life and Times of John J. Pershing,* 2 vols. (College Station: Texas A&M Univ. Press, 1977).

5. There is no full modern biography of Bliss, but see David Trask, "Tasker H. Bliss" (forthcoming), and *The United States in the Supreme War Council.* See also Frederick Palmer's older *Bliss, Peacemaker: The Life and Letters of General Tasker Howard Bliss* (New York: Dodd, Mead, 1934).

6. Edward Parsons, *Wilsonian Diplomacy: Allied-American Rivalries in War and Peace* (St. Louis, Mo.: Forum, 1978).

7. Ray Stannard Baker, *Woodrow Wilson, Life and Letters,* 8 vols. (Garden City, N.J.: Doubleday, Page, and Doran, 1927–39), 6:496; memo from Assistant Chief of Staff Tasker

H. Bliss for Chief of Staff Hugh Scott, Mar. 31, 1917, in the Papers of Tasker Howard Bliss, Library of Congress; William Redfield to W. Wilson, Apr. 6, 1917, in the Papers of Woodrow Wilson, Library of Congress; Tasker H. Bliss to Hugh L. Scott, May 4, 1917, in the Bliss Papers; Tasker H. Bliss to Newton D. Baker, May 25, 1917, in the Bliss Papers; Secretary of War Baker to Woodrow Wilson, May 2, 1917, in the Baker Papers; President Wilson to Secretary Baker, May 3, 1917, in the Baker Papers; minutes of a conference with the Secretary of War, May 14, 1917, transmitted to the French government by Marshal Joffre, in *The United States Army in the World War, 1917–1919,* 17 vols. (Washington, D.C.: Center of Military History, 1948), 2:5.

8. *United States Army in the World War, 1917–1919,* 1:1–153.

9. Tasker H. Bliss to Hugh L. Scott, Mar. 31, 1917, in the Bliss Papers.

10. Brigadier General Joseph E. Kuhn, President of the War College, to Acting Chief of Staff Tasker H. Bliss, June 7, 1917, transmitting War College Document 10050–30, "Plan for a Possible Expeditionary Force in France," with accumulated appendixes and additional mobilization plans, War College Files, Records of the War Department General Staff, RG 165. For the recommendations of the War Department/AEF Board, see "Report on Organization" July 10, 1917, *U.S. Army in the World War,* 1:91–115, 144–54. The two best discussions of the Balfour Mission and the American debate over a "Western" strategy before Nov. 1917 are in Beaver, *Baker,* 22–49; and David R. Woodward, *Trial by Friendship: Anglo-American Relations, 1917–1918* (Lexington: Univ. Press of Kentucky, 1993), 45–111.

11. Planning began on the basis of the 1915–16 mobilization program, which called for a million men composed of the regular army, the National Guard, and a body of U.S. volunteers. For the decision to go to conscription, see John W. Chambers III, *To Raise an Army: The Modern Draft Comes to America* (New York: Free Press, 1987). Local draft resistance is dealt with in Peter Nitty's "Uncle Sam's Little War in the Arkansas Ozarks," in Peter Karsten, ed., *The Military in America: From the Colonial Era to the Present* (New York: Free Press, 1980); and Christopher C. Gibbs, "Missouri Farmers and World War I: Resistance to Mobilization," *Bulletin of the Missouri Historical Society* 35 (Oct. 1978): 17–27.

12. Beaver, *Baker,* 198–99; Harvey DeWeerd, *President Wilson Fights His War: World War I and the American Intervention* (New York: MacMillan, 1968), 389–94. DeWeerd accepts uncritically Leonard Ayres's statistical analysis of the training of American soldiers as published in his *The War with Germany: A Statistical Summary* (Washington, D.C.: GPO, 1919). For a peculiar interpretation of conditions in the army and the training requirements for battle in World War I, see March, *The Nation at War,* 231–72. For the consolidation of the army, see *War Department General Order 73,* Aug. 7, 1918. For the wartime turbulence in the United States, see the first three volumes of *The Order of Battle of the United States Land Forces in the World War,* 4 vols. (Washington, D.C.: GPO, 1931–1949), which deal with the forces at home. Vol. 4 covers the AEF.

13. James J. Cooke, *The All-Americans at War: The 82nd Division in the Great War, 1917–1918* (Westport, Conn.: Praeger, 1999); Lonnie J. White, *Panthers to Arrowheads: The 36th Texas-Oklahoma Division in World War I* (Austin, Tex.: Presidial Press, 1984).

14. War College Division of the General Staff WCD 13485, June 3, 1917; WCD 13390, June 16, 1917, War College Division of the General Staff, RG 165; cited in Trask, "Tasker H. Bliss," 8.

15. Risch, *Quartermaster Support of the Army,* 625; Benedict Crowell and Robert Wilson, *How America Went to War,* 6 vols. (New Haven, Conn: Yale Univ. Press, 1921), 2:652–54.

16. *The Order of Battle of United States Land Forces in the World War,* vol. 1, *Zone of the Interior.* For the standardization of motor trucks, see Cary, "Uses of the Motor Vehicle."

17. Beaver, *Baker,* 59–60.

18. Sharpe's book, *The Quartermaster Corps in the Year 1917 in the World War* (New York: Century, 1921), is an expanded version of his annual report for 1917.

19. In mid-March 1917, he wrote the chief of staff, "Clothing and equipment for one million men can, under existing conditions, be procured within ten months with the understanding that it might be necessary to purchase some blankets which do not conform to existing specifications, but . . . closely approximate standard quality and color." QMG Sharpe to Chief of Staff Scott, Mar. 13, 1917, in WCD Report 14930, Jan. 2, 1918, RG 165, National Archives.

20. Memorandum, Henry G. Sharpe to Chief of Staff Hugh Scott, Apr. 2, 1917, Records of the War Department General Staff, RG 165, National Archives.

21. Memorandum, QMG Sharpe to Chief of Staff Scott, Apr. 16, 1917, Records of the War Department General Staff, RG 165, National Archives.

22. Memorandum, QMG Sharpe to Tasker H. Bliss, July 21, 1917, Records of the War Department General Staff, RG 165, National Archives.

23. Memorandum, QMG Sharpe to Tasker H. Bliss, Oct. 9, 1917, Records of the War Department General Staff, RG 165, National Archives.

24. James G. Harbord, in *Leaves from a War Diary* (New York: Dodd, Mead, 1925), writes of what he called the disorganization in Washington. For the storage problem and efforts to solve it, see the lecture of O.D. Street at the War College, (Aug. 1917) Records of the War Department General Staff, RG 165, National Archives; and Risch, *Quartermaster Support of the Army,* 630.

25. Risch, *Quartermaster Support of the Army,* 602–3.

26. *War Department Annual Reports, 1917: Annual Report of the Secretary of War,* 26; *War Department General Order 102,* Aug. 4, 1917.

27. Lockridge's comments are in WDGS Report 14930, Jan. 2, 1918, "Quartermaster General Explains Delay in Finding Personnel and Supplies for the Expeditionary Force in France," Records of the War Department General Staff, RG 165, National Archives.

28. "The Quartermaster Corps during the Great War" (1919?), Quartermaster Historical File, RG 92, NA.

29. Crowell and Wilson, *How America Went to War,* 2:48–49.

30. Beaver, *Baker,* 53–57; *War Department Annual Reports, 1917: Report of the Chief of Ordnance,* 1:807. For contemporary discussions of the mobilization effort, see Crowell and Wilson, *How America Went to War;* and Grosvenor B. Clarkson, *Industrial America in the World War: The Strategy behind the Lines* (Boston: Houghton Mifflin, 1923). The story of the Enfield contract can be found in the papers of Frank A. Scott, located with those of Bernard Baruch in the Firestone Library, Princeton University.

31. Harvey A. De Weerd, "Production Lag in the American Ordnance Program, 1917–1918," 5–36. De Weerd's volume, previously cited as a source for ordnance procurement during the war with Spain and based on a careful study of ordnance archival material, is the only detailed, critical history of the World War army armaments program.

32. Acting Chief of Staff Tasker H. Bliss to Chief of Ordnance William Crozier, June 9, 1917, Ordnance Historical File, Office of the Chief of Ordnance, RG 156, National Archives.

33. Apparently the Americans had increased their forging and casting capacity considerably since Crozier had been compelled to import foreign materials to complete the artillery modernization project of 1903–08.

34. Bliss to Crozier, June 21, 1917, Chief of Staff's File, RG 165, National Archives; Pershing, *My Experiences in the World War,* 1:10; Harvey De Weerd, "The American Adoption of French Artillery, 1917–1918," *Journal of the American Military Institute* 3 (Summer 1939): 104–16.

35. *War Department Annual Reports, 1917: Annual Report of the Chief of Ordnance,* 1:793–814. Crozier concluded with an admonition that production in the United States was still far from adequate to meet the immediate needs of the army.

36. The best general discussion of the aircraft program is in Irving B. Holley, *Ideas and Weapons: The Exploitation of the Air Weapon by the United States in World War I* (New Haven, Conn.: Yale Univ. Press, 1957).

37. *War Department Annual Reports, 1917: Annual Report of the Secretary of War,* 1:838–45; Major William Mitchell to Brigadier General Joseph E. Kuhn, President of the War College, May 17, 1917; General Kuhn to Howard Coffin, June 13, 1917; Howard Coffin to General Kuhn, June 13, 1917; Records of the War College Division of the General Staff, RG 165, National Archives. The approved War College Aircraft Plan was released on June 23, 1917.

38. *War Department Annual Reports, 1918: Annual Report of the Chief Signal Officer.* (Washington, D.C.: GPO, 1918), 1:1074–76.

39. See Holley, *Ideas and Weapons.* For the work of Squier and Foulois, see Clark, "George Owen Squier," and John F. Shiner, *Foulois and the U.S. Army Air Corps* (Washington, D.C.: Office of Air Force History, 1983), 8–9.

40. *New York Times,* Oct. 5, 1917, cited in Beaver, *Baker,* 59.

41. *United States Army in the World War,* 1:1–116.

6. Reorganizing the War Department and Building the American Expeditionary Forces, 1917–1918

1. For the thirty-division plan, see *United States Army in the World War,* 1:117–54. For the War Department fifty-four-division program and the war program of Apr. 2, 1918, see "Report of the War Council," Records of the War Department General Staff, RG 165, National Archives. For Baker, March, and the development of the eighty-division program, see Beaver, *Baker,* 156–59.

2. For Crowder's career and place in the history of War Department reform, see David A. Lockmiller, *Enoch H. Crowder: Soldier, Lawyer, and Statesman* (Columbia: Univ. of Missouri Press, 1955).

3. Among the general discussions of the reforms of the fall and winter of 1917–18 are Edward M. Coffman, *The War to End All War: The American Military Experience in World War I* (New York: Oxford Univ. Press, 1968), 20–53; Beaver, *Baker,* 79–109; Daniel R. Beaver, "George W. Goethals and the Problem of Military Supply," in Daniel R. Beaver, ed., *Some Pathways in Twentieth-Century History: Essays in Honor of Reginald Charles McGrane* (Detroit, Mich.: Wayne State Univ. Press, 1969), 95–109; and Phyllis A. Zimmerman, *The Neck of the Bottle: George W. Goethals and the Reorganization of the U.S. Army Supply System, 1917–1918* (College Station: Texas A&M Univ. Press, 1992). See also Hewes, *From Root to McNamara,*

21–35; Robert D. Cuff, *The War Industries Board: Business-Government Relations during World War I* (Baltimore, Md.: Johns Hopkins Univ. Press, 1973), 113–47; and John K. Ohl, "Old Iron Pants: The Wartime Career of General Hugh S. Johnson, 1917–1918," (Ph.D. diss., Univ. of Cincinnati, 1971), 64–102.

4. Beaver, *Baker,* 165–72.

5. *New York Times,* Dec. 20, 1917. Crozier was an effective chief of ordnance. His work in negotiating with the British and French for artillery and ammunition was outstanding, and his appointment to the War Council was not to get him out of the way. He worked hard there until June 1918 when the council was abolished. He then served as military and technical adviser to Edward R. Stettinius Sr., who led the American industrial mission to Paris in the summer of 1918. Sharpe served on the war council until June 1918 and was then promoted to major general and assigned to command the Southeastern Department.

6. *New York Times,* Jan. 18, 1918.

7. March, *Nation at War,* 39–42. For the change in the Wilson administration's attitude during the next six months, see Beaver, *Baker,* 79–109.

8. *War Department Annual Reports 1919; Annual Report of the Chief of Staff* (Washington, D.C.: GPO, 1919), 1:148–50.

9. "Report of the Committee of Three," Apr. 18, 1918, in Records of the Chief of Staff, RG 165, National Archives; Beaver, "George W. Goethals," 98–101; Daniel R. Beaver, "The Problem of Military Supply," in B. Franklin Cooling, ed., *War Business and American Society: Historical Perspectives on the Military Industrial Complex* (Port Washington, N.Y.: Kennikat, 1977), 78–81.

10. March, *Nation at War,* 74, 196.

11. The legislation was first drafted by Judge Advocate General Enoch Crowder in the War Department in Feb. 1918. The Overman Act of May 20, 1918, simply legalized the massive reorganizations that had been underway since mid-December 1917.

12. Coffman, *Hilt of the Sword,* 119–33.

13. Beaver, "George W. Goethals," 101–8.

14. Ibid., 98.

15. *War Department Annual Reports, 1919: Annual Report of the Secretary of War,* 1:350–52.

16. Ibid., 1:350.

17. The Diary of George W. Goethals, June 15, 1918, in the papers of George W. Goethals, Library of Congress. Thorne remained in the Quartermaster Corps with Wood. Swope assumed Thorne's role as adviser and troubleshooter for Goethals.

18. G. W. Goethals to Peyton C., Mar., July 18, 1918, General Staff Historical File, RG 165, NA. This is the "July memorandum" that set the stage for the consolidation of procurement in the PS and T division of the general staff.

19. Goethals Diary, July 19, 1918, Goethals Papers. See also Goethals to T. Goethals, Aug. 5, 1918, Goethals Papers.

20. For a differently focused discussion of the summer War Department reforms, see Zimmerman, *Neck of the Bottle,* 126–35.

21. Trask, "Tusker H. Bliss," 19.

22. Palmer, *Newton D. Baker,* 1:172, 180. The infamous two sets of instructions are analyzed in Smythe, *Pershing,* 5–12.

23. Beaver, *Baker;* Coffman, *Hilt of the Sword;* and Smythe, *Pershing* all cover the conflict for command between March and Pershing, which lasted from Mar. 1918 to the armistice.

24. March, *The Nation at War,* 40, 48–49.

25. Coffman, *The War to End All War,* 20–53; Beaver, *Baker,* 79–109; Beaver "George W. Goethals," 95–109; and Zimmerman, *Neck of the Bottle,* 114–35. See also Hewes, *From Root to McNamara,* 21–35. The most recent accounts of the effects of the wartime Baker-March-Pershing connection are Father Donald Smythe's two articles, "Your Authority in France Shall Be Supreme: The Baker-Pershing Relationship in World War I," *Parameters* 9 (Sept. 1979): 38–45; and "The Pershing-March Conflict" *Parameters* 11 (Dec. 1981): 53–62.

26. *United States Army in the World War,* "Schedule of Priority Shipment of Personnel," 2:53–55.

27. Pershing, *My Experiences,* 1:144.

28. Smythe, *Pershing,* 41, 58.

29. Pershing, *My Experiences,* 1:146. See also Johnson Hagood, *The Services of Supply: A Memoir of the Great War* (Boston: Houghton Mifflin, 1927), 27.

30. Pershing, *My Experiences,* 1:147; Smythe, *Pershing,* 41–43.

31. Smythe, *Pershing,* 42–44.

32. *Report of the General Purchasing Agent of the American Expeditionary Forces to the Commander in Chief* (Feb. 28, 1919), in *Report of the Military Board of Allied Supply,* 2 vols. (Washington, D.C.: GPO, 1924–1925), 1:229–31. See also Charles G. Dawes, *A Journal of the Great War,* 2 vols. (Boston: Houghton Mifflin, 1921).

33. James G. Harbord, *The American Army in France, 1917–1919* (Boston, Little, Brown, 1936), 160.

34. Sharp to Lansing, Nov. 12, 1917, in *Papers Relating to the Foreign Relations of the United States, 1917,* supplement 2, *The World War,* 2 vols. (Washington, D.C.: GPO, 1932), 2:1212. The *Foreign Relations* series will be cited as *Foreign Relations* for 1917 or 1918 and, when appropriate, additional volumes will be indicated as supplements.

35. Marshal Ferdinand Foch, *The Memoirs of Marshal Foch,* trans. Col. T. Bentley Mott (New York: Doubleday, Doran, 1931), 345.

36. Harbord, *The American Army in France,* 183.

37. Hagood, *The Services of Supply,* 138.

38. Harbord, *American Army in France,* 360–61; Hagood, *The Services of Supply,* 150.

39. Pershing, *My Experiences,* 2:320–21.

40. Charles G. Dawes, foreword, *The Report of the Military Board of Allied Supply,* vol. 1, part 1, 28. For Dawes's work on inter-Allied supply, see Edward A. Goedeken, "Charles Dawes and the Military Board of Allied Supply" *Military Affairs* 50 (Jan. 1986): 1–6.

41. *The United States Army in the World War,* 2:354–55.

42. *Report of the Military Board of Allied Supply,* 2:454.

43. For the continuing debate over the 1919 program, the size of the AEF, and the rejection of Goethals, see Beaver, *Baker,* 165–68; and Smythe, *Pershing,* 161–68. For Pershing's plan to replace Goethals with Rogers, see Beaver, "The Problem of American Military Supply," 87–89.

44. The most recent work on the AEF in battle is Paul F. Brain, *The Test of Battle: The American Expeditionary Forces in the Meuse-Argonne Campaign, 26 September–11 November, 1918*

(Newark: Univ. of Delaware Press, 1987), whereas Pershing's command system and methods have been most recently discussed in James J. Cooke, *Pershing and His Generals: Command and Staff in the A.E.F* (Westport, Conn.: Praeger, 1997). The best analysis, however, is Timothy K. Nenninger, "American Military Effectiveness in the First World War," in Allan R. Millett and Williamson Murray, eds., *Military Effectiveness*, 3 vols. (Boston: Allen and Unwin, 1988). See also Nenninger's "Unsystematic as a Mode of Command: Commanders and the Process of Command in the American Expeditionary Forces," *Journal of Military History* 64, no.3 (July 2000): 739–68. The description of Pershing's breakdown is in Richard O'Connor, *Black Jack Pershing* (New York: Doubleday, 1961), 182. For a sensitive analysis of the stress of command on Pershing, see Frank Vandiver, "Haig and Pershing," in Hugh Cecil and Peter H. Liddle, eds., *Facing Armageddon: The First World War Experienced* (London: Leo Cooper, for Pen and Sword Books Ltd., 1996), 67–78.

45. "Final Report of Assistant Chief of Staff, G-5, June 30, 1919" in *United States Army in the First World War*, 14:289–442.

46. Douglas V. Johnson II and Rolfe L. Hillman Jr., *Soissons 1918* (College Station: Texas A&M Univ. Press, 1999). See also Robert H. Ferrell, *Collapse at Meuse-Argonne: The Failure of the Missouri-Kansas Division* (Columbia: Univ. of Missouri Press, 2004). For Pershing's views on the effectiveness of AEF doctrine, see Smythe, *Pershing*, 31.

47. "Final Report of Assistant Chief of Staff, G-5, June 30, 1919," in *The United States Army in the First World War*, 14:310.

48. See Beaver, *Baker*, 205–11; and David F. Trask, "Tasker H. Bliss." Bullitt Lowry, "Pershing and the Armistice," *Journal of American History* 55 (Mar. 1968): 281–91, adds a fresh dimension to the events of Oct. 1918. For Lowry's final views on the negotiations, see his *Armistice 1918* (Kent, Ohio: Kent State Univ. Press, 1996).

49. See Smythe, *Pershing*, 223–37; Beaver, *Baker*, 208–11. To a soldier such as Pershing, the honor of the army was an idea that extended far beyond his own personal ego and ambition. The AEF commander was determined, in a way not completely understood by civilians such as Wilson, House, and Baker, or even another soldier such as Bliss, to press the battle to a successful conclusion.

7. Coordinating Industry and Transportation

1. For a general introduction to the official sources on industrial mobilization, see Waldo G. Leland and Newton D. Mereness, comp., *Introduction to the American Official Sources for the Economic and Social History of the World War* (New Haven, Conn.: Yale Univ. Press, 1926). There is a large reservoir of published documents covering the American industrial war effort in *United States Army in the First World War*. The *Annual Reports of the War Department* includes everything from the reports of the secretary of war and the bureau chiefs, with critical comments on war materials, to those of the commander of the AEF. Benedict Crowell's *America's Munitions, 1917–1918: The Report of the Director of Munitions* (Washington, D.C.: GPO, 1919) contains much information on industrial production. The Nye Committee, *Hearings: Munitions Industry* (Washington, D.C.: GPO, 1935–37), which is a gold mine of primary documents, contains more than forty volumes of critical materials, including the *Minutes of the General Munitions Board* and *Minutes of the War Industries Board*. Bernard

Baruch, the chairman of the WIB, published his account of events in *American Industry in the War* (Washington, D.C.: GPO, 1921). Another group of books on the American industrial effort, which should be considered primary sources, were published in the first decade after the war ended. Assistant Secretary of War Crowell (with Robert Forrest Wilson) republished and expanded his annual report for 1919 in six volumes titled *How America Went to War;* and Grosvenor Clarkson, a former head of the Council of National Defense and a colleague of Baruch, gave industry's side of the story in *Industrial America in the World War* (Boston: Houghton Mifflin, 1923). A few years later, Thomas Frothingham put the best light possible on War and Navy Department efforts in *The American Reinforcement* (Garden City, N.J.: Doubleday, Page, 1927); and in *The Naval History of the World War,* 3 vols. (Cambridge, Mass.: Harvard Univ. Press, 1924–26). There is significant American literature written during the 1920s on wartime rail transportation and sealift. Walker Hines, who was active in the war administration, wrote the *War History of American Railroads* (New Haven, Conn.: Yale Univ. Press, 1928), a defense of Director General of Railroads William G. McAdoo and the railroad administration. Edward N. Hurley, in *The Bridge to France* (Philadelphia, Pa.: J. B. Lippincott, 1927); and Rear Admiral Albert Gleaves, in *A History of the Transport Service* (New York: George H. Doran, 1921), wrote apologias for their records in shipping troops and cargo to France. Among the best of the critical secondary literature on the war effort is Frederick Paxson's three-volume *American Democracy and the World War* (Boston: Houghton Mifflin, 1936–48), which contains information available nowhere else. Among the best recent works on the American war effort at home are David Kennedy, *Over Here* (New York: Oxford Univ. Press, 1980); and Hawley, *The Great War;* Skowronek, *Building a New American State;* and Weinstein, *The Corporate Ideal,* which takes the currently popular corporatist and state-building approach. Ronald Shaffer's *America in the Great War: The Rise of the War Welfare State* (New York: Oxford Univ. Press, 1991) is not as comprehensive as its title indicates. David A. Hounshell discusses American manufacturing during the war in *From the American System to Mass Production, 1800–1932* (Baltimore, Md.: Johns Hopkins, 1984). A critical study of the railroads is Austin K. Kerr, *American Railroad Politics, 1914–1920* (Pittsburgh, Pa.: Univ. of Pittsburgh Press, 1968). William J. Williams, *The Wilson Administration and the Shipbuilding Crisis of 1917* (Lewiston, N.Y.: Edwin Mellen Press, 1992), is critical of the Wilson administration's maritime programs. For the so-called military-industrial complex and the Great War, see Paul A. C. Koistinen, *Mobilizing for Modern War;* and Robert Cuff, *The War Industries Board.* B. F. Cooling, in *Grey Steel and Blue Water* (Hamden, Conn.: Archon Books, 1979); and Beaver, in "George W. Goethals" and "The Problem of Military Supply," give a somewhat different historical perspective to the controversy.

2. Transcript of proceedings of the National Defense Conference, held under the auspices of the Council of National Defense, May 2–3, 1917, in the Daniels Papers. The best work on the State and Local Councils of National Defense is William J. Breen, *Uncle Sam at Home: Civilian Mobilization, Wartime Federalism, and the Council of National Defense, 1917–1919* (Westport, Conn.: Greenwood, 1984). James E. Cebula, in *James A. Cox: Journalist and Politician* (New York: Garland, 1985), reveals the Wilson administration's aggressive use of federal executive power in his discussion of Governor Cox's abortive attempt to impose state control on economic mobilization in Ohio. In July 1917, the president also blocked Senator

Henry Cabot Lodge's attempt to establish a joint congressional committee on the conduct of the war. The Wilson administration had an excellent institutional memory.

3. Baker never hesitated to act because he thought that he, or anyone else, lacked power. See, for example, Baker's letter to President Wilson of Nov. 17, 1917, quoted in Palmer, *Newton D. Baker,* 1:379.

4. Hugh Scott to W. J. Nicholson, Apr. 5, 1917, in the Papers of Major General Hugh Scott, Library of Congress.

5. Testifying before a House committee after the war, Eisenman stated that in the early months he located the bidders and the quartermaster general's office signed the contracts to make them legal. See J. Franklin Crowell, *Government War Contracts* (New York: Oxford Univ. Press, 1920), 54.

6. *New York Times,* July 11, 1917.

7. McAdoo to Wilson, May 16, 1917, the Papers of William G. McAdoo, Library of Congress. The best study of Baruch is Jordan A. Schwarz, *The Speculator: Bernard M. Baruch in Washington, 1917–1965* (Chapel Hill: Univ. of North Carolina Press, 1981.) Baruch's recommendations were representative of the contemporary conventional managerial wisdom.

8. Bernard Baruch, *The Public Years* (New York: Holt, Rinhardt, and Winston, 1960), 1–17.

9. Baker to Wilson, May 28, 1917, in the Baker Papers.

10. Baker to Wilson, June 13, 1917, in the Baker Papers; Bernard M. Baruch to Wilson, July 11, 1917, in the Wilson Papers; Diary of Josephus Daniels, July 9, 1917, in the Daniels Papers; Baker to Wilson, July 14, 1917, in the Wilson Papers; Wilson to Baker, July 17, 1917, in the Baker Papers; the War Diary of Josephus Daniels, July 28, 1917, in the Daniels Papers; McAdoo to Wilson, July 30, 1917, in the Wilson Papers; Baker to Wilson, Aug. 1, 1917, in the Baker Papers. For Wilson's letter on the duties of the WIB, see Clarkson, *Industrial America in the World War,* 37. For a good discussion of the work of the supply committees during the summer and autumn of 1917 and their connections with the War Department, see Clarkson's interviews with Herbert E. Peabody of April 11, 1921, and Charles Otis of May 19, 1920, in "Statements of Men in War Work," the Papers of Bernard Baruch, Firestone Library, Princeton University. I have written at length on the politics of the summer reorganizations in *Newton D. Baker.*

11. Wilson to Baker, Sept. 18, 1917, in the Baker Papers; Baker to Wilson, Sept. 21, 1917, in the Wilson Papers; Clarkson, *Industrial American in the World War,* 82–85; Baker to Wilson, Sept. 21, 1917, in the Wilson Papers; Diary of Josephus Daniels, Nov. 7 and 12, 1917, in the Daniels Papers. Although anti-Semitism was widespread in the United States at the time, there is no evidence that Baker himself was an anti-Semite.

12. Baker to Wilson, Nov. 17, 1917, quoted in Frederick Palmer, *Newton D. Baker,* 1:379.

13. The best study of activities of the War Congress is Seward W. Livermore, *Politics is Adjourned: Woodrow Wilson and the War Congress, 1916–1918* (Middletown, Conn.: Wesleyan Univ. Press, 1966). Some members of the WIB, who believed that the War Department, particularly by the Stettinius appointment, was circumventing them to make unnecessary any further delegation of power, supported Chamberlain's move. See Clarkson, *Industrial America in the World War,* 52–54.

14. *New York Times,* Jan. 21, 1918.

15. Baruch, *The Public Years,* 46; Margaret L. Coit, *Mr. Baruch* (Boston: Houghton Mifflin, 1957), 166–72. Appointment of Baruch as secretary of war would also make him chairman of the CND and, as far as McAdoo was concerned, kill two birds with one stone and make Baruch, except for President Wilson and, perhaps indirectly, McAdoo himself, the most powerful man in the United States.

16. I have analyzed the Jan.–Feb. management crisis in *Newton D. Baker,* 104–9, and also in "Newton D. Baker and the Genesis of the War Industries Board," *Journal of American History* 52, no. 1 (June 1965): 43–58. For the critical primary sources, see Daniels Diary, Jan. 24, 1918, in the Daniels Papers; Baker to Wilson, Jan. 24, 1918, in the Wilson Papers; McAdoo to Wilson, Jan. 27, 1918, in the Wilson Papers.

17. Alpheus Thomas Mason, *Brandeis: A Free Man's Life* (New York: Viking, 1946), 524; House to Wilson, Feb. 6, 1918, in the Wilson Papers.

18. Baker to Wilson, Feb. 2, 1918, in the Wilson Papers; Wilson to McAdoo, Feb. 26, 1918, in the Wilson Papers; Wilson to Baker, Mar. 4, 1918, in the Baker Papers.

19. Baruch, *The Pubic Years,* 74. See also Robert D. Cuff, "Bernard Baruch: Symbol and Myth in Industrial Mobilization," *Business History Review* 43 (Summer 1969): 115–33. Baruch emerged from the war with an enhanced reputation. He was ambivalent about carrying the WIB into the postwar era. Unlike George Peek, he sought to end national controls as quickly as possible. He resigned as chairman of the WIB shortly after the armistice. Later, during the mid-1930s, when things in Washington were not so much to his liking, Baruch would think again about the "analogue of war" and revise his views about the effectiveness of government economic regulation.

20. Hawley, *The Great War,* 25; Zimmerman, *Neck of the Bottle,* 108. On May 28, 1918, after the passage of the Overman Act, President Wilson formally separated the WIB from the CND.

21. Edward R. Stettinius to Bernard Baruch Mar. 10, 1918, the Papers of Bernard Baruch; Coit, *Mr. Baruch,* 201.

22. Wilson to Baruch, Mar. 4, 1918, Records of the War Industries Board, RG 61, National Archives. There is an excellent discussion of the work of the WIB during 1918 in Cuff, *War Industries Board.*

23. Ohl, "Old Iron Pants."

24. P. E. Foerderer to George N. Peek, May 24, 1918; Hugh Johnson to George Peek, June 18, 1918, Requirements Division File, WIB Records, RG 61, National Archives.

25. Hugh Johnson to Alex Legge, June 14, 1918; Pope Yeatman to James Inglis, July 9, 1918; Requirements Division File, Records of the WIB, RG 61, National Archives.

26. Minutes of Priorities Board Meeting, July 22, 1918, Priorities Division File, Records of the WIB, RG 61, National Archives.

27. Office Review Memorandum, Division of Purchase and Supply, July 24, 1918, Records of the PS and T Division, General Staff, RG 165, National Archives.

28. Assignment of H. R. Hatfield, reported in Hugh Johnson to W. W. Guylee, Aug. 12, 1918, and Guylee to Major H. R. Hayes (P and S Section, PS and T), Sept. 21, 1918, Requirements Division File, Records of the WIB, RG 61, National Archives.

29. As Edward Morse of the brass section of the WIB wrote in mid-September, "Speaking generally, our own idea of requirements is based on our own guess, and while the guess

is not intelligent, it is as reliable as any information that is to be furnished with a program in each department that changes every week." Edward Morse to Edwin Gay, WIB Division of Planning and Statistics, Sept. 12, 1918, Requirements Division File, Records of the WIB, RG 61, National Archives.

30. Grosvenor Clarkson, interview with Charles A. Otis, president of the Cleveland Chamber of Commerce, and the Otis Elevator Co., May 19, 1920, in "Statements of Men in War Work," the Papers of Bernard Baruch.

31. Gibbs to Aldrich, July 10, 1918; Crabb to Gibbs, Sept. 14, 1918; Meeting of the Special Requirements Committee, Oct. 24, 1918, Requirements Division File, WIB Records, RG 61, National Archives. See also Beaver, "George W. Goethals," 95–110.

32. *Minutes of the WIB,* Sept. 26, 1917; Feb. 7, 1918; *Iron Age,* Feb. 7, 1918, 101:266; *Minutes of the WIB,* Feb. 7, 1918, 205–6; *Iron Age,* 101:266. See also E. H. Gary to Bernard Baruch, Apr. 2, 1918, Records of the Shipping Board, RG 32, National Archives.

33. Memorandum of a meeting with the Washington representatives of the American Iron and Steel Institute, May 17, 1918, PS and T Division File, Records of the General Staff, RG 165, National Archives; History of the Priorities Division of the WIB, Priorities File, Records of the WIB, RG 61, National Archives.

34. Priorities Division; Meeting of June 3, 1918, Priorities File, Records of the WIB, RG 61, National Archives.

35. *Minutes of the War Industries Board, 1917–1918* (Washington, D.C.: GPO, 1935), 205–6.

36. *Iron Age,* Apr. 18, 1918, CI, 1016.

37. Priorities History; Meeting of Sept. 20, 1918; Judge Parker to commodity chiefs and section heads, Sept. 24, 1918, Priorities Division File, Records of the WIB, RG 61, National Archives.

38. Baruch to Crowell, Sept. 5, 1918, in *Minutes of the WIB,* 466–67; Crowell to March, Sept. 5, 1918, Files of the Office of the Adjutant General, RG 94; National Archives; General Order 86, Sept. 18, 1918.

39. For an analysis of the steel situation at the end of 1917, see Replogle to Baruch, Dec. 6, 1917, Records of the WIB, RG 61, National Archives.

40. For conditions in the mines, see Edward Hurley to Charles R. Tower, Apr. 12, 1918, Records of the United States Shipping Board, RG 32, National Archives.

41. James Inglis to William Ritter, July 25, 1918, Requirements Division File; Records of the WIB, RG 61, National Archives.

42. Hard, *New Republic,* July 1918.

43. Hard, *New Republic,* Sept. 1918; David Montgomery, *The Fall of the House of Labor: The Workplace, the State, and American Labor Activism, 1865–1925* (New York: Cambridge Univ. Press, 1987), 330–410.

44. The best study of the railroad situation is Kerr, *American Railroad Politics.*

45. Crowell and Wilson, *How America Went to War,* 4:115–16.

46. Walker Hines, *War History of American Railroads.* For public discussion of the 1917 crisis, see the *Literary Digest* 5 (Oct. 20, 1917): 22. Another contemporary report is that of T.C. Powell to George N. Peek, Nov. 4, 1918, Requirements Division File, Records of the WIB, RG 61, National Archives.

47. Annual Report of the Inland Traffic Service, Sept. 7, 1918, General Rogers's File; Records of the Quartermaster General's Office, RG 92, National Archives.

48. McAdoo to Wilson, Mar. 25, 1918, in the Baruch Papers; Baruch to Assistant Secretary of War Benedict Crowell, Apr. 2, 1918; Crowell to Baruch, Apr. 5, 1918, in the Baruch Papers.

49. James Inglis to Hodell, [June 16 ?], 1918, Requirements Division File, WIB Records, RG 61, National Archives.

50. James Inglis to Alfred S. Kellogg, July 19, 1918, Requirements Division File, WIB Records, RG 61, National Archives.

51. Guylee to Johnson, Sept. 12, 1918, Requirements Division File, WIB Records, RG 61; Supply Bulletin 20, Sept. 23, 1918, Records of the PS and T Division, General Staff, RG 165, National Archives.

52. Supply Bulletin 28, Oct. 24, 1918, Records of the PS and T Division, General Staff, RG 165, National Archives.

53. Memorandum from George W. Goethals on the appointment of H.M. Adams to head the Inland Traffic Service, Jan. 15, 1918, Records of the Office of the Adjutant General, RG 94, National Archives. Inland Traffic Service Order 1, Feb. 18, 1918, "Rules and Regulations of the Division of Inland Transportation of the Storage and Traffic Service," General Rogers's File, Records of the QMG, RG 92, National Archives.

54. *New York Times,* June 21, 1918; Report of T. C. Powell to George Peek, Nov. 4, 1918, Requirements Division File, Records of the WIB, RG 61, National Archives.

55. The greatest logistical tests of the war still lay in the future. For a description of conditions at ports of embarkation in the fall of 1918, see Crowell and Wilson, *How America Went to War;* and Hines, *War History of American Railroads.*

56. Tasker H. Bliss to Newton D. Baker, May 31, 1917, in the Bliss Papers.

57. Beaver, *Baker,* 85–87.

58. For the War Board, see George Soule, *Prosperity Decade: From War to Depression, 1917–1929,* vol. 8 of Henry David et al., eds., *The Economic History of the United States* (New York: Rinhart, 1947), 29–59. The War Board formed the nucleus for the Shipping-Control Committee, which began in New York and expanded its authority later over all American ports of embarkation.

59. Edward M. Hurley to Carry, Jan. 31, 1918, copy in the Records of the Office of the Chief of Staff, 1917–1918, RG 165, National Archives.

60. Goethals to Biddle, Jan. 23, 1918; and Goethals to Biddle, Feb. 4, 1918, Records of the Office of the Chief of Staff, RG 165, National Archives.

61. *Iron Age,* 101:21.

62. For Schwab's connections with the Allies, see Gaddis Smith, *Britain's Clandestine Submarines* (New Haven, Conn.: Yale Univ. Press, 1964). Frederick Lewis Allen tells one version of Schwab's role in the creation of U.S. Steel in *The Lords of Creation* (New York: Harpers, 1935), 18–34. The best version is in Robert Hessen, *Steel Titan: The Life of Charles M. Schwab* (New York: Oxford Univ. Press, 1975).

63. Alex Legge to James Inglis, June 15, 1918 Requirements Division File, WIB Records, RG 61, National Archives; Alex Legge to Charles Piez, June 11, 1918, Piez File, Shipping Board Records, RG 32, National Archives.

64. Charles Piez to George W. Goethals, June 12, 1918; and Goethals to Piez June 12, 1918, Piez File, Shipping Board Records, RG 32, National Archives.

65. Baker to Hurley, July 22, 1918, War College Division Records, Records of the General Staff, RG 165, National Archives.

66. "Army Cargo Situation," Oct. 7, 1918, with background material, Division of Planning and Statistics, Shipping Board Records, RG 32, National Archives.

67. L. P. Alford to John R. Dunlap [of the EFC], Nov. 4, 1918, Piez File, Shipping Board Records, RG 32, National Archives.

68. "Report of the Investigation of Hog Island," Sept. 1918, Piez File, Shipping Board Records, RG 32, National Archives.

69. Edward N. Hurley, *The Bridge to France*.

70. From the beginning, the logistical infrastructure of the home base was overburdened. The removal of even half a million men meant an immediate labor shortage in an industrial economy that was still labor intensive and at full employment. The railroads, which had almost collapsed under the weight of eastward-moving agricultural goods in the fall of 1916 and collapsed again in Dec. 1917, were notoriously short of locomotives and cars, even in normal times. In Sept. 1917, shipping was already in short supply and conditions got worse. If nothing had changed, ad hoc volunteer organizations and the existing federal agencies might have muddled through, but the war's dimensions changed and wrought changes in Wilsonian war-making timetables that confronted soldiers, businessmen, and government officials with brutal new realities.

71. Ohl, "Old Iron Pants," 64–183.

72. Priority Committee minutes, May 25, 1918, Priorities Division File, WIB Records, RG 61, National Archives.

73. Johnson to March, Aug. 1, 1918, Chief of Staff's Correspondence File, 1917–21, RG 165, National Archives.

74. Hurley to Schwab, July 18, 1918, General Files of the U.S. Shipping Board, RG 32, National Archives.

75. Statement of Samuel Vauclain, Locomotive Committee, July 11, 1918, WIB Records, RG 61, National Archives.

76. Circular letter from President Woodrow Wilson to all concerned department heads, July 24, 1918, WIB Resources and Conversion Division Files, RG 61, National Archives.

77. William McNeill, *The Pursuit of Power: Technology, Armed Force, and Society since A.D. 1000* (Chicago: Univ. of Chicago Press, 1982), 306.

78. It was a Progressive truism that information was power. Progressives had a passion for numbers and percentages. The Bureau of the Census, the first national statistical agency, had existed in some form since the beginnings of the republic, and its 1880 figures were the best available on the growth of industry in the nineteenth century. After 1890 more specialized statistical agencies emerged in the Bureau of Standards, the Department of Labor, the Bureau of Mines, the Department of Agriculture, and other official organizations. In 1906 the new Department of Commerce became a central depository for business data, and, as part of the quest for scientific management and efficiency, the War Department bureaus developed their own statistical sections before the First World War. There was, however, no central repository where all the information could be assembled and made into a useful management tool. The industrial inventory undertaken in 1915 accumulated some preliminary figures before the declaration of war, but in the spring of 1918 its work was far from complete. See Jerry Israel, "A Diplomatic Machine: Scientific Management in the State Department, 1906–1924," in Galambos, ed., *Building the Organizational Society*, 183–96. Coffman, at the end of the most recent edition of his study of

the United States Army in the Great War, *The War to End All Wars,* writes succinctly about the problem of securing reliable statistics for the First World War (396).

79. *Foreign Relations, 1917,* vol. 1, supplement 2 (Washington, D.C.: GPO, 1931–32), 437.

80. Leland and Mereness, comp., *Economic and Social History of the World War,* 68.

81. There is no general history of the development of statistical methods during the First World War. For a start, however, see Robert D. Cuff, "Creating Control Systems: Edwin F. Gay and the Central Bureau of Planning and Statistics, 1917–1918," *Business History Review* 63 (Autumn 1989): 588–613; and William J. Breen, "Foundations, Statistics, and State Building: Leonard P. Ayres, the Russell Sage Foundation, and U.S. Government Statistics in the First World War," *Business History Review* 68 (Winter 1994): 451–82. For the notes between the Allied and Associated Powers, see *Foreign Relations,* 1918, supplement 1, 576.

8. Coalition War-making, 1917–1918

1. Beaver, *Baker,* 165–68; Smythe, *Pershing,* 161–68. The two most recent studies of inter-Allied diplomacy are David R. Woodward, *Trial by Friendship;* and David F. Trask, *The A.E.F. and Coalition War Making, 1917–1918* (Lawrence: Univ. Press of Kansas, 1993). The best example of this suspicion involved the question of the amalgamation of American forces into the British and French armies.

2. Wilson to Edward M. House, July 17, 1917, quoted in David F. Trask, *Captains and Cabinets: Anglo-American Naval Relations, 1917–1918* (Columbia: Univ. of Missouri Press, 1972), 126. See also Huston, *The Sinews of War;* Walter Millis, *The Road to War: America, 1914–1917* (Boston: Houghton Mifflin, 1935); Burton Kauffman, *Efficiency and Expansion, Foreign Trade in the Wilson Administration, 1913–1921* (Westport, Conn.: Greenwood, 1974); and Carl P. Parrini, *Heir to Empire: United States Economic Diplomacy, 1916–1923* (Pittsburgh, Pa.: Univ. of Pittsburgh Press, 1969).

3. Cecil Spring-Rice to Alfred [Lord] Balfour, Sept. 21, 1917, quoted in Trask, *Captains and Cabinets,* 168.

4. The best account of inter-Allied financial dealings is Kathleen Burk, *Britain, America, and the Sinews of War, 1914–1918* (Boston: Allen and Unwin, 1985). Edward R. Stettinius, who would become surveyor general of supply in the War Department in early Jan. 1918, coordinated prewar activity for the Morgan interests. William G. McAdoo, *Crowded Years: The Reminiscences of William Gibbs McAdoo* (Boston: Houghton Mifflin, 1931), has a good discussion of the early financial mobilization effort. Cuff, *The War Industries Board,* analyzes early economic mobilization. See also Beaver, *Baker,* 50–78.

5. Army War College Report 14004, accompanied by a memorandum for the chief of staff from Lieutenant Colonel C. Bentley Mott, Sept. 12, 1917, Records of the War Department General Staff, RG 165, National Archives.

6. Newton D. Baker to Chief of Staff Tasker H. Bliss, Sept. 14, 1917, Records of the War Department General Staff, RG 165, National Archives.

7. On American arrogance and the inter-Allied economic committees, see Crowell and Wilson, *How America Went to War,* 1:143; and Clarkson, *Industrial America in the World War,* 485.

8. John T. Sumida, "Forging the Trident: British Naval Industrial Logistics, 1914–1918," in John A. Lynn, ed., *Feeding Mars: Logistics in Western Warfare from the Middle Ages to the*

Present (Boulder, Colo.: Westview, 1993), 227. In 1918 the British actually reduced their production of artillery shell and reallocated steel to other uses.

9. For the French effort to build an assembly plant, one which remained uncompleted in Nov. 1918, see Albert G. Stern, *Tanks: 1914–1918: The Logbook of a Pioneer* (London: Hodder and Soughton, 1919).

10. *Foreign Relations,* 1917, supplement 1, 2:413–30, 561–62.

11. Tasker H. Bliss to Acting Chief of Staff [John Biddle], Dec. 14, 1917, Records of the Supreme War Council, RG 120, National Archives; *Foreign Relations,* 1917, supplement 2, 1:419–20, 423–31, 441.

12. *Foreign Relations,* 1917, supplement 2, 1:418–19.

13. "Summary of Preliminary Estimates of Probable Shipments of Troops, Animals, and Cargo from November 1917–June 1918," Records of the Council of National Defense, RG 62, National Archives; "Moving American Troops to France," Jan. [20 ?], 1918, Planning and Statistics Division, United States Shipping Board, RG 32, National Archives.

14. Goethals to Biddle, "For the Secretary of War," Feb. 4, 1918, Records of the War Department General Staff, RG 165, National Archives.

15. Green to Gay, Mar. 14, 1918; Rublee to Gay, Apr. 1, 1918, Records of the Division of Planning and Statistics of the United States Shipping Board, RG 32, National Archives.

16. Beaver, *Baker,* 110–50. The entire affair was part of the amalgamation controversy that had been simmering since the Americans entered the war.

17. Chief of Ordnance C. C. Williams to Chief of Staff Peyton C. March, July 19, 1918, Historical Records of the Ordnance Department, RG 156, National Archives. The Ordnance Department notes were prepared in part to brief Assistant Secretary of War Stettinius for his European trip.

18. The Office Diary of George W. Goethals, Mar. 27, 1918, Papers of George W. Goethals, Library of Congress, Washington, D.C.; "Extracts from Conferences on the Movement of Troops Abroad, March 14–21, 1918," War Department Historical Files, RG 120, National Archives. Hurley, *The Bridge to France,* contains a good discussion of the shipping situation in the United States.

19. For examples of the unanswered cables, see Stevens, Hurley, Gay, McAdoo, McCormick, and Hoover, May 25, 1918, in *Foreign Relations,* 1918, supplement 1, 1:577–78, 583–84.

20. *Foreign Relations,* 1918, supplement 1, 1:599–600.

21. American historians have neglected the summer and early autumn meetings of the inter-Allied councils. The only sustained published accounts are in Clarkson, *Industrial America in the World War;* and Crowell and Wilson, *How America Went to War.*

22. *Foreign Relations,* 1918, supplement 1, 1:605–8.

23. Ibid., 1:606.

24. Ibid., 1:609, 611–12.

25. Beaver, *Baker,* 175.

26. Ibid., 175–76. For the Foch incident, see Palmer, *Newton D. Baker,* 2:348.

27. *New York Times,* Oct. 3, 1918.

28. *Foreign Relations,* 1918, supplement 1, 1:528–29; Lansing to Laughlin, Oct. 26, 1918; Stanley King to Baker, Nov. 8, 1918; Bernard Baruch to Baker, Nov. 2, 1918, Papers of Newton D.

Baker; Donald Scott to Edwin Gay, Oct. 18, 1918, Records of the Division of Planning and Statistics, United States Shipping Board, RG 32, National Archives.

29. Bliss to March, Oct. 14, 1918, in the Bliss Papers; Crowell and Wilson, *How America Went to War,* 1:143; Clarkson, *Industrial America in the World War,* 485.

30. Goethals to Thomas J. Goethals, Oct. 27, 1918; Nov. 10, 1918, Papers of George W. Goethals, Library of Congress, Washington, D.C.

31. *Foreign Relations, 1917,* supplement 2, 1:357.

9. General Supplies, Artillery, and Smokeless Powder

1. *War Department General Order 80,* Aug. 26, 1918 (Washington, D.C.: GPO, 1918).

2. See chap. 6 (above) for the details of Goethals's work as director of the PS and T division of the general staff.

3. *War Department Annual Reports 1919; Annual Report of the Quartermaster General* in full. For accounts of Goethals's work see Risch, *Quartermaster Support of the Army,* 630–36; Beaver "George W. Goethals and the Problem of Military Supply," 95–109; and Zimmerman, *The Neck of the Bottle.*

4. Interview of Grosvenor Clarkson with Herbert R. Peabody, President of the Association of American Woolen and Worsted Manufactures, Apr. 11, 1921, in Clarkson's "Statements of Men in War Work," in the Papers of Bernard Baruch, Firestone Library, Princeton University. See also annual report of the quartermaster general for 1918 and 1919 and Risch, *Quartermaster Support of the Army.*

5. Desk Diary of George W. Goethals, June 13, 1918, Papers of George W. Goethals, Library of Congress.

6. Newton. D. Baker to Thomas Nelson Page, June 22, 1918, Baker Papers, Library of Congress.

7. For Pershing's November recommendations, see *My Experiences in the World War,* 1:221–22. For the Bliss cable, see Beaver, *Baker,* 117.

8. The development of the artillery program can be followed in Crozier to Bliss, June 20, 1917; Crozier to Biddle, Nov. 8, 1917; P. D. Lockridge to Biddle, Nov. 26, 1917; War College to Biddle, Feb. 6, 1918; and Biddle to Wheeler, Feb. 28, 1918, Records of the Adjutant General's Office, RG 94, National Archives.

9. For the appointment of Wheeler, see *Annual Report of the Chief of Ordnance,* in *War Department Annual Reports, 1918,* 1:1043. Baker is quoted in Harvey DeWeerd, *President Wilson Fights His War: World War I and the American Intervention* (New York: Macmillan, 1968), 224; and *Report of the Chief of Ordnance,* in *War Department Annual Reports, 1919,* vol. 1, part 4, 3868–69. The Kernan Board had reported in 1916, "For the first six months after a war emergency arose, the delivery of complete field artillery would be limited practically to that previously under manufacture at the one arsenal engaged in the fabrication of field gun carriages and vehicles. Increased output of consequence should begin in nine months to a year. It would probably be eighteen months or more before all the output *which had been foreseen and arranged for in the beginning could be obtained"* (emphasis mine). Crozier had stated categorically in 1916, "The time required for an unprepared adaptation of this kind is sometimes surprising and in the case of an emergency would be serious."

10. The discussion of the reorganization of the Ordnance Bureau is based on the historical section of a memorandum, prepared in 1922 in the Office of the Chief of Ordnance, titled "Information that Each Executive Assistant to an Ordnance District Chief Should Possess," June 22, 1922, Records of the Office of the Chief of Ordnance Historical File, RG 156, National Archives.

11. *War Department Annual Reports 1919: Report of the Chief of Ordnance.* vol. 1, part 4; Constance M. Green, Harry C. Thompson, and Peter C. Roots, *The Ordnance Department: Planning Munitions for War* (Washington, D.C.: Office of the Chief of Military History, 1955), 27–29.

12. For a discussion of Wheeler's reassignment, see Ordnance History [1919], RG 156, National Archives. See also Crowell and Wilson, *How America Went to War.* For the quotation on Wheeler, see March, *The Nation at War,* 369. Wheeler served as AEF chief of ordnance until Sept. 1918, when he became the American military representative on the Inter-Allied Ordnance Committee.

13. Green, Thompson, and Roots, *The Ordnance Department,* 29.

14. *War Department Annual Reports, 1919: Report of the Chief of Ordnance,* vol. 1, part 4, 3892–93.

15. Ibid., 3893.

16. For the special case of Bridgeport, see Montgomery's article on the Bridgeport strike, in *Workers' Control in America.*

17. *War Department Annual Reports, 1919,* vol.3, *Annual Report of the Chief of Ordnance,* includes an extensive discussion of the arms and equipment produced by each of the major ordnance districts.

18. Discussion of the artillery program is based on the material contained in the report of a special artillery board convened in June 1918 to analyze the progress of the program and make recommendations, and a general "History of the Artillery Program" prepared for the chief of ordnance and submitted on Jan. 10, 1919. The artillery board report was intended in part to rationalize the program at home and in part to prepare Assistant Secretary of War Stettinius for his mission to Europe. See "General Conditions Concerning the Manufacture of 75mm Gun Carriages," May 1, 1918; "Historical Statement in Connection with the 155mm Howitzer Material"; "Effective Utilization of Existing Facilities for Manufacturing Artillery Material," Aug. 10, 1918; and "Present and Prospective Deliveries for 75mm and 155mm Guns and Howitzers," Sept. 10, 11, and 12, 1918, Records of the Office of the Chief of Ordnance, Ordnance Historical File, RG 156, National Archives.

19. *War Department Annual Reports, 1919: Report of the Chief of Ordnance,* vol. 1, part 4, 3869.

20. For the war records of the chief government arsenals, see *The History of Picatinny Arsenal* (Picatinny, N.J.: War Plans Division, Plant Engineering Plant, n.d.); *A History of the Watertown Arsenal, Watertown, Massachusetts, 1816–1967* (Watertown, Mass.: Army Materials and Mechanics Research Center, 1977); *History of Watervliet Arsenal, 1813–1968* (Troy, N.Y.: U.S. Army, Watervliet Arsenal, 1969); *A Short History of the Island of Rock Island, 1816–1966* (Rock Island, Ill.: Rock Island Arsenal, 1967), 870–71; and *War's Greatest Workshop: Rock Island Arsenal* (Rock Island, Ill.: Arsenal, 1922).

21. *General History of the Artillery Program,* Jan. 10, 1919, Office of the Chief of Ordnance, Historical Records Branch, RG 156, National Archives. For example, on Nov. 11, 1918, twenty-two firms were building the tubes, carriages, and recuperators for the 155 mm GF gun and the 155 mm howitzer, and 127 firms were building smaller component parts. All elements in the program were to be interchangeable. That ideal was never met.

22. *New York Times,* Dec. 12, 1917.

23. For a discussion of the poor quality of clothing, web and leather equipment, small arms, artillery, and ammunition supplied by the Americans to the British during the first two years of the war, see Peter Simkins, *Kitchener's Armies: The Raising of the New Armies, 1914–1916* (Manchester, U.K,: Manchester Univ. Press, 1988), 256–95.

24. DeWeerd, "Production Lag," 170–71.

25. *History of 155mm Howitzer Production,* Ordnance Historical File, RG 156, National Archives.

26. *History of the District Offices,* June 22, 1922, Ordnance Historical File, RG 156, National Archives. The memorandum "Information that Each Executive Assistant to an Ordnance District Chief Should Possess," prepared in 1922, tells the Mosler and Dodge stories as well as the story of the conflicts among the district managers and their chiefs in Washington.

27. "Effective Utilization of Existing Facilities for Manufacturing Artillery Material: 75mm Shrapnel," memorandum, July 29, 1918, Office of the Chief of Ordnance, Ordnance Historical File, RG 156, National Archives.

28. Hogg did not follow the story of the split-trail carriage to its conclusion in the summer of 1918. See Ian Hogg, *The Guns, 1914–1918* (New York: Ballantine, 1972).

29. It took Willis-Overland six months to retool. For a discussion of recuperator production for the "75," see DeWeerd, "Production Lag," 169. This was the same system that allegedly had been offered earlier to Isaac Lewis by the French government and rejected by the Ordnance Department.

30. DeWeerd, "Production Lag," 77–83, 159–74. Deweerd's account is incomplete. Apparently the shift to the model 1897 production program was considered a temporary solution. Production of the model 1916 carriage did not stop. According to the *General History of the Artillery Program,* reinforced by the Artillery Board report of July 2, 1918, and Colonel James W. Benét's *Annual Report for 1919,* a modest parallel program for the model 1916 gun and carriage continued at Watervliet Arsenal throughout the war. AEF Chief of Ordnance Wheeler must have known about it, but there is no evidence that he ever mentioned it to anyone. There is also no evidence that Williams informed Pershing's headquarters that a shift in production might be undertaken in the fall of 1918.

31. Alfred D. Chandler and Stephen Salsbury, *Pierre S. Du Pont,* 396–98. In 1924 the Historical Division of the Ordnance Department prepared another extensively documented and somewhat different history, which reflected the story from the perspective of Secretary Baker and the War Department. That paper, which comprises the institutional memory of the Ordnance Department and supplements the DuPont version of affairs, can be found in Major P. J. O'Shaughnessy, "History of the Old Hickory Powder Plant," May 24, 1924. Together with another, more contemporary, document, "Financing the Ordnance Department" (June 1919 [?], in the Ordnance Historical File, Records of the Office of the Chief of

Ordnance, RG 156, National Archives), it constitutes a significant part of the archival support for this portion of the chapter.

32. Acting Chief of Staff Tasker H. Bliss to Chief of Ordnance William Crozier, June 9, 1917, Ordnance Historical File, Office of the Chief of Ordnance, RG 156, National Archives; Bliss to Crozier, 21 June 1917, Chief of Staff's File, RG 165, National Archives. See also Harvey De Weerd, "The American Adoption of French Artillery, 1917–1918," *Journal of the American Military Institute* 3 (Summer 1939): 104–16.

33. Petain memos of May 19, 1917, and Dec. 15, 1917; Memorandum, "Attacks with Limited Objectives," 3rd section, General Staff, GHQ, French Armies of the North and Northeast, cited in *The United States Army in the World War,* vol. 1, *Policy Making Documents,* 101–2.

34. Pershing, *My Experiences in the World War,* 1:107, 143–44; *The United States Army in the World War,* vol. 2, *Policy Documents,* 96. For one view of the solution to the nitrate issue, see Baruch, *The Public Years,* 44–45; *Annual Report of the Chief of Ordnance,* in *War Department Annual Reports, 1917,* 1:812. The cable advising that it was possible that the French as well as the Americans would have to be supplied is in O'Shaughnessy, "History of the Old Hickory Powder Plant."

35. Chief of Ordnance Clarence C. Williams to Chief of Staff Peyton C. March, July 19, 1918, Ordnance Historical File, RG 156, National Archives. The general wrote, "The rates of fire provided by our existing programs are considerably in excess of what the British and French experience is understood to justify." Williams believed the situation had become ludicrous, and, when Assistant Secretary of War Edward R. Stettinius Sr. went abroad to attend inter-Allied munitions meetings in late July 1918, he took with him a request from the chief of ordnance that something be done to get control of the run-amuck smokeless-powder program.

36. Chandler and Salsbury, *Pierre S. Du Pont,* 248; 400–410; O'Shaughnessy, "History of the Old Hickory Powder Plant"; and "Financing the Ordnance Department." See also "Council of National Defense: Munitions Standards Board," minutes of Mar. 21 and Apr. 15 and 20, 1917, Records of the Council of National Defense, RG 62, National Archives. The results of the meetings of Frank Scott, Colonel Buckner, and Major General William Crozier during Apr. 1917 are also quoted in O'Shaughnessy, "History of the Old Hickory Powder Plant," 36.

37. "Financing the Ordnance Department." Similar arrangements had been made during the construction of the Panama Canal, and contracts with the Emergency Fleet Corporation during the last months of peace and the first months 1916–17 had already created the so-called GOCO (Government Owned, Contractor Operated) system that the conventional wisdom attributes to the mobilization period before the Second World War. During the First World War such contracts, only used in particular circumstances when rapid expansion of facilities of little peacetime use by private industry was required, were called "agency contracts," and their use was widespread.

38. Chandler and Salsbury, *Pierre S. Du Pont,* 404–9.

39. Newton D. Baker to Pierre DuPont, Oct. 31, 1917, Records of the Office of the Secretary of War, RG 107, National Archives.

40. Chandler and Salisbury, *Pierre S. Du Pont,* 414.

41. O'Shaughnessy, "History of the Old Hickory Powder Plant."

42. Ibid.

43. Chandler and Salsbury, *Pierre S. Du Pont,* 424–25. According to Chandler, DuPont believed Baker had approved the new negotiations and that their antagonisms were starting

to dissipate in the common effort to win the war. The presence of Samuel McRoberts on the negotiating committee may have been the result of an earlier War Department attempt to balance Stettinius, a member of J. P. Morgan and Company, with an important former member of the Rockefeller organization.

44. O'Shaughnessy, "History of the Old Hickory Powder Plant." Ironically, the Hercules Powder Company, a DuPont subsidiary, contracted to operate the plant at Nitro, West Virginia.

45. Paul A. C. Koistinen includes a comprehensive, though controversial, discussion on interwar investigations of the munitions industry in the third volume of his series on war and American business, *Planning War, Pursuing Peace: The Political Economy of American Warfare, 1920–1939* (Lawrence: Univ. Press of Kansas, 1998). For a discussion of twentieth-century conspiracy theories, see Anne Trotter, "Development of the 'Merchants of Death' Theory," in Cooling, ed., *War Business and American Society.*

46. Green, Thompson, and Roots, *Planning Munitions for War,* 25–27.

10. Motor Transport, Tanks, Aircraft, and Communications Equipment

1. Norman Cary, "Motor Vehicles in the US Army," 253–54; *War Department Annual Reports 1916: Report of the Secretary of War,* 1:23. The quartermasters, ordnance, engineers, signals, and surgeon general all ordered trucks.

2. See Beaver, "Politics and Policy," 101–8.

3. For conditions on the Western Front and the response of the belligerents to them, see Shelford Bidwell and Dominick Graham, *Fire-Power,* 39–148. This discussion of the American tank program relies for the most part on published reports in the *United States Army in the World War,* contemporary articles in journals of opinion, and, especially, the reports and appendixes in Major R. E. Carlson, ORC., "Memorandum on the Development of Tanks," Mar. 16, 1921, Records of the Office of the Chief of Ordnance, RG 156, National Archives.

4. For Pershing, see his *My Experiences,* 1:68. For the report of the tank committee, see *United States Army in the World War,* 1:138–39. The report recommended the creation of five battalions of heavy and twenty battalions of light tanks. Like visionaries in all armies, there were Americans who believed tanks were capable of revolutionizing warfare. One officer on the Baker Board, which was then in France representing the War Department, argued that tanks were a new weapon and should be a new branch of service, but Colonel Frank Parker of Pershing's staff considered the suggestion to be inappropriate and self-serving.

5. "Report on the Development of the Tank Corps," *The United States Army in the World War,* 15:220–25.

6. Tasker H. Bliss to Newton D. Baker, Dec. 14, 1917, Supreme War Council Records, RG 120, National Archives.

7. "Agreement between the British and U.S. Governments for the Production of Tanks," Jan. 22, 1918, *United States Army in the World War,* 15:223–24.

8. General Charles B. Wheeler to Benedict Crowell, Apr. 10, 1918: Attention Mr. Stettinius, Records of the Adjutant General's Office, RG 94, National Archives. This was part of a general report on all ordnance programs including light- and heavy-artillery manufacturing for 1919.

9. *War Department Annual Reports, 1918: Report of the Secretary of War,* 1:1394.

10. Robert J. Icks, *Tanks and Armored Vehicles,* ed. Philip Andrews (New York: Duell, Sloan, and Pearce, 1945), 45.

11. Icks, *Tanks,* 45.

12. O'Shaughnessy, "Ordnance History," May 24, 1922, Ordnance Historical File, RG 156, National Archives.

13. Notes of Conference of Division Chiefs, Office of the Chief of Ordnance, Aug. 16, 1918, Ordnance Historical File, Record Group 156. National Archives.

14. David A. Hounsell, "Ford Eagle Boats and Mass Production during World War I," in Smith, ed., *Military Enterprise and Technological Change.*

15. Production figures are from Director of Munitions and Assistant Secretary of War Benedict Crowell's *America's Munitions, 1917–1918: Report of Benedict Crowell, The Assistant Secretary of War and Director of Munitions* (Washington, D.C.: GPO, 1919), 157.

16. See Robert Icks, *Tanks,* 45, for the story of mild-steel tanks; for Rockenbach's comments as Chief of the Tank Corps in the AEF, see *United States Army in the World War,* 15:222; for Rockenbach's comments as Chief of the Army Tank Corps, see *War Department Annual Reports 1920: Annual Report of the Secretary of War,* 1:1894.

17. The most recent work on General Squier and his associates is Charles J. Gross, "George Owen Squier and the Origins of American Military Aviation," *Journal of Military History* 54 (July 1990): 281–305.

18. Secretary of Commerce William Redfield to Woodrow Wilson, Nov. 3, 1917, in the Wilson Papers.

19. Beaver, *Baker,* 161–65.

20. Benedict Crowell and Wilson, *How America Went to War,* 2:345.

21. Pershing, *My Experiences,* 1:161, 2:50.

22. Crowell and Wilson, *How America Went to War,* 1:378–80.

23. For a discussion of the Liberty engine, see Herschel Smith, *Aircraft Piston Engines: From the Manly Baltzer to the Continental Tira* (New York: McGraw Hill, 1981); and Paul S. Dickey III, *The Liberty Engine, 1918–1942,* in *Smithsonian Annals of Flight,* vol. 1, no. 3 (Washington, D.C.: Smithsonian Institution Press, 1968). For a discussion of attempts to improve the engine, see above and also *Material Research and Development in the Army Air Arm, 1914–1945,* Army Air Forces Historical Studies no. 50, AAF Historical Office, Headquarters, Army Air Forces, 1946.

24. Crowell, *America's Munitions,* 257.

25. For the situation in the air program in the summer of 1918 and Ryan's appointment, see Holley, *Ideas and Weapons,* 130; see also *New York Times,* July 30 and Aug. 28, 1918. For March's attitude, see March, *Nation at War,* 283–84.

26. Holley, *Ideas and Weapons,* 106.

27. *War Department Annual Reports, 1919: The Report of the Chief Signal Officer,* vol. 1, part 1, 886.

28. Ibid., 1152–55.

29. Clark, "George Owen Squier," 296–313.

30. *War Department Annual Reports, 1919: Report of the Chief Signal Officer,* 1:1120.

31. Ibid., 1:986–89.

32. Clark, "George Owen Squier," 342; "Oral Interview by Dr. G. R. Thompson with Fred Lack and William A. MacDonald, April 4 and May 20, 1960, at the Hezeltine, Long

Island Factory of the Little Neck Corporation," Signal Corps Historical Division Files in the archives at the United States Army Military History Institute, Carlisle Barracks, Pennsylvania. There is a fascinating short article on Squier's postwar career by David Lindsay, "The Muzak Man," in *Invention and Technology* 14, no. 2 (Fall 1998): 52–57.

11. Digesting the War Experience, 1919–1940

1. Beaver, "The Problem of American Military Supply," 87–89; undated interview with Hugh Johnson by Grosvenor Clarkson in "Statements of Men in War Work," the papers of Bernard M. Baruch, 6 and 7. Clarkson sanitized many of the interviews for his book, *Industrial America in the World War.*

2. Baker to Wilson, July 10, 1918, cited in Beaver, *Baker,* 173. Baker had suggested such a group in early Dec. 1917. Hoover and Baruch also claimed they originated the idea. See Francis W. O'Brien, ed., *The Hoover-Wilson Wartime Correspondence, September 24, 1914, to November 11, 1918* (Ames: Iowa State Univ. Press, 1974), 164; and Baruch, *The Public Years,* 85–86.

3. Baruch, *Public Years,* 87.

4. "Report of the Labor-Relations Committee of the Emergency Fleet Corporation, February 2, 1919: Selected Documents concerning Charles Piez and Charles Schwab," Records of the United States Shipping Board, RG 32, National Archives.

5. David Chandler, "John Churchill, First Duke of Marlborough," in *Soldier Statesmen of the Age of the Enlightenment* (Manhattan: Kansas State Univ. Press, 1984), 215. See also *Army and Navy Register,* Feb. 1919. Looking back in 1927, Johnson Hagood observed that "never within the memory of those now living who are conversant with military affairs has there been so much unrest, discontent, distrust and manifestations of grievances as now exists in the War Department."

6. Hewes, *From Root to McNamara,* 52–53; Matloff, *American Military History,* 407–12; Weigley, *History of the United States Army,* 309. The National Defense Act of 1920 formally ended the coalition era. It not only retained the "dual oath" but also affirmed the March consolidation of Aug. 1918 and labeled the three components of the emergency force the Army of the United States.

7. *War Department General Order 50,* Aug. 20, 1920. The War Department abolished the nineteenth-century territorial administrative system at the same time and replaced it with a regional corps and army mobilization-based organization.

8. Hewes, *From Root to McNamara,* 53.

9. This discussion of the postwar situation is based on Coffman, *Hilt of the Sword;* Beaver, *Baker;* Beaver, "The Problem of Military Supply"; Smythe, *Pershing;* and Holley, *John M. Palmer.* For a discussion of the work of the army-navy munitions board after its creation in 1922, especially the navy's reluctance to cooperate during the interwar years, see Green, Thomson, and Roots, *Planning Munitions for War,* 50–59. For the joint army-navy board, as well as other insights into the effectiveness of the munitions board, see Weigley, *History of the United States Army,* 405–8. For critical discussions of the addition of combat-arms branch chiefs, see two recent books, David E. Johnson, *Fast Tanks and Heavy Bombers: Innovation in the U.S. Army, 1917–1945* (Ithaca, N.Y.: Cornell Univ. Press, 1998); and William O. Odom, *After the Trenches: The Transformation of U.S. Army Doctrine, 1918–1939* (College Station: Texas A&M Univ. Press, 1998).

10. See "Testimony of Benedict Crowell before the House Committee on Military Affairs," Jan. 9, 1920, in *Army Reorganization: Hearings before the Committee on Military Affairs* (Washington, D.C.: GPO, 1920), 2:1,803–4.

11. Ibid., 1802.

12. Testimony of Secretary of War Newton D. Baker, *Hearings before the Senate Military Affairs Committee: Reorganization of the Army, 1919* (Washington, D.C.: GPO, 1919), 1:191–92.

13. Testimony of Secretary of War Newton D. Baker, *Hearings before the House Committee on Military Affairs: Army Reorganization, 1919,* 2:2106.

14. Testimony of Secretary of War Newton D. Baker, *Hearings before the Senate Committee on Military Affairs: Reorganization of the Army 1919,* 3:173.

15. Ibid., 3:174.

16. The most recent discussions of the creation of the industrial college are two excellent articles by Terrence J. Gough, "Origins of the Army Industrial College: Military-Business Tensions after World War I," *Armed Forces and Society* 17 (Winter 1991): 259–73; and "Soldiers, Businessmen, and U.S. Industrial Mobilization Planning between the World Wars," *War and Society* 9 (May 1991): 63–98. Edward M. Coffman, in *The Regulars: The American Army, 1898–1941* (Cambridge, Mass.: Belknap Press of Harvard Univ. Press, 2004), 233–89, brilliantly analyses the role of interwar army advanced schools in maintaining historically significant memories and critical "lessons learned" from the Great War that proved important in the early preparations for the Second World War.

17. Brigadier General William D. Connor, "Supply and Transportation from the Point of View of the G-4 War Department," lecture delivered at the Army War College, Apr. 13, 1922, Major General H. L. Rogers's Private Papers, Records of the Office of the Quartermaster General, RG 92, National Archives.

18. Draft paper, "The Problem of Requirements: What an Ordnance Officer Should Know," June 22, 1922, Ordnance Historical File, RG 156, National Archives.

19. James A. Douglas, "The War's Lessons with Regard to the Supply System of the Army," June 1919, Records of the Chief of Staff, RG 165, National Archives.

20. James G. Harbord, *The American Army in France,* 160–61.

21. Ray S. Cline, *Washington Command Post: The Operations Division* (Washington, D.C.: GPO, 1951), 1–7, 258–61.

22. See Richard M. Leighton and Robert W. Coakley, *Global Logistics and Strategy,* 2 vols. (Washington, D.C.: Center of Military History, 1955–68), 1:26–27.

23. Green, Thomson, and Roots, *The Ordnance Department,* 157. For example, Benedict Crowell never left the ordnance reserve. When he returned to government service in 1940, he came as a brigadier general of ordnance.

24. Johnson, *Fast Tanks and Heavy Bombers;* and Odom, *After the Trenches.* See also Chandler and Salsbury, *Pierre S. Du Pont,* 546–49. Marshall knew that the approaching military emergency with its significant time restraints would transform administrative priorities and practices and require, just as it had during the First World War, a substantially modified and simplified organizational structure.

25. The army 1923 *Field Regulations* recognized the training and doctrinal shortcomings of the AEF. They incorporated the experience of the last two years of the First World War and acknowledged the importance of combined arms. For an overview of interwar techno-

logical and doctrinal developments, see Ronald Spector, "The Military Effectiveness of the U.S. Armed Forces, 1919–1939," in Millett and Murray, eds., *Military Effectiveness*, 2:70–97. For artillery, the best short discussion is Janice McKenney, "More Bang for the Buck in the Inter-War Army: The 105 mm Howitzer," *Military Affairs* 42 (Apr. 1978): 80–86. For armor, see George F. Hofmann, "The Demise of the U.S. Tank Corps and Medium Tank Development Program," *Military Affairs* (Feb. 1973): 34:20–25, and "Combat Arms vs. Combined Arms," *Armor* 54 (Jan.–Feb. 1997): 6–13, 51–52. See also his discussion of the doctrinal issues involved in the tank debate in "The Tactical and Strategic Use of Attaché Intelligence: The Spanish Civil War and the U.S. Army's Misguided Quest for a Modern Tank Doctrine," *Journal of Military History* 62 (Jan. 1998): 101–34. For further insights into debates about armored doctrine in the interwar military, see Johnson, *Fast Tanks and Heavy Bombers*.

26. For the quartermaster truck program, see Daniel R. Beaver, "Deuce and a Half": Selecting U.S. Army Trucks, 1920–1945," in John A. Lynn, ed., *Feeding Mars: Logistics in Western Warfare from the Middle Ages to the Present* (Boulder, Colo.: Westview, 1993), 251–70.

27. For a discussion of the movement to create a government aircraft plant and the history of the Naval Aircraft Factory, see William F. Trimble, "The Naval Aircraft Factory, the American Aviation Industry, and Government Competition, 1919–1928," *Business History Review* 60, no. 2 (Summer 1986): 175–98.

28. The postwar careers of George W. Goethals, whose engineering firm was very successful, Hugh Johnson, who joined George Peek at the Moline Plow Corporation, and Robert E. Wood, who first assisted Robert J. Thorne at Montgomery Ward and moved on to Sears and Roebucks, were only three examples of successful transfer from military to civilian life. Although many businessmen retained reserve commissions, no civilians of comparable private business stature joined the regular army officer corps.

29. For a discussion of air corps procurement policies, see Irving B. Holley, *Buying Aircraft: Materiel Procurement for the Army Air Forces* (Washington, D.C.: Office of the Chief of Military History, Department of the Army, 1964). For the pioneer civilian industrial developers, see Wayne Biddle, *Barons of the Sky: The Story of the American Aerospace Industry* (New York: Simon and Schuster, 1991). Professor Holley notes that Louis Johnson proposed the construction of seven government-owned aircraft factories in 1938 that would have created a traditional mixed manufacturing-and-procurement system, but the plan was not implemented. See Holley, *Buying Aircraft*, 175–93.

30. Leighton and Coakley, *Global Logistics and Strategy*, 1:10.

31. Huston, *Sinews of War*, 413–14; Millett and Maslowski, *For the Common Defense*, 361–92; Hewes, *From Root to McNamara*, 50–56. On Dec. 7, 1941, army combat forces in the United States were organized into twenty-seven infantry divisions, five armored divisions, two cavalry divisions, and about two hundred incomplete air squadrons, but equipment and shipping shortages made few of them immediately available for overseas deployment. A big new naval building program was in progress, but new combat vessels would not begin to join the fleet for at least six months. By early 1942, however, the United States was far better prepared to make war than it had been at the end of eighteen frenzied months in Nov. 1918.

32. Michael M. Boll, *National Security Planning: Roosevelt through Reagan* (Lexington: Univ. of Kentucky Press, 1988), 10–12; Henry G. Gole, "War Planning at the War College in the Mid-Thirties," *Parameters* 15 (Spring 1985): 52–64.

33. In *Commander In Chief: Franklin Delano Roosevelt, His Lieutenants, and Their War* (New York: Harper & Row, 1987), Eric Larrabee writes persuasively of Roosevelt's resistance, at least initially, to any changes in traditional, informal leadership methods. For the best discussion of Roosevelt's approach to national-security organization, see Calvin L. Christman, "Franklin D. Roosevelt and the Craft of Strategic Assessment," in Allan R. Millett and Williamson Murray, eds., *Calculations: Net Assessment and the Coming of World War II* (New York: Free Press, 1992), 216–57. In the spring of 1941 the war council included the president's friend and personal troubleshooter Harry Hopkins, Army Chief of Staff George C. Marshall, Chief of Naval Operations Harold R. Stark, Under Secretary of State Sumner Welles, Secretary of the Treasury Henry Morgenthau, Secretary of War Henry L. Stimson, and Secretary of the Navy Frank Knox. Before Pearl Harbor those closest to the president were Hopkins, Stimson, and Welles.

34. Paul A. C. Koistinen has now published the final volume of his five-volume study, *The Political Economy of American Warfare*, to 1945, which examines American military industrial connections from a corporate perspective. Stephen Skowronek takes a similar position. In *Building a New American State,* he states, "The American army of the 1870's and the American Army of the 1920's were two entirely different institutions. . . . The army had become a powerful bureaucratic institution in its own right, able to claim a distinctive place in the national government, the corporate economy, and the universities" (246). Skowonek is correct that the War Department was reorganized and expanded, but, on the other hand, it always had considerable political power and occupied a distinctive place in the national government. Certain bureaus had long-standing connections with American higher education. In 1920 there was notable professional and cultural authority left from the 1870s, and the army was not an entirely different institution.

35. Stephen E. Ambrose gives eloquent support to that view and to the importance of small-unit connections and personal loyalties in *Citizen Soldiers: The U.S. Army from the Normandy Beaches to the Bulge to the Surrender of Germany, June 7, 1944–May 7, 1945* (New York: Simon and Schuster, 1997), 17–23.

36. *The Executive Office Building, 17th Street and Pennsylvania Avenue, NW* (Washington, D.C.: General Services Administration Historical Monograph no.3, GPO, 1970), 1–23.

37. For a description of the War, Navy, State Building and the history of its construction, see *Executive Office Building*, 54–57.

38. Fernand Braudel, *The Perspective of the World* (New York: Harper & Row, 1984), vol. 3 of *Civilization and Capitalism: 15th–18th Century*, 19. Braudel reminds us, "The past always counts . . . the world is the result of structural realities at once slow to take shape and slow to fade away."

ESSAY ON SOURCES

Although this book concentrates on the 1890s and the Progressive Era, the broader context within which it has been written requires substantial knowledge of sources whose length and breadth simply boggle the mind. The unpublished and published primary sources cited reflect the mass of material available for the study of War Department and army organization. I do not claim that I have seen everything, but I have worked in portions of all the manuscript collections indicated and used substantial parts of the printed documents listed. In many ways, however, I have merely scratched the surface. Leonard White reflected many years ago that, when studying government organization after 1890, one person simply cannot see everything; one can only do one's best. The discussion of secondary sources does not reproduce every book and article cited in the notes, but it does contain full citations for those publications that do not appear in the main body of the book. It also connects the War Department with the larger themes of American organizational history.

Primary Published and Unpublished Sources

At the Library of Congress, I used the papers of Theodore Roosevelt, William Howard Taft, Woodrow Wilson, Newton D. Baker, George W. Goethals, John J. Pershing, Peyton C. March, Elihu Root, William Howard Taft, Leonard Wood, Hugh S. Scott, Tasker H. Bliss, and Josephus Daniels. At Case Western Reserve University in Cleveland, Ohio, I used the small collection of Benedict Crowell papers. At Firestone Library at Princeton University, I consulted the papers of Bernard Baruch, Grosvenor Clarkson, and Frank Scott. At the United States Army Military History Institute at Carlisle Barracks, Pennsylvania, I found the manuscripts and reports involving John Schofield, Nelson Miles, Johnson Hagood, Brainerd Taylor, William Crozier, Fred Ainsworth, Henry Stimson, Walter Gifford, and Lindley M. Garrison, the most useful materials available for the period before the First World War. The curriculum assignments and war-planning papers prepared by faculty and students at the Army War College before the First World War and during the interwar period were especially useful.

At the National Archives I worked first in the various department and office records and then worked my way toward the Records of the Adjutant General (Record Group 94), the general file for the great mass of military correspondence. I found the records of the secretary of war (Record Group 107), especially those from the record card period (1890–1913) and the decimal correspondence period (1913–42), very helpful. Record Group 107 also contains some materials from the office of the assistant secretary of war and some planning materials from the interwar period. The records of the Ordnance Bureau from 1890–1940 (Record Group 156) and the records of the quartermaster general 1890–1940 (Record Group 92) are especially valuable for their historical files, many of which were written to support annual reports, which guide the researcher into the masses of records maintained by both bureaus. The records of the general staff, war plans, and War College to 1921 (Record Group 165) and the records of the American Expeditionary Forces, 1917–19 (Record Group 120) contain essential documents, including, among other materials, the Records of the Supreme War Council. I have also surveyed the records of the Council of National Defense, 1916–20 (Record Group 62), the records of the War Industries Board, 1917–20 (Record Group 61), and the records of the War Shipping Board, 1917–20 (Record Group 32).

For the period before the Civil War, I have examined the old *American State Papers: Military Affairs,* 7 vols. (Washington, D.C.: Gales and Seaton, 1832–61), as well as the new edition of the military volumes edited for Scholarly Resources by B. Franklin Cooling. I have read the *War Department Annual Reports* (Washington, D.C.: GPO, printed annually) from 1838 to 1940 very carefully. The *Annual Reports* from the end of the Civil War to 1920 are much more useful than those published later. Indeed, the multivolume reports to the secretary of war from the various bureau chiefs and from the president of the Board of Ordnance and Fortification, established by the Endicott Board in 1887, contain a history of late-nineteenth- and early-twentieth-century American manufacturing and technology unavailable anywhere else. The four-volume collection of nineteenth-century ordnance reports compiled at the command of Chief of Ordnance Stephen Vincent Benét between 1882 and 1892, *Ordnance Reports and Other Important Papers Relating to the Ordnance Department* (Washington, D.C.: GPO, 1882–92), provide invaluable background. The annual *Hearings of the House Military Affairs Committee* (Washington, D.C.: GPO, printed annually), especially those on appropriations, contain revealing remarks from the bureau chiefs that give insights into their connections with the rest of the War Department and the civilian community. I have used the *Hearings* in depth, particularly for the period from 1906 to 1916. Other important sets of congressional hearings of great value include the 1916 *Hearings before the Committee on Military Affairs, House of Representatives: To Increase the Military Effectiveness of the Military Establishment of the United States,* 2 vols. (Washington, D.C.: GPO, 1916); *United States Senate: Investigation of the War Department, 1917–1918* (Washington, D.C.: GPO, 1918); *Hearings before the Committee on Military Affairs, House of Representatives: Army Reorganization, 1919–1920* (Washington, D.C.: GPO, 1920); and the *War Policy Commission Hearings* (Washington, D.C.: GPO, 1930). Volumes 40–53 of the *Papers of Woodrow Wilson* (Princeton, N.J.: Princeton University Press, 1970–1986), ed. Arthur S. Link and his colleagues, cover the preparedness movement and the First World War. The seventeen-volume *United States Army in the First World War* (Washington, D.C.: Historical Division, Department of the Army, 1948) is indispensable for the war period, as are *Papers Relating to the Foreign Relations of the United States* for 1917 and 1918 (Washington, D.C.: GPO, 1926 and 1930) and their World War I *Supplements* for 1917 (3 vols., 1931–32) and 1918 (3 vols., 1933). I have used four army professional journals—*Ordnance*

Notes (vols. 1–12); *Journal of the Military Service Institution; Infantry Journal;* and *Field Artillery Journal,* originally *Journal of Artillery*—to gain insight into the thinking of army officers on matters of organization, training, technology, and doctrine. I have also used *Iron Age,* the public voice of the iron and steel industry in the United States from 1890 to the end of the First World War, and *North American Review,* which was used on occasion by both Democrats and Republicans as a vehicle to test War Department thinking on the educated public. The *Independent* and the *New Republic* both advocated military reform during the years before the United States entered the Great War.

Secondary Sources: The Historical Content

For a general approach to the idea of modernization as incremental, see Fernand Braudel, *The Structure of Everyday Life; The Wheels of Commerce; The Perspective of the World;* and *Civilization and Capitalism, 15th–18th Century,* translated by Siân Reynolds (New York: Harper & Row, 1981–84); David S. Landes, *The Unbound Prometheus: Technological Change and Industrial Development in Western Europe from 1750 to the Present* (Cambridge: Cambridge Univ. Press, 1969); Cyril Black, *The Dynamics of Modernization: A Study in Contemporary History* (New York: Harper & Row, 1966); and William McNeill, *The Pursuit of Power: Technology, Armed Forces, and Society since A.D. 1000* (Chicago: Univ. of Chicago Press, 1982). I have adopted a definition of modernization which combines those of Braudel, Landes, Black, and McNeill. I use the term to describe a western phenomenon involving those political changes in society and the state that emerged during the French Revolution and blended with the somewhat later intellectual and organizational impact of industrialization (1775–1890). It includes nationalism and self-determination of peoples, representative government, and a profound individualism accompanied by a thrust toward political and social equality. It also involves laissez faire and corporate capitalism and Marxism in all their various modes and guises. Landes writes that it entails the reorganization and rebuilding of the state itself to put in place "that combination of changes—in the mode of production and government, in the social and institutional order, in the corpus of knowledge, and in attitudes and values—that make it possible for a society to hold its own in the twentieth century." Black emphasizes the idea of planning and describes it as an effort to mobilize and rationalize the resources of society to achieve greater control, efficiency, and production. McNeill describes the condition as incremental, ironic, and paradoxical, and he writes about the relationships between technology, military power, and the modernizing process with more sensitivity and understanding than most contemporary scholars. See also John U. Nef, *War and Human Progress* (Cambridge, Mass.: Harvard Univ. Press, 1950), and Lewis Mumford, *Technics and Civilization* (New York: Harcourt, Brace, 1934). David J. Jeremy, *The Transatlantic Industrial Revolution* (Cambridge, Mass.: Harvard Univ. Press, 1981) adds an American dimension to the essentially European perspective of the other books.

The writing about American modernization has often been simplified in a "nationalist–states' rights" dichotomy. The most effective traditional, linear approaches to the issues are Allan Nevins' *The Emergence of Modern America, 1865–1878* (New York: MacMillan, 1927); Arthur M. Schlesinger and Dixon Ryan Fox, eds., *A History of American Life;* the concluding four volumes of Nevins' *The War for the Union* (New York: Scribner, 1959–1971); and Mary and Charles Beard's *The Rise of American Civilization* (New York: MacMillan, 1927). The Beards' volume is among the premier expressions of a general "cultural conflict" approach to change in American society. Charles Sellers' *The Market Revolution: Jacksonian America, 1815–1846* (New York: Oxford Univ. Press, 1991) is the most recent and well-argued traditional approach to the issues. Less conflict oriented but still linear, Thomas C. Cochran and William Miller's *The Age of Enterprise: A Social History of Industrial America* (New York: MacMillan, 1942), introduces the general theme of incremental incorporation, which did not attract much attention until the 1950s, when Richard Hofstadter, in *The Age of Reform: From Bryan to FDR* (New York: Knopf, 1955), and John Kenneth Galbraith, in *The New Industrial State* (Boston: Houghton Mifflin, 1967), began to synthesize it. Frederick Jackson Turner's *The United States, 1830–1850, The Nation and Its Sections* (New York: Holt, 1935), ed. M. H. Crissey, Max Farrand, and Avery Craven, stresses the persistence of local and regional power bases and the importance of pluralistic perspectives in studying a modernizing American society. In the early 1960s Robert Dahl published *Who Governs?* (New Haven, Conn.: Yale Univ. Press, 1961), which notes the pluralistic nature of American society and the diffusion of power within its institutions. A similar theme is developed by James MacGregor Burns in *The Deadlock of Democracy: Four-Party Politics in America* (Englewood Cliffs, N.J.: Prentice-Hall, 1963). Pluralistic themes are reinforced by Rowland Bertoff in *An Unsettled People: Social Order and Disorder in American History* (New York: Harper & Row, 1971). In the late 1970s Ellis W. Hawley, in an outstanding book, *The Great War and the Search for a Modern Order: A History of the American People and Their Institutions, 1917–1933* (New York: St. Martin's, 1979), integrates the two themes into the history of the early twentieth century. Robert Wiebe, in *The Opening of American Society: From the Adoption of the Constitution to the Eve of Disunion* (New York: Alfred J. Knopf, 1984) and *The Search for Order* (New York: Hill and Wang, 1967), with his consolidationist-localist focus, balances change and continuity across the American national experience.

The general study of organizational modernization begins with Max Weber's formalistic description found in *The Theory of Social and Economic Organization* (New York: Oxford Univ. Press, 1947). Michael Crozier, *The Bureaucratic Phenomenon* (Chicago: Univ. of Chicago Press, 1964), modifies Weber in accord with very real organizational experience. American organizational history has received considerable scholarly attention during the last generation. Alfred D. Chandler's *Strategy and Structure: Chapters in the History of the Industrial Enterprise* (Cambridge, Mass.: MIT Press, 1962); *The Visible Hand: The Managerial Revolution in American Business* (Cambridge, Mass.: Harvard Univ. Press, 1977); and *Scale and Scope: The Dynamics of Industrial Capitalism* (Cambridge, Mass.: Belknap Press of Harvard Univ. Press, 1994) mark a most sophisticated approach to the study of organizational systems and the role of the corporation in modern societies. Stephen Skowronek's *Building a New American State: The Expansion of National Administrative Capacity, 1877–1920* (Cambridge: Cambridge University Press, 1982) is an important contribution to the ongoing discussion. Kenneth Boulding, "Intersects: The Peculiar Organizations," in *Challenge to Leadership* (New York: Conference Board, 1973), explains elegantly how some organizations are formed. Finally, a very significant piece, Irvin H. Anderson Jr.'s "Methodological Note" is found in appendix A of his *Aramco, The United States, and Saudi Arabia: A Study of the Dynamics of Foreign Oil Policy, 1933–1950* (Princeton, N.J.: Princeton Univ. Press, 1981).

Technology and Military Doctrine

The best general history of technology is Charles Singer et al., eds., *A History of Technology*, 5 vols. (New York and London: Oxford Univ. Press, 1954–1958). Martin Van Creveld's, *Supplying War: Logistics from Wallenstein to Patton* (London: Cambridge Univ. Press, 1977); *Command in War* (Cambridge, Mass.: Harvard Univ. Press, 1985); and *Technology and War* provide excellent general introductions to the history of technology, logistics, and communications. His periodization based on means of propulsion is interesting, but J. F. C. Fuller's, *Armaments and History* (New York: Charles Scribner and Sons, 1945), is much more persuasive. See also Bernard and Fawn Brodie, *From Crossbow to H-Bomb*, rev. ed. (Bloomington: Indiana Univ. Press, 1973); Daniel R. Headrick, *The Tools of Empire: Technology and European Imperialism in the Nineteenth Century* (New York: Oxford Univ. Press, 1981); and Merritt Roe Smith's introduction in *Military Enterprise and Technological Change: Perspectives of the American Experience* (Cambridge, Mass.: MIT Press, 1985). For manufacturing systems, read David A. Hounshell, *From the American System to Mass Production, 1800–1932: The Development of Manufacturing Technology in the United States* (Baltimore, Md.: Johns Hopkins Univ. Press, 1984). A. Hunter Dupree deals with the institutionalization of science in *Science in the Federal Government: A History of Policies and Activities* (Baltimore, Md.: Johns Hopkins Univ. Press, 1986). For technology and supply in the United States Army, read James A. Huston, *The Sinews of War: Army Logistics, 1775–1953* (Washington, D.C.: Office of the Chief of Military History, 1966), Marvin A. Kreidberg and Merton G. Henry, *History of Military Mobilization in the United States Army, 1775–1945* (Washington, D.C.: GPO, 1955); and Erna Risch, *Quartermaster Support of the Army: A History of the Corps* (Washington, D.C.: Quartermaster General's Office, 1962). For technology and the human factor, see Elting E. Morison, *Men and Machines* (Cambridge, Mass.: MIT Press, 1968). An excellent book about integrating weapons and doctrine with implications for American affairs is Sheldon Bidwell and Dominick Graham's *Firepower: British Army Weapons and Theories of War, 1904–1945* (London: Allen and Unwin, 1982). For the intimate connections between technology and battle, John Keegan's *The Face of Battle* (New York: Viking, 1976) and Paddy Griffith's provocative *Forward into Battle: Fighting Tactics from Waterloo to Vietnam* (Chichester: Anthony Bird, 1981) are indispensable. For the American experience during the first half of the nineteenth century, see Merritt Roe Smith, *Harpers Ferry and the New Technology* (Ithaca, N.Y.: Cornell Univ. Press, 1977). His "Military Arsenals and Industry before World War I," in B. F. Cooling, ed., *War Business and American Society: Historical Perspectives on the Military Industrial Complex* (Port Washington, N.Y.: Kennikat, 1977), is the only survey of that significant era. Richard I. Wolf, "Arms and Innovation: The United States Army and the Repeating Rifle," (Ph.D. diss., Boston Univ., 1981), and David Armstrong, *Bullets and Bureaucrats: The Machine Gun and the United States Army, 1861–1916* (Westport, Conn.: Greenwood, 1982), deal with the development and use of specific weapons and the interlocking interests that in some cases prevented their rapid assimilation into the American army. John Ellis's brilliant *The Social History of the Machine Gun* (New York: Random House, 1975) is one of the few attempts to show the impact of weapon systems on societies. Hugh G. J. Aitken has written a groundbreaking study of the introduction of scientific management into the Ordnance Department arsenal system, *Taylorism at the Watertown Arsenal* (Cambridge, Mass.: Harvard Univ. Press, 1960). For the interwar period, see Daniel R. Beaver, "Politics and Policy: The War Department

Motorization and Standardization Program, 1920–1940" *Military Affairs* 47 (Oct. 1983) and George Hofmann, "A Yankee Inventor and the Military Establishment: The Cristie Tank Controversy," *Military Affairs* 39 (Feb. 1975). Ralph B. Baldwin's *The Deadly Fuze: The Secret Weapon of World War II* (San Rafael, Calif.: Presidio, 1980) deals with a later period but provides excellent insight into cooperation between scientific, technological, and military communities in creating new weapons. Edward C. Ezell sums up the issues involving small arms superbly in *The Great Rifle Controversy: Search for the Ultimate Infantry Weapon through Vietnam and Beyond* (Harrisburg, Pa.: Stackpole Press, 1985). The introductory chapters of Constance Green, Harry C. Thomson, and Peter C. Roots, *The Ordnance Department: Planning Munitions for War* (Washington, D.C.: Office of the Chief of Military History, 1955) take the story up to 1940.

In dealing with the connections between technology and military doctrine, I use a "systems-subsystems" approach that integrates Thomas Kuhn's *The Structure of Scientific Revolutions* (Chicago: Univ. of Chicago Press, 1962), Thomas P. Hughes's *Networks of Power: Electrification in Western Society, 1880–1930* (Baltimore, Md.: Johns Hopkins Univ. Press, 1983), and J. F. C. Fuller's *Armaments and History* (New York: Charles Scribner and Sons, 1945). Kuhn is considered old-fashioned by some scholars who, like Steven Fuller, in his *Thomas Kuhn: A Philosophical History for Our Times* (Chicago: Univ. of Chicago Press, 2000), label him a philosophical posturer. Some sociologists, such as Anthony Giddens in *The Constitution of Society: Outline of the Theory of Structuration* (Berkeley: Univ. of California Press, 1984), have formulated other theories of technological change that have persuaded younger scholars to go so far as to reduce its organization to an acronym (SCOT—Social Construction of Technology), but Kuhn still offers a useful approach to the study of technology and military doctrine, and his description of change over time, including the significant idea of "informational supersaturation," is very persuasive. Mumford's *Technics and Civilization;* Nef's *War and Human Progress;* McNeill's *The Pursuit of Power;* Brodie and Brodie's *From Crossbow to H-Bomb;* and Walter Millis's *Arms and Men: A Study in American Military History* (New York: G. P. Putnam, 1956) are all essential to reaching any kind of understanding about the connections between warfare and technology. Martin Van Creveld's *Technology and War from 2000 B.C. to the Present* (New York: Free Press, 1989); Elting E. Morison's *Men, Machines, and Modern Times;* and Merritt Roe Smith's introduction to *Military Enterprise and Technological Change* are important recent additions that support my general approach. I also incorporate the insights developed by Irving B. Holley in *Ideas and Weapons: Exploitation of the Aerial Weapon by the United States during World War I: A Study in the Relationships of Technological Advance, Military Doctrine, and the Development of Weapons* (New Haven, Conn.: Yale Univ. Press, 1953) and *Buying Aircraft: Military Procurement for the Army Air Forces* (Washington, D.C.: Center of Military History, 1964). Connections between specific weapons design, production, development, and deployment after the Civil War are explored by David Armstrong, *Bullets and Bureaucrats,* but also look at John Ellis's *Social History of the Machine Gun.* Edward C. Ezell describes late-nineteenth-century weapons-development issues in *The Great Rifle Controversy.* The best introduction to interwar supply and technology is in Thompson, Green, and Roots's *Planning Munitions for War.* Beaver 's "Politics and Policy" discusses the Quartermaster Corps truck program, and Hofmann's "A Yankee Inventor and the Military

Establishment" examines the difficulties of wedding technology with armored doctrine. There is a masterful summary of the literature and a fine bibliography on science, technology, and the military in Alex Roland's "Science and War," in Sally Gregory Kohlstedt and Margaret W. Rossiter, eds., *Historical Writing on American Science: Perspectives and Prospects* (Baltimore, Md.: Johns Hopkins Univ. Press, 1985).

The War Department and the Army

There is no great war-and-society tradition in American historiography, but John E. Jessup and Louise B. Katz, eds., *Encyclopedia of the American Military: Studies of the History, Traditions, Policies, Institutions, and Roles of the Armed Forces in War and Peace,* 3 vols. (New York: Charles Scribner's Sons, 1994) contains articles by specialists on almost every aspect of army history. Two sets of essays, J. L. Granatstein and R. D. Cuff eds., *War and Society in North America* (Toronto: Thomas Nelson, 1971), and Jerry Israel, ed., *Building the Organizational Society* (New York: Free Press, 1972), can be of value to the student of American military affairs. Walter Millis, *Arms and Men: A Study of American Military History,* is the only American work to integrate armed forces, supply, logistics, and technology within a general framework of developing American institutions, and the volume still powerfully influences the writing of American military history. Allan R. Millett and Peter Maslowski, *For the Common Defense: A Military History of the United States* (New York: Free Press, 1984), contains the best recent discussion of military policy. Peter Karsten, ed., *The Military in America from the Colonial Era to the Present* (New York: Free Press, 1980), gives some attention to the second theme of diffusion and pluralism. Joseph Bernardo and Eugene H. Bacon, *American Military Policy: Its Development since 1775* (New York: Greenwood, 1977), should also be consulted. There is no history of the Congress and the army; nor is there any general study of the House and Senate Military Affairs committees before 1948. Elias Huzar's *The Purse and the Sword: Control of the Army by Congress through Military Appropriations, 1933–1950* (Ithaca, N.Y.: Cornell Univ. Press, 1950) shows what a general study might reveal. The development of the American army itself can be traced through William A. Ganoe, *A History of the United States Army,* rev. ed. (New York: Appleton-Century, 1942); Oliver L. Spaulding, *The United States Army in Peace and War* (New York: Putnam, 1937); and John M. Palmer, *America in Arms: The Experience of the United States with Military Organization* (New Haven, Conn.: Yale Univ. Press, 1941). Russell F. Weigley has placed the army into the framework of American society in his *History of the United States Army,* rev. ed. (Bloomington: Indiana Univ. Press, 1984). John Shy, *A People Numerous and Armed: Reflections on the Military Struggle for American Independence* (New York: Oxford Univ. Press, 1976), gives a social insight into that war, while James K. Martin and Mark E. Lender, *A Respectable Army: The Military Origins of the Republic, 1763–1789* (Arlington Heights., Ill.: Harlan-Davidson, 1982) has an excellent bibliography. Richard Kohn, *Eagle and Sword: The Federalists and the Creation of the Military Establishment in America, 1783–1802* (New York: Free Press, 1975), is unexcelled in its treatment of the military policy of the early period. Francis Paul Prucha's *The Sword of the Republic: The United States Army on the Frontier, 1783–1846* (New York: MacMillan, 1969) and Robert Utley's *Frontiersmen in Blue: The United States Army and the Indian, 1848–1865* (New York: MacMillan, 1967) and *Frontier Regulars: The United States Army and the Indian, 1866–1890* (New York: MacMillan, 1973) treat soldiers as nation builders and members of frontier societies. William H. Goetzmann, *Army Exploration in the American West* (New Haven, Conn.: Yale Univ. Press, 1959) develops the same theme and adds insight into the army engineer's role in economic expansion.

The best introduction to the themes of diffusion and pluralism in the American military establishment comes through the study of the militia. Marcus Cunliffe's *Soldiers and Civilians: The Martial Spirit in America, 1775–1865* (Boston: Little, Brown, 1968) contains a good discussion of anticonsolidationist thinking in local America, and John Mahon's *History of the Militia and National Guard* (New York: MacMillan, 1983) includes an excellent bibliography on the National Guard. Jerry Cooper's *The Rise of the National Guard: The Evolution of the American Militia, 1865–1920* (Lincoln: Univ. of Nebraska Press, 1997) is the most insightful institutional study of the armies of the states. Readers would also profit by reading Jack D. Foner, *The United States Soldier between Two Wars: Army Life and Reforms, 1865–1898* (New York: Humanities Press, 1970), and Martha Derthick, *The National Guard in Politics* (Cambridge, Mass.: Harvard Univ. Press, 1963). Gerald Linderman, in two beautiful books, *Embattled Courage: The Experience of Combat in the American Civil War* (New York: Free Press, 1987) and *The Mirror of War: American Society and the Spanish-American War* (Ann Arbor: Univ. of Michigan Press, 1974), describes nineteenth-century American attitudes toward war and soldiering. James Abrahamson, *America Arms for a New Century: The Making of a Great Military Power* (New York: Free Press, 1981), and John P. Finnegan, *Against the Specter of a Dragon: The Campaign for American National Preparedness, 1914–1917* (Westport, Conn.: Greenwood, 1979), place the military within the framework of early-twentieth-century progressive reform. Both David M. Kennedy, *Over Here: The First World War and American Society* (New York: Oxford Univ. Press, 1980), and Ronald Schaffer, *America in the Great War: The Rise of the War Welfare State* (New York: Oxford Univ. Press, 1991) have useful bibliographies for the war period and place organizational issues within a broad social context. For the later Progressive period and the First World War, see Hawley, *The Great War and the Search for a Modern Order;* Robert Cuff, *The War Industries Board: Business-Government Relations during World War One* (Baltimore, Md.: Johns Hopkins Univ. Press, 1973); and Daniel R. Beaver, *Newton D. Baker and the American War Effort, 1917–1919* (Lincoln: Univ. of Nebraska Press, 1966). For national and local power relationships and manpower questions, see John W. Chambers II's two volumes, *Draftees or Volunteers: A Documentary History of the Debate over Military Conscription in the United States, 1787–1973* (New York: Garland, 1975) and *To Raise an Army: The Draft Comes to Modern America* (New York: Free Press, 1987). See also John Garry Clifford's *The Citizen Soldiers: The Plattsburg Training Camp Movement, 1913–1920* (Lexington: Univ. of Kentucky Press, 1972). For discussions of the ideas of reform and reorganization, see Otto M. Nelson, *National Security and the General Staff* (Washington, D.C.: Infantry Journal Press, 1946); Paul Y. Hammond, *Organizing for Defense: The American Military Establishment in the Twentieth Century* (Princeton, N.J.: Princeton Univ. Press, 1961); and James E. Hewes, *From Root to McNamara: Army Organization and Administration, 1900–1963* (Washington, D.C.: Center of Military History, 1975).

Command and control has always attracted the attention of scholars. Louis Smith, *American Democracy and Military Power: A Study of Civil Control of Military Power in the United States* (Chicago: Univ. of Chicago Press, 1951), is still the best book on civil-military relations. Ernest R. May, *The Ultimate Decision: The President as Commander in Chief* (New

York: Braziller, 1960), although inadequate on Woodrow Wilson, is still a most impressive study on presidential control of the military. Joseph G. Dawson III, ed., *Commanders in Chief: Presidential Leadership in Modern Wars* (Lawrence: Univ. Press of Kansas, 1992), is more insightful for the Wilson era. Changes in informed opinion, from 1940 to the present, on presidential power can be seen by comparing Edwin S. Corwin's *The President: Office and Powers, 1781–1957* (New York: New York Univ. Press, 1957) to Arthur M. Schlesinger Jr.'s *The Imperial Presidency* (New York: Popular Library, 1974). There is no general monograph on War Department command-and-control systems, but Weigley covers the issues in *History of the United States Army*. Another balanced general history is Allan R. Millett and Peter Maslowski, *For the Common Defense*. Leonard White's *The Jeffersonians, 1801–1829: A Study in Administrative History* (New York: Free Press, 1951) and *The Jacksonians, 1829–1861: A Study in Administrative History* (New York: Free Press, 1954) are excellent surveys of antebellum administration, while Charles M. Wiltse's *John C. Calhoun,* 3 vols. (Indianapolis, Ind.: Bobbs-Merrill, 1944–1951) is the best study of the great nineteenth-century administrator. For the history of the office of the commanding general in the nineteenth century, see three works by William B. Skelton: "The United States Army, 1821–1842: An Institutional History" (Ph.D. diss., Northwestern Univ., 1968); "The Commanding General and the Problem of Command in the United States Army," *Military Affairs* (Dec. 1970); and *An American Profession of Arms: The Army Officer Corps, 1784–1861* (Lawrence: Univ. Press of Kansas, 1992). For the latter part of the nineteenth century, see Robert F. Stohlman Jr., *The Powerless Position* (Manhattan: Kansas State Univ. Press, 1975). For internal War Department affairs before the Civil War, see Charles F. O'Connell, "The United States Army and the Origins of Modern Management, 1818–1860" (Ph. D. diss., Ohio State University, 1982), and William R. Roberts, "Loyalty and Expertise: The Transformation of the American Nineteenth Century General Staff and the Creation of the Modern Military Establishment" (Ph.D. diss., Johns Hopkins Univ., 1979). See also K. Jack Bauer, *The Mexican War* (New York: MacMillan, 1974). For connections between the army and the militia, read Mahon, *Militia and National Guard*. Nevins, *The War for the Union,* is the most useful survey of Civil War institutional growth. For Civil War military organization, see Fred D. Shannon, *Organization and Administration of the Union Army, 1861–1865,* 2 vols. (Cleveland: Clark, 1928) and Alexander H. Meneely, *The United States War Department, 1861: A Study in Mobilization and Administration* (New York: Columbia Univ. Press, 1928). For the development of the Civil War command system, the best book is T. Harry Williams, *Lincoln and His Generals* (New York: Alfred A. Knopf, 1952). Harold M. Hyman's *Stanton: The Life of Lincoln's Secretary of War* (New York: Alfred A. Knopf, 1962) is the best biography of Lincoln's controversial associate. For new approaches to Civil War command-and-control issues, see Herman Hattaway and Archer Jones, *How the North Won: A Military History of the Civil War* (Urbana: Univ. of Illinois Press, 1983), and Richard E. Beringer, Herman Hattaway, Archer Jones, and William N. Still Jr., *Why the South Lost the Civil War* (Athens: Univ. of Georgia Press, 1986). Command and control in the Spanish-American War have been carefully discussed in David Trask, *The War with Spain in 1898* (New York: MacMillan, 1981), and Graham A. Cosmas, *An Army For Empire: The United States Army in the Spanish-American War* (Columbia: Univ. of Missouri Press, 1971). Frank Freidel's *The Splendid Little War* (New York: Bramhall House, 1958) is an excellent source for pictures as well as a good introduction to the conduct of the war. For postwar reorganization, see

Graham A. Cosmas, "Military Reorganization after the Spanish-American War: The Army Reorganization of 1898–1899," *Military Affairs* 35 (Feb. 1971). For insight into the Progressive Era, see Abrahamson, *America Arms for a New Century*, and Peter Karsten, "Armed Progressives: The Military Reorganizes for the American Century," in Jerry Israel, ed., *Building the Organizational Society* (New York: Free Press, 1972). Three other books, Otto M. Nelson, *National Security and the General Staff*; Paul Y. Hammond, *Organizing for Defense: The American Military Establishment in the Twentieth Century*; and the best of the lot, James E. Hewes, *From Root to McNamara: Army Organization and Administration, 1900–1963*, champion the case for the development of a hierarchical general-staff system in the early twentieth century. The consultative tradition can be traced through Bauer's *The Mexican War, 1846–1848*; Cosmas's *Army For Empire: The United States Army in the Spanish-American War*; and David Trask's *The War with Spain in 1898*. Jones and Hattaway's *How the North Won* contains important information on Civil war staff consultation and cooperation. James A. Huston, *The Sinews of War: Army Logistics, 1775–1953* and Erna Risch, *Quartermaster Support of the Army: A History of the Corps*, are sympathetic to the bureaus. Works on the bureau chiefs include *Maligned General* (San Rafael, Cal.: Presidio, 1979), a biography of Thomas Jesup by Chester L. Kieffer; Russell F. Weigley, *Quartermaster General of the Union Army: A Biography of Montgomery C. Meigs* (New York: Columbia Univ. Press, 1959); Mabel E. Deutrich, *Struggle for Supremacy: The Career of General Fred C. Ainsworth* (Washington, D.C.: Public Affairs Press, 1962); and Paul Clark, "Major General George Owen Squier: Military Scientist" (Ph.D. diss., Case Western Reserve Univ., 1974). The best introduction to War Department organizational problems during the First World War is Edward M. Coffman, *The War to End All Wars: The American Military Experience in World War I* (New York: MacMillan, 1968). For another general view, see Robert H. Ferrell, *Woodrow Wilson and the World War, 1917–1921* (New York: Harper & Row, 1985). More details can be found in Edward M. Coffman, *The Hilt of the Sword: The Career of Peyton C. March* (Madison: Univ. of Wisconsin Press, 1966); Beaver, *Newton D. Baker and the American War Effort; 1917–1919*; and Donald Smythe, *Pershing: General of the Armies* (Bloomington: Indiana Univ. Press, 1986). Interallied affairs can be followed in David F. Trask's *The United States in the Supreme War Council* (Middletown, Conn.: Wesleyan Univ. Press, 1961) and *Captains and Cabinets: Anglo-American Naval Relations, 1917–1918* (Columbia: Univ. of Missouri Press, 1972). See also Walter Millis, *The Road to War: America, 1914–1917* (Boston: Houghton Mifflin, 1935); Burton Kauffman, *Efficiency and Expansion: Foreign Trade in the Wilson Administration, 1913–1921* (Westport, Conn.: Greenwood, 1974); Carl P. Parrini, *Heir to Empire, United States Economic Diplomacy, 1916–1923* (Pittsburgh, Pa.: Univ. of Pittsburgh Press, 1969); and Kathleen Burk, *Britain, America, and the Sinews of War, 1914–1918* (Boston: Allen and Unwin, 1985). For the best introduction to the interwar period, see Mark Watson, *Chief of Staff: Pre-War Plans and Policies* (Washington, D.C.: Office of the Chief of Military History, 1950), and Hewes, *From Root to McNamara*. There is a small bibliography on the National Defense Act of 1920 and on command-and-control problems in the interwar period. See also Alfred A. Blum, "Birth and Death of the M-Day Plan," in Harold Stein, ed., *American Civil-Military Decisions* (Birmingham: Univ. of Alabama Press, 1963).

The conventional definition of military professionalism is found in Samuel Huntington, *The Soldier and the State: The Theory and Politics of Civil-Military Relations* (Cambridge, Mass.: Harvard Univ. Press, 1957), which employs a "Neo-Hamiltonian–Neo-Jeffersonian" approach to American organizational matters and adopts, to my mind, a simplistic definition of military culture. For a brilliant and far more insightful analysis, see Morris Janowitz, *The Professional Soldier: A Social and Political Study* (New York: Free Press, 1960). See also Russell F. Weigley, *The American Way of War: A History of United States Strategy and Military Policy* (New York: Columbia Univ. Press, 1973). A thoughtful critique of Huntington, Janowitz, and Weigley is Mark R. Grandstaff, "Preserving the Habits and Usages of War: William Tecumseh Sherman, Professional Reform, and the U.S. Army Officer Corps, 1865–1881, Revisited," *Journal of Military History* 62 (July 1998): 521–45. For the connections between army education and military professionalism, see John W. Masland and Lawrence I. Radway, *Soldiers and Scholars: Military Education and National Policy* (Princeton, N.J.: Princeton Univ. Press, 1957). The best history of West Point is Stephen E. Ambrose, *Duty, Honor, Country: A History of West Point* (Baltimore, Md.: Johns Hopkins Univ. Press, 1966). The most recent history of the Army War College is Harry P. Ball, *Of Responsible Command: A History of the U.S. Army War College* (Carlisle, Pa.: U.S. Army War College, 1983). Timothy K. Nenninger has written three excellent works on the Leavenworth schools and military professionalization and modernization during the half century before the Second World War. *The Leavenworth Schools and the Old Army: Education, Professionalism, and Officer Corps of the United States Army, 1881–1918* (Westport, Conn.: Greenwood, 1978); "Creating Officers: The Leavenworth Experience, 1920–1940," *Military Review* 69 (Nov. 1989): 58–68; and "Leavenworth and Its Critics: The U.S. Army Command and General Staff School, 1920–1940," *Journal of Military History* 58 (Apr. 1994): 199–231. See also Carol Reardon's *Soldiers and Scholars: The U.S. Army and the Uses of Military History, 1865–1920* (Lawrence: Univ. Press of Kansas, 1990). The ROTC is discussed by John W. Masland and Gene D. Lyons in *Education and Military Leadership: A Study of the R.O.T.C.* (Princeton, N.J.: Princeton Univ. Press, 1959). For useful definitions of military culture, see Peter Karsten, *The Naval Aristocracy: The Golden Age of Annapolis and the Emergence of Modern American Navalism* (New York: Free Press, 1972), and Edward M. Coffman, *The Old Army: A Portrait of the American Army in Peacetime, 1784–1898* (New York: Oxford Univ. Press, 1986).

Connections with the Civilian Sector

Any general study of military-industrial relations should begin with Paul A. C. Koistinen's recently published volumes, *Beating Ploughshares into Swords; Mobilizing for Modern War;* and *The Interwar Years*. His earlier, *The Military Industrial Complex: An Historical Perspective* (New York: Praeger, 1980), describes the controversies over military-industrial questions during the last two generations and introduces the contemporary historiography. For the nineteenth century, the army's role in building the antebellum national infrastructure is analyzed in Paul Francis Prucha's *Broadaxe and Bayonet: The Role of the United States Army in the Development of the Northwest, 1815–1860* (Madison: State Historical Society of Wisconsin, 1953) and Louis C. Hunter's *Steamboats on the Western Waters* (Cambridge, Mass.: Harvard Univ. Press, 1949). See also Forest G. Hill, *Roads, Rails, and Waterways: The Army Engineers and Early Transportation* (Norman: Univ. of Oklahoma Press, 1957); William Goetzman, *Army Exploration in the American West, 1803–1863* (New Haven, Conn.: Yale Univ. Press, 1959); and Harold L. Nelson, "Military Roads for War and Peace, 1791–1836," *Military Affairs* 19 (1955). For nineteenth-century military and industrial developments, read Giles Cromwell, *The Virginia Manufactory of Arms* (Charlottesville: Univ. of Virginia Press, 1975); Felicia J.

Deyrup, *Arms Makers of the Connecticut Valley: A Regional Study of Economic Development in the Arms Industry* (Northampton, Mass.: Smith College Studies in History 23, 1948); David Freeman Hawke, *Nuts and Bolts of the Past: A History of American Technology, 1776–1860* (New York: Harper & Row, 1988); and Smith, *The Harpers Ferry Armory and the New Technology*. Coffman's *The Old Army, 1784–1898*, gives insight into the impact of supply and logistics on everyday military life. Few authors have dealt with the organization of Civil War supply and technology in a systematic way. For new approaches, see Hattaway and Jones, *How the North Won*, and Beringer, Hattaway, Jones, and Still, *Why the South Lost*. For transportation, see George Edgar Turner, *Victory Road the Rails: The Strategic Place of the Railroads in the Civil War* (Indianapolis, Ind.: Bobbs-Merrill, 1953), and Francis A. Lord, *Lincoln's Railroad Man: Herman Haupt* (Rutherford, N.J.: Fairleigh Dickinson Univ. Press, 1969). The best book on weapons development is Robert V. Bruce, *Lincoln and the Tools of War* (Indianapolis, Ind.: Bobbs-Merrill, 1956), but see also Carl L. Davis, *Arming the Union: Small Arms in the Civil War* (Port Washington, N.Y.: Kennikat, 1974), and Claude E. Fuller, *The Breechloader in the Service* (Topeka, Ks.: Arms Reference Club of America, 1933). For logistics and supply, see Weigley, *Montgomery Meigs*. Confederate supply and logistics are carefully discussed in Robert C. Black III, *The Railroads of the Confederacy* (Chapel Hill: Univ. of North Carolina Press, 1952); Frank E. Vandiver, *Ploughshares into Swords: Josiah Gorgas and Confederate Ordnance* (Austin: Univ. of Texas Press, 1952); Richard D. Goff, *Confederate Supply* (Durham, N.C.: Duke Univ. Press, 1969), and Charles B. Dew, *Ironmaker to the Confederacy: Joseph R. Anderson and the Tradager Iron Works* (New Haven, Conn.: Yale Univ. Press, 1965). The best studies of the economic impact of the war are Victor Clark, *History of American Manufactures in the United States* (New York: McGraw-Hill, 1929); Thomas Corcoran, *Frontiers of Change: Early Industrialization in America* (New York: Oxford Univ. Press, 1981); Douglas C. North and Robert Paul Thomas, eds., *The Growth of the American Economy to 1860* (Columbia: Univ. of South Carolina Press, 1968); and, in particular, Corcoran's, "Did the Civil War Retard Industrialization?" in Ralph Adreano, ed., *The Economic Impact of the American Civil War,* 2nd ed.(Cambridge, Mass.: Schenkman, 1967). For the post–Civil War effects of army supply and technology on American expansion, see Darlis A. Miller, *Soldiers and Settlers: Military Supply in the Southwest, 1961–1885* (Albuquerque: Univ. of New Mexico Press, 1989). Merritt Roe Smith deals with the work of army arms makers in the 1870s and 1880s in "Military Arsenals and Industry Before World War I," in Cooling, ed., *War, Business, and American Society*, while Cooling himself investigates industrial modernization on a broader scale in *Grey Steel and Blue Water: The Formative Years of America's Military-Industrial Complex, 1881–1917* (New York: Archon Books, 1979). For the Progressive Era, the preparedness movement, and the First World War, see Aitken, *Taylorism at Watertown Arsenal,* and Finnegan, *Against the Specter of a Dragon*.

Most of the literature on American military requirements and their connection with industrial and technological capacity during the First World War was published in the first decade after the war ended. Chief of Ordnance William Crozier's testimony before Congress is included in his *Ordnance and the World War* (New York: Scribner's, 1920). Edward N. Hurley, *The Bridge to France* (Philadelphia, Pa.: J. B. Lippincott, 1927), and Rear Admiral Albert Gleaves, *A History of the Transport Service* (New York: Doran, 1921), give good insights into wartime problems involved in shipping troops and cargo to France. Johnson Hagood, *The Services of Supply: A*

Memoir of the Great War (Boston: Houghton Mifflin, 1927); William J. Wilgus, *Transporting the A.E.F. in Western Europe* (New York: Columbia Univ. Press, 1931); and Charles G. Dawes, *A Journal of the Great War,* 2 vols. (Boston: Houghton Mifflin, 1921), praise the AEF's Walker Hines, *War History of American Railroads* (New Haven, Conn.: Yale Univ. Press, 1928), who defends the Railroad Administration, while Grosvenor Clarkson gives industry's side of the story in *Industrial America in the World War: The Strategy Behind the Lines, 1917–1918* (Boston: Houghton Mifflin, 1923). Thomas Frothingham provides the official War Department defense in *The American Reinforcement* (New York: Doubleday, Page, 1927). Benedict Crowell and Robert F. Wilson, *How America Went to War,* 6 vols. (New Haven, Conn.: Yale Univ. Press, 1921), includes a vast amount of detail on production and transportation. Cuff, *The War Industries Board;* Kennedy, *Over Here;* Daniel R. Beaver, "George W. Goethals and the PS and T," in Daniel R. Beaver, ed., *Some Pathways in Twentieth-Century History* (Detroit: Wayne State Univ. Press, 1969); and "The Problem of Military Supply, 1890–1920," in B. Franklin Cooling ed., *War, Business, and American Society,* give some historical perspective to the controversy. For interwar military industrial relations, see Harry B. Yoshpe, "Economic Mobilization between the Wars," *Military Affairs* 15 (winter 1951), and Paul A. C. Koistinen, "The 'Industrial Military Complex' in Historical Perspective: The Interwar Years," *Journal of American History* 55 (Mar. 1970). Anne Trotter discusses conspiracy theories in "Development of the Merchant of Death Theory," in Cooling, ed., *War Business and American Society.* Carroll Pursell, ed., *The Military-Industrial Complex* (New York: Harper & Row, 1972), deals with military-industrial relations in the twentieth century.

INDEX

Modernizing the American War Department

was designed and composed by Darryl ml Crosby

in 10.75/13.5 Adobe Garamond Pro with display type in Univers;

printed on 55# Natures Natural stock by Sheridan Books, Inc.

of Ann Arbor, Michigan; and published by

The Kent State University Press

Kent, Ohio 44242